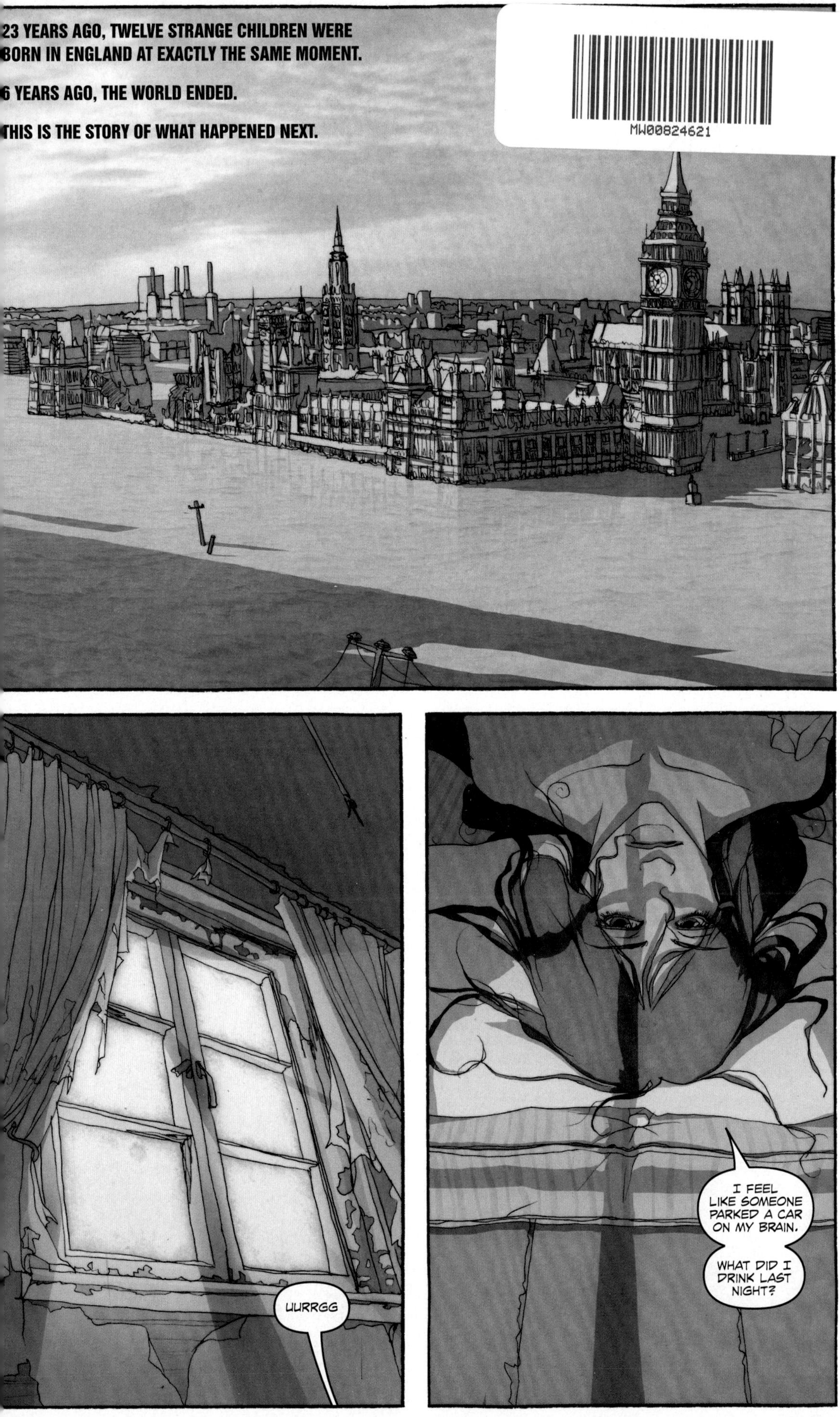
23 YEARS AGO, TWELVE STRANGE CHILDREN WERE BORN IN ENGLAND AT EXACTLY THE SAME MOMENT.
6 YEARS AGO, THE WORLD ENDED.
THIS IS THE STORY OF WHAT HAPPENED NEXT.
UURRGG
I FEEL LIKE SOMEONE PARKED A CAR ON MY BRAIN.
WHAT DID I DRINK LAST NIGHT?

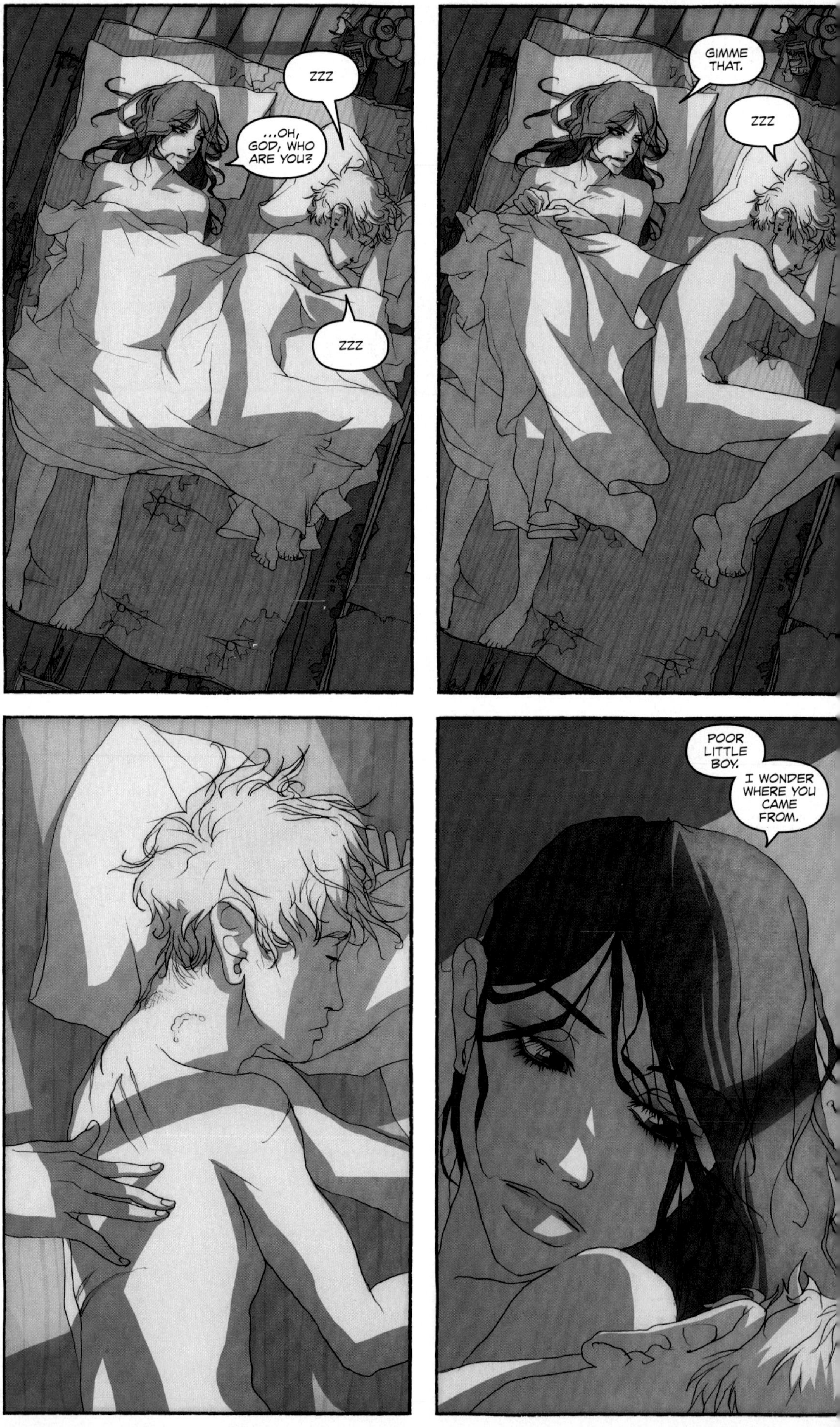
ZZZ
...OH, GOD, WHO ARE YOU?
ZZZ
GIMME THAT.
ZZZ
POOR LITTLE BOY.
I WONDER WHERE YOU CAME FROM.

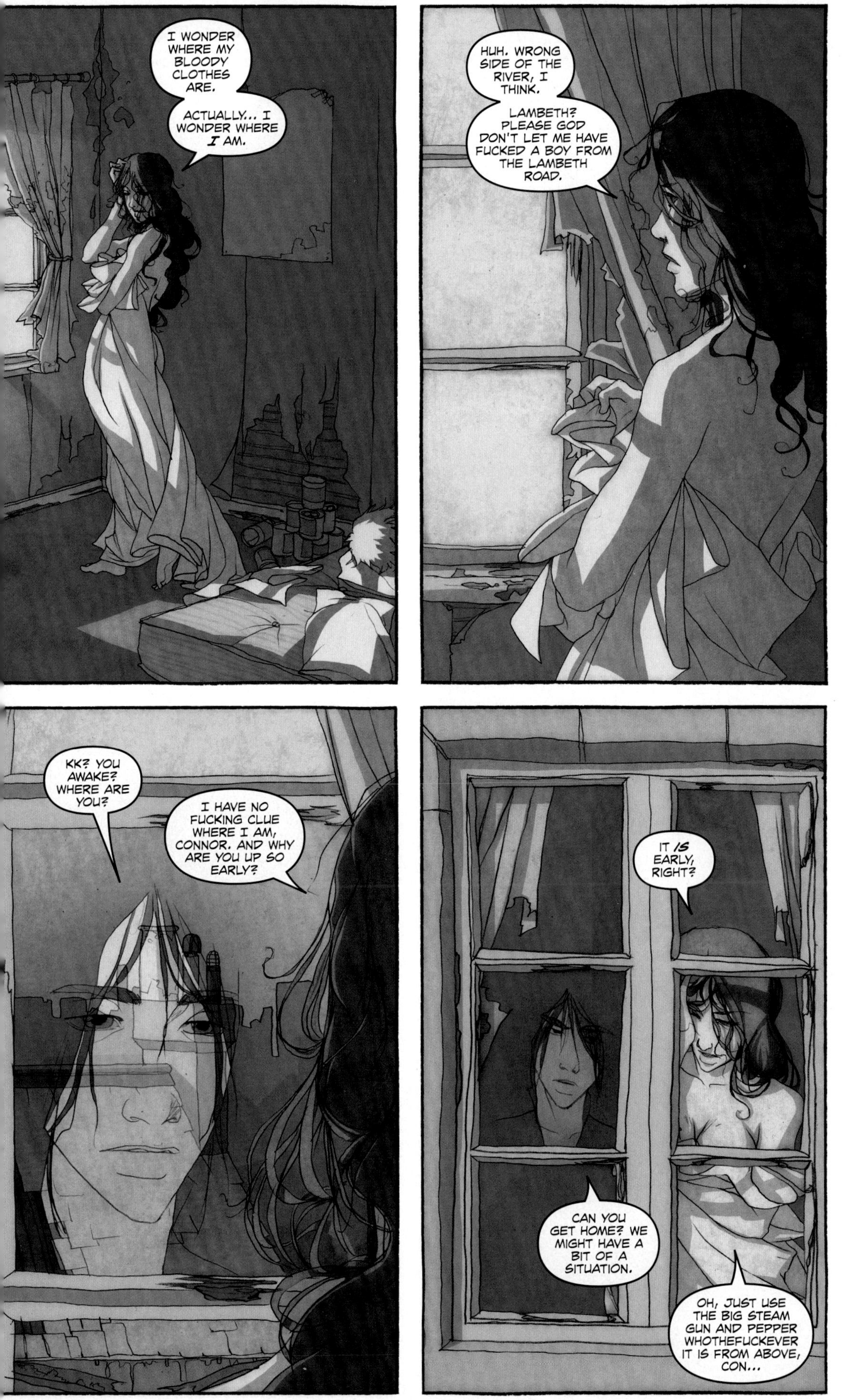
I WONDER WHERE MY BLOODY CLOTHES ARE.
ACTUALLY... I WONDER WHERE *I* AM.
HUH. WRONG SIDE OF THE RIVER, I THINK.
LAMBETH? PLEASE GOD DON'T LET ME HAVE FUCKED A BOY FROM THE LAMBETH ROAD.
KK? YOU AWAKE? WHERE ARE YOU?
I HAVE NO FUCKING CLUE WHERE I AM, CONNOR. AND WHY ARE YOU UP SO EARLY?
IT *IS* EARLY, RIGHT?
CAN YOU GET HOME? WE MIGHT HAVE A BIT OF A SITUATION.
OH, JUST USE THE BIG STEAM GUN AND PEPPER WHOTHEFUCKEVER IT IS FROM ABOVE, CON...

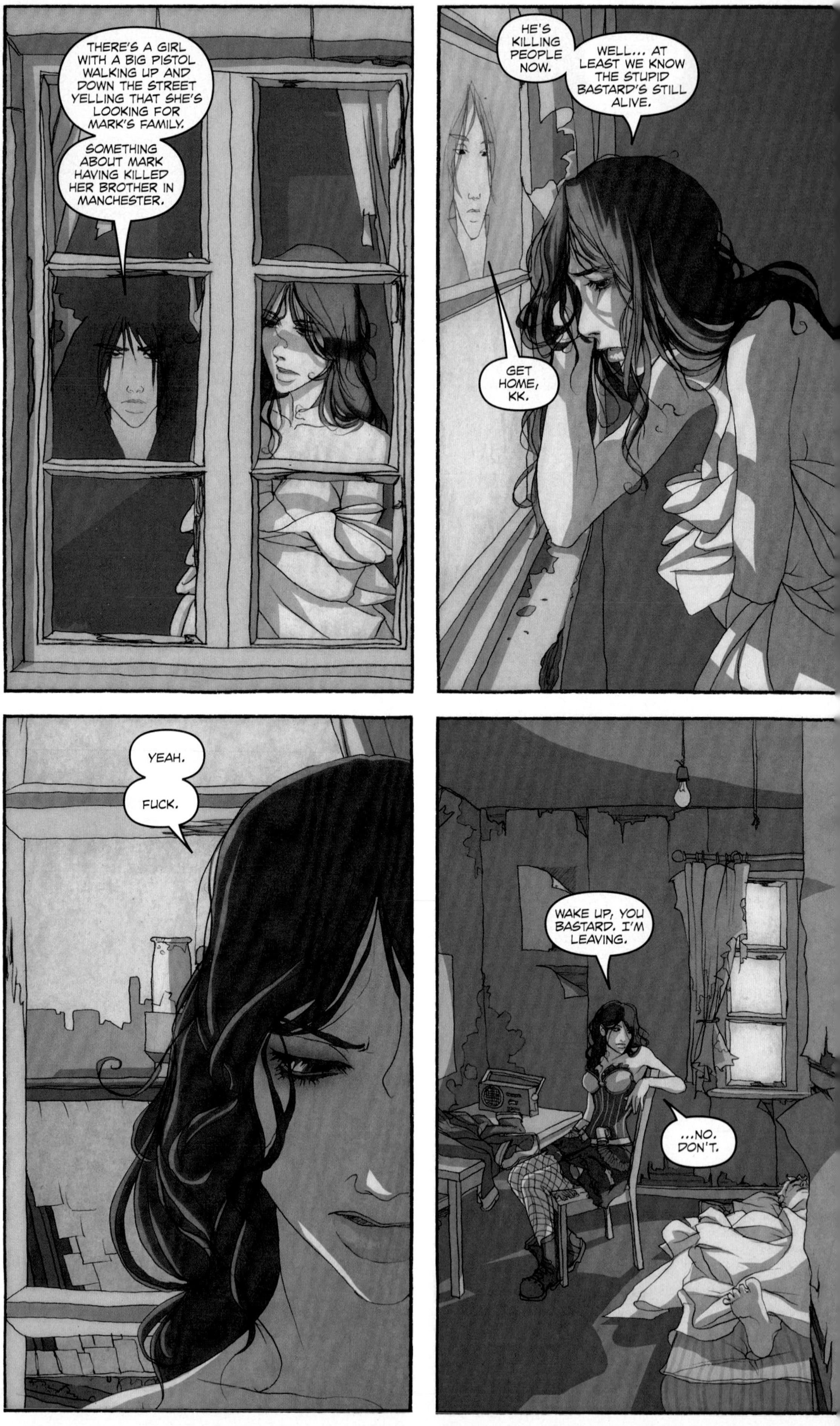
THERE'S A GIRL WITH A BIG PISTOL WALKING UP AND DOWN THE STREET YELLING THAT SHE'S LOOKING FOR MARK'S FAMILY.
SOMETHING ABOUT MARK HAVING KILLED HER BROTHER IN MANCHESTER.
HE'S KILLING PEOPLE NOW.
WELL... AT LEAST WE KNOW THE STUPID BASTARD'S STILL ALIVE.
GET HOME, KK.
YEAH.
FUCK.
WAKE UP, YOU BASTARD. I'M LEAVING.
...NO. DON'T.

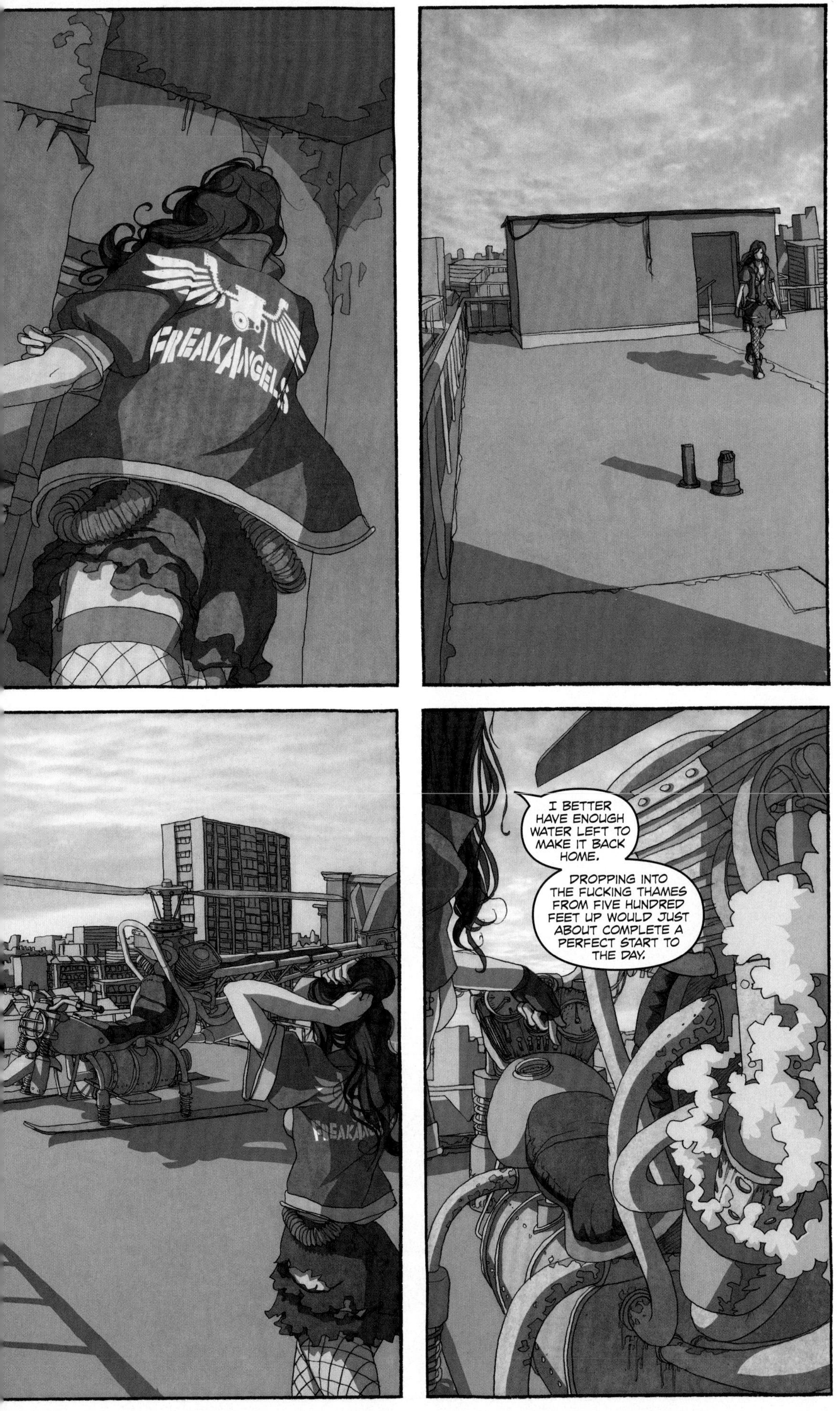
FREAKANGELS
I BETTER HAVE ENOUGH WATER LEFT TO MAKE IT BACK HOME.
DROPPING INTO THE FUCKING THAMES FROM FIVE HUNDRED FEET UP WOULD JUST ABOUT COMPLETE A PERFECT START TO THE DAY.

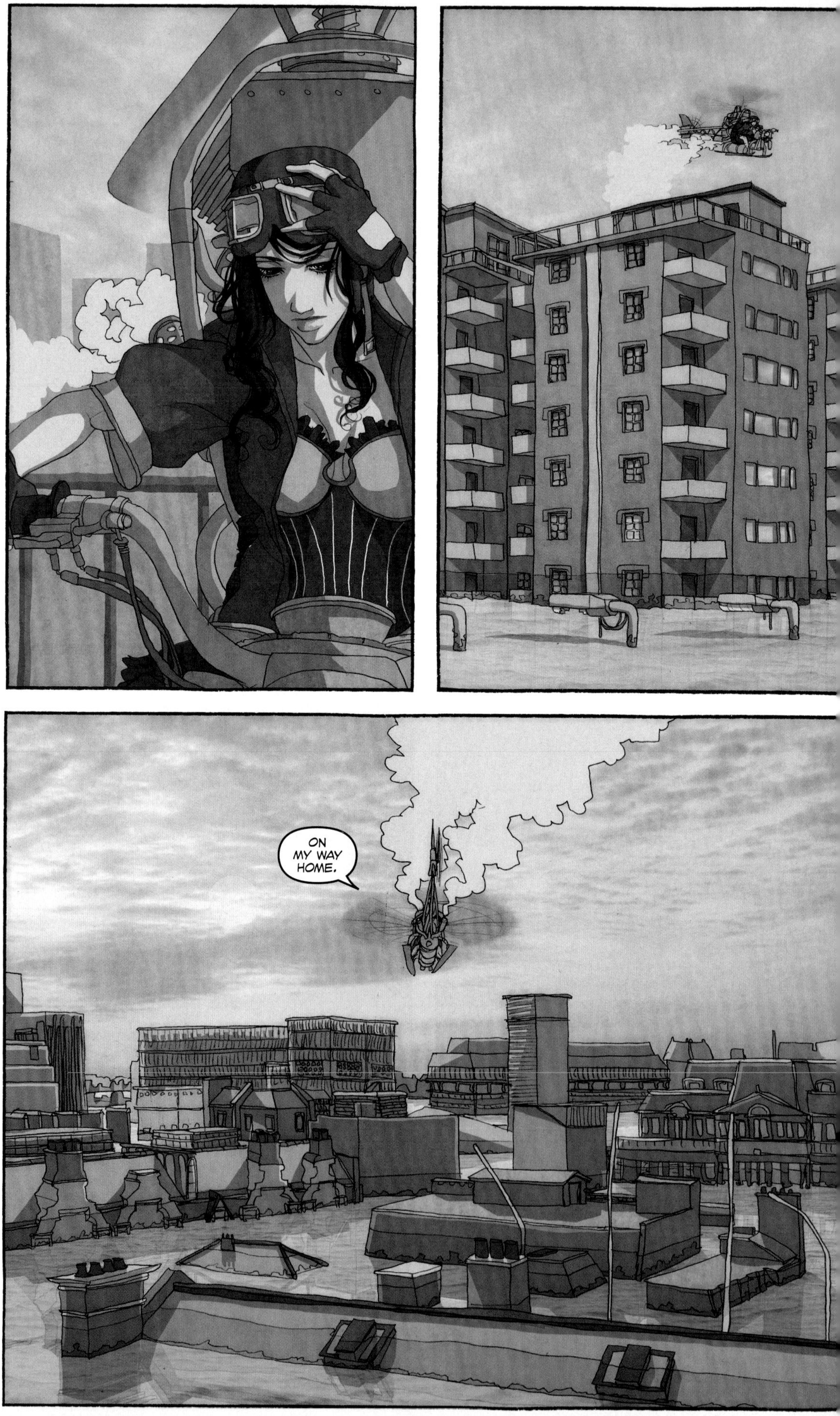
ON MY WAY HOME.

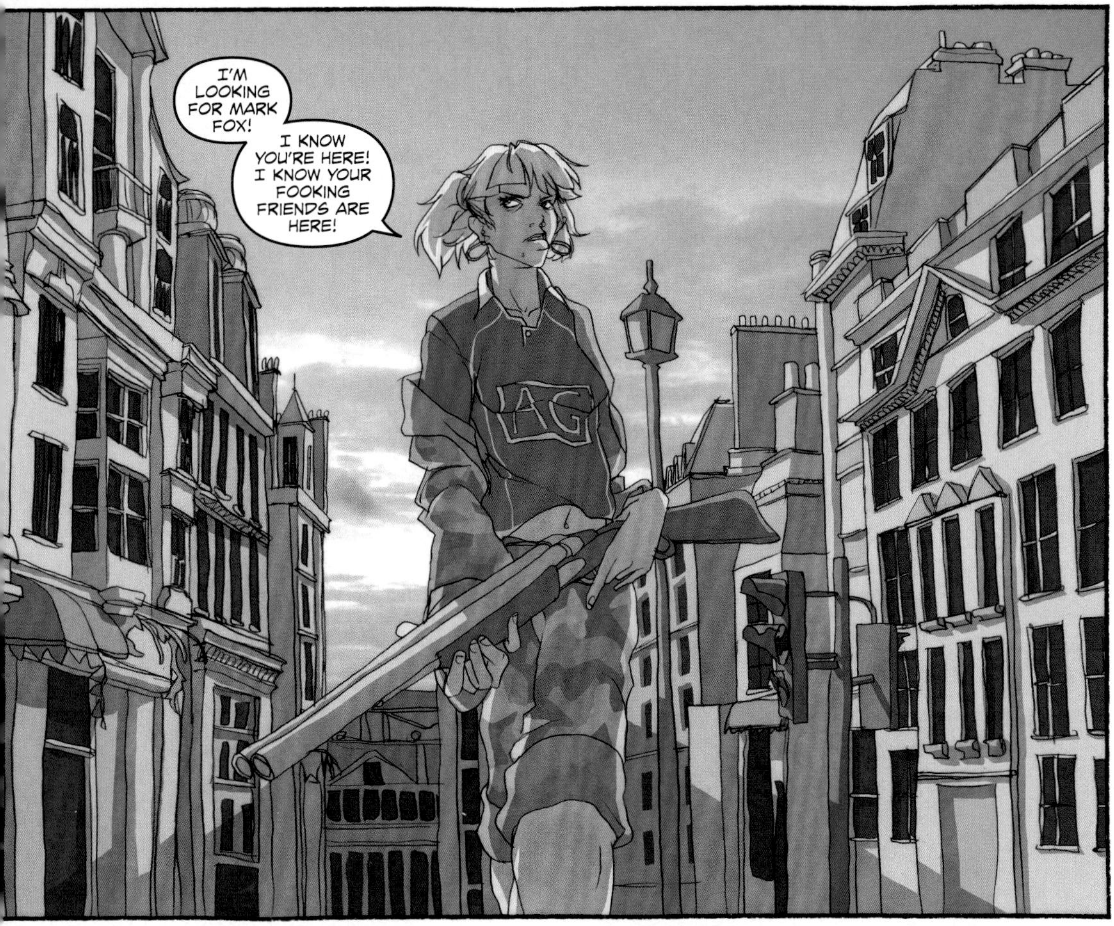
I'M LOOKING FOR MARK FOX!
I KNOW YOU'RE HERE! I KNOW YOUR FOOKING FRIENDS ARE HERE!
AG

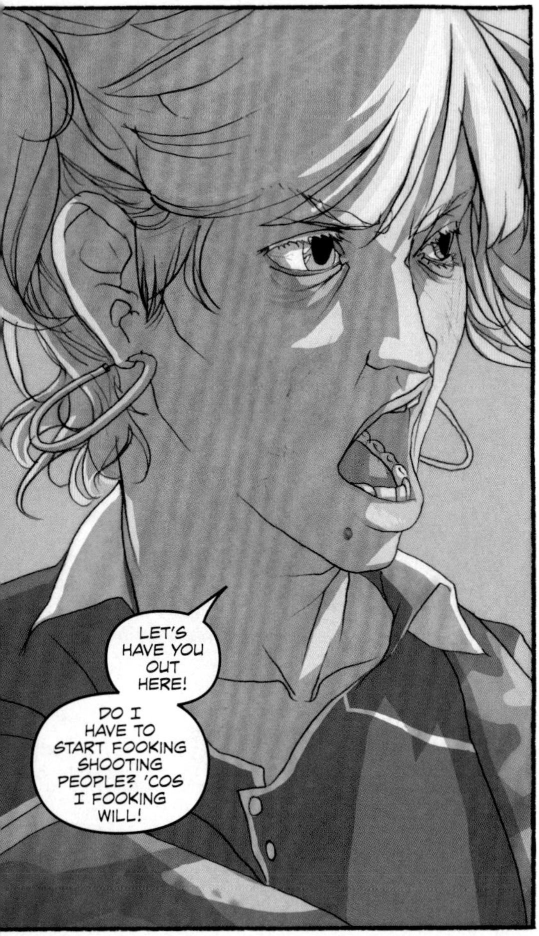
LET'S HAVE YOU OUT HERE!
DO I HAVE TO START FOOKING SHOOTING PEOPLE? 'COS I FOOKING WILL!

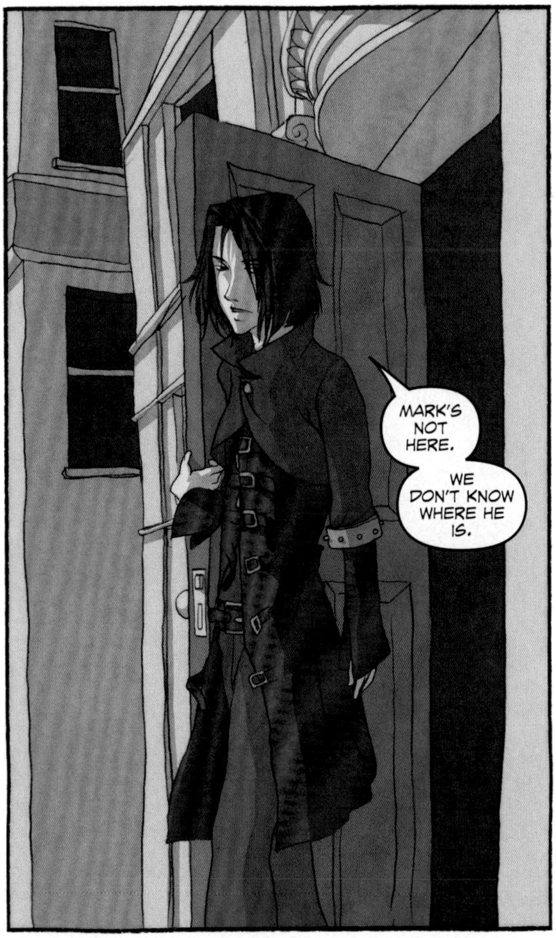
MARK'S NOT HERE.
WE DON'T KNOW WHERE HE IS.

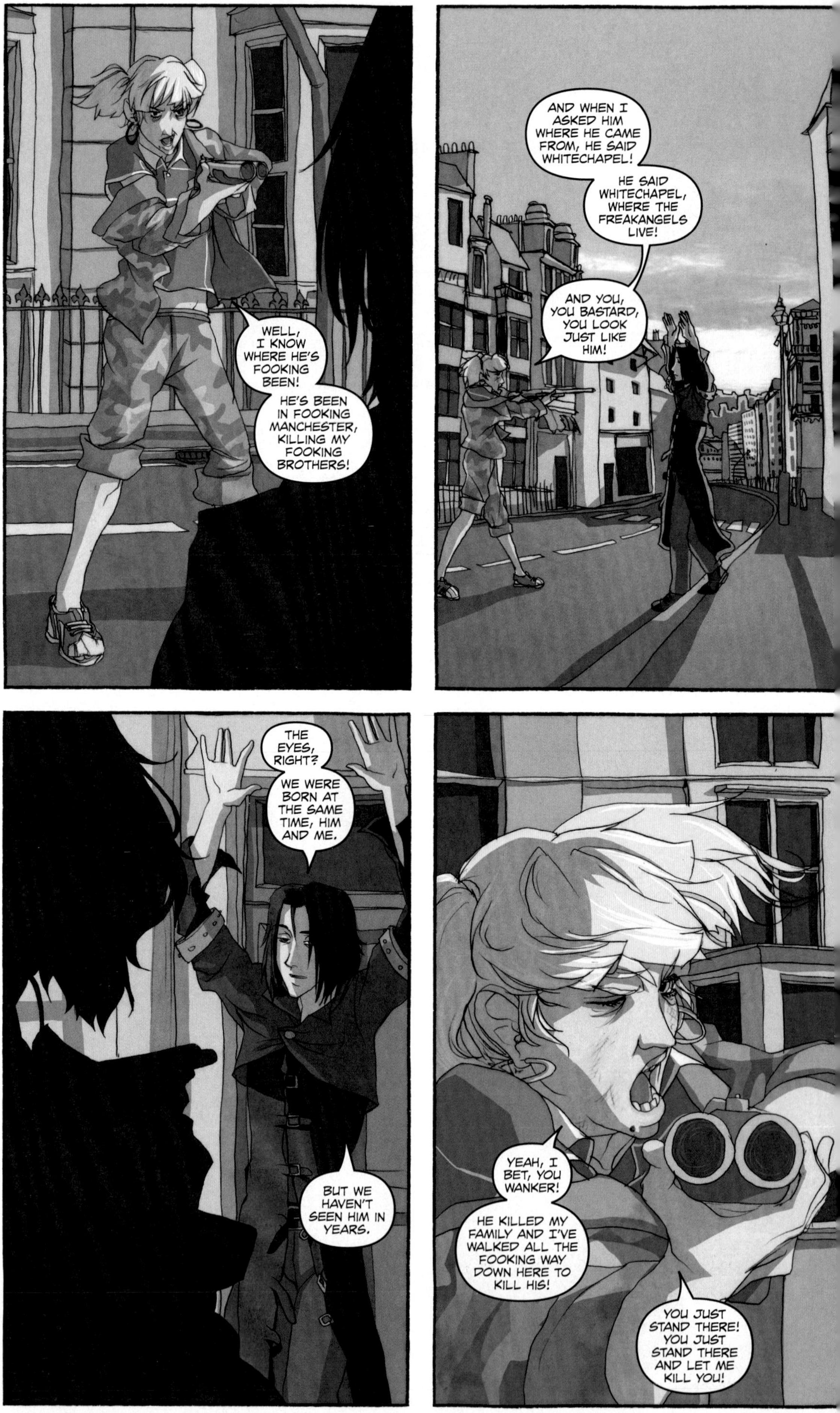
WELL, I KNOW WHERE HE'S FOOKING BEEN!
HE'S BEEN IN FOOKING MANCHESTER, KILLING MY FOOKING BROTHERS!
AND WHEN I ASKED HIM WHERE HE CAME FROM, HE SAID WHITECHAPEL!
HE SAID WHITECHAPEL, WHERE THE FREAKANGELS LIVE!
AND YOU, YOU BASTARD, YOU LOOK JUST LIKE HIM!
THE EYES, RIGHT?
WE WERE BORN AT THE SAME TIME, HIM AND ME.
BUT WE HAVEN'T SEEN HIM IN YEARS.
YEAH, I BET, YOU WANKER!
HE KILLED MY FAMILY AND I'VE WALKED ALL THE FOOKING WAY DOWN HERE TO KILL HIS!
YOU JUST STAND THERE! YOU JUST STAND THERE AND LET ME KILL YOU!

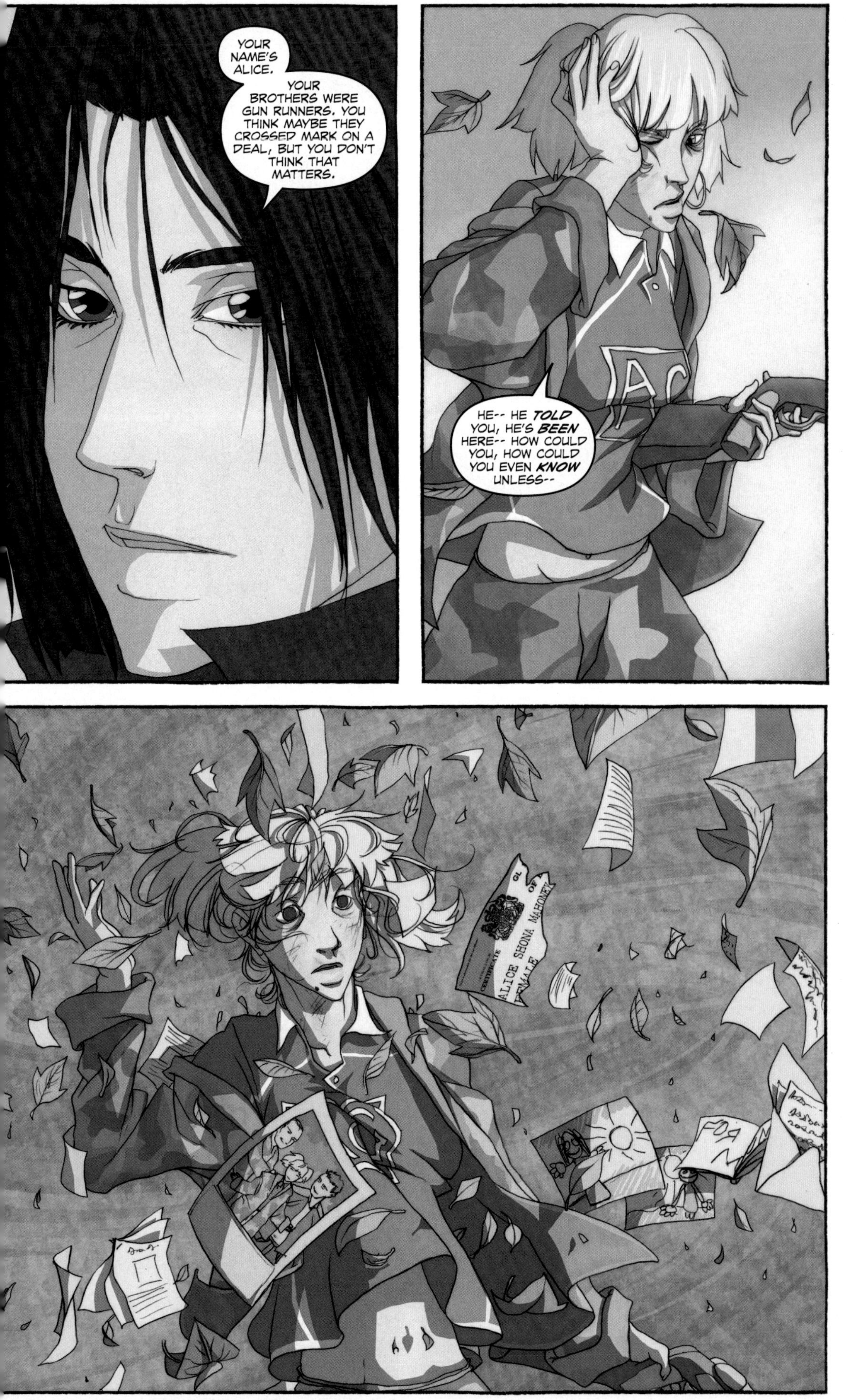
YOUR NAME'S ALICE.
YOUR BROTHERS WERE GUN RUNNERS. YOU THINK MAYBE THEY CROSSED MARK ON A DEAL, BUT YOU DON'T THINK THAT MATTERS.
HE-- HE **TOLD** YOU, HE'S **BEEN** HERE-- HOW COULD YOU, HOW COULD YOU EVEN **KNOW** UNLESS--
ALICE SHONA MAHONEY

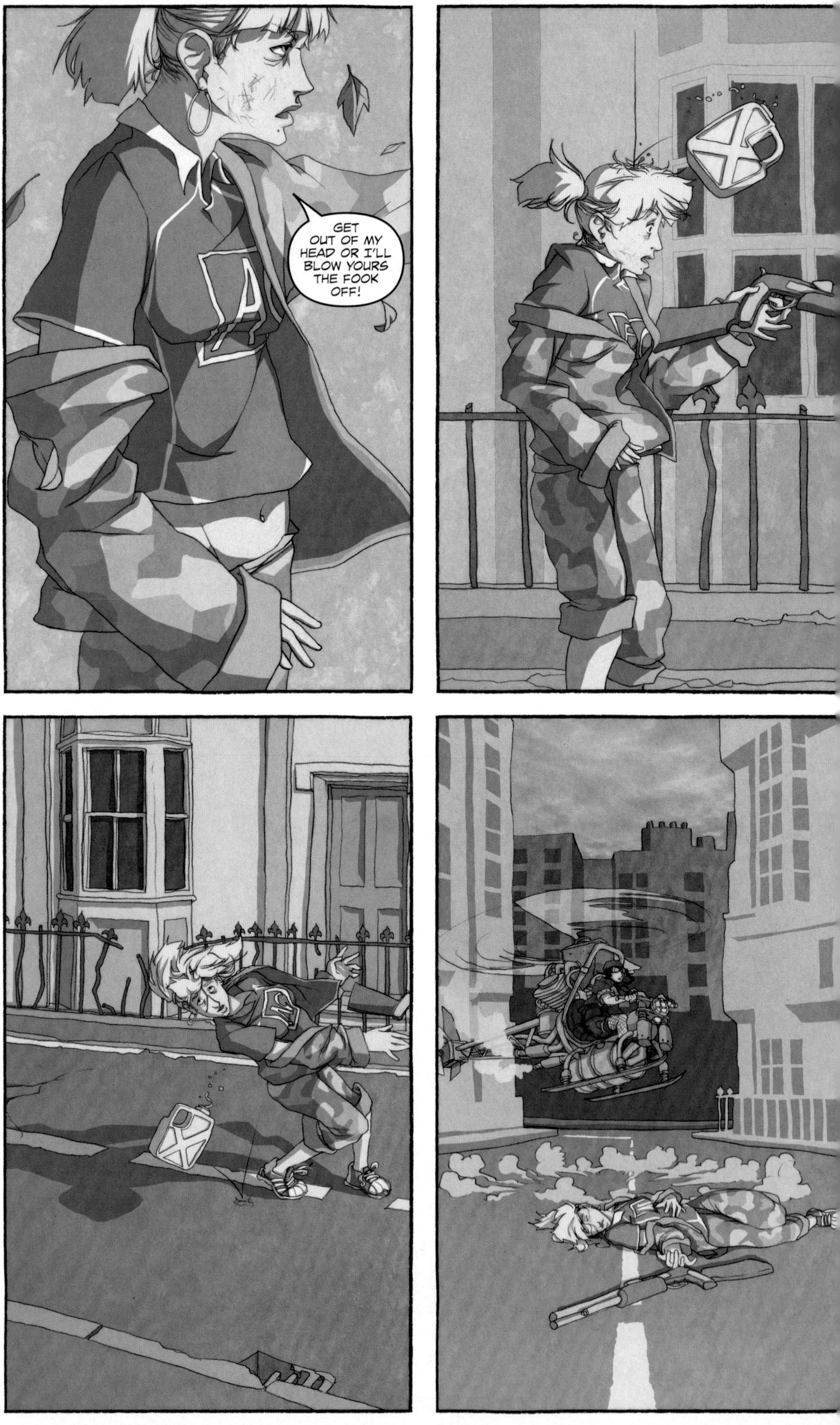
GET OUT OF MY HEAD OR I'LL BLOW YOURS THE FOOK OFF!

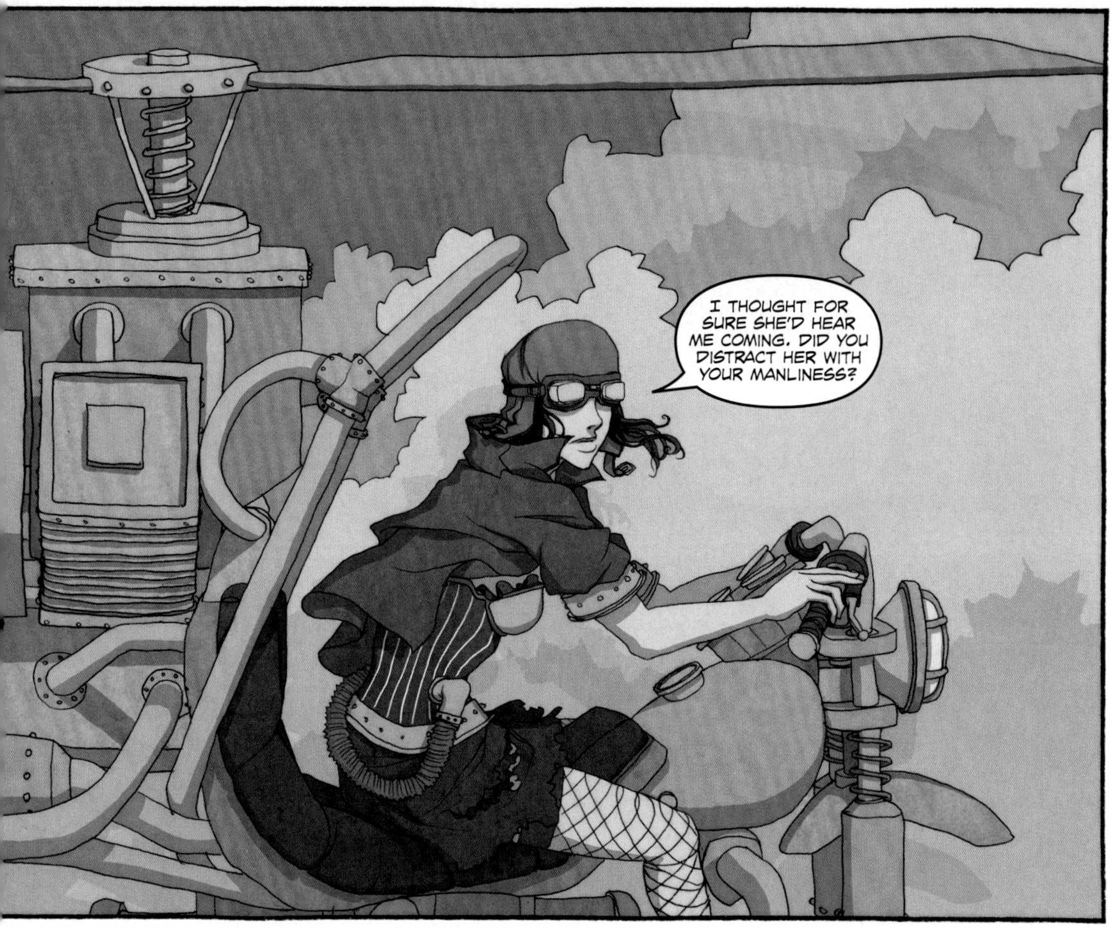
I THOUGHT FOR SURE SHE'D HEAR ME COMING. DID YOU DISTRACT HER WITH YOUR MANLINESS?

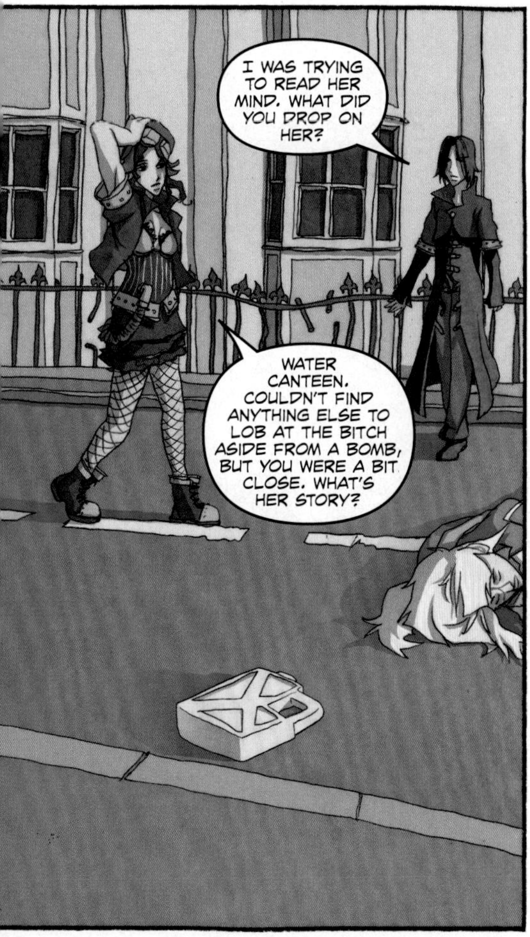
I WAS TRYING TO READ HER MIND. WHAT DID YOU DROP ON HER?
WATER CANTEEN. COULDN'T FIND ANYTHING ELSE TO LOB AT THE BITCH ASIDE FROM A BOMB, BUT YOU WERE A BIT CLOSE. WHAT'S HER STORY?

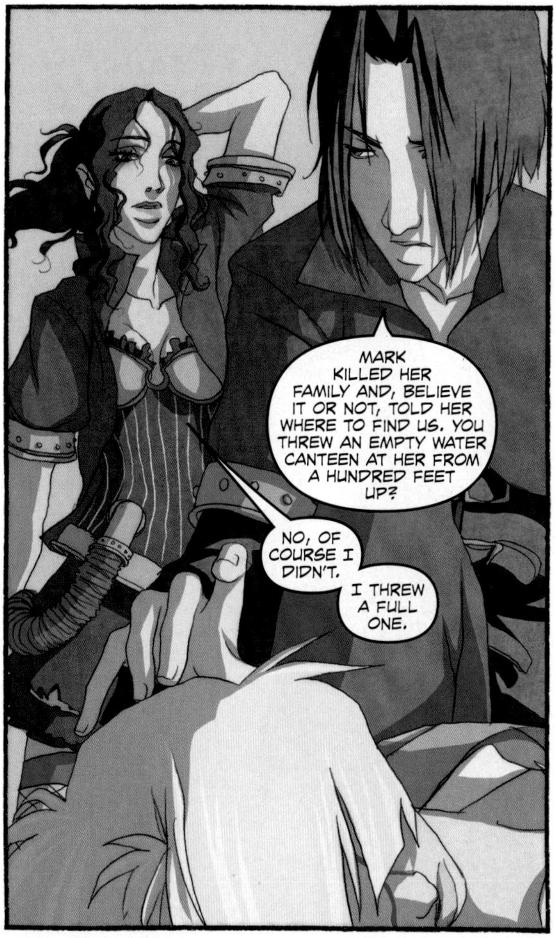
MARK KILLED HER FAMILY AND, BELIEVE IT OR NOT, TOLD HER WHERE TO FIND US. YOU THREW AN EMPTY WATER CANTEEN AT HER FROM A HUNDRED FEET UP?
NO, OF COURSE I DIDN'T.
I THREW A FULL ONE.

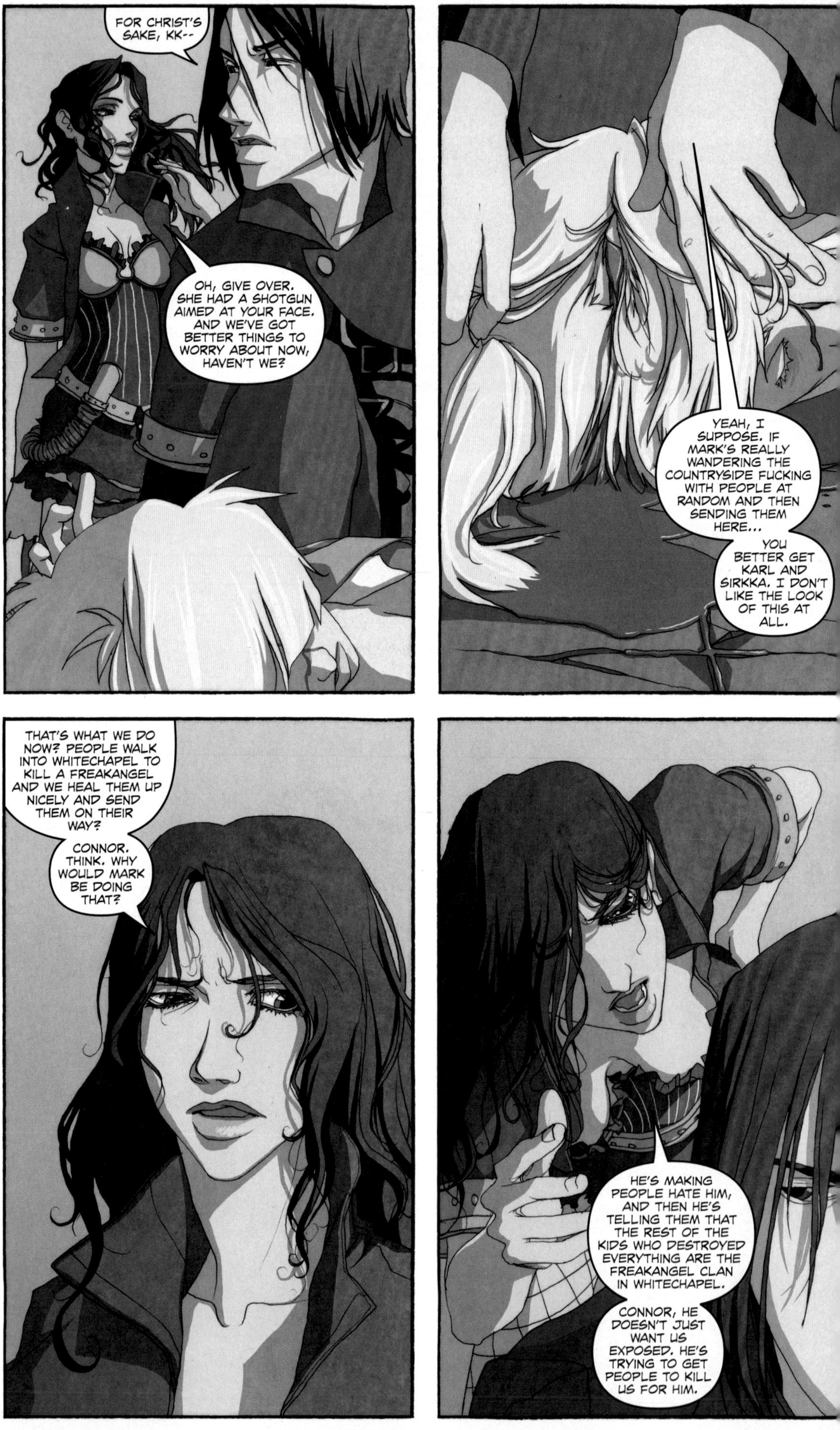
FOR CHRIST'S SAKE, KK--
OH, GIVE OVER. SHE HAD A SHOTGUN AIMED AT YOUR FACE. AND WE'VE GOT BETTER THINGS TO WORRY ABOUT NOW, HAVEN'T WE?
YEAH, I SUPPOSE. IF MARK'S REALLY WANDERING THE COUNTRYSIDE FUCKING WITH PEOPLE AT RANDOM AND THEN SENDING THEM HERE...
YOU BETTER GET KARL AND SIRKKA. I DON'T LIKE THE LOOK OF THIS AT ALL.
THAT'S WHAT WE DO NOW? PEOPLE WALK INTO WHITECHAPEL TO KILL A FREAKANGEL AND WE HEAL THEM UP NICELY AND SEND THEM ON THEIR WAY?
CONNOR. THINK. WHY WOULD MARK BE DOING THAT?
HE'S MAKING PEOPLE HATE HIM, AND THEN HE'S TELLING THEM THAT THE REST OF THE KIDS WHO DESTROYED EVERYTHING ARE THE FREAKANGEL CLAN IN WHITECHAPEL.
CONNOR, HE DOESN'T JUST WANT US EXPOSED. HE'S TRYING TO GET PEOPLE TO KILL US FOR HIM.

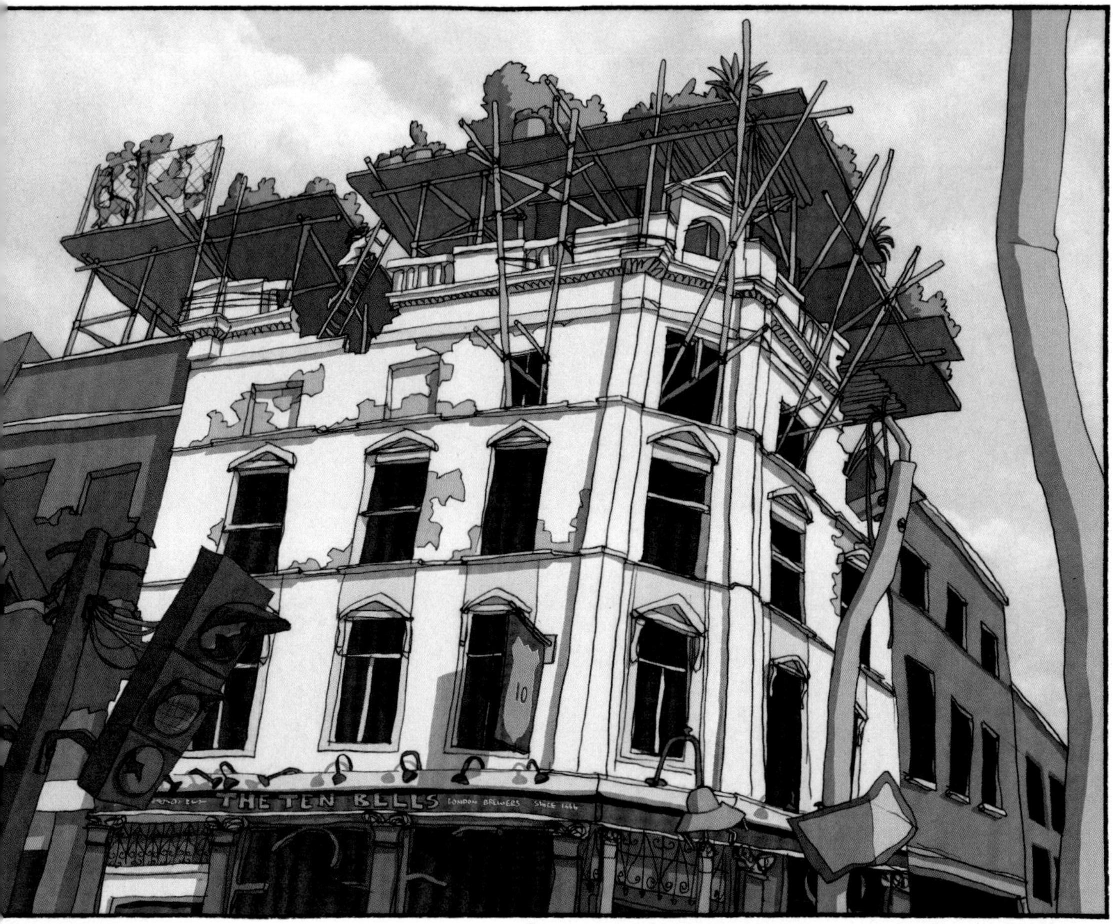
10
THE TEN BELLS
LONDON BREWERS

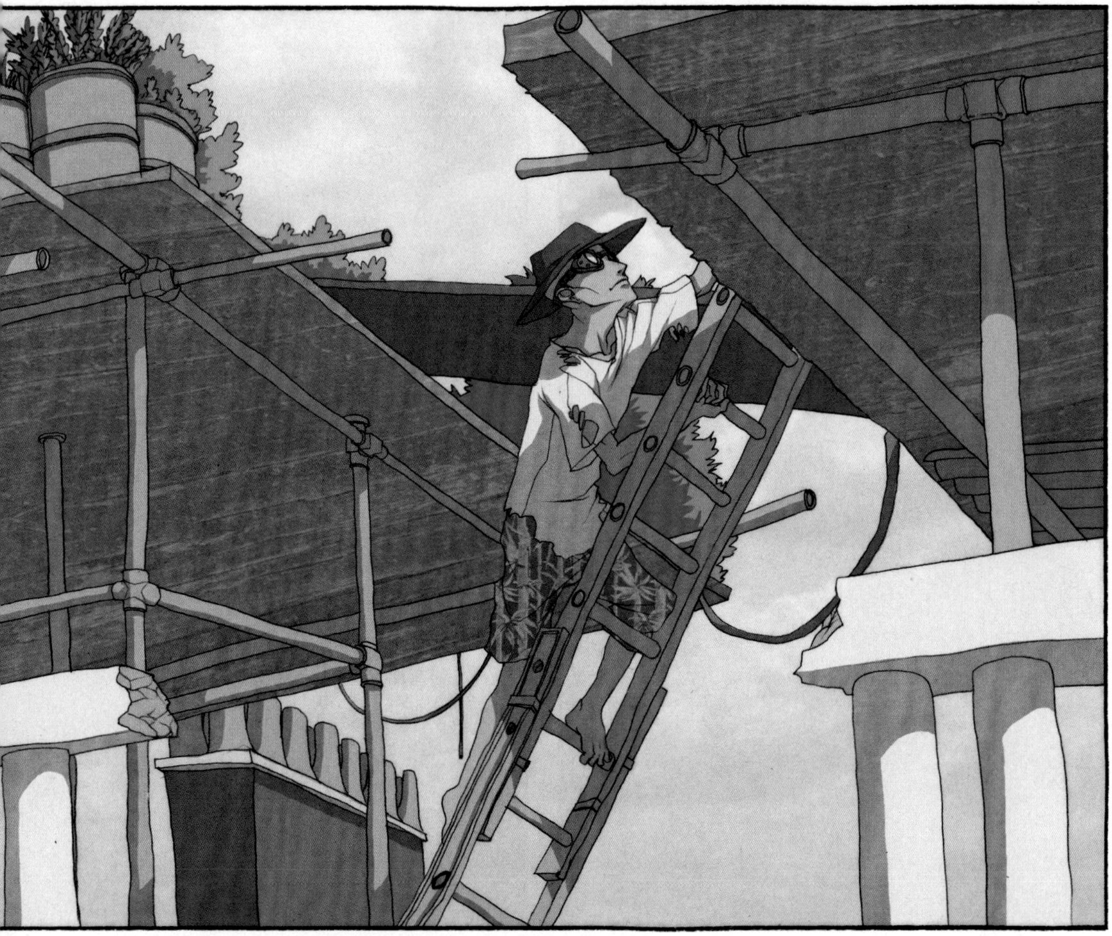

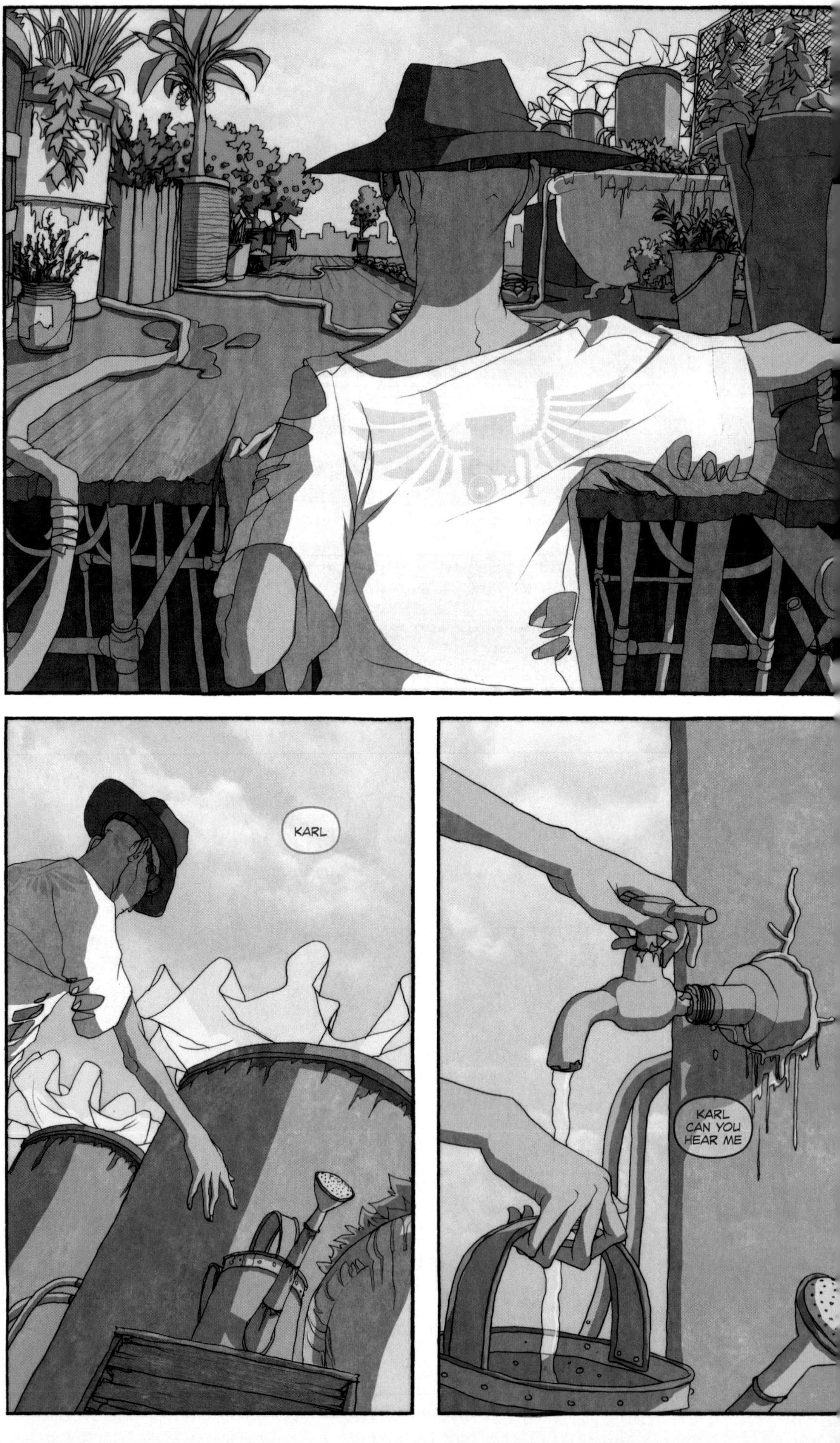
KARL
KARL CAN YOU HEAR ME

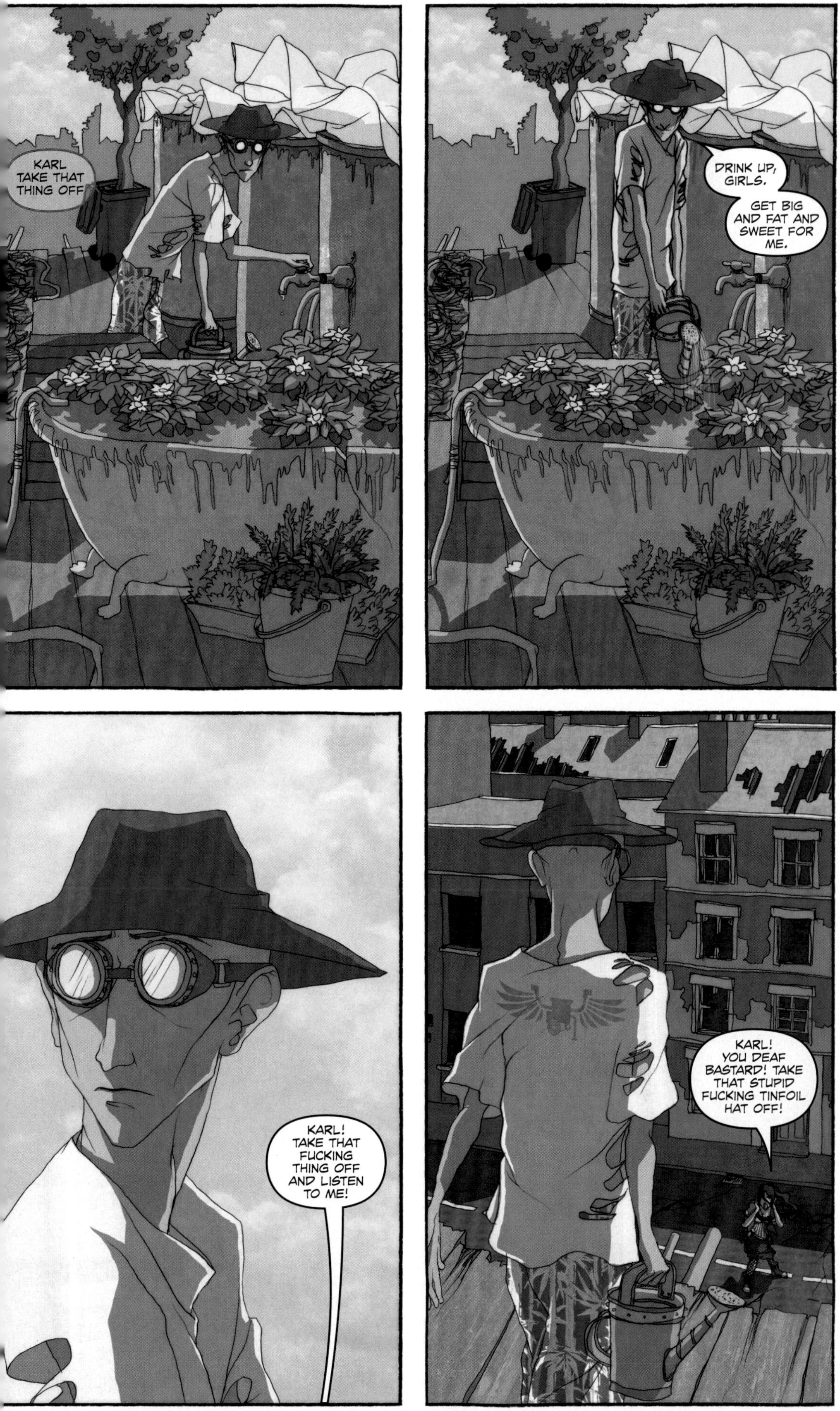
KARL TAKE THAT THING OFF
DRINK UP, GIRLS.
GET BIG AND FAT AND SWEET FOR ME.
KARL! TAKE THAT FUCKING THING OFF AND LISTEN TO ME!
KARL! YOU DEAF BASTARD! TAKE THAT STUPID FUCKING TINFOIL HAT OFF!

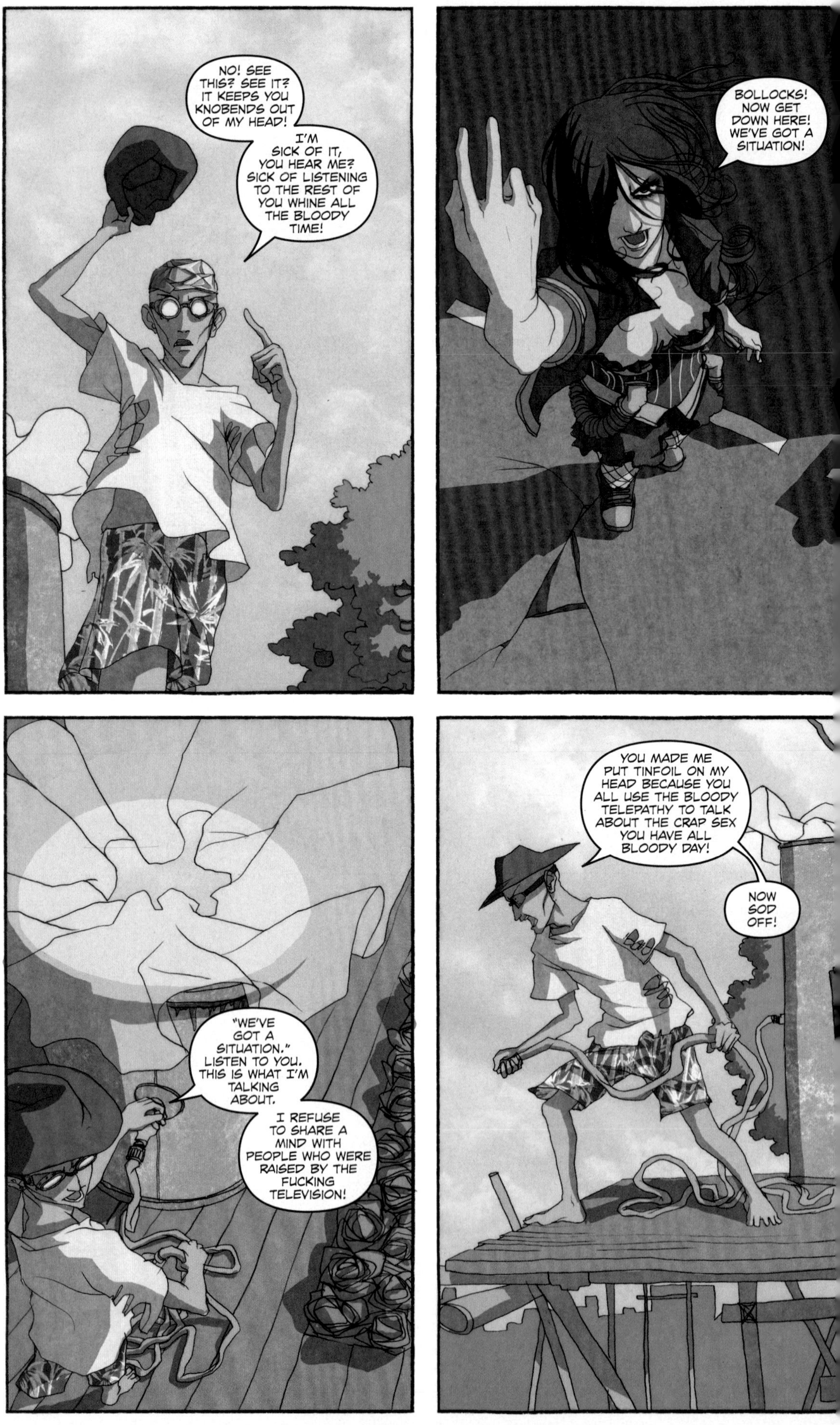
NO! SEE THIS? SEE IT? IT KEEPS YOU KNOBENDS OUT OF MY HEAD!
I'M SICK OF IT, YOU HEAR ME? SICK OF LISTENING TO THE REST OF YOU WHINE ALL THE BLOODY TIME!
BOLLOCKS! NOW GET DOWN HERE! WE'VE GOT A SITUATION!
"WE'VE GOT A SITUATION." LISTEN TO YOU. THIS IS WHAT I'M TALKING ABOUT.
I REFUSE TO SHARE A MIND WITH PEOPLE WHO WERE RAISED BY THE FUCKING TELEVISION!
YOU MADE ME PUT TINFOIL ON MY HEAD BECAUSE YOU ALL USE THE BLOODY TELEPATHY TO TALK ABOUT THE CRAP SEX YOU HAVE ALL BLOODY DAY!
NOW SOD OFF!

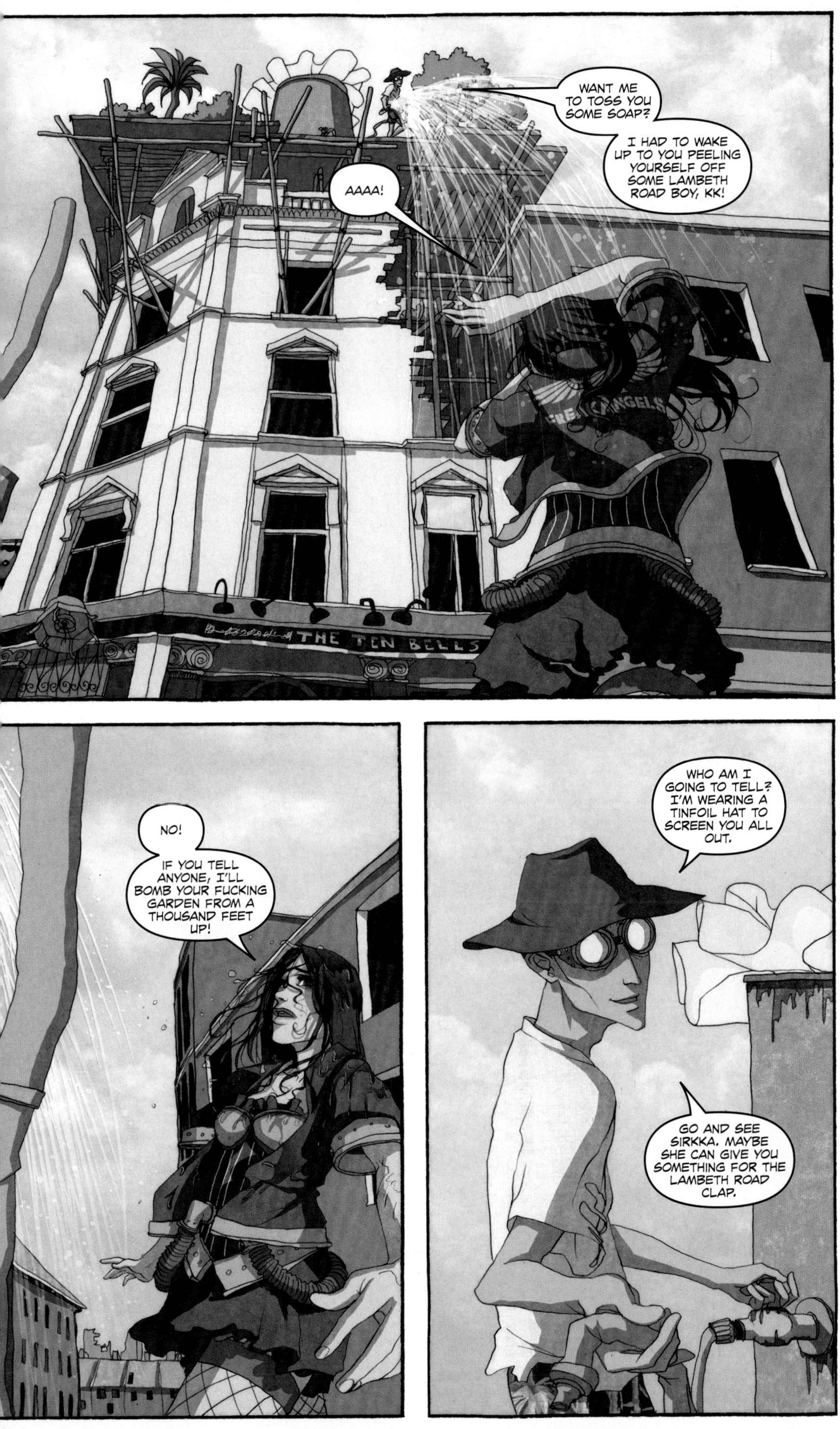
WANT ME TO TOSS YOU SOME SOAP?
I HAD TO WAKE UP TO YOU PEELING YOURSELF OFF SOME LAMBETH ROAD BOY, KK!
AAAA!
THE TEN BELLS
NO!
IF YOU TELL ANYONE, I'LL BOMB YOUR FUCKING GARDEN FROM A THOUSAND FEET UP!
WHO AM I GOING TO TELL? I'M WEARING A TINFOIL HAT TO SCREEN YOU ALL OUT.
GO AND SEE SIRKKA. MAYBE SHE CAN GIVE YOU SOMETHING FOR THE LAMBETH ROAD CLAP.

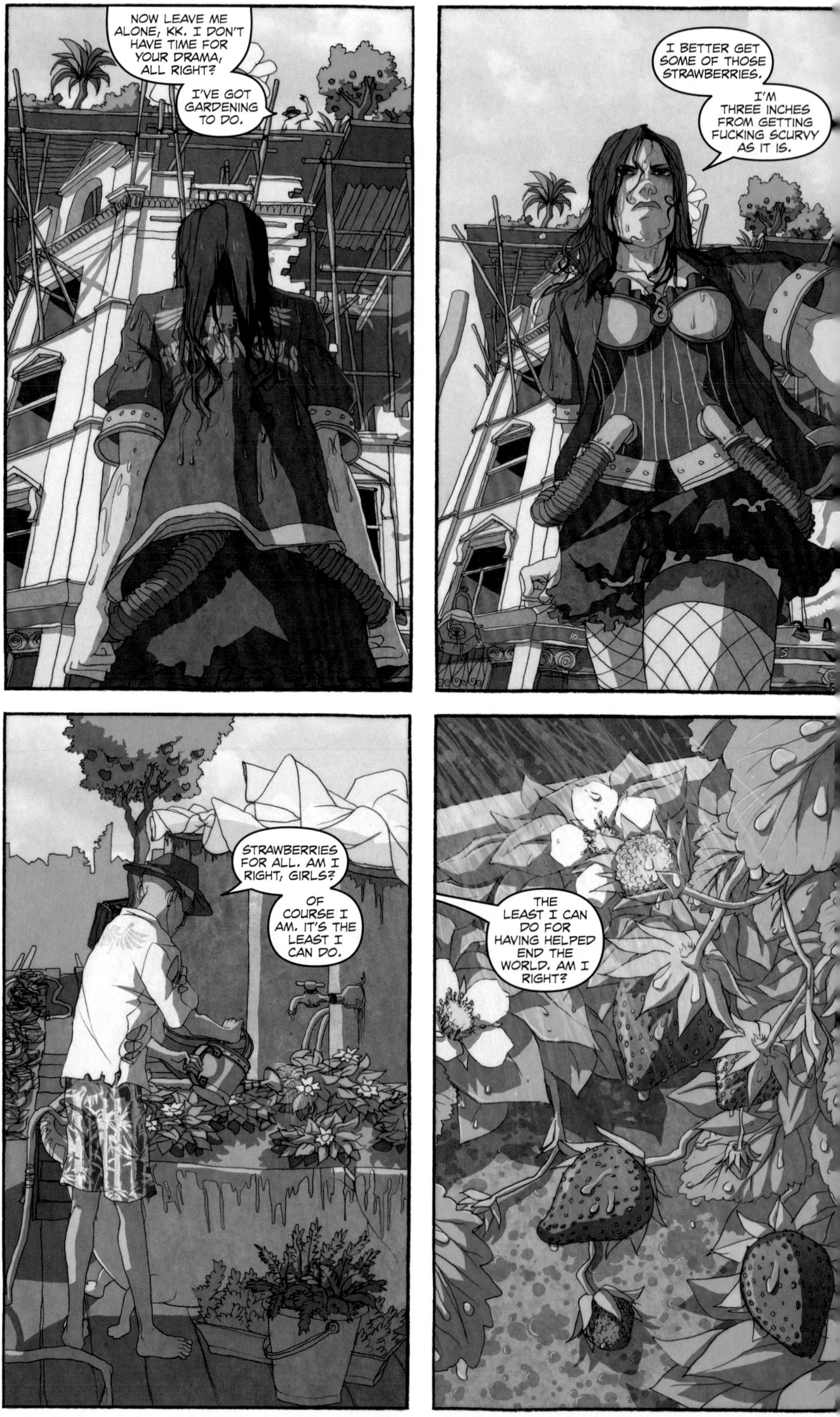
NOW LEAVE ME ALONE, KK. I DON'T HAVE TIME FOR YOUR DRAMA, ALL RIGHT?
I'VE GOT GARDENING TO DO.
I BETTER GET SOME OF THOSE STRAWBERRIES.
I'M THREE INCHES FROM GETTING FUCKING SCURVY AS IT IS.
STRAWBERRIES FOR ALL. AM I RIGHT, GIRLS?
OF COURSE I AM. IT'S THE LEAST I CAN DO.
THE LEAST I CAN DO FOR HAVING HELPED END THE WORLD. AM I RIGHT?

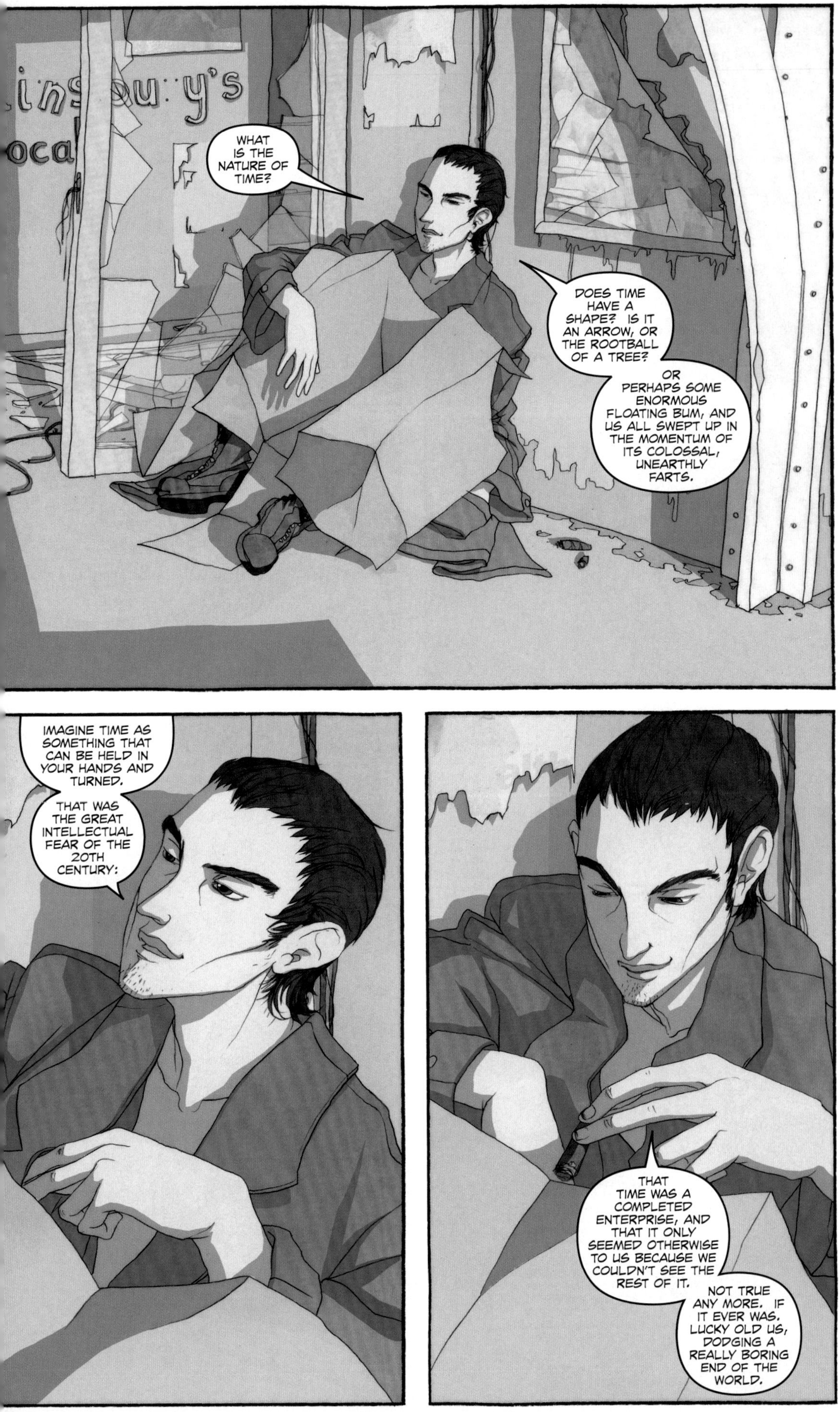
WHAT IS THE NATURE OF TIME?
DOES TIME HAVE A SHAPE? IS IT AN ARROW, OR THE ROOTBALL OF A TREE?
OR PERHAPS SOME ENORMOUS FLOATING BUM, AND US ALL SWEPT UP IN THE MOMENTUM OF ITS COLOSSAL, UNEARTHLY FARTS.
IMAGINE TIME AS SOMETHING THAT CAN BE HELD IN YOUR HANDS AND TURNED.
THAT WAS THE GREAT INTELLECTUAL FEAR OF THE 20TH CENTURY:
THAT TIME WAS A COMPLETED ENTERPRISE, AND THAT IT ONLY SEEMED OTHERWISE TO US BECAUSE WE COULDN'T SEE THE REST OF IT.
NOT TRUE ANY MORE. IF IT EVER WAS. LUCKY OLD US, DODGING A REALLY BORING END OF THE WORLD.

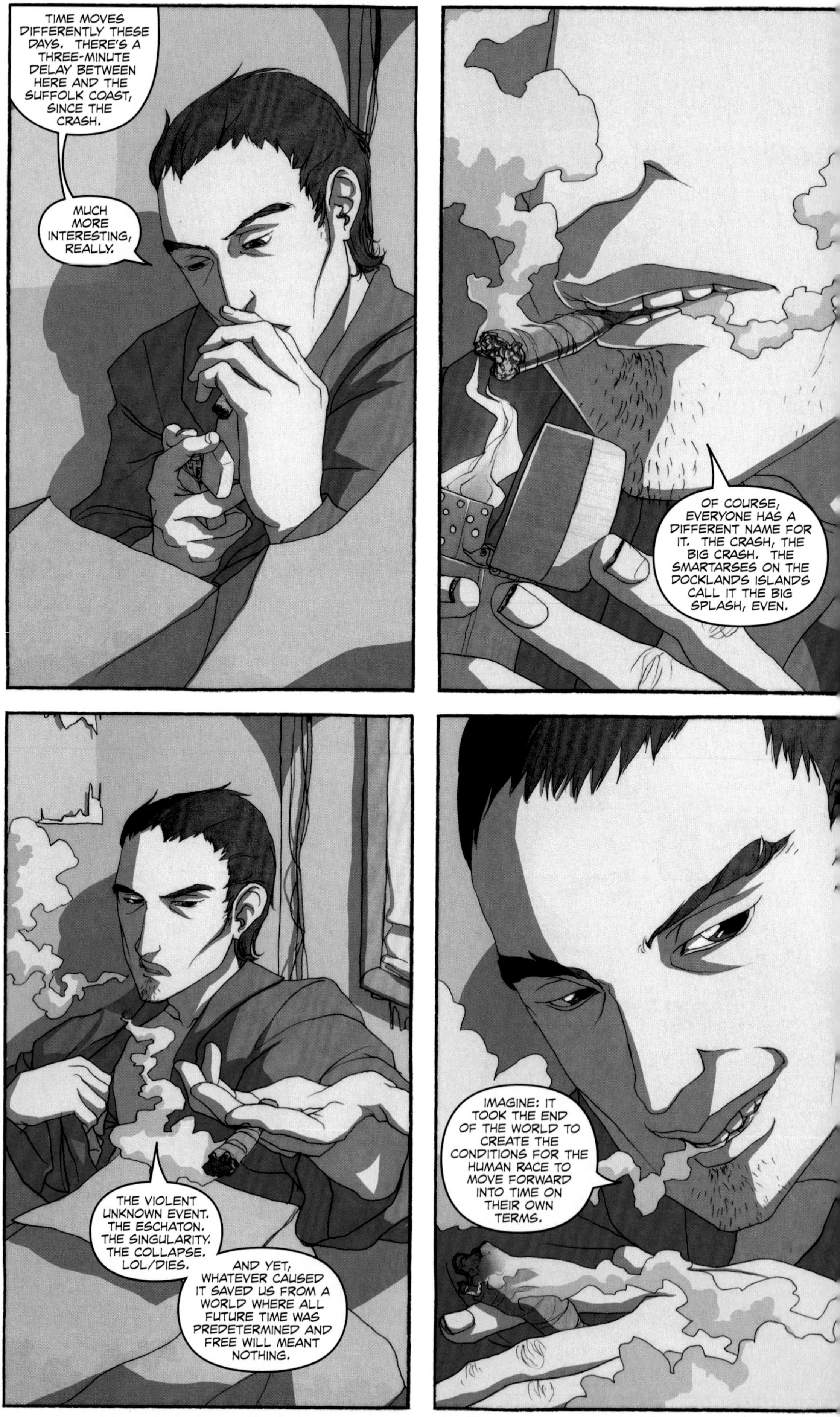
TIME MOVES DIFFERENTLY THESE DAYS. THERE'S A THREE-MINUTE DELAY BETWEEN HERE AND THE SUFFOLK COAST, SINCE THE CRASH.
MUCH MORE INTERESTING, REALLY.
OF COURSE, EVERYONE HAS A DIFFERENT NAME FOR IT. THE CRASH, THE BIG CRASH. THE SMARTARSES ON THE DOCKLANDS ISLANDS CALL IT THE BIG SPLASH, EVEN.
THE VIOLENT UNKNOWN EVENT. THE ESCHATON. THE SINGULARITY. THE COLLAPSE. LOL/DIES.
AND YET, WHATEVER CAUSED IT SAVED US FROM A WORLD WHERE ALL FUTURE TIME WAS PREDETERMINED AND FREE WILL MEANT NOTHING.
IMAGINE: IT TOOK THE END OF THE WORLD TO CREATE THE CONDITIONS FOR THE HUMAN RACE TO MOVE FORWARD INTO TIME ON THEIR OWN TERMS.

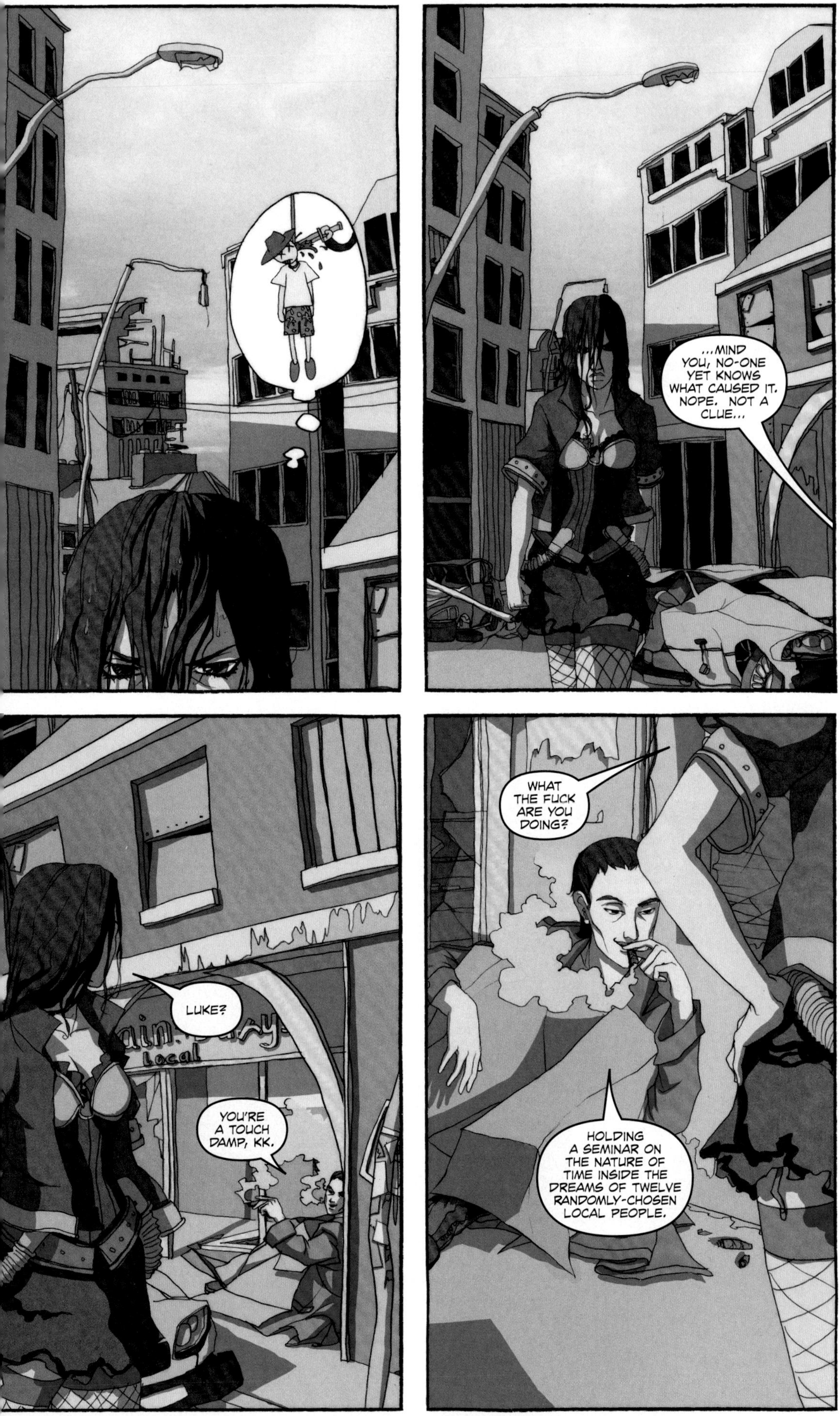
...MIND YOU, NO-ONE YET KNOWS WHAT CAUSED IT. NOPE. NOT A CLUE...
LUKE?
Local
YOU'RE A TOUCH DAMP, KK.
WHAT THE FUCK ARE YOU DOING?
HOLDING A SEMINAR ON THE NATURE OF TIME INSIDE THE DREAMS OF TWELVE RANDOMLY-CHOSEN LOCAL PEOPLE.

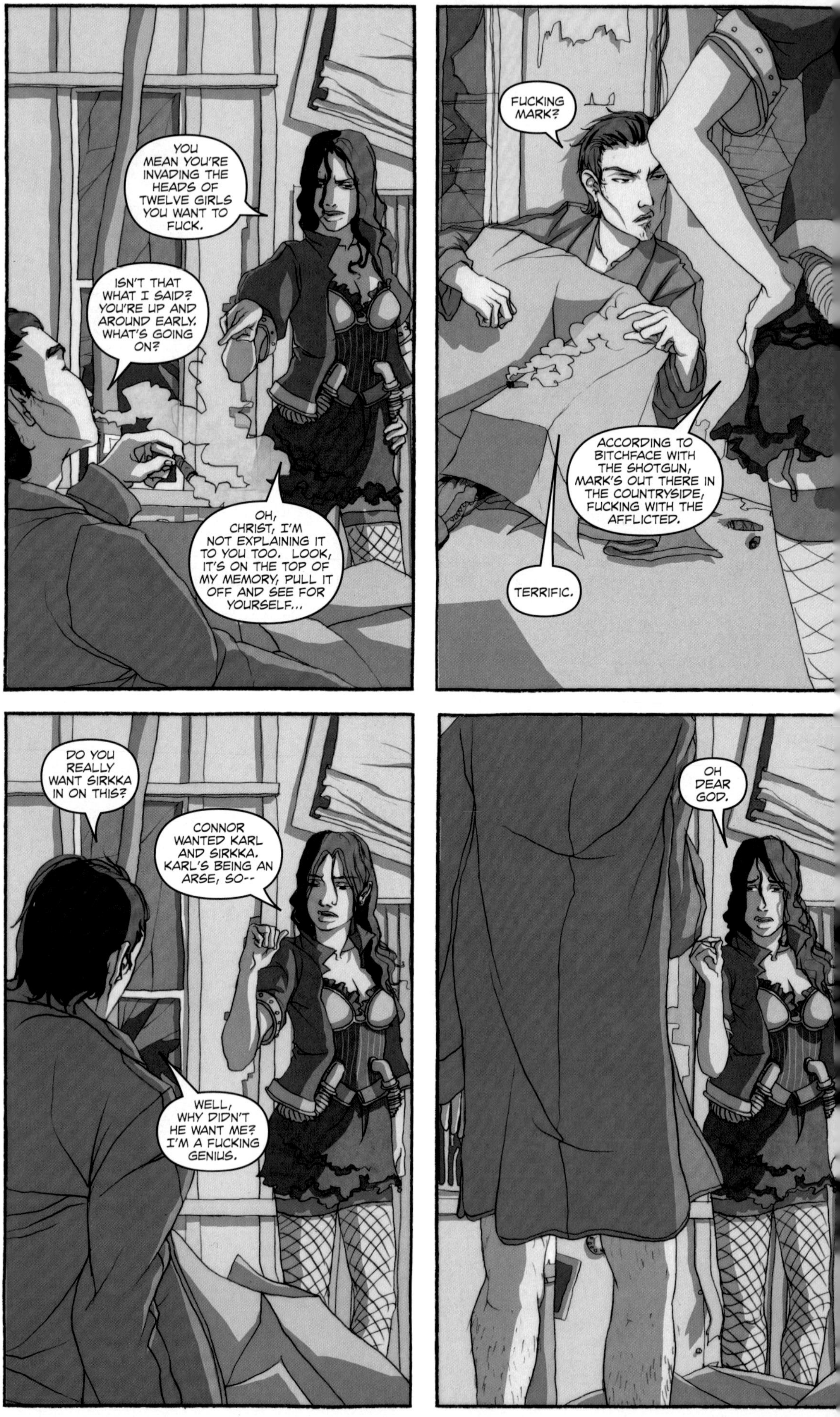
YOU MEAN YOU'RE INVADING THE HEADS OF TWELVE GIRLS YOU WANT TO FUCK.
ISN'T THAT WHAT I SAID? YOU'RE UP AND AROUND EARLY. WHAT'S GOING ON?
OH, CHRIST, I'M NOT EXPLAINING IT TO YOU TOO. LOOK, IT'S ON THE TOP OF MY MEMORY, PULL IT OFF AND SEE FOR YOURSELF...
FUCKING MARK?
ACCORDING TO BITCHFACE WITH THE SHOTGUN, MARK'S OUT THERE IN THE COUNTRYSIDE, FUCKING WITH THE AFFLICTED.
TERRIFIC.
DO YOU REALLY WANT SIRKKA IN ON THIS?
CONNOR WANTED KARL AND SIRKKA. KARL'S BEING AN ARSE, SO--
WELL, WHY DIDN'T HE WANT ME? I'M A FUCKING GENIUS.
OH DEAR GOD.

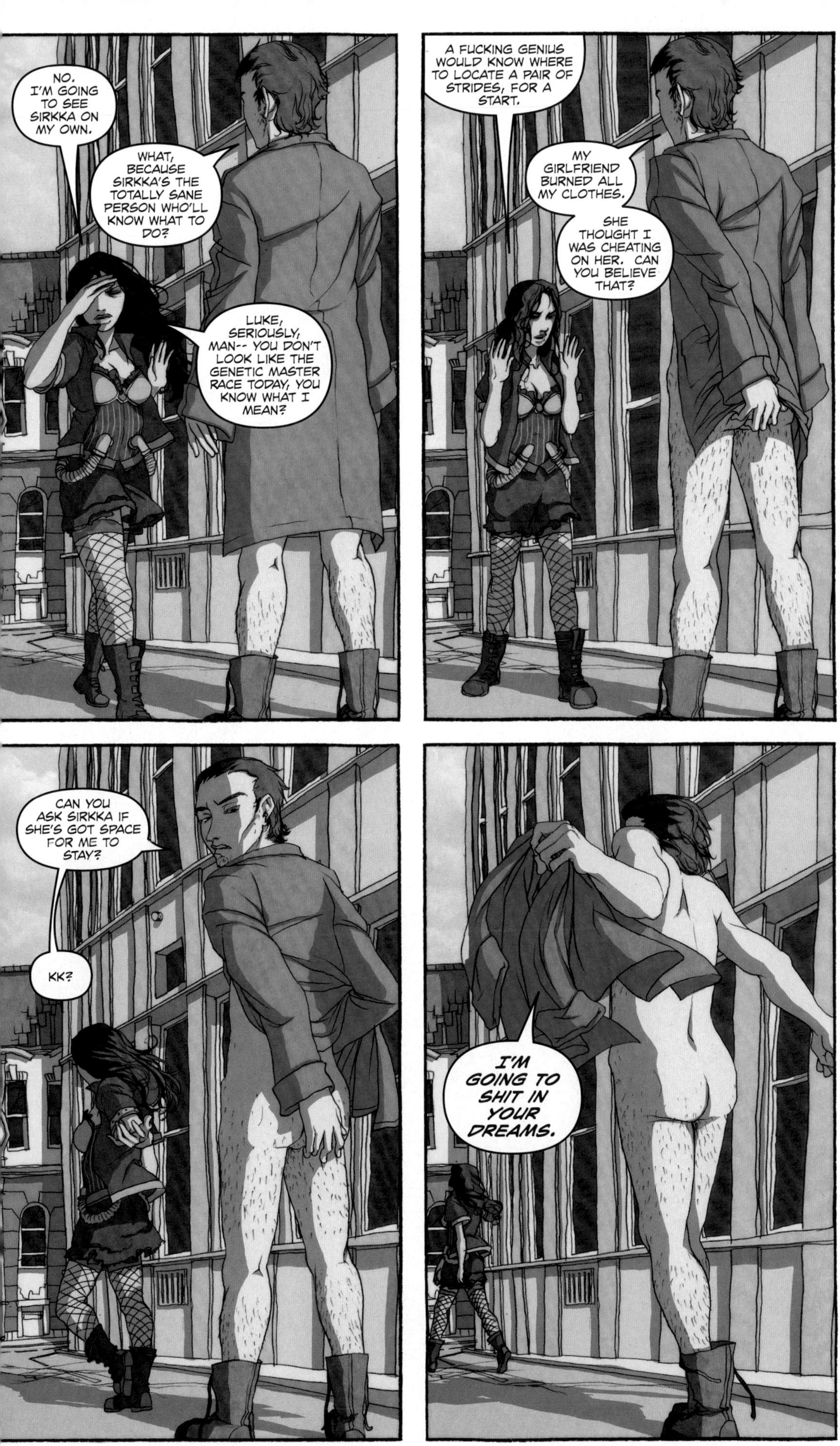
NO. I'M GOING TO SEE SIRKKA ON MY OWN.
WHAT, BECAUSE SIRKKA'S THE TOTALLY SANE PERSON WHO'LL KNOW WHAT TO DO?
LUKE, SERIOUSLY, MAN-- YOU DON'T LOOK LIKE THE GENETIC MASTER RACE TODAY, YOU KNOW WHAT I MEAN?
A FUCKING GENIUS WOULD KNOW WHERE TO LOCATE A PAIR OF STRIDES, FOR A START.
MY GIRLFRIEND BURNED ALL MY CLOTHES.
SHE THOUGHT I WAS CHEATING ON HER. CAN YOU BELIEVE THAT?
CAN YOU ASK SIRKKA IF SHE'S GOT SPACE FOR ME TO STAY?
KK?
I'M GOING TO SHIT IN YOUR DREAMS.

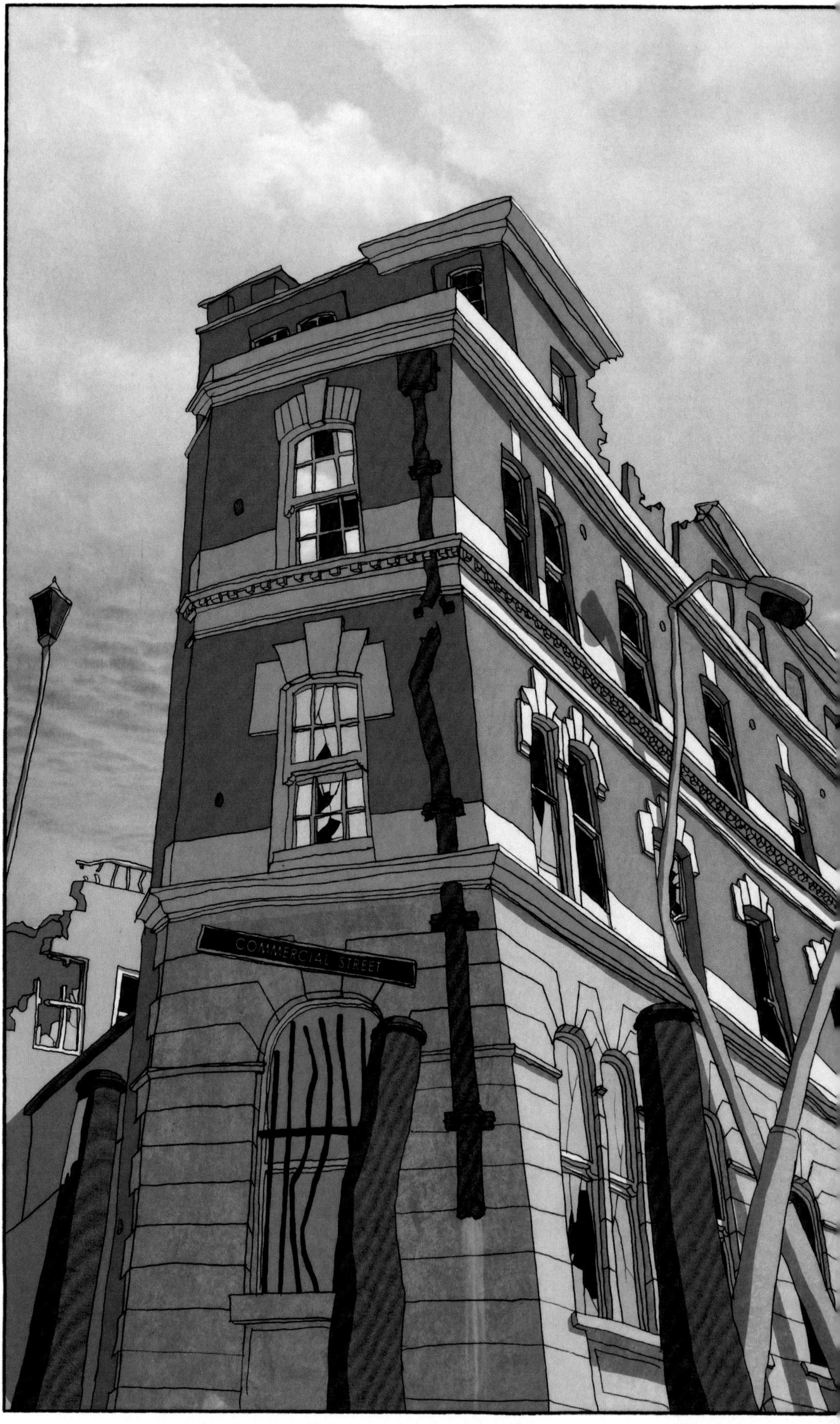
COMMERCIAL STREET

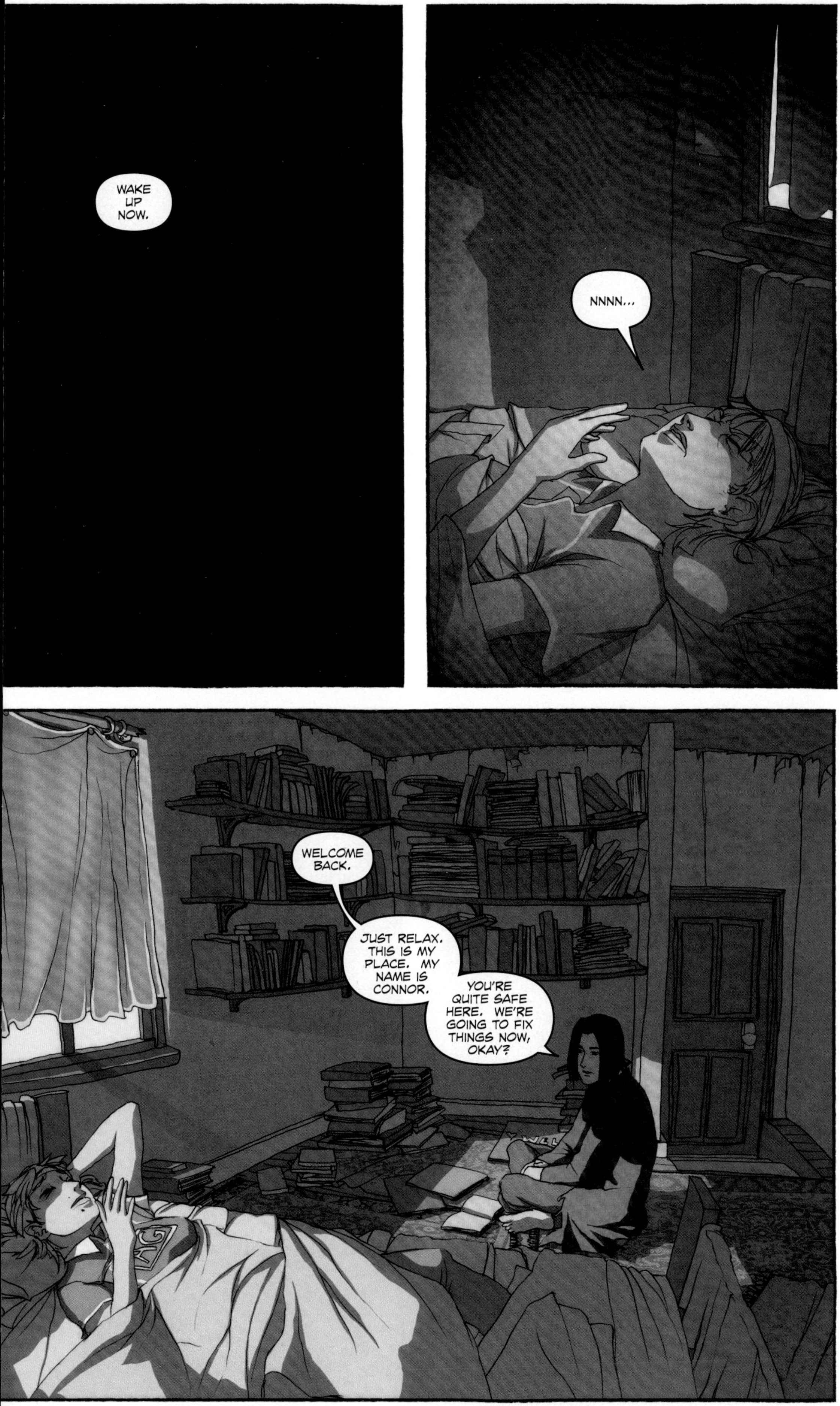
WAKE UP NOW.
NNNN...
WELCOME BACK.
JUST RELAX. THIS IS MY PLACE. MY NAME IS CONNOR.
YOU'RE QUITE SAFE HERE. WE'RE GOING TO FIX THINGS NOW, OKAY?

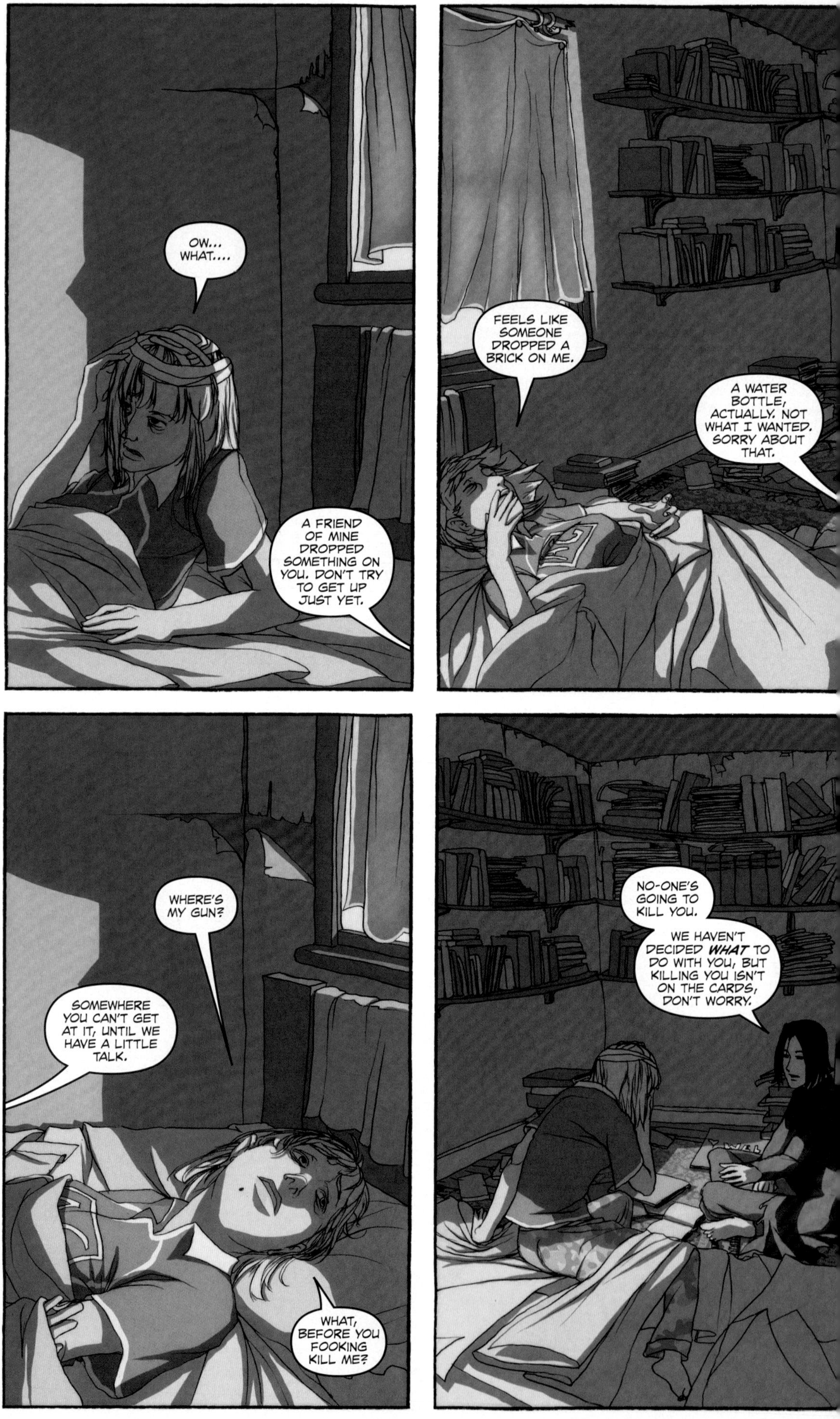
OW... WHAT....
A FRIEND OF MINE DROPPED SOMETHING ON YOU. DON'T TRY TO GET UP JUST YET.
FEELS LIKE SOMEONE DROPPED A BRICK ON ME.
A WATER BOTTLE, ACTUALLY. NOT WHAT I WANTED. SORRY ABOUT THAT.
WHERE'S MY GUN?
SOMEWHERE YOU CAN'T GET AT IT, UNTIL WE HAVE A LITTLE TALK.
WHAT, BEFORE YOU FOOKING KILL ME?
NO-ONE'S GOING TO KILL YOU.
WE HAVEN'T DECIDED *WHAT* TO DO WITH YOU, BUT KILLING YOU ISN'T ON THE CARDS, DON'T WORRY.

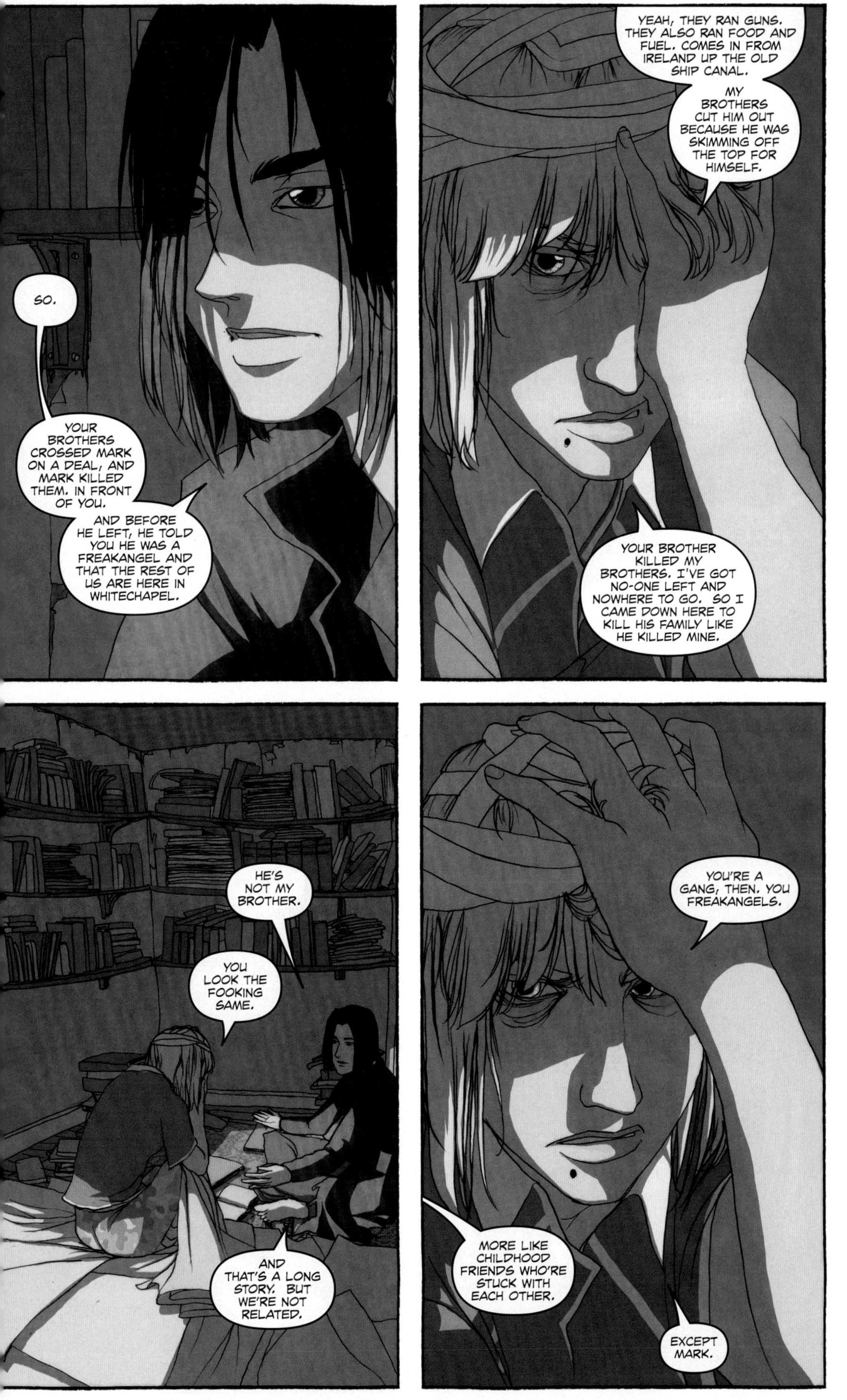
SO.
YOUR BROTHERS CROSSED MARK ON A DEAL, AND MARK KILLED THEM. IN FRONT OF YOU.
AND BEFORE HE LEFT, HE TOLD YOU HE WAS A FREAKANGEL AND THAT THE REST OF US ARE HERE IN WHITECHAPEL.
YEAH, THEY RAN GUNS. THEY ALSO RAN FOOD AND FUEL. COMES IN FROM IRELAND UP THE OLD SHIP CANAL.
MY BROTHERS CUT HIM OUT BECAUSE HE WAS SKIMMING OFF THE TOP FOR HIMSELF.
YOUR BROTHER KILLED MY BROTHERS. I'VE GOT NO-ONE LEFT AND NOWHERE TO GO. SO I CAME DOWN HERE TO KILL HIS FAMILY LIKE HE KILLED MINE.
HE'S NOT MY BROTHER.
YOU LOOK THE FOOKING SAME.
AND THAT'S A LONG STORY. BUT WE'RE NOT RELATED.
YOU'RE A GANG, THEN. YOU FREAKANGELS.
MORE LIKE CHILDHOOD FRIENDS WHO'RE STUCK WITH EACH OTHER.
EXCEPT MARK.

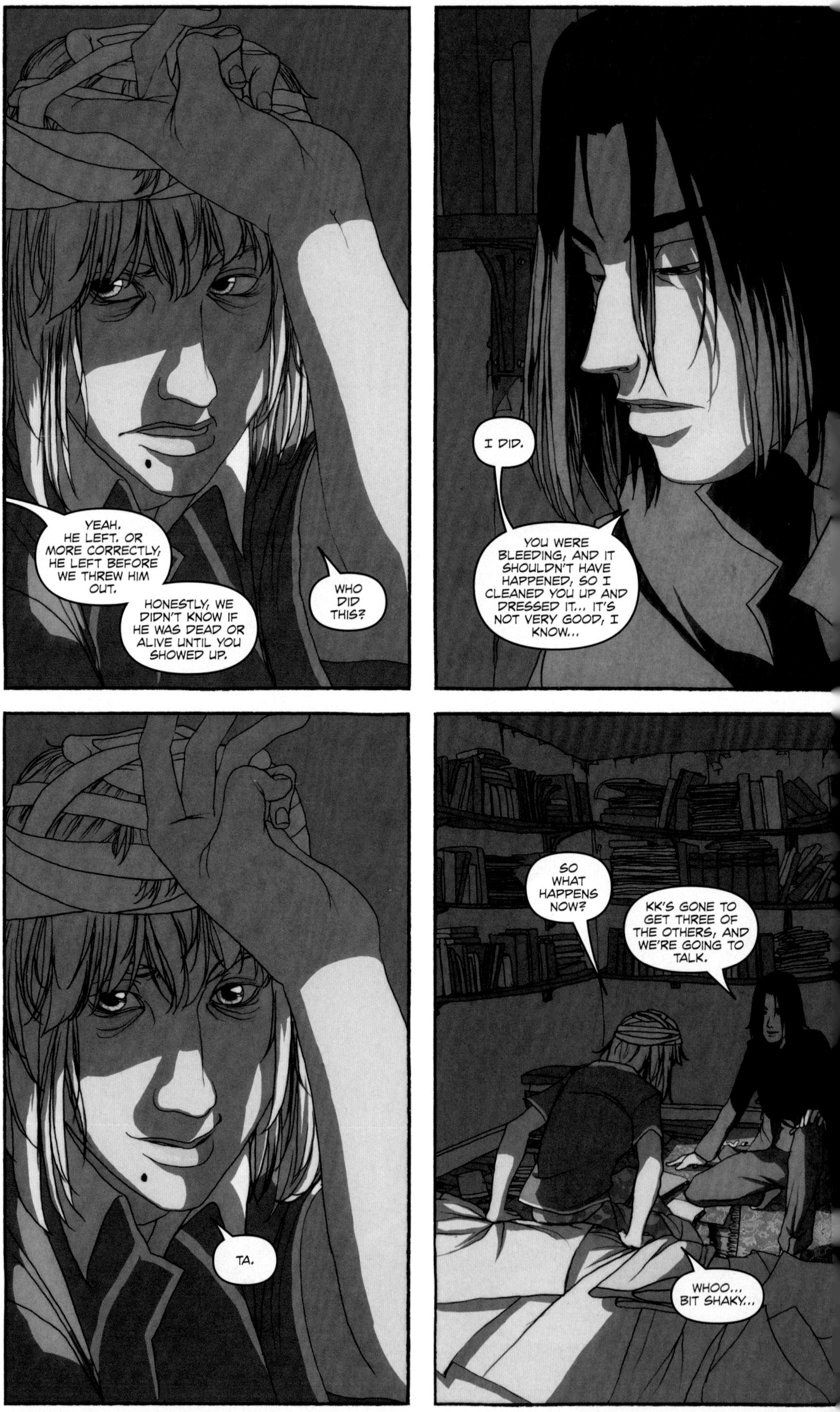
YEAH. HE LEFT. OR MORE CORRECTLY, HE LEFT BEFORE WE THREW HIM OUT.
HONESTLY, WE DIDN'T KNOW IF HE WAS DEAD OR ALIVE UNTIL YOU SHOWED UP.
WHO DID THIS?
I DID.
YOU WERE BLEEDING, AND IT SHOULDN'T HAVE HAPPENED, SO I CLEANED YOU UP AND DRESSED IT... IT'S NOT VERY GOOD, I KNOW...
TA.
SO WHAT HAPPENS NOW?
KK'S GONE TO GET THREE OF THE OTHERS, AND WE'RE GOING TO TALK.
WHOO... BIT SHAKY...

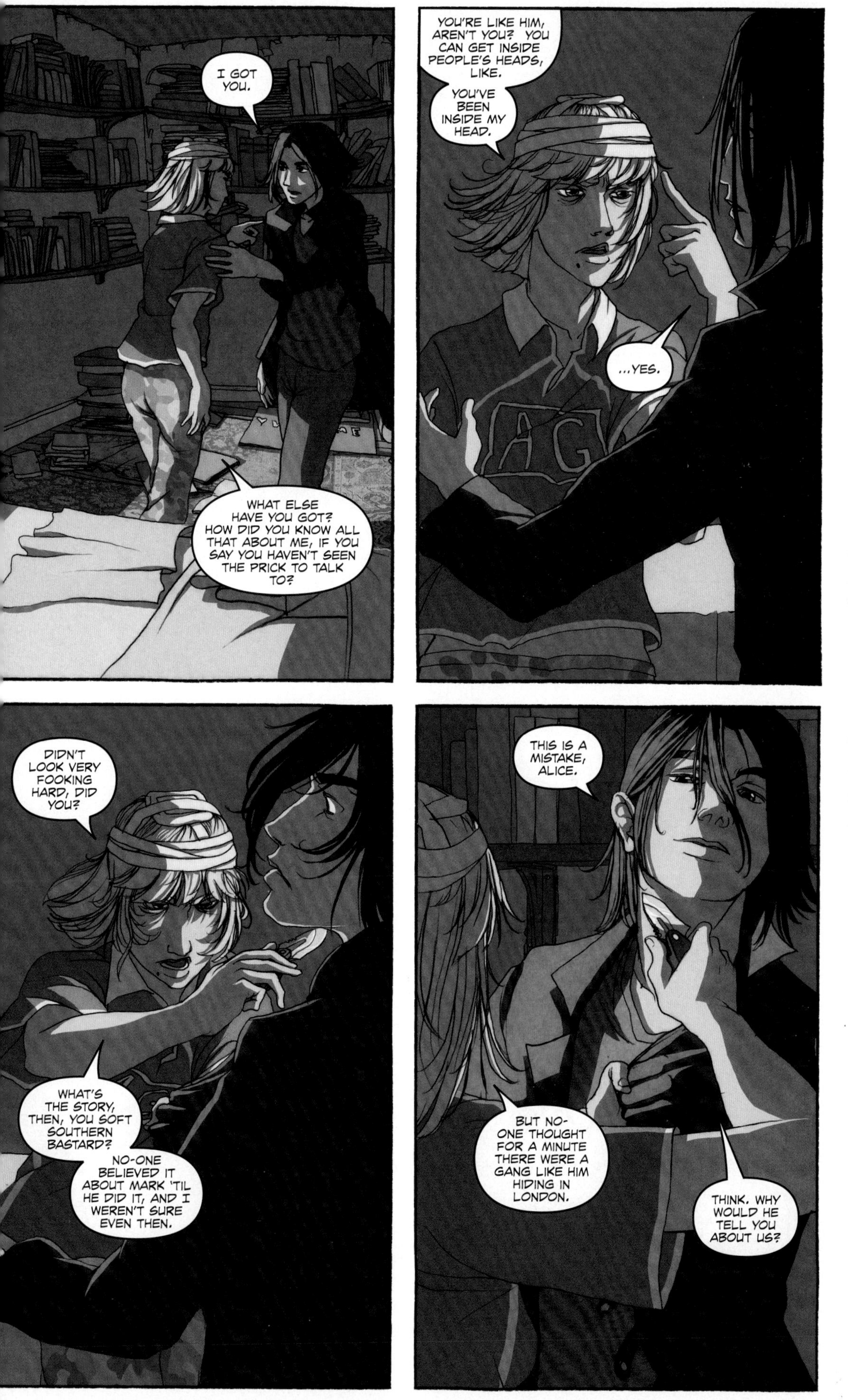
I GOT YOU.
WHAT ELSE HAVE YOU GOT? HOW DID YOU KNOW ALL THAT ABOUT ME, IF YOU SAY YOU HAVEN'T SEEN THE PRICK TO TALK TO?
YOU'RE LIKE HIM, AREN'T YOU? YOU CAN GET INSIDE PEOPLE'S HEADS, LIKE.
YOU'VE BEEN INSIDE MY HEAD.
...YES.
DIDN'T LOOK VERY FOOKING HARD, DID YOU?
WHAT'S THE STORY, THEN, YOU SOFT SOUTHERN BASTARD?
NO-ONE BELIEVED IT ABOUT MARK 'TIL HE DID IT, AND I WEREN'T SURE EVEN THEN.
THIS IS A MISTAKE, ALICE.
BUT NO-ONE THOUGHT FOR A MINUTE THERE WERE A GANG LIKE HIM HIDING IN LONDON.
THINK. WHY WOULD HE TELL YOU ABOUT US?

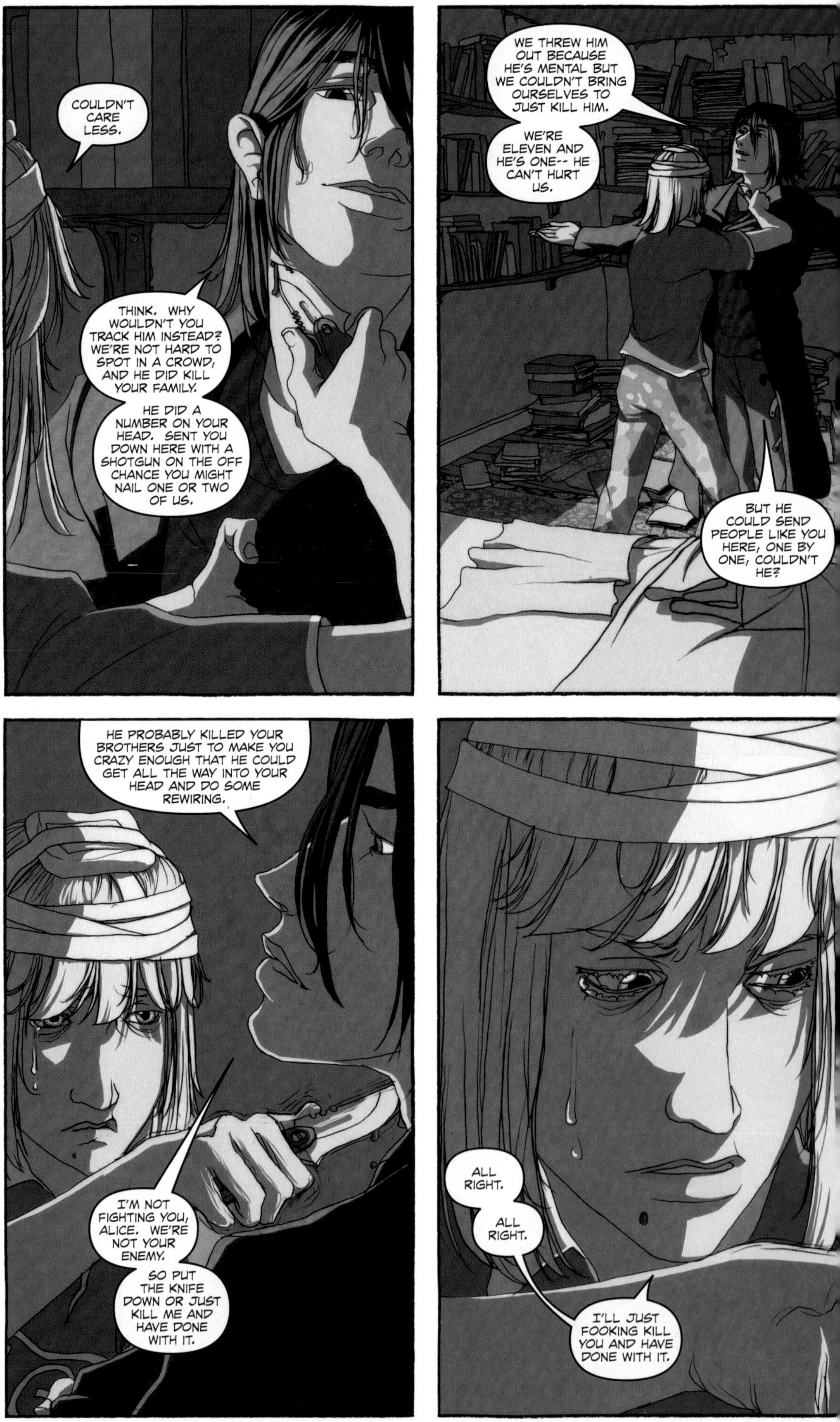
COULDN'T CARE LESS.
THINK. WHY WOULDN'T YOU TRACK HIM INSTEAD? WE'RE NOT HARD TO SPOT IN A CROWD, AND HE DID KILL YOUR FAMILY.
HE DID A NUMBER ON YOUR HEAD. SENT YOU DOWN HERE WITH A SHOTGUN ON THE OFF CHANCE YOU MIGHT NAIL ONE OR TWO OF US.
WE THREW HIM OUT BECAUSE HE'S MENTAL BUT WE COULDN'T BRING OURSELVES TO JUST KILL HIM.
WE'RE ELEVEN AND HE'S ONE-- HE CAN'T HURT US.
BUT HE COULD SEND PEOPLE LIKE YOU HERE, ONE BY ONE, COULDN'T HE?
HE PROBABLY KILLED YOUR BROTHERS JUST TO MAKE YOU CRAZY ENOUGH THAT HE COULD GET ALL THE WAY INTO YOUR HEAD AND DO SOME REWIRING.
I'M NOT FIGHTING YOU, ALICE. WE'RE NOT YOUR ENEMY.
SO PUT THE KNIFE DOWN OR JUST KILL ME AND HAVE DONE WITH IT.
ALL RIGHT.
ALL RIGHT.
I'LL JUST FOOKING KILL YOU AND HAVE DONE WITH IT.

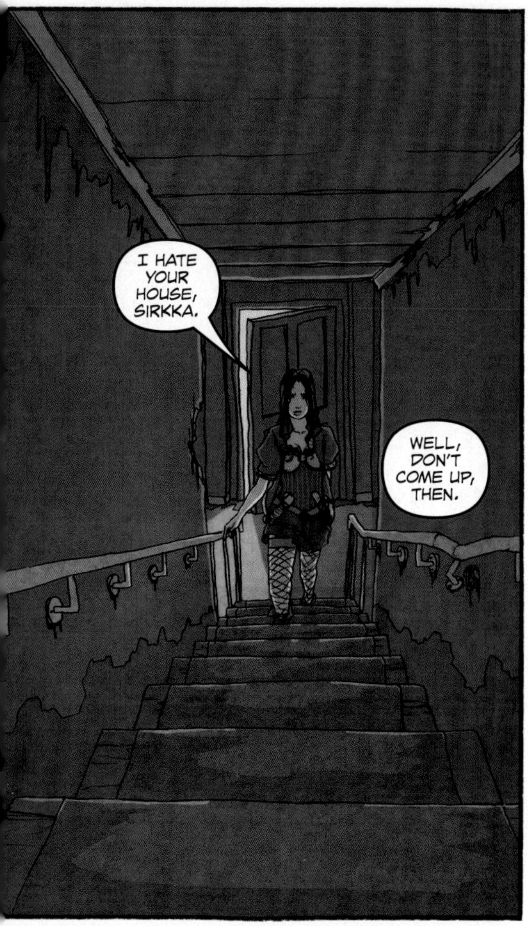
I HATE YOUR HOUSE, SIRKKA.
WELL, DON'T COME UP, THEN.

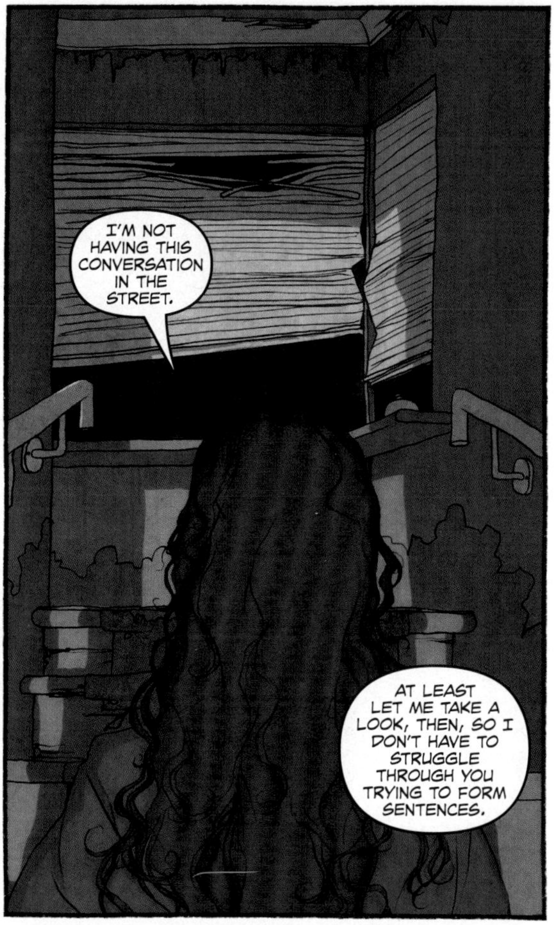
I'M NOT HAVING THIS CONVERSATION IN THE STREET.
AT LEAST LET ME TAKE A LOOK, THEN, SO I DON'T HAVE TO STRUGGLE THROUGH YOU TRYING TO FORM SENTENCES.

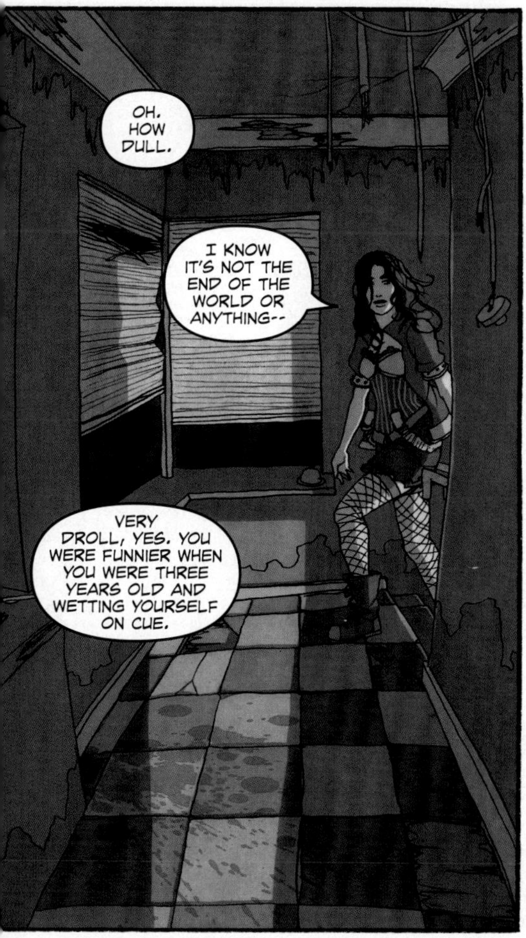
OH. HOW DULL.
I KNOW IT'S NOT THE END OF THE WORLD OR ANYTHING--
VERY DROLL, YES. YOU WERE FUNNIER WHEN YOU WERE THREE YEARS OLD AND WETTING YOURSELF ON CUE.

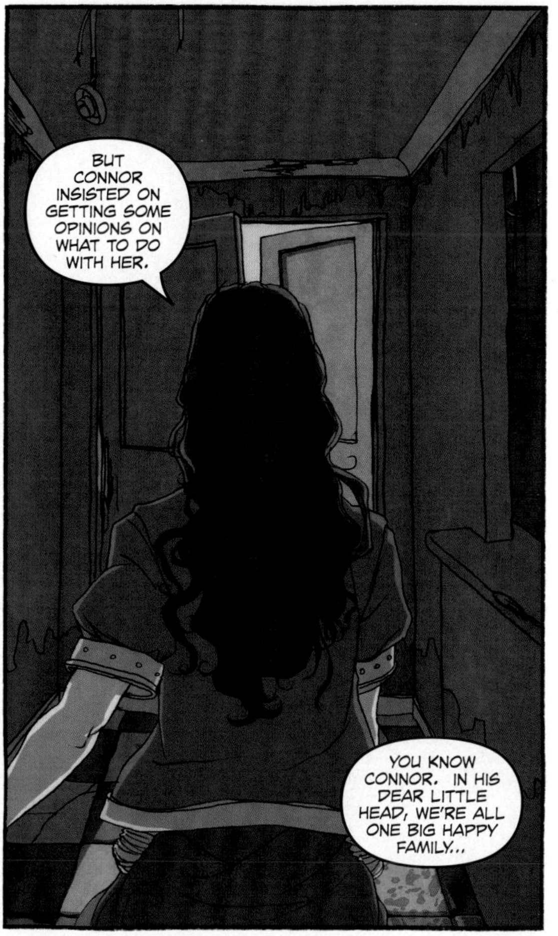
BUT CONNOR INSISTED ON GETTING SOME OPINIONS ON WHAT TO DO WITH HER.
YOU KNOW CONNOR. IN HIS DEAR LITTLE HEAD, WE'RE ALL ONE BIG HAPPY FAMILY...

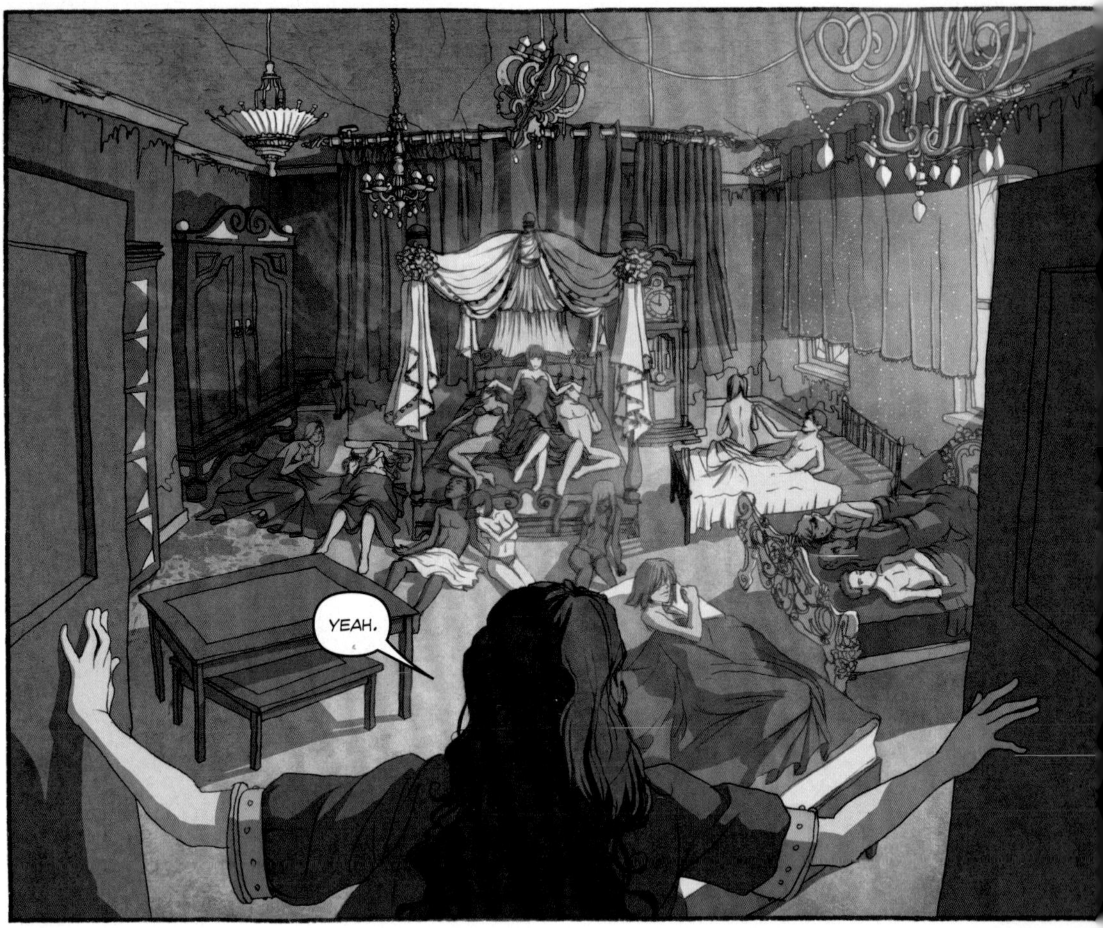
YEAH.

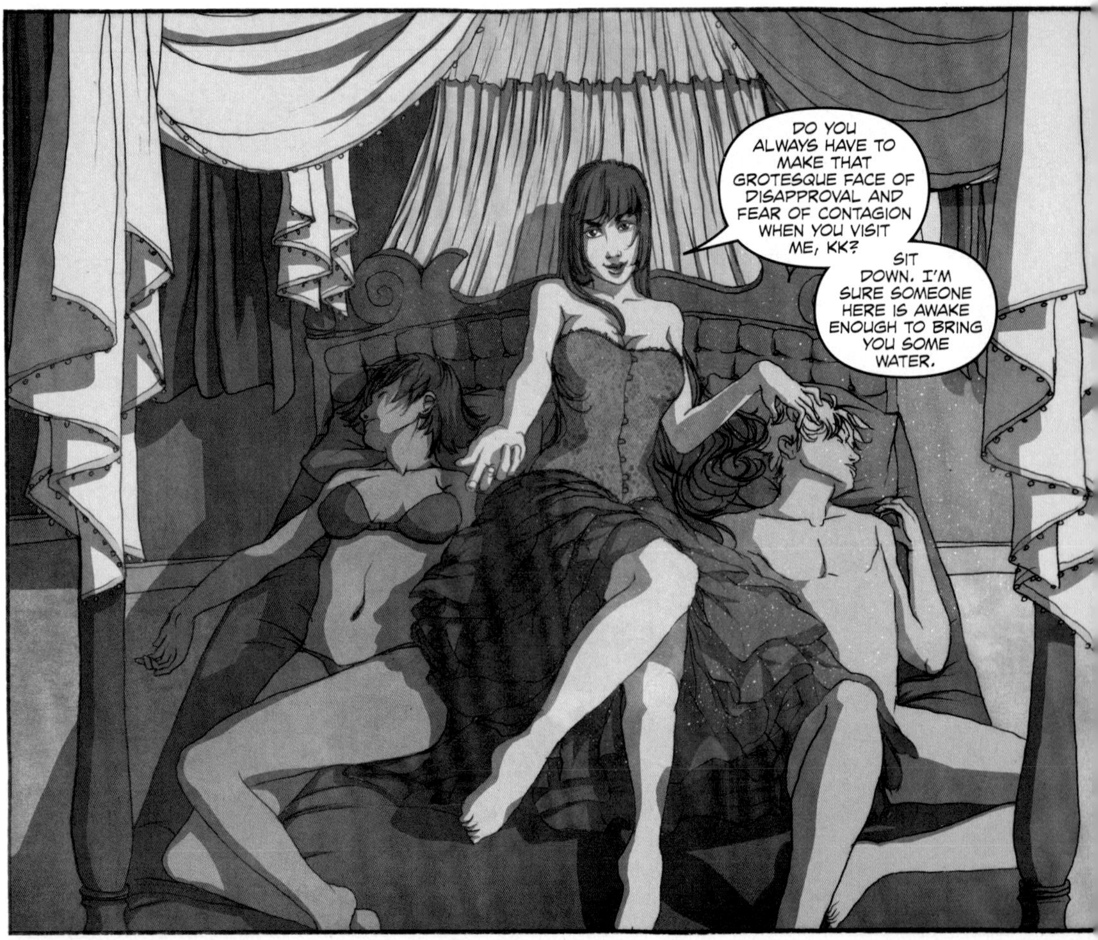
DO YOU ALWAYS HAVE TO MAKE THAT GROTESQUE FACE OF DISAPPROVAL AND FEAR OF CONTAGION WHEN YOU VISIT ME, KK?
SIT DOWN. I'M SURE SOMEONE HERE IS AWAKE ENOUGH TO BRING YOU SOME WATER.

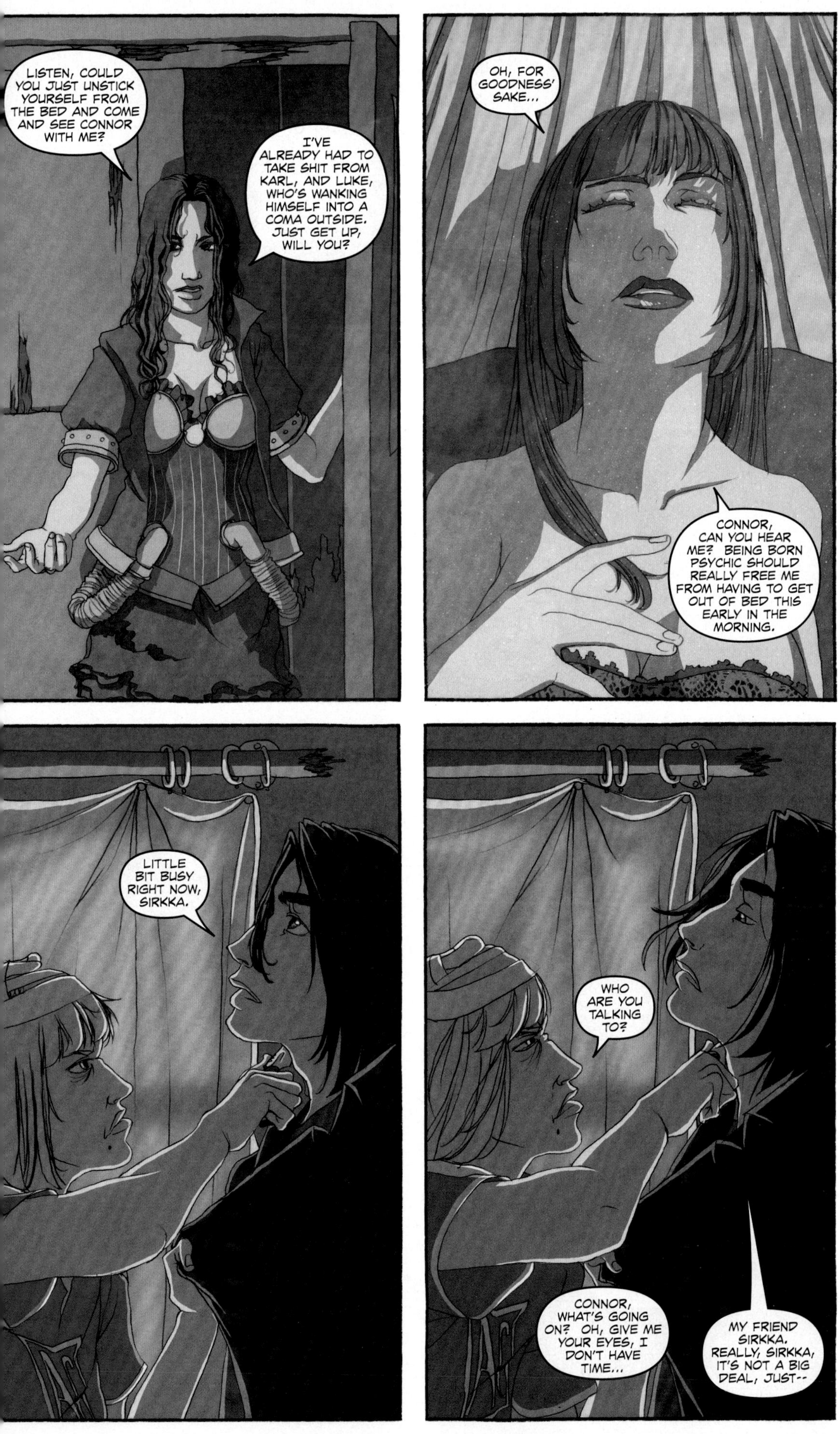

LISTEN, COULD YOU JUST UNSTICK YOURSELF FROM THE BED AND COME AND SEE CONNOR WITH ME?
I'VE ALREADY HAD TO TAKE SHIT FROM KARL, AND LUKE, WHO'S WANKING HIMSELF INTO A COMA OUTSIDE. JUST GET UP, WILL YOU?
OH, FOR GOODNESS' SAKE...
CONNOR, CAN YOU HEAR ME? BEING BORN PSYCHIC SHOULD REALLY FREE ME FROM HAVING TO GET OUT OF BED THIS EARLY IN THE MORNING.
LITTLE BIT BUSY RIGHT NOW, SIRKKA.
WHO ARE YOU TALKING TO?
CONNOR, WHAT'S GOING ON? OH, GIVE ME YOUR EYES, I DON'T HAVE TIME...
MY FRIEND SIRKKA. REALLY, SIRKKA, IT'S NOT A BIG DEAL, JUST--

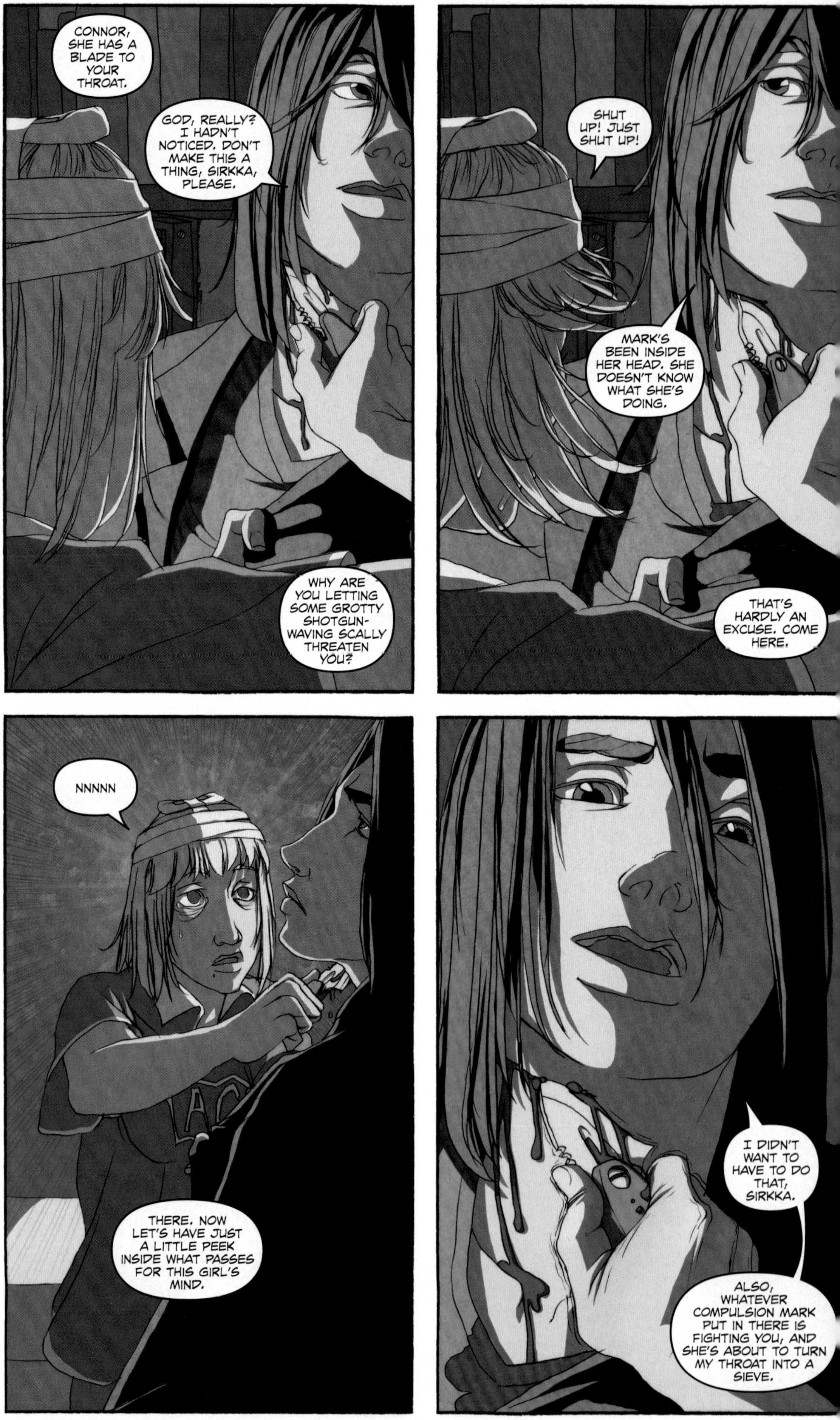
CONNOR, SHE HAS A BLADE TO YOUR THROAT.
GOD, REALLY? I HADN'T NOTICED. DON'T MAKE THIS A THING, SIRKKA, PLEASE.
WHY ARE YOU LETTING SOME GROTTY SHOTGUN-WAVING SCALLY THREATEN YOU?
SHUT UP! JUST SHUT UP!
MARK'S BEEN INSIDE HER HEAD. SHE DOESN'T KNOW WHAT SHE'S DOING.
THAT'S HARDLY AN EXCUSE. COME HERE.
NNNNN
THERE. NOW LET'S HAVE JUST A LITTLE PEEK INSIDE WHAT PASSES FOR THIS GIRL'S MIND.
I DIDN'T WANT TO HAVE TO DO THAT, SIRKKA.
ALSO, WHATEVER COMPULSION MARK PUT IN THERE IS FIGHTING YOU, AND SHE'S ABOUT TO TURN MY THROAT INTO A SIEVE.

ALL RIGHT, I'M COMING IN...

KK, SHE'S PISSED OFF ENOUGH ABOUT MY TALKING TO THIN AIR AS IT IS--

DON'T GIVE ME THAT. YOU JUST DON'T WANT TO HURT HER.

I'M NOT DOING THAT. MY FINGERS ARE MOVING AND I'M NOT DOING IT.

I KNOW. IT'S MY FRIENDS. JUST LET GO.

I... I CAN'T LET GO, BUT I DIDN'T MOVE THOSE FINGERS--

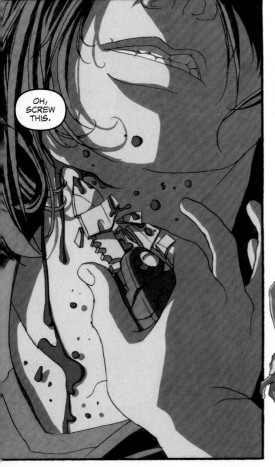

OH, SCREW THIS.

WE'RE FLUSHING HER BRAIN OUT, CONNOR.

WHATEVER'S LEFT AFTERWARDS IS ALL HER. WHICH KK AND I DOUBT WILL BE ANY MORE CHARMING, BUT STILL.

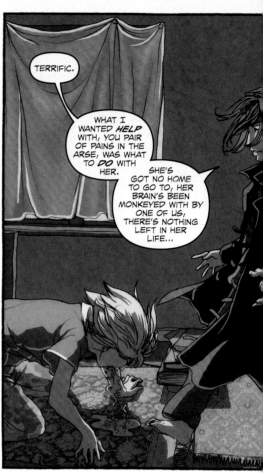

TERRIFIC.

WHAT I WANTED *HELP* WITH, YOU PAIR OF PAINS IN THE ARSE, WAS WHAT TO *DO* WITH HER.

SHE'S GOT NO HOME TO GO TO, HER BRAIN'S BEEN MONKEYED WITH BY ONE OF US, THERE'S NOTHING LEFT IN HER LIFE...

HE WANTS TO RESCUE HER.

STILL, I SUPPOSE HE NEEDS A HOBBY. ALSO, HE HASN'T BEEN LAID SINCE NOAH WAS A BOY.

ALL RIGHT, CONNOR...

...WE'VE BEEN LOOKING FOR SOMEONE TO SPELL KIRK ON THE LOOKOUT POSTS.

IF SHE APPEARS AT ALL SENTIENT AFTER SHE'S FINISHED PURGING, THEN WE MAY AS WELL GIVE THE GIRL A JOB.

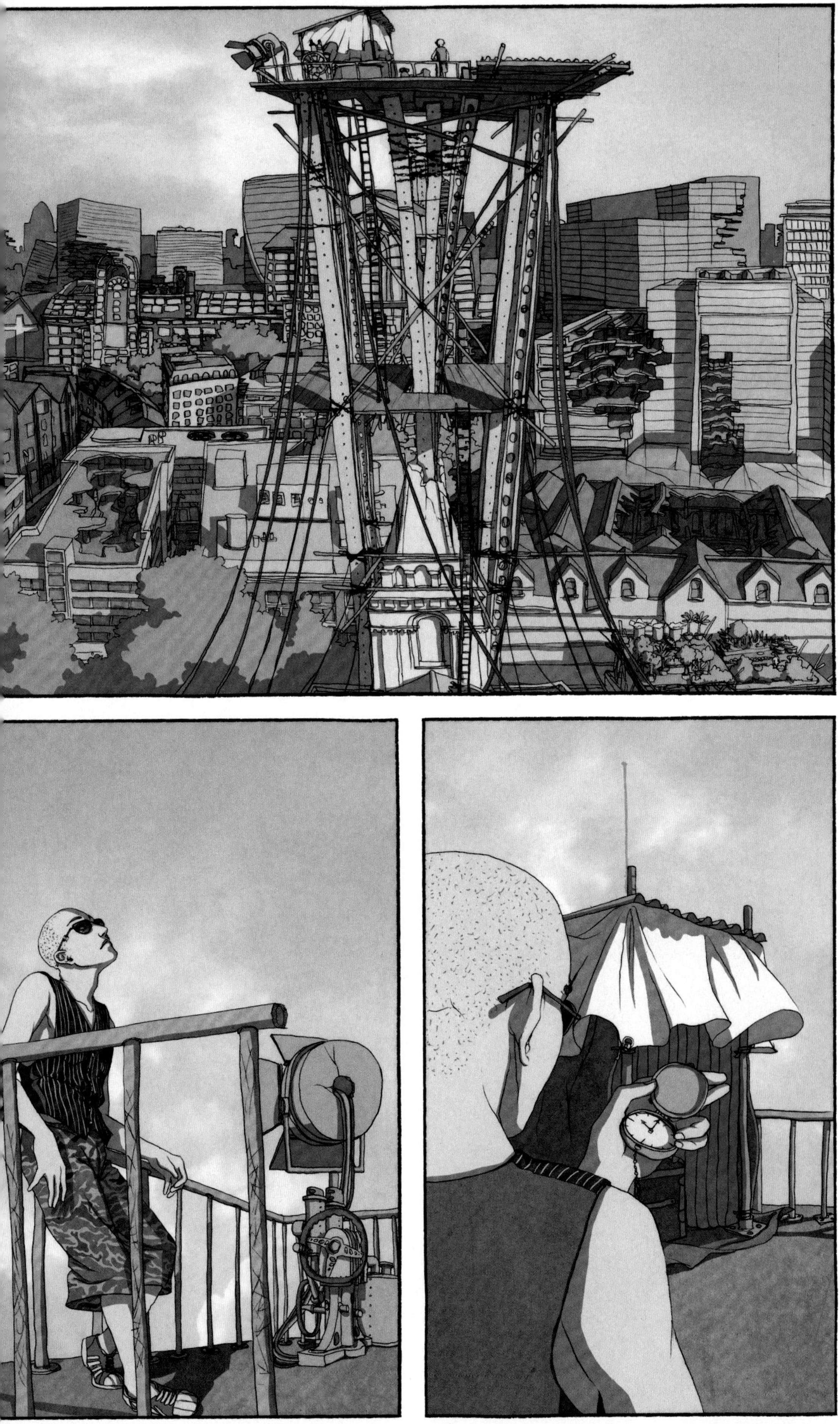

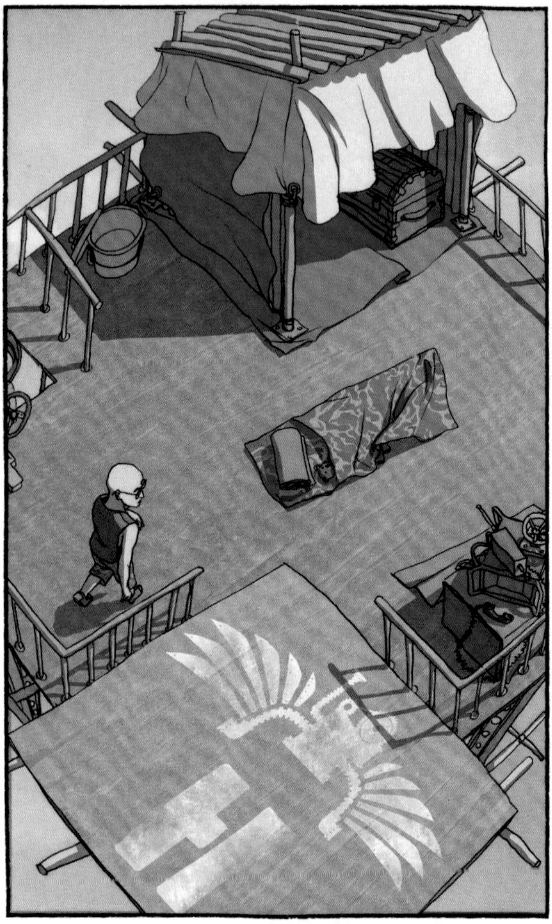

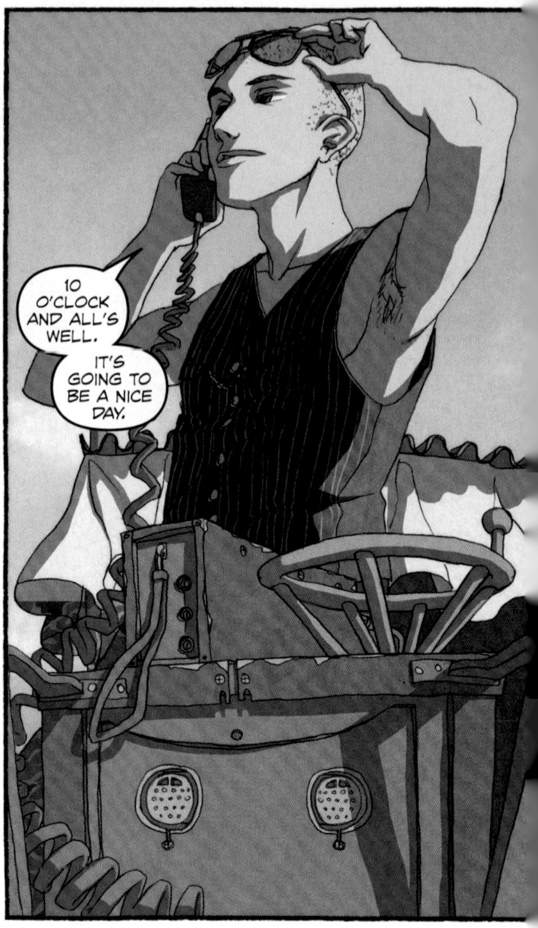
10 O'CLOCK AND ALL'S WELL.
IT'S GOING TO BE A NICE DAY.

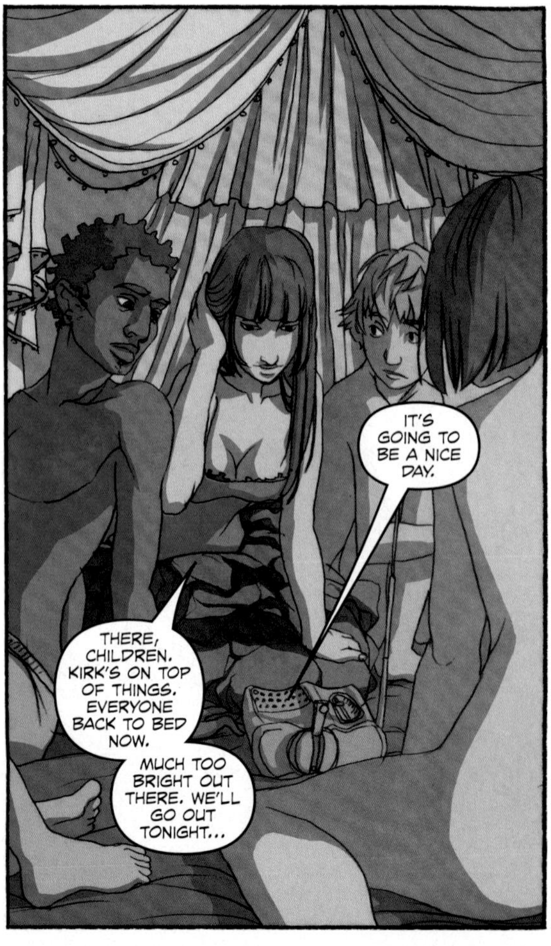
IT'S GOING TO BE A NICE DAY.
THERE, CHILDREN. KIRK'S ON TOP OF THINGS. EVERYONE BACK TO BED NOW.
MUCH TOO BRIGHT OUT THERE. WE'LL GO OUT TONIGHT...

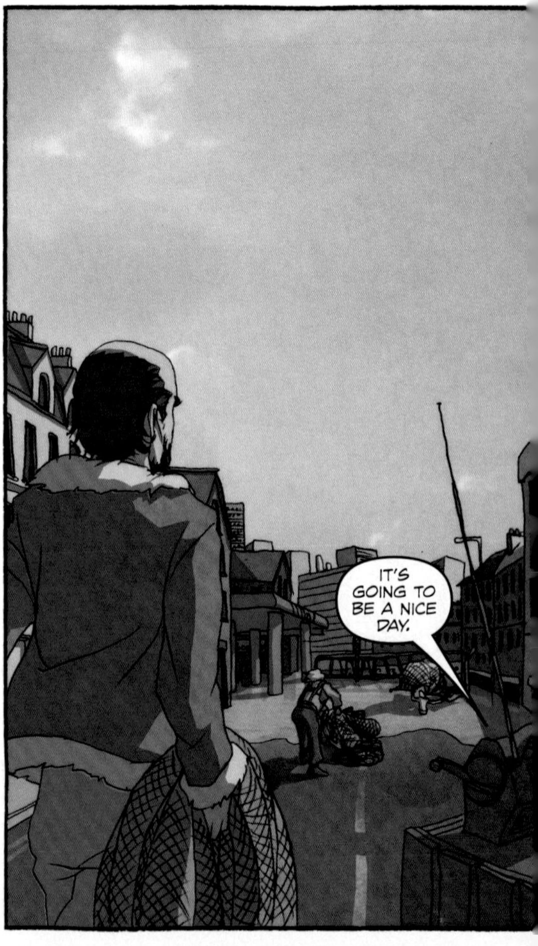
IT'S GOING TO BE A NICE DAY.

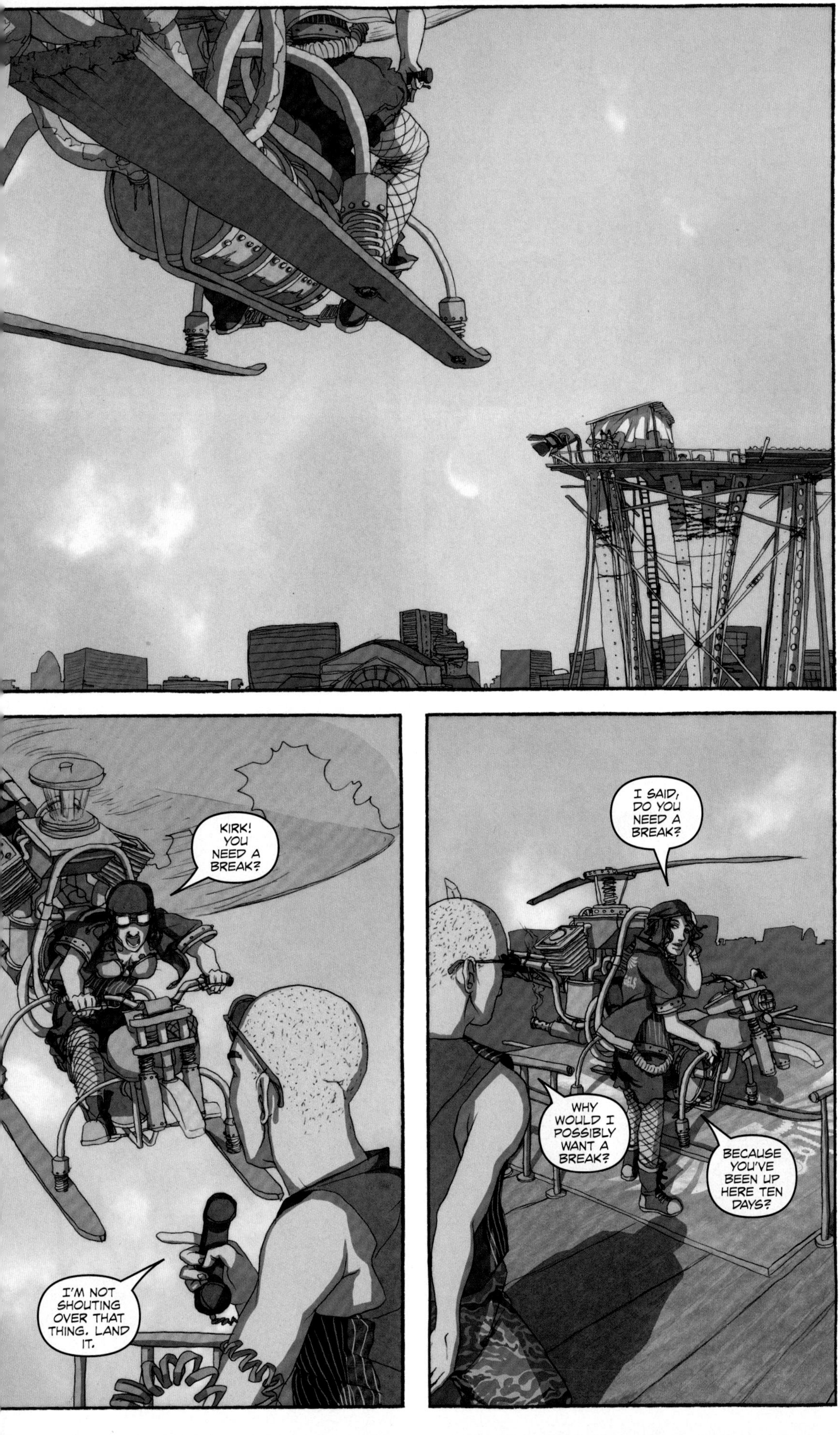
KIRK! YOU NEED A BREAK?
I'M NOT SHOUTING OVER THAT THING. LAND IT.
I SAID, DO YOU NEED A BREAK?
WHY WOULD I POSSIBLY WANT A BREAK?
BECAUSE YOU'VE BEEN UP HERE TEN DAYS?

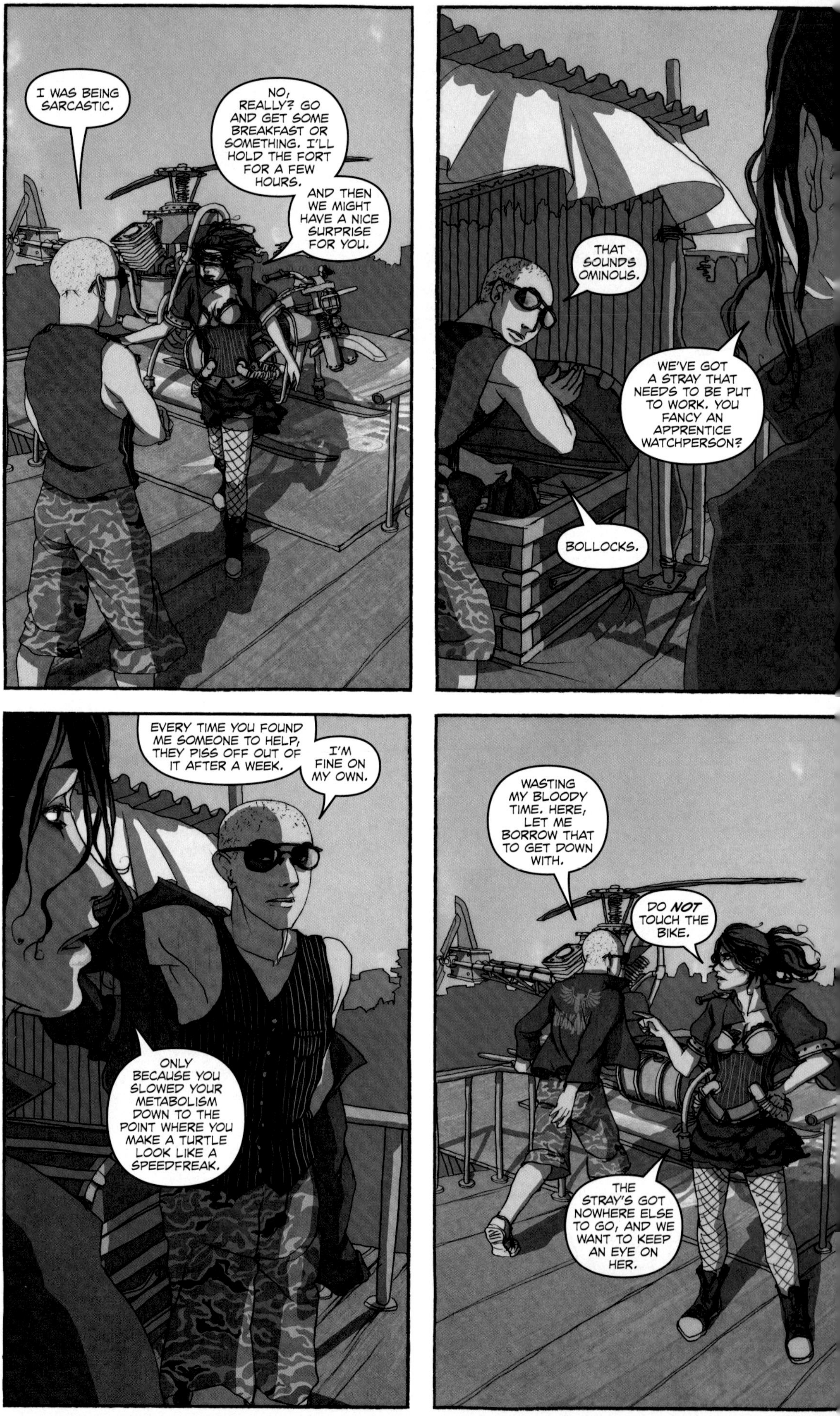
I WAS BEING SARCASTIC.
NO, REALLY? GO AND GET SOME BREAKFAST OR SOMETHING. I'LL HOLD THE FORT FOR A FEW HOURS.
AND THEN WE MIGHT HAVE A NICE SURPRISE FOR YOU.
THAT SOUNDS OMINOUS.
WE'VE GOT A STRAY THAT NEEDS TO BE PUT TO WORK. YOU FANCY AN APPRENTICE WATCHPERSON?
BOLLOCKS.
EVERY TIME YOU FOUND ME SOMEONE TO HELP, THEY PISS OFF OUT OF IT AFTER A WEEK.
I'M FINE ON MY OWN.
ONLY BECAUSE YOU SLOWED YOUR METABOLISM DOWN TO THE POINT WHERE YOU MAKE A TURTLE LOOK LIKE A SPEEDFREAK.
WASTING MY BLOODY TIME. HERE, LET ME BORROW THAT TO GET DOWN WITH.
DO **NOT** TOUCH THE BIKE.
THE STRAY'S GOT NOWHERE ELSE TO GO, AND WE WANT TO KEEP AN EYE ON HER.

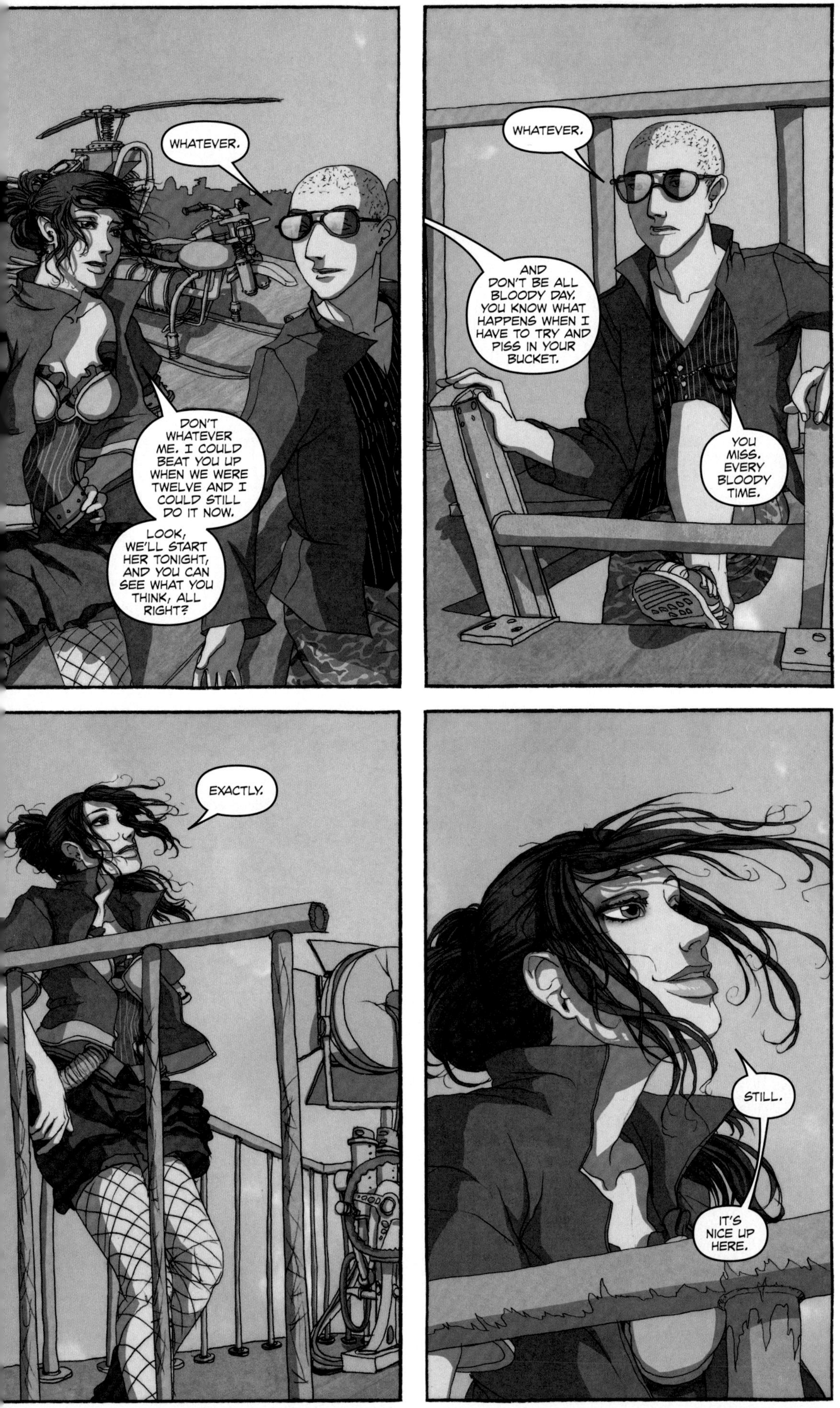
WHATEVER.
DON'T WHATEVER ME. I COULD BEAT YOU UP WHEN WE WERE TWELVE AND I COULD STILL DO IT NOW.
LOOK, WE'LL START HER TONIGHT, AND YOU CAN SEE WHAT YOU THINK, ALL RIGHT?
WHATEVER.
AND DON'T BE ALL BLOODY DAY. YOU KNOW WHAT HAPPENS WHEN I HAVE TO TRY AND PISS IN YOUR BUCKET.
YOU MISS. EVERY BLOODY TIME.
EXACTLY.
STILL.
IT'S NICE UP HERE.

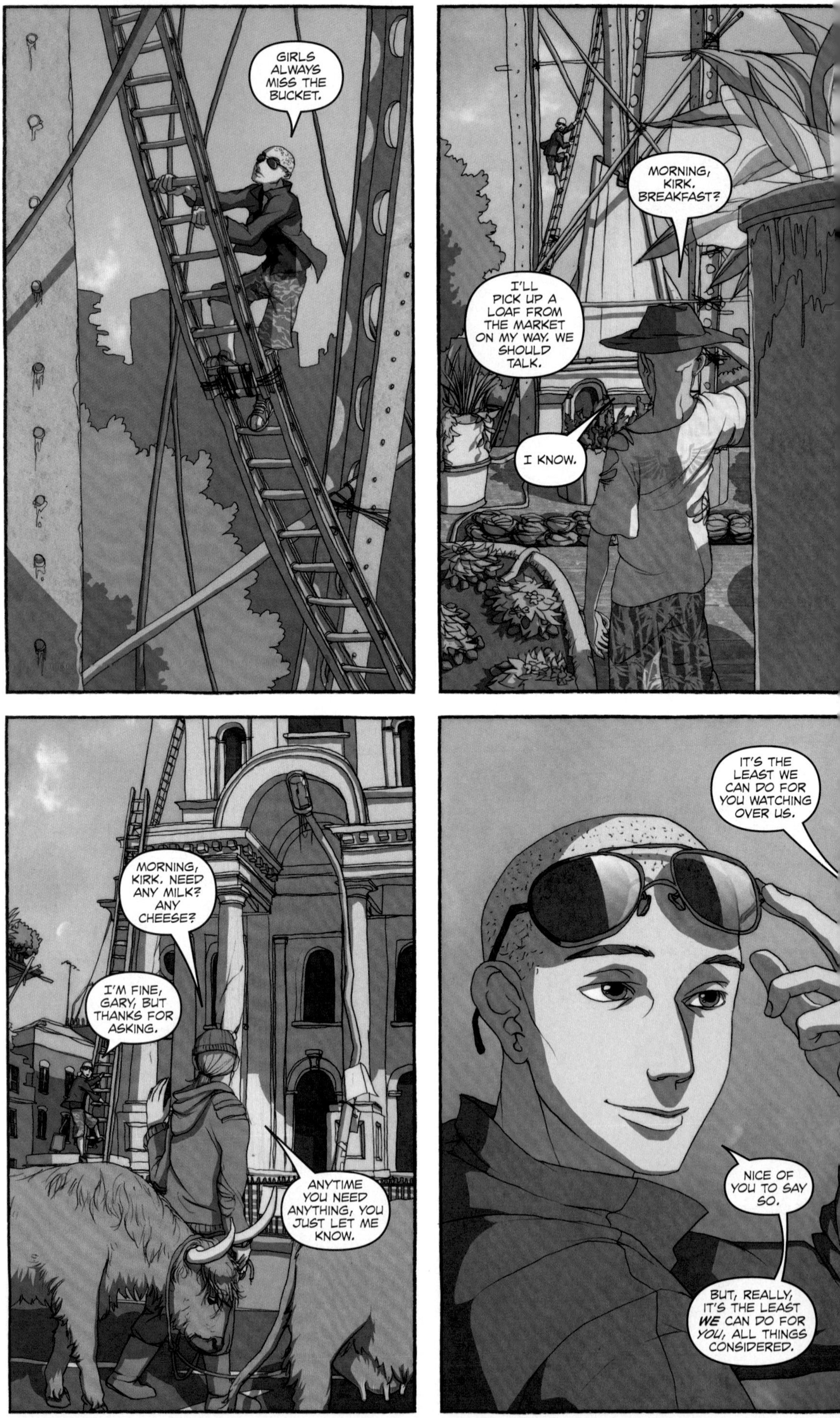
GIRLS ALWAYS MISS THE BUCKET.
MORNING, KIRK. BREAKFAST?
I'LL PICK UP A LOAF FROM THE MARKET ON MY WAY. WE SHOULD TALK.
I KNOW.
MORNING, KIRK. NEED ANY MILK? ANY CHEESE?
I'M FINE, GARY, BUT THANKS FOR ASKING.
ANYTIME YOU NEED ANYTHING, YOU JUST LET ME KNOW.
IT'S THE LEAST WE CAN DO FOR YOU WATCHING OVER US.
NICE OF YOU TO SAY SO.
BUT, REALLY, IT'S THE LEAST *WE* CAN DO FOR *YOU*, ALL THINGS CONSIDERED.

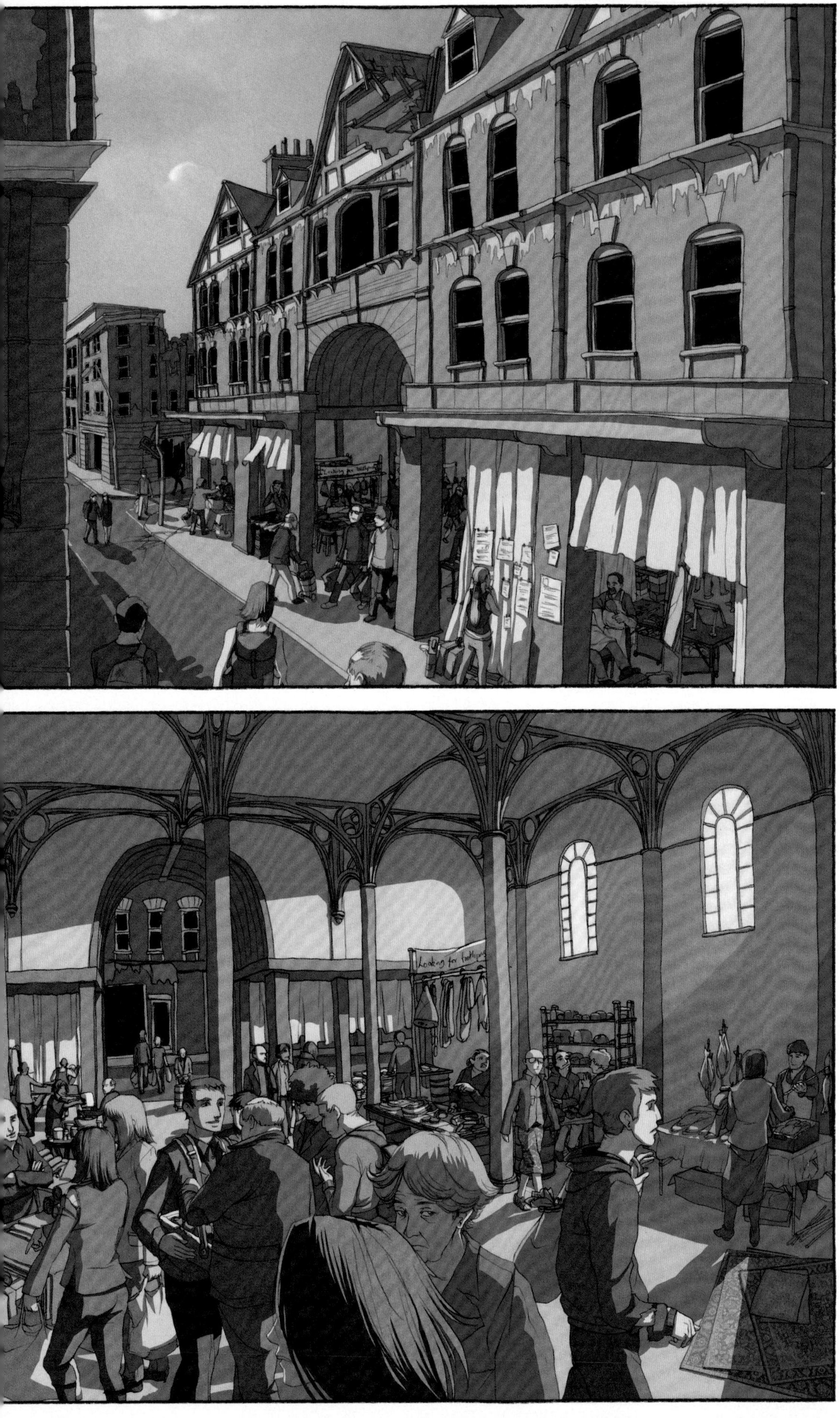
Looking for

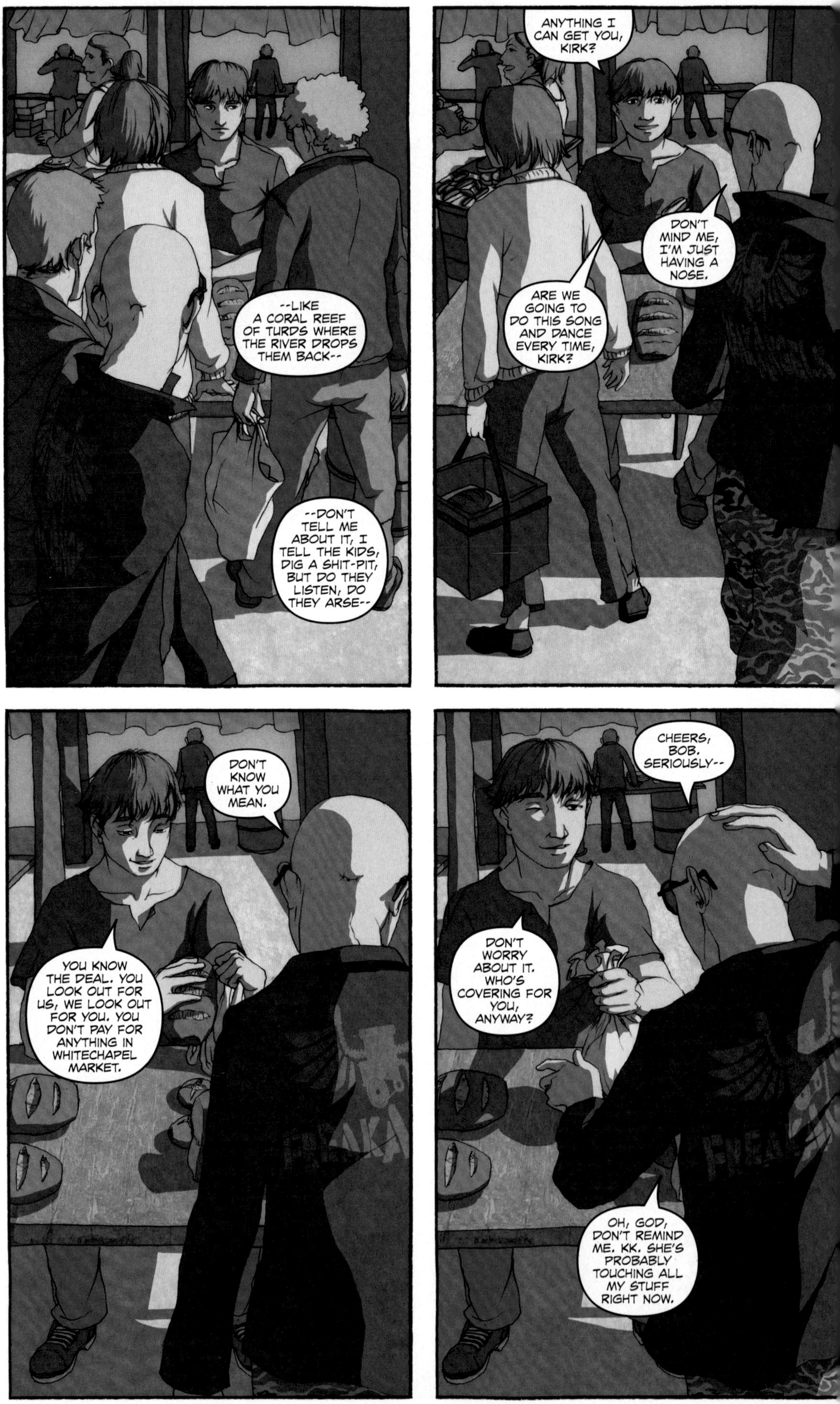
--LIKE A CORAL REEF OF TURDS WHERE THE RIVER DROPS THEM BACK--
--DON'T TELL ME ABOUT IT, I TELL THE KIDS, DIG A SHIT-PIT, BUT DO THEY LISTEN, DO THEY ARSE--
ANYTHING I CAN GET YOU, KIRK?
DON'T MIND ME, I'M JUST HAVING A NOSE.
ARE WE GOING TO DO THIS SONG AND DANCE EVERY TIME, KIRK?
DON'T KNOW WHAT YOU MEAN.
YOU KNOW THE DEAL. YOU LOOK OUT FOR US, WE LOOK OUT FOR YOU. YOU DON'T PAY FOR ANYTHING IN WHITECHAPEL MARKET.
CHEERS, BOB. SERIOUSLY--
DON'T WORRY ABOUT IT. WHO'S COVERING FOR YOU, ANYWAY?
OH, GOD, DON'T REMIND ME. KK. SHE'S PROBABLY TOUCHING ALL MY STUFF RIGHT NOW.

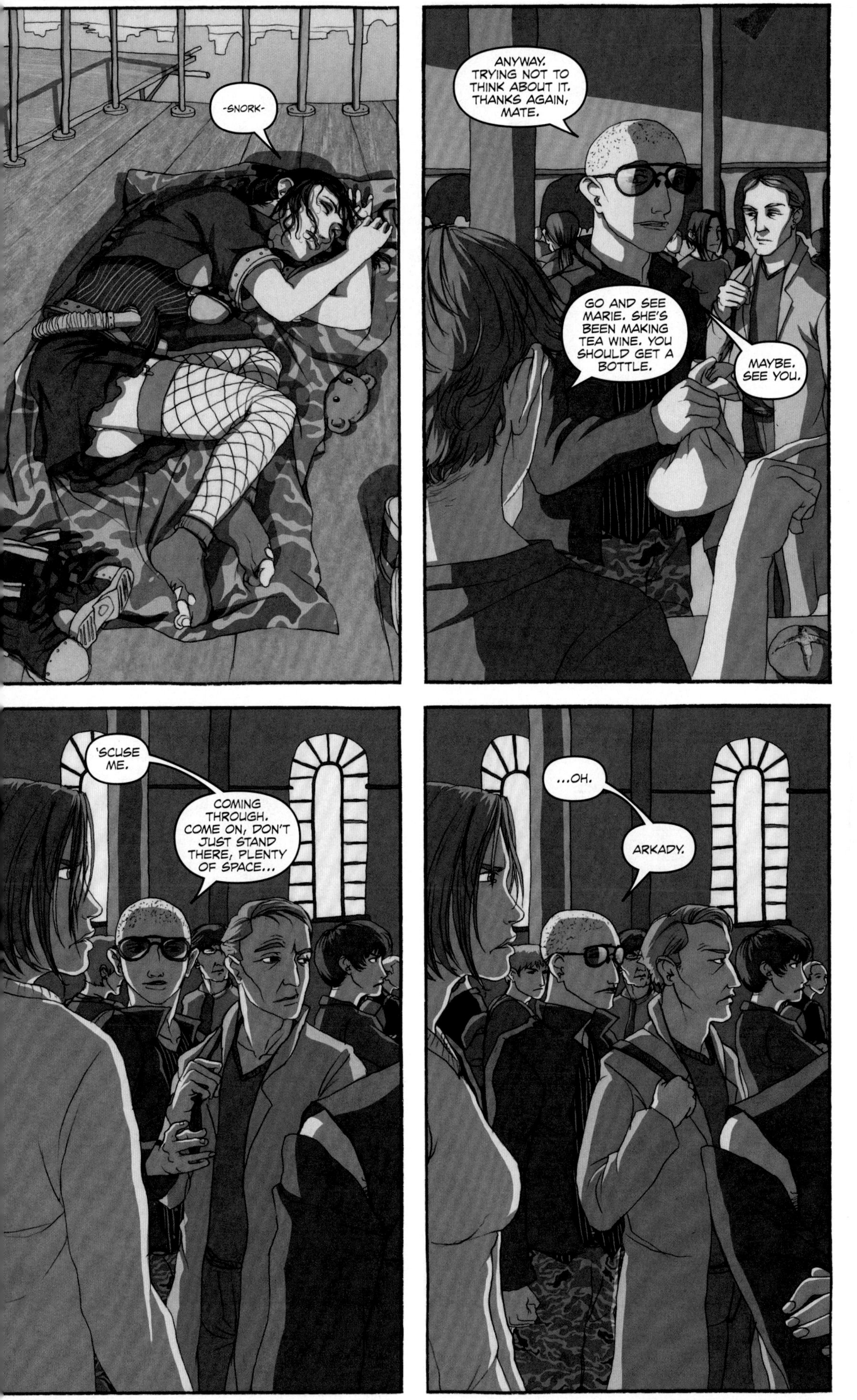
-SNORK-
ANYWAY. TRYING NOT TO THINK ABOUT IT. THANKS AGAIN, MATE.
GO AND SEE MARIE. SHE'S BEEN MAKING TEA WINE. YOU SHOULD GET A BOTTLE.
MAYBE. SEE YOU.
'SCUSE ME.
COMING THROUGH. COME ON, DON'T JUST STAND THERE, PLENTY OF SPACE...
...OH.
ARKADY.

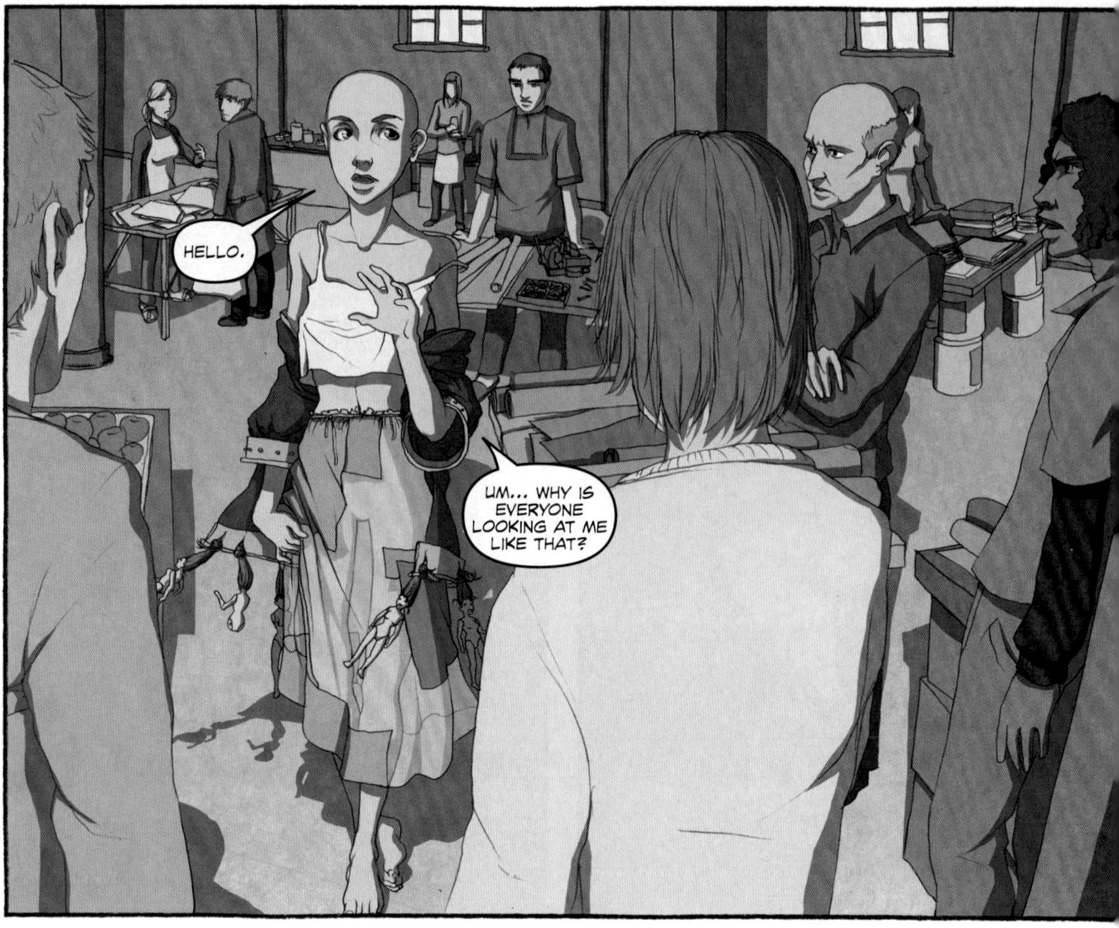
HELLO.
UM... WHY IS EVERYONE LOOKING AT ME LIKE THAT?

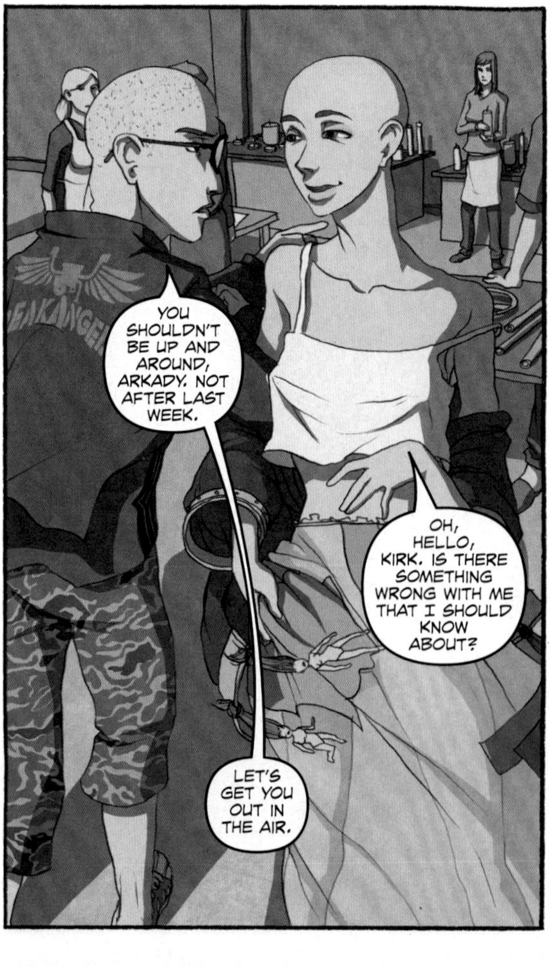
YOU SHOULDN'T BE UP AND AROUND, ARKADY. NOT AFTER LAST WEEK.
OH, HELLO, KIRK. IS THERE SOMETHING WRONG WITH ME THAT I SHOULD KNOW ABOUT?
LET'S GET YOU OUT IN THE AIR.

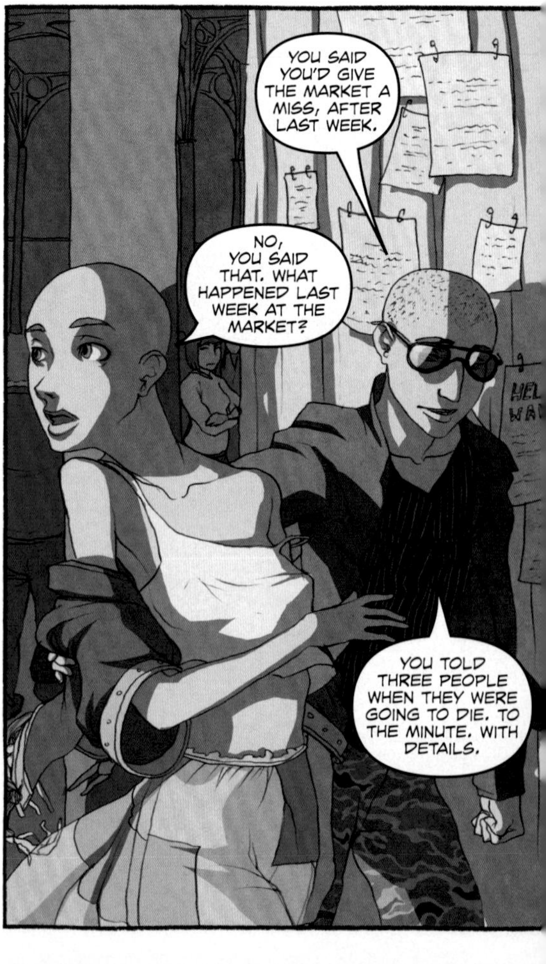
YOU SAID YOU'D GIVE THE MARKET A MISS, AFTER LAST WEEK.
NO, YOU SAID THAT. WHAT HAPPENED LAST WEEK AT THE MARKET?
YOU TOLD THREE PEOPLE WHEN THEY WERE GOING TO DIE. TO THE MINUTE. WITH DETAILS.

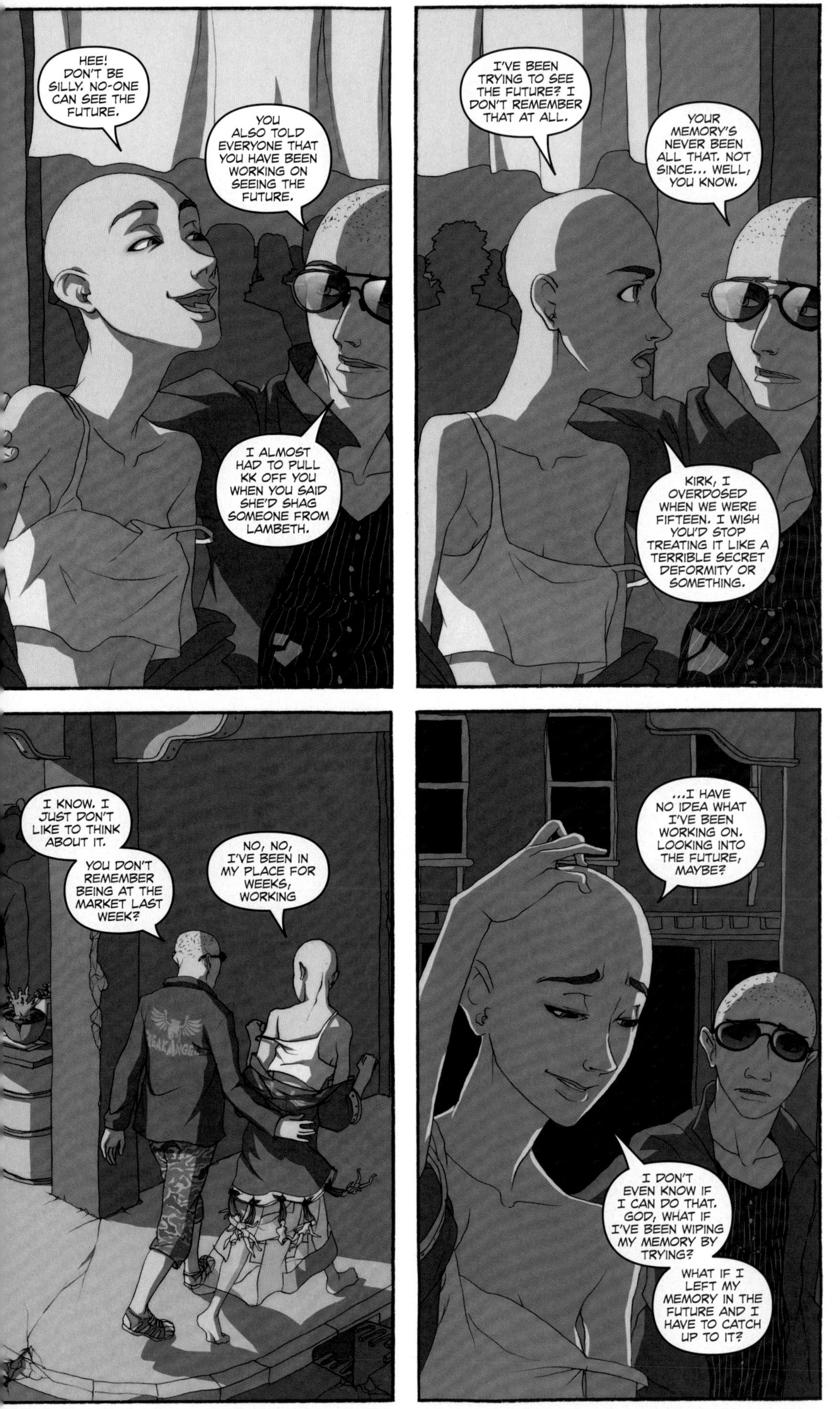
HEE! DON'T BE SILLY. NO-ONE CAN SEE THE FUTURE.
YOU ALSO TOLD EVERYONE THAT YOU HAVE BEEN WORKING ON SEEING THE FUTURE.
I ALMOST HAD TO PULL KK OFF YOU WHEN YOU SAID SHE'D SHAG SOMEONE FROM LAMBETH.
I'VE BEEN TRYING TO SEE THE FUTURE? I DON'T REMEMBER THAT AT ALL.
YOUR MEMORY'S NEVER BEEN ALL THAT. NOT SINCE... WELL, YOU KNOW.
KIRK, I OVERDOSED WHEN WE WERE FIFTEEN. I WISH YOU'D STOP TREATING IT LIKE A TERRIBLE SECRET DEFORMITY OR SOMETHING.
I KNOW. I JUST DON'T LIKE TO THINK ABOUT IT.
YOU DON'T REMEMBER BEING AT THE MARKET LAST WEEK?
NO, NO, I'VE BEEN IN MY PLACE FOR WEEKS, WORKING
...I HAVE NO IDEA WHAT I'VE BEEN WORKING ON. LOOKING INTO THE FUTURE, MAYBE?
I DON'T EVEN KNOW IF I CAN DO THAT. GOD, WHAT IF I'VE BEEN WIPING MY MEMORY BY TRYING?
WHAT IF I LEFT MY MEMORY IN THE FUTURE AND I HAVE TO CATCH UP TO IT?

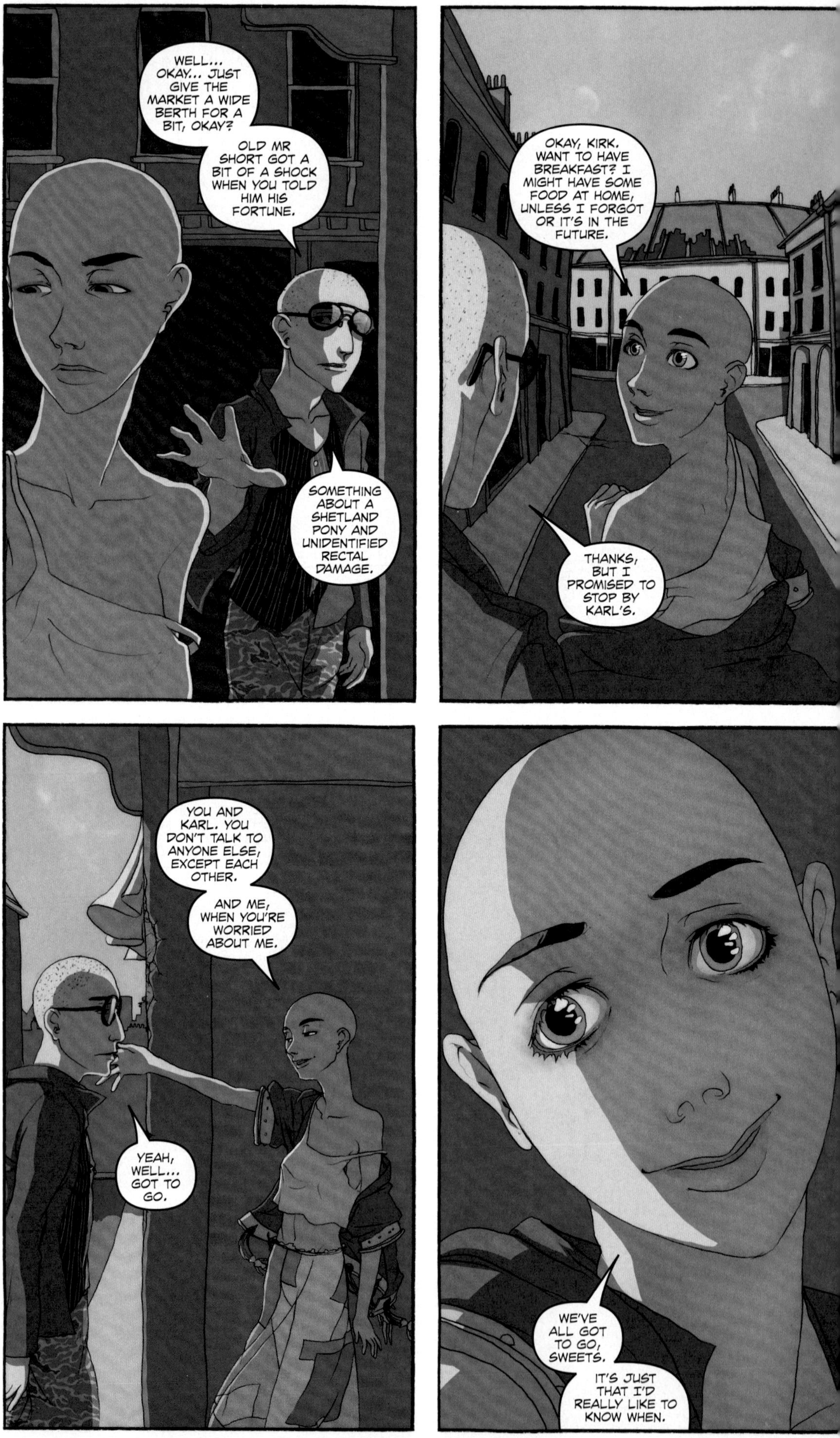

WELL... OKAY... JUST GIVE THE MARKET A WIDE BERTH FOR A BIT, OKAY?
OLD MR SHORT GOT A BIT OF A SHOCK WHEN YOU TOLD HIM HIS FORTUNE.
SOMETHING ABOUT A SHETLAND PONY AND UNIDENTIFIED RECTAL DAMAGE.
OKAY, KIRK. WANT TO HAVE BREAKFAST? I MIGHT HAVE SOME FOOD AT HOME, UNLESS I FORGOT OR IT'S IN THE FUTURE.
THANKS, BUT I PROMISED TO STOP BY KARL'S.
YOU AND KARL. YOU DON'T TALK TO ANYONE ELSE, EXCEPT EACH OTHER.
AND ME, WHEN YOU'RE WORRIED ABOUT ME.
YEAH, WELL... GOT TO GO.
WE'VE ALL GOT TO GO, SWEETS.
IT'S JUST THAT I'D REALLY LIKE TO KNOW WHEN.

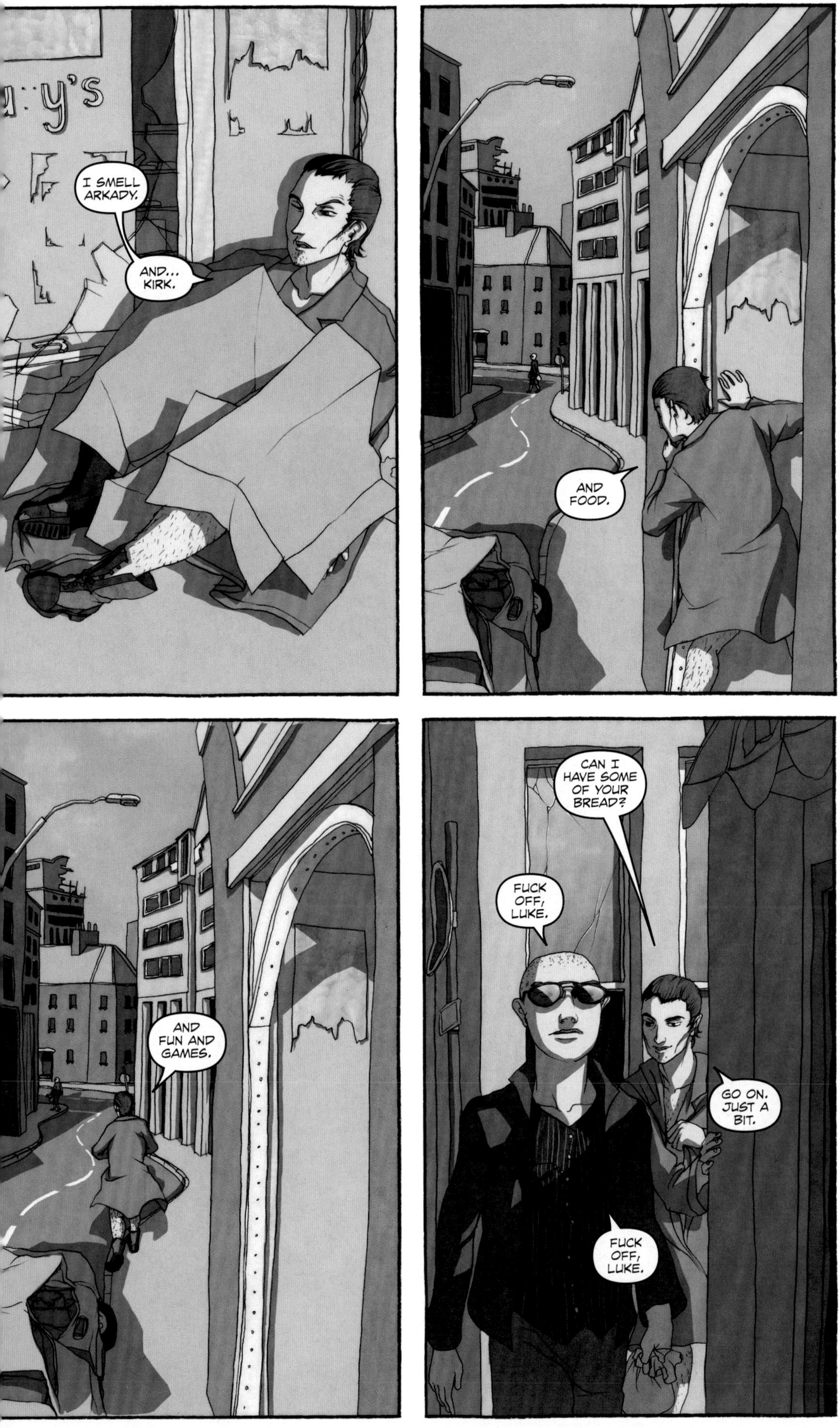

I SMELL ARKADY.
AND... KIRK.
AND FOOD.
AND FUN AND GAMES.
CAN I HAVE SOME OF YOUR BREAD?
FUCK OFF, LUKE.
GO ON. JUST A BIT.
FUCK OFF, LUKE.

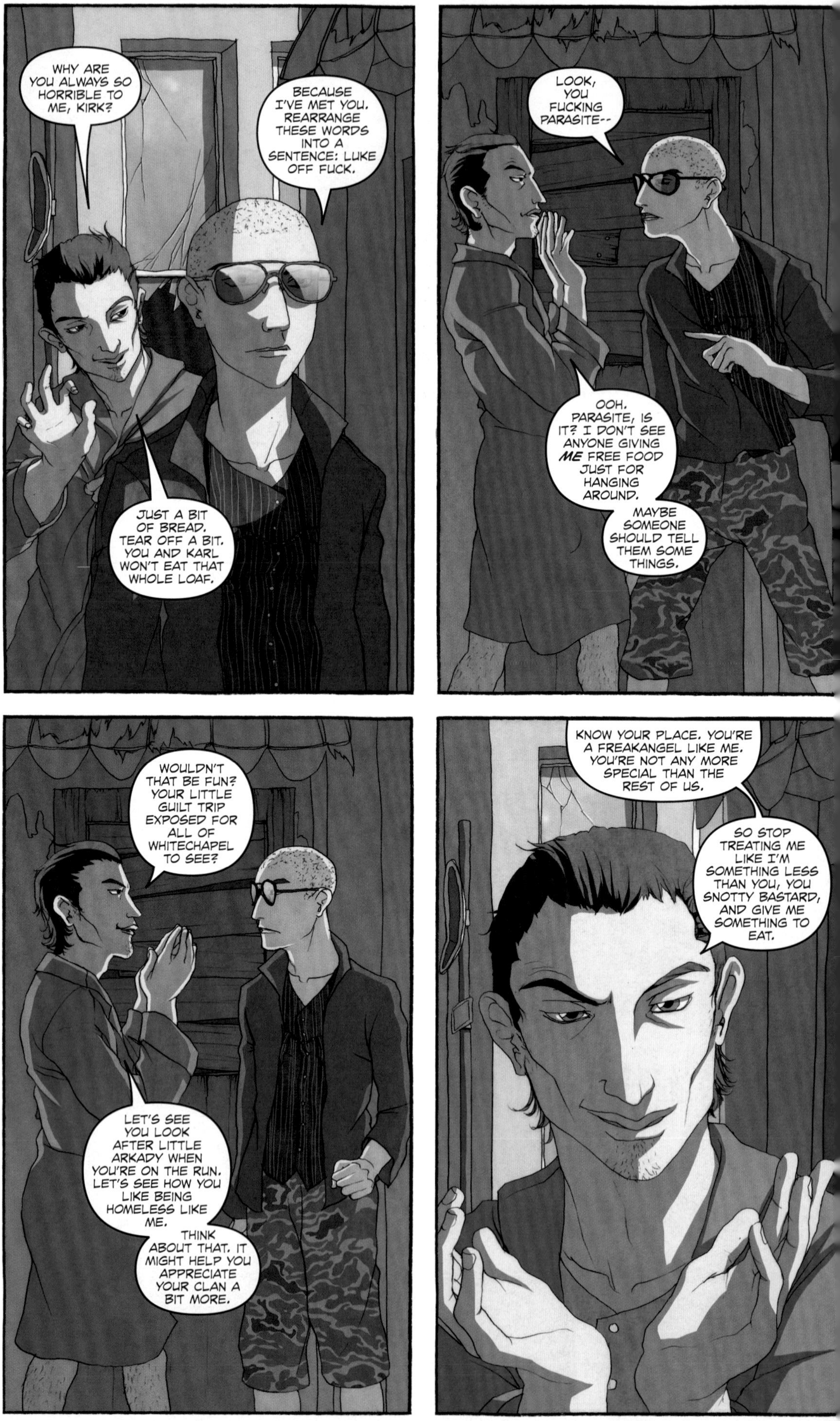

WHY ARE YOU ALWAYS SO HORRIBLE TO ME, KIRK?
BECAUSE I'VE MET YOU. REARRANGE THESE WORDS INTO A SENTENCE: LUKE OFF FUCK.
JUST A BIT OF BREAD. TEAR OFF A BIT. YOU AND KARL WON'T EAT THAT WHOLE LOAF.
LOOK, YOU FUCKING PARASITE--
OOH. PARASITE, IS IT? I DON'T SEE ANYONE GIVING *ME* FREE FOOD JUST FOR HANGING AROUND.
MAYBE SOMEONE SHOULD TELL THEM SOME THINGS.
WOULDN'T THAT BE FUN? YOUR LITTLE GUILT TRIP EXPOSED FOR ALL OF WHITECHAPEL TO SEE?
LET'S SEE YOU LOOK AFTER LITTLE ARKADY WHEN YOU'RE ON THE RUN. LET'S SEE HOW YOU LIKE BEING HOMELESS LIKE ME.
THINK ABOUT THAT. IT MIGHT HELP YOU APPRECIATE YOUR CLAN A BIT MORE.
KNOW YOUR PLACE. YOU'RE A FREAKANGEL LIKE ME. YOU'RE NOT ANY MORE SPECIAL THAN THE REST OF US.
SO STOP TREATING ME LIKE I'M SOMETHING LESS THAN YOU, YOU SNOTTY BASTARD, AND GIVE ME SOMETHING TO EAT.

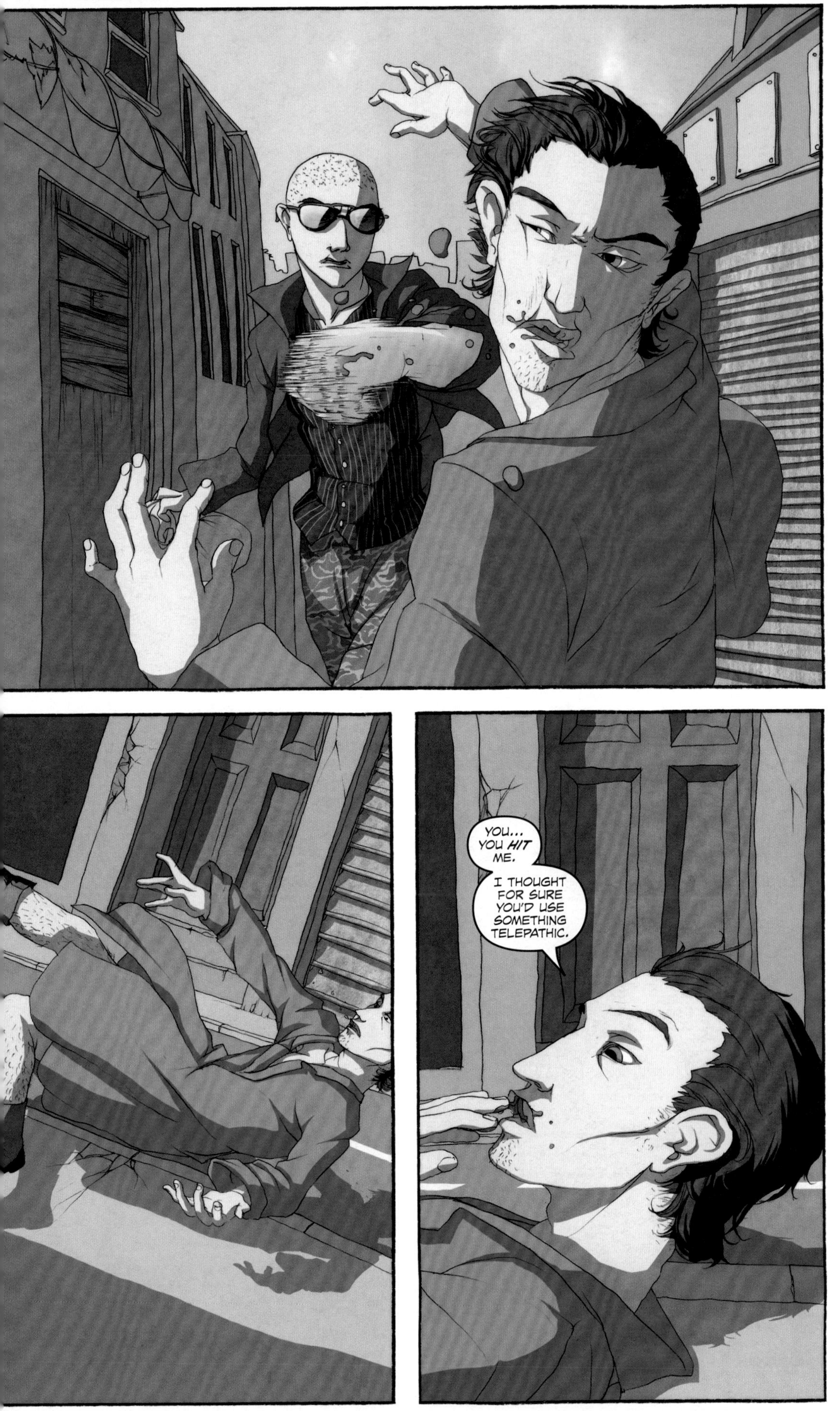
YOU... YOU HIT ME.
I THOUGHT FOR SURE YOU'D USE SOMETHING TELEPATHIC.

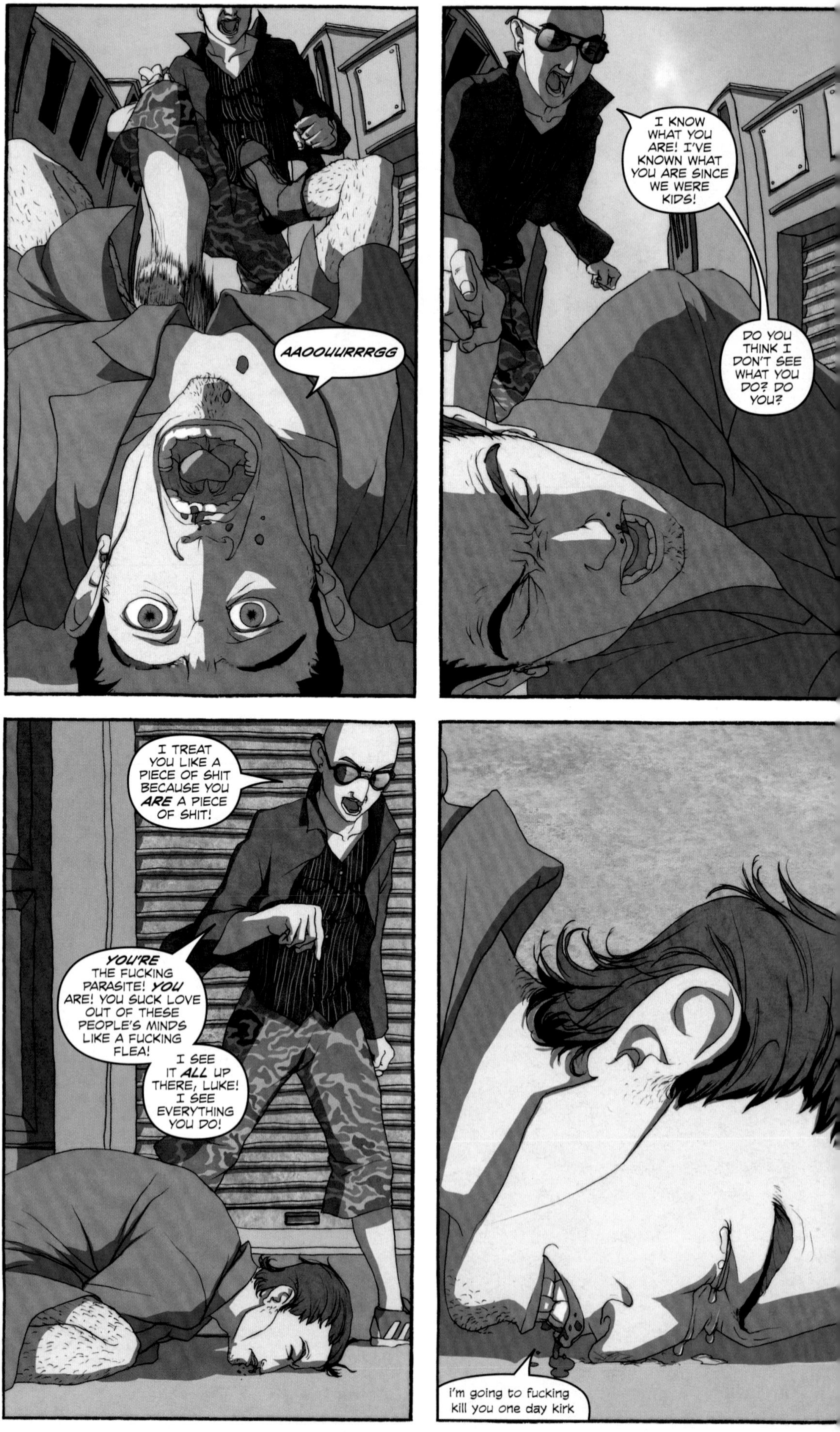
AAOOUURRRGG
I KNOW WHAT YOU ARE! I'VE KNOWN WHAT YOU ARE SINCE WE WERE KIDS!
DO YOU THINK I DON'T SEE WHAT YOU DO? DO YOU?
I TREAT YOU LIKE A PIECE OF SHIT BECAUSE YOU ARE A PIECE OF SHIT!
YOU'RE THE FUCKING PARASITE! YOU ARE! YOU SUCK LOVE OUT OF THESE PEOPLE'S MINDS LIKE A FUCKING FLEA!
I SEE IT ALL UP THERE, LUKE! I SEE EVERYTHING YOU DO!
i'm going to fucking kill you one day kirk

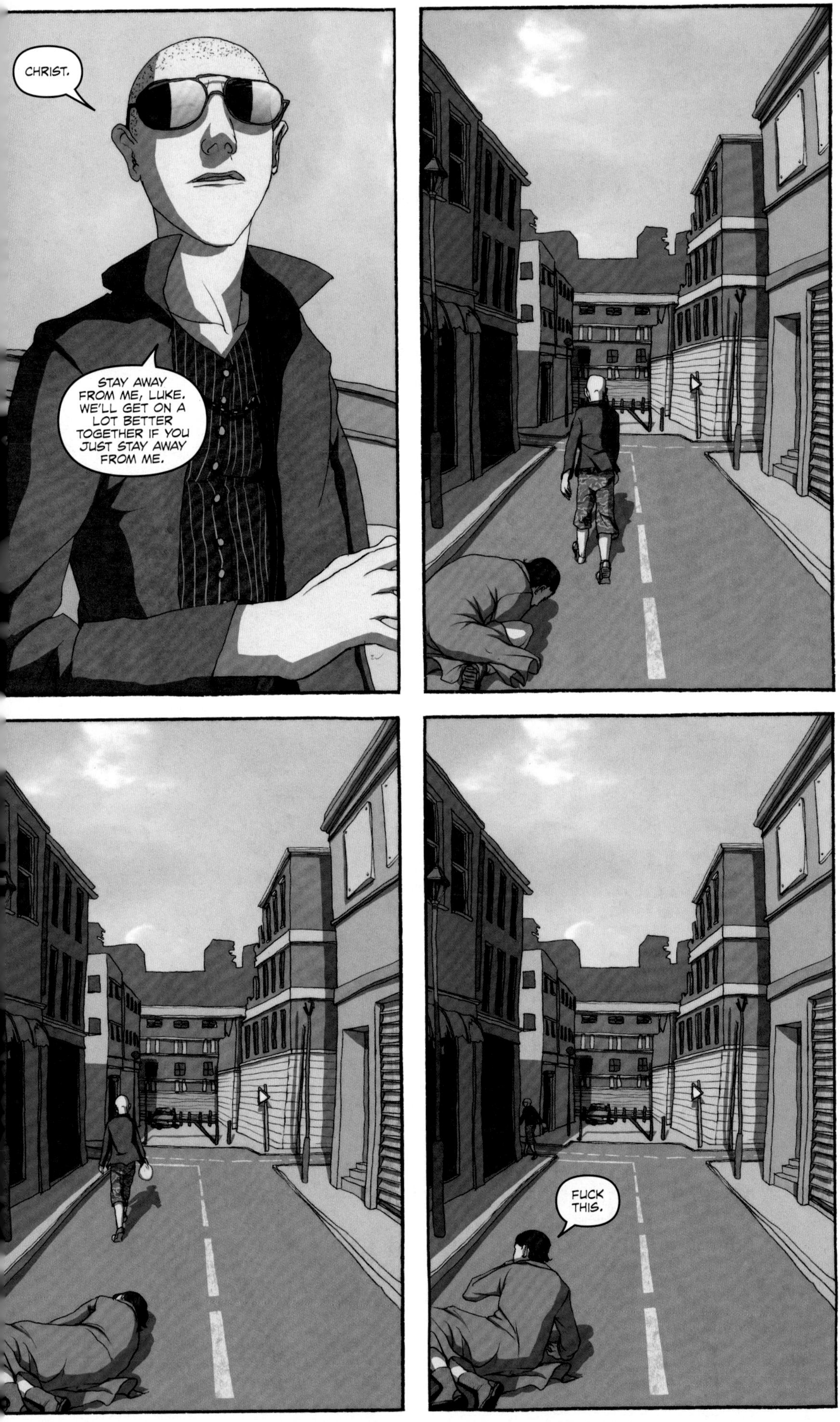
CHRIST.
STAY AWAY FROM ME, LUKE. WE'LL GET ON A LOT BETTER TOGETHER IF YOU JUST STAY AWAY FROM ME.
FUCK THIS.

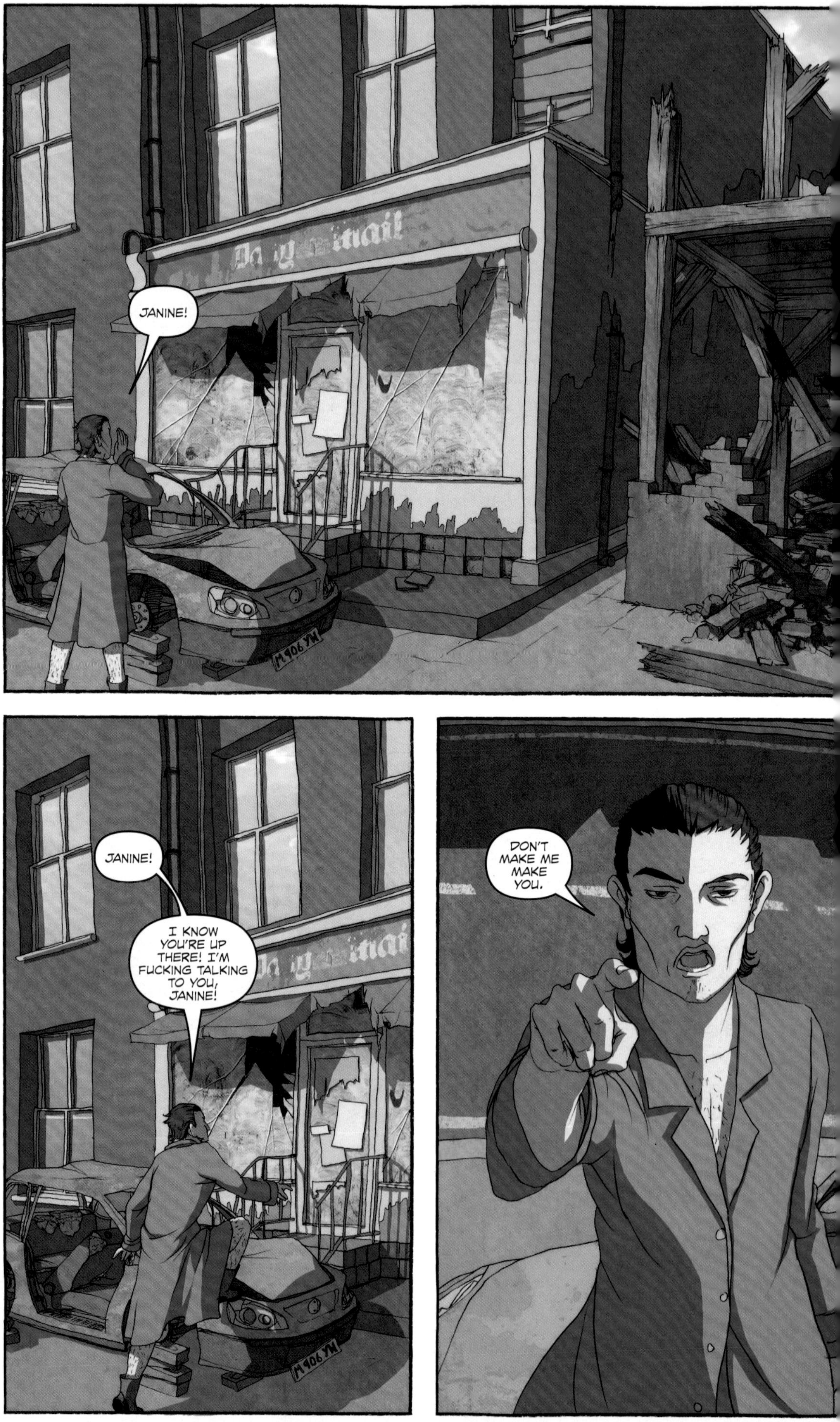
JANINE!
JANINE!
I KNOW YOU'RE UP THERE! I'M FUCKING TALKING TO YOU, JANINE!
DON'T MAKE ME MAKE YOU.

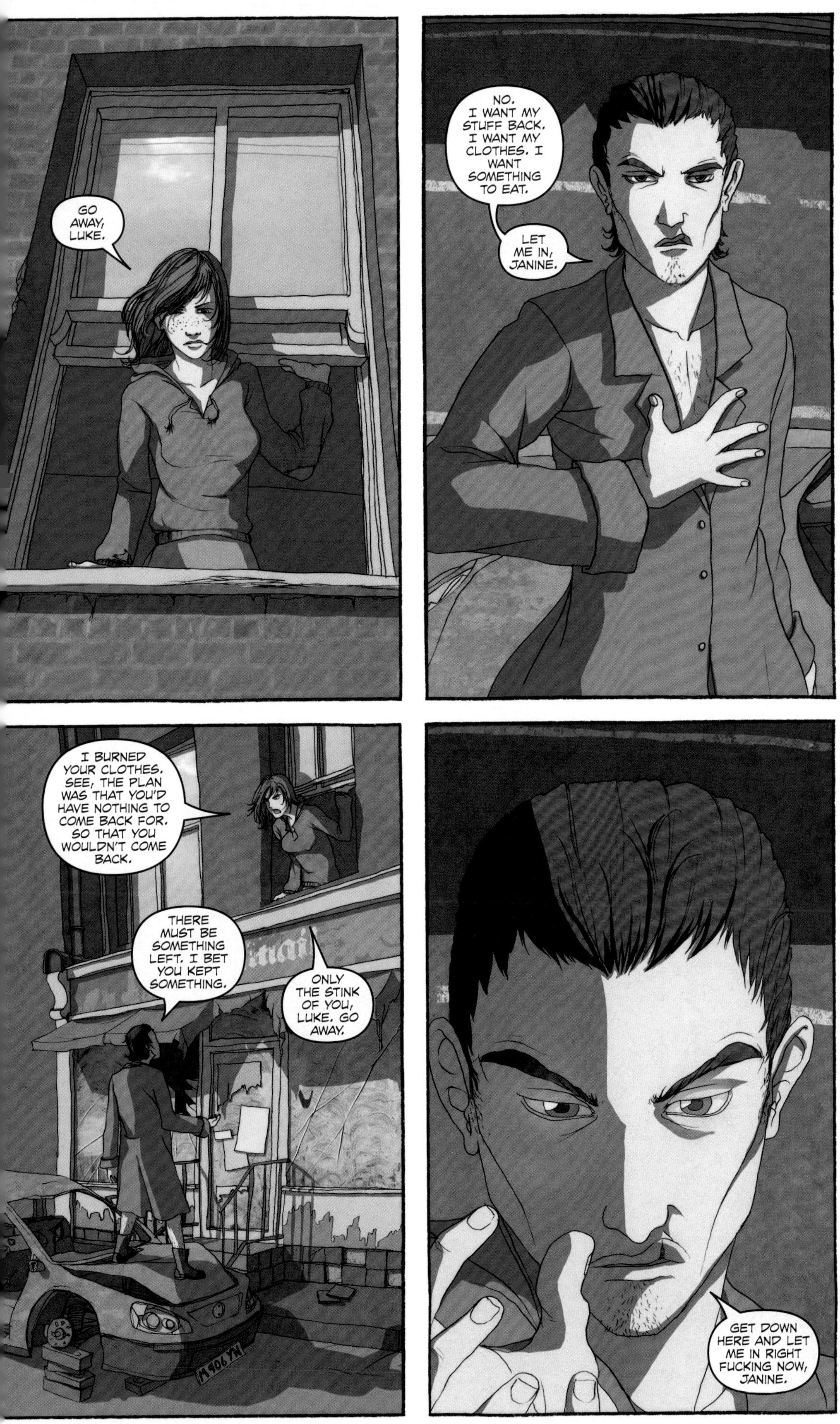
GO AWAY, LUKE.
NO. I WANT MY STUFF BACK. I WANT MY CLOTHES. I WANT SOMETHING TO EAT.
LET ME IN, JANINE.
I BURNED YOUR CLOTHES. SEE, THE PLAN WAS THAT YOU'D HAVE NOTHING TO COME BACK FOR. SO THAT YOU WOULDN'T COME BACK.
THERE MUST BE SOMETHING LEFT. I BET YOU KEPT SOMETHING.
ONLY THE STINK OF YOU, LUKE. GO AWAY.
GET DOWN HERE AND LET ME IN RIGHT FUCKING NOW, JANINE.

uh

THAT'S IT. I DON'T KNOW WHY I NEVER DID IT BEFORE.

CALL *ME* A PARASITE, YOU PIECE OF SHIT...

HM.

THAT'S VERY GOOD, JANINE.

NOW WHY DON'T YOU MAKE ME SOME BREAKFAST WHILE I HAVE A LOOK AROUND FOR MY STUFF?

AND THEN... WELL, WE'LL SEE.

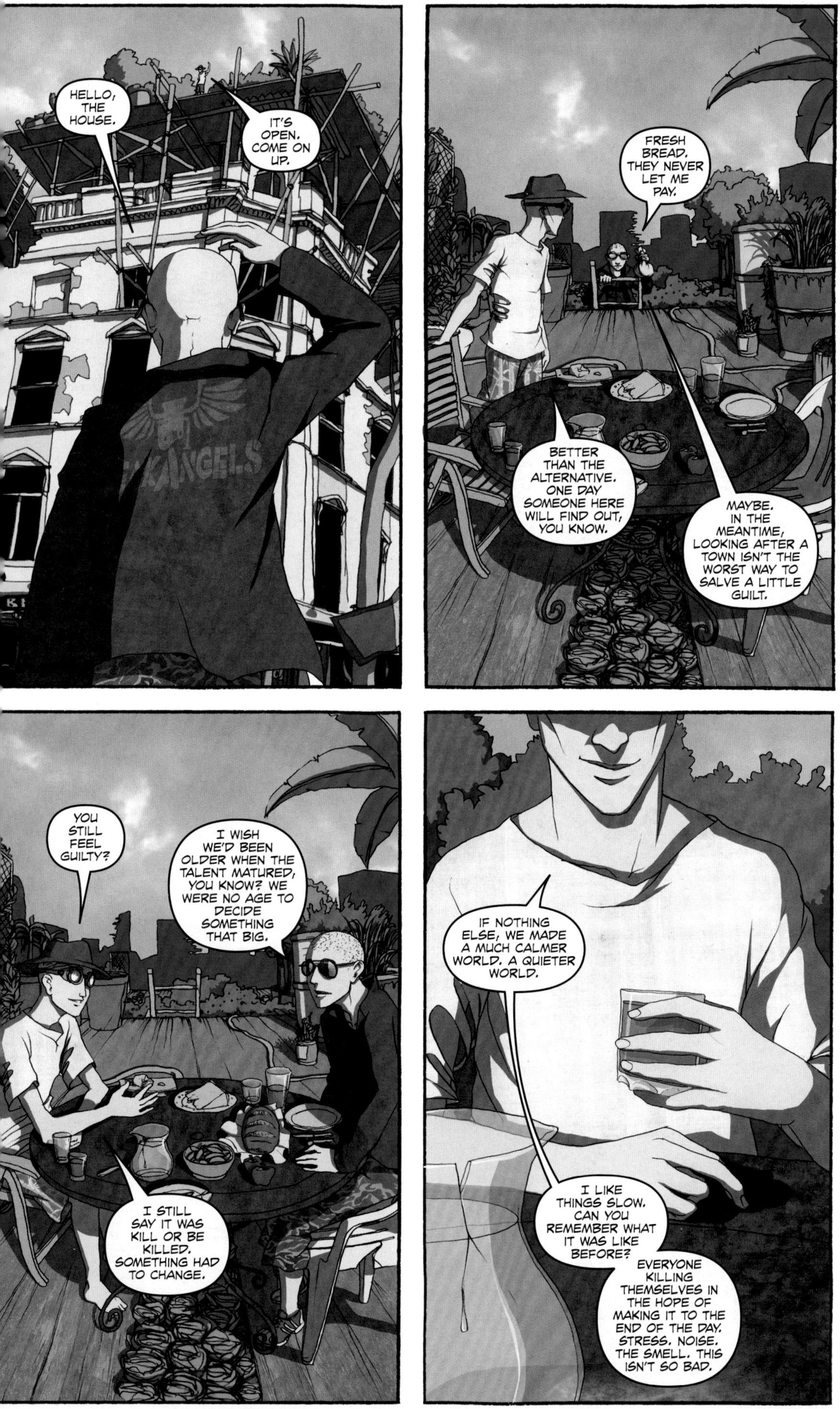
HELLO, THE HOUSE.
IT'S OPEN. COME ON UP.
FRESH BREAD. THEY NEVER LET ME PAY.
BETTER THAN THE ALTERNATIVE. ONE DAY SOMEONE HERE WILL FIND OUT, YOU KNOW.
MAYBE. IN THE MEANTIME, LOOKING AFTER A TOWN ISN'T THE WORST WAY TO SALVE A LITTLE GUILT.
YOU STILL FEEL GUILTY?
I WISH WE'D BEEN OLDER WHEN THE TALENT MATURED, YOU KNOW? WE WERE NO AGE TO DECIDE SOMETHING THAT BIG.
I STILL SAY IT WAS KILL OR BE KILLED. SOMETHING HAD TO CHANGE.
IF NOTHING ELSE, WE MADE A MUCH CALMER WORLD. A QUIETER WORLD.
I LIKE THINGS SLOW. CAN YOU REMEMBER WHAT IT WAS LIKE BEFORE?
EVERYONE KILLING THEMSELVES IN THE HOPE OF MAKING IT TO THE END OF THE DAY. STRESS. NOISE. THE SMELL. THIS ISN'T SO BAD.

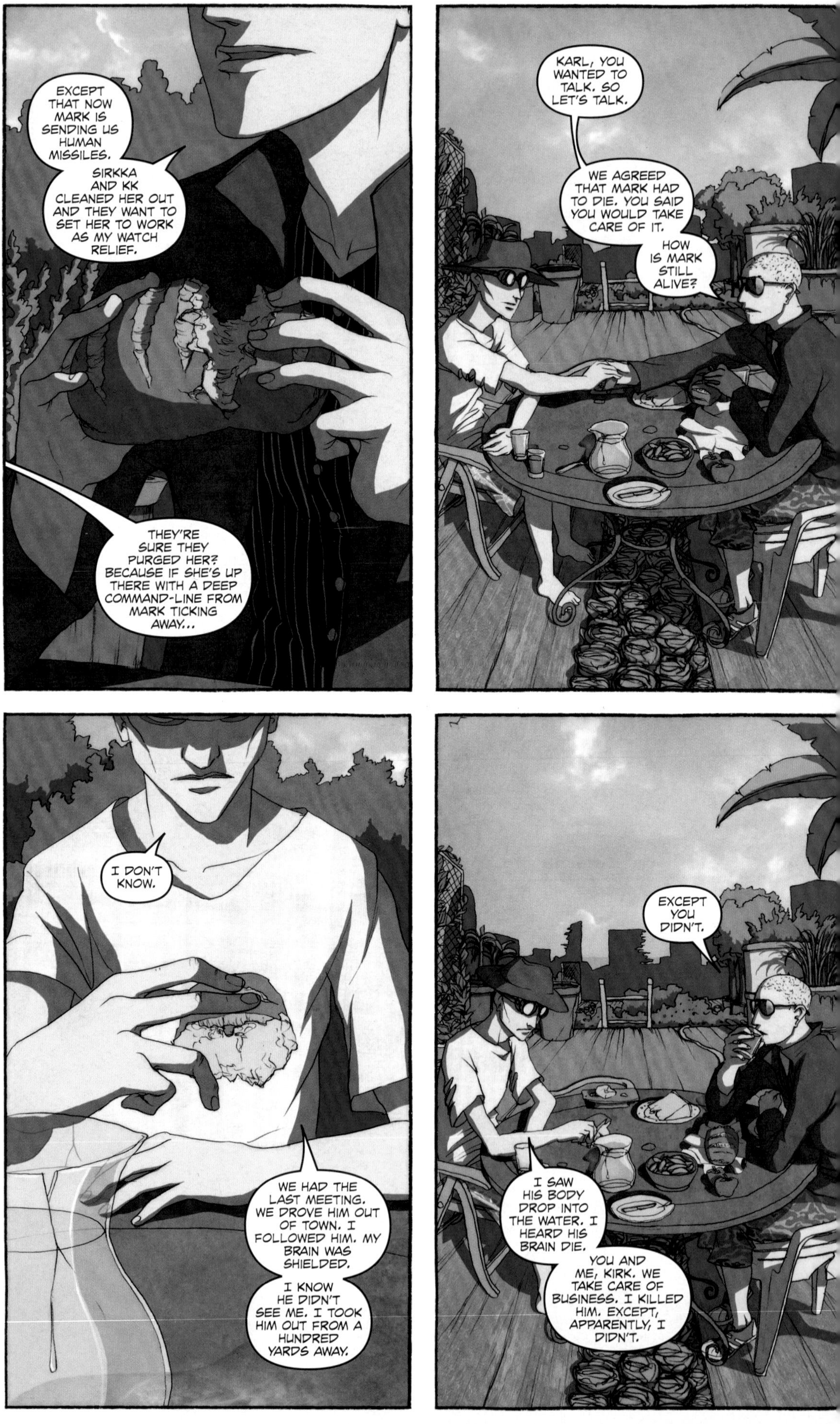
EXCEPT THAT NOW MARK IS SENDING US HUMAN MISSILES.
SIRKKA AND KK CLEANED HER OUT AND THEY WANT TO SET HER TO WORK AS MY WATCH RELIEF.
THEY'RE SURE THEY PURGED HER? BECAUSE IF SHE'S UP THERE WITH A DEEP COMMAND-LINE FROM MARK TICKING AWAY...
KARL, YOU WANTED TO TALK. SO LET'S TALK.
WE AGREED THAT MARK HAD TO DIE. YOU SAID YOU WOULD TAKE CARE OF IT.
HOW IS MARK STILL ALIVE?
I DON'T KNOW.
WE HAD THE LAST MEETING. WE DROVE HIM OUT OF TOWN. I FOLLOWED HIM. MY BRAIN WAS SHIELDED.
I KNOW HE DIDN'T SEE ME. I TOOK HIM OUT FROM A HUNDRED YARDS AWAY.
EXCEPT YOU DIDN'T.
I SAW HIS BODY DROP INTO THE WATER. I HEARD HIS BRAIN DIE.
YOU AND ME, KIRK. WE TAKE CARE OF BUSINESS. I KILLED HIM. EXCEPT, APPARENTLY, I DIDN'T.

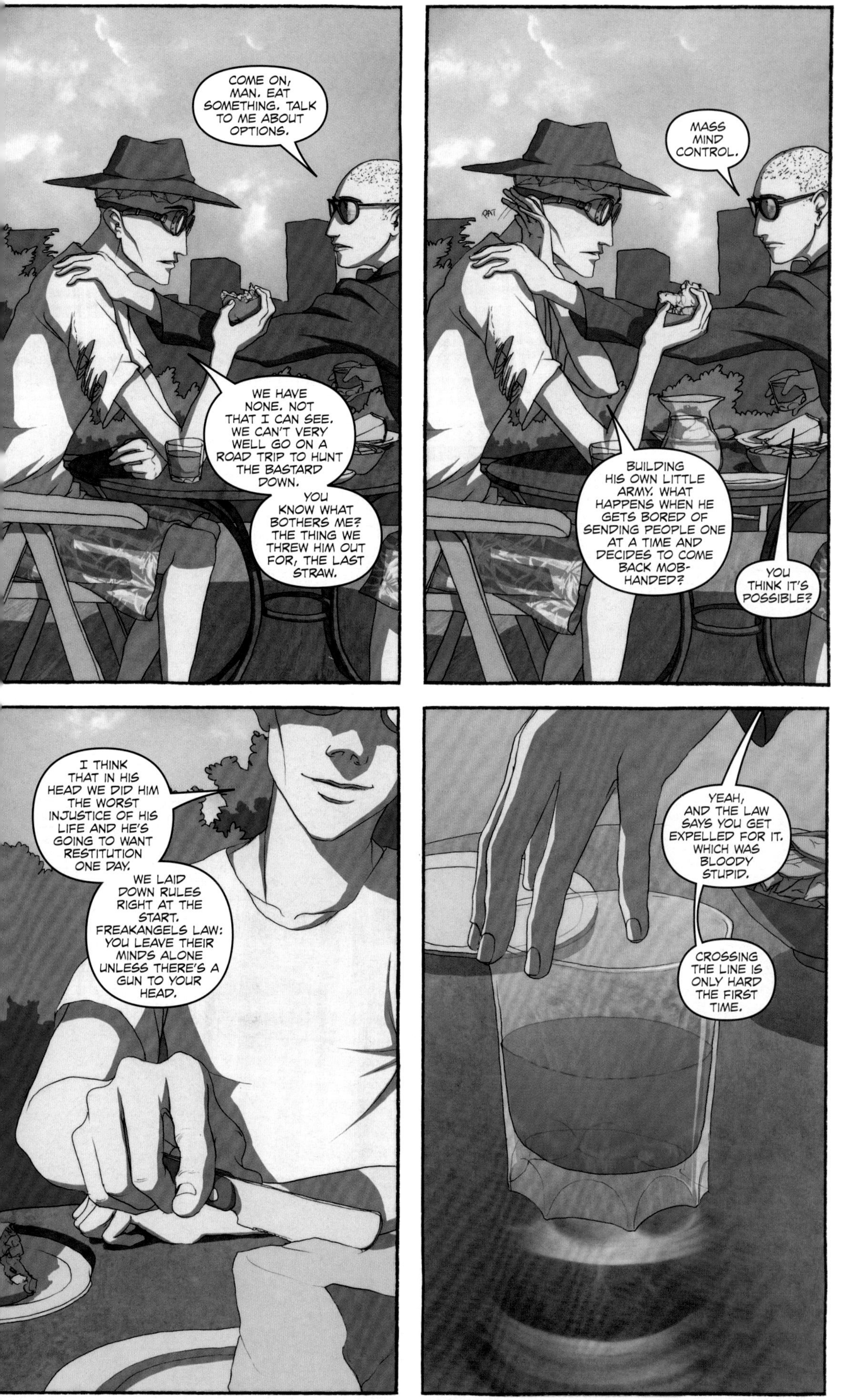
COME ON, MAN. EAT SOMETHING. TALK TO ME ABOUT OPTIONS.
WE HAVE NONE. NOT THAT I CAN SEE. WE CAN'T VERY WELL GO ON A ROAD TRIP TO HUNT THE BASTARD DOWN.
YOU KNOW WHAT BOTHERS ME? THE THING WE THREW HIM OUT FOR, THE LAST STRAW.
PAT
MASS MIND CONTROL.
BUILDING HIS OWN LITTLE ARMY. WHAT HAPPENS WHEN HE GETS BORED OF SENDING PEOPLE ONE AT A TIME AND DECIDES TO COME BACK MOB-HANDED?
YOU THINK IT'S POSSIBLE?
I THINK THAT IN HIS HEAD WE DID HIM THE WORST INJUSTICE OF HIS LIFE AND HE'S GOING TO WANT RESTITUTION ONE DAY.
WE LAID DOWN RULES RIGHT AT THE START. FREAKANGELS LAW: YOU LEAVE THEIR MINDS ALONE UNLESS THERE'S A GUN TO YOUR HEAD.
YEAH, AND THE LAW SAYS YOU GET EXPELLED FOR IT. WHICH WAS BLOODY STUPID.
CROSSING THE LINE IS ONLY HARD THE FIRST TIME.

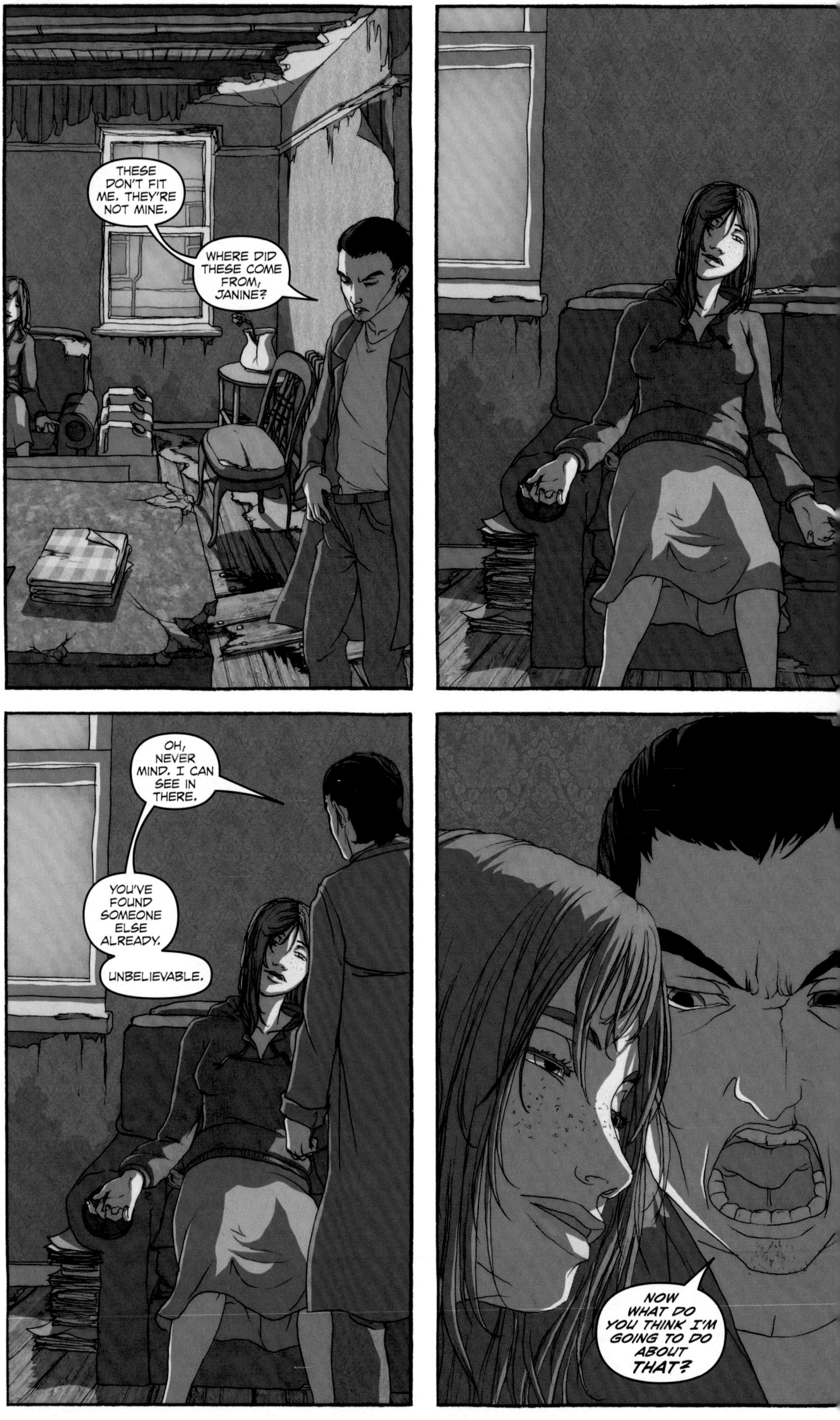

THESE DON'T FIT ME. THEY'RE NOT MINE.
WHERE DID THESE COME FROM, JANINE?
OH, NEVER MIND. I CAN SEE IN THERE.
YOU'VE FOUND SOMEONE ELSE ALREADY.
UNBELIEVABLE.
NOW WHAT DO YOU THINK I'M GOING TO DO ABOUT THAT?

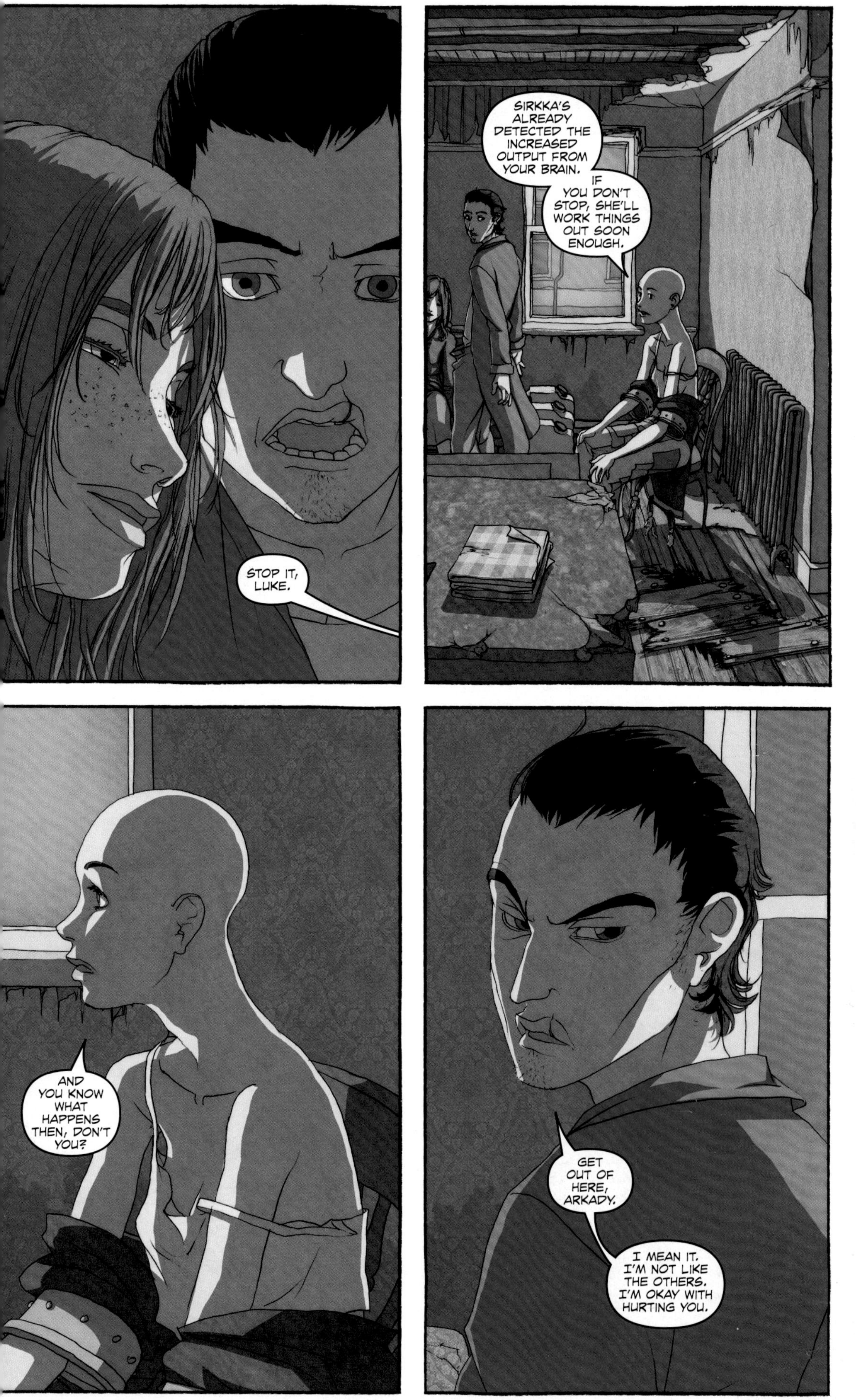
STOP IT, LUKE.
SIRKKA'S ALREADY DETECTED THE INCREASED OUTPUT FROM YOUR BRAIN.
IF YOU DON'T STOP, SHE'LL WORK THINGS OUT SOON ENOUGH.
AND YOU KNOW WHAT HAPPENS THEN, DON'T YOU?
GET OUT OF HERE, ARKADY.
I MEAN IT. I'M NOT LIKE THE OTHERS. I'M OKAY WITH HURTING YOU.

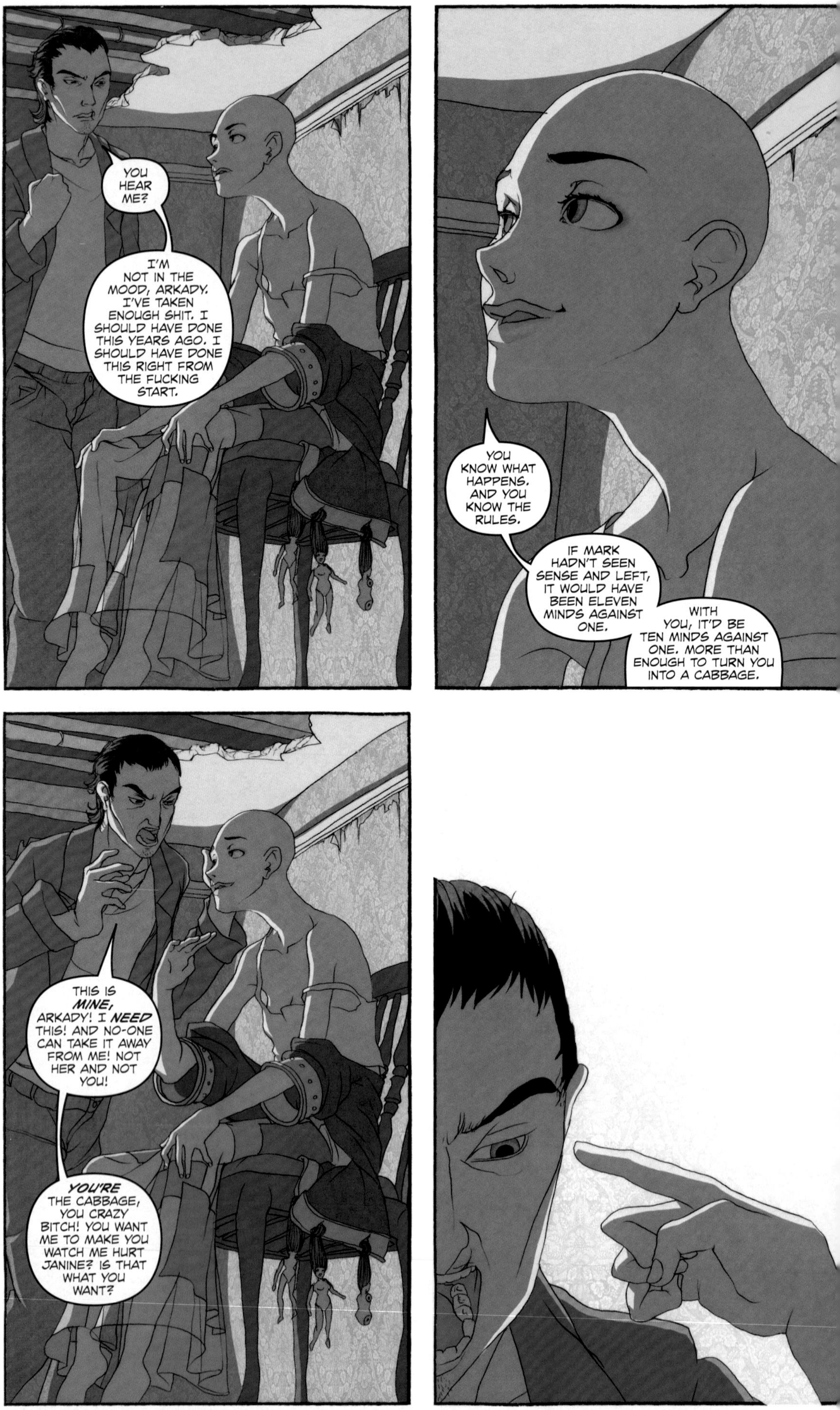
YOU HEAR ME?
I'M NOT IN THE MOOD, ARKADY. I'VE TAKEN ENOUGH SHIT. I SHOULD HAVE DONE THIS YEARS AGO. I SHOULD HAVE DONE THIS RIGHT FROM THE FUCKING START.
YOU KNOW WHAT HAPPENS. AND YOU KNOW THE RULES.
IF MARK HADN'T SEEN SENSE AND LEFT, IT WOULD HAVE BEEN ELEVEN MINDS AGAINST ONE.
WITH YOU, IT'D BE TEN MINDS AGAINST ONE. MORE THAN ENOUGH TO TURN YOU INTO A CABBAGE.
THIS IS ***MINE,*** ARKADY! I ***NEED*** THIS! AND NO-ONE CAN TAKE IT AWAY FROM ME! NOT HER AND NOT YOU!
***YOU'RE*** THE CABBAGE, YOU CRAZY BITCH! YOU WANT ME TO MAKE YOU WATCH ME HURT JANINE? IS THAT WHAT YOU WANT?

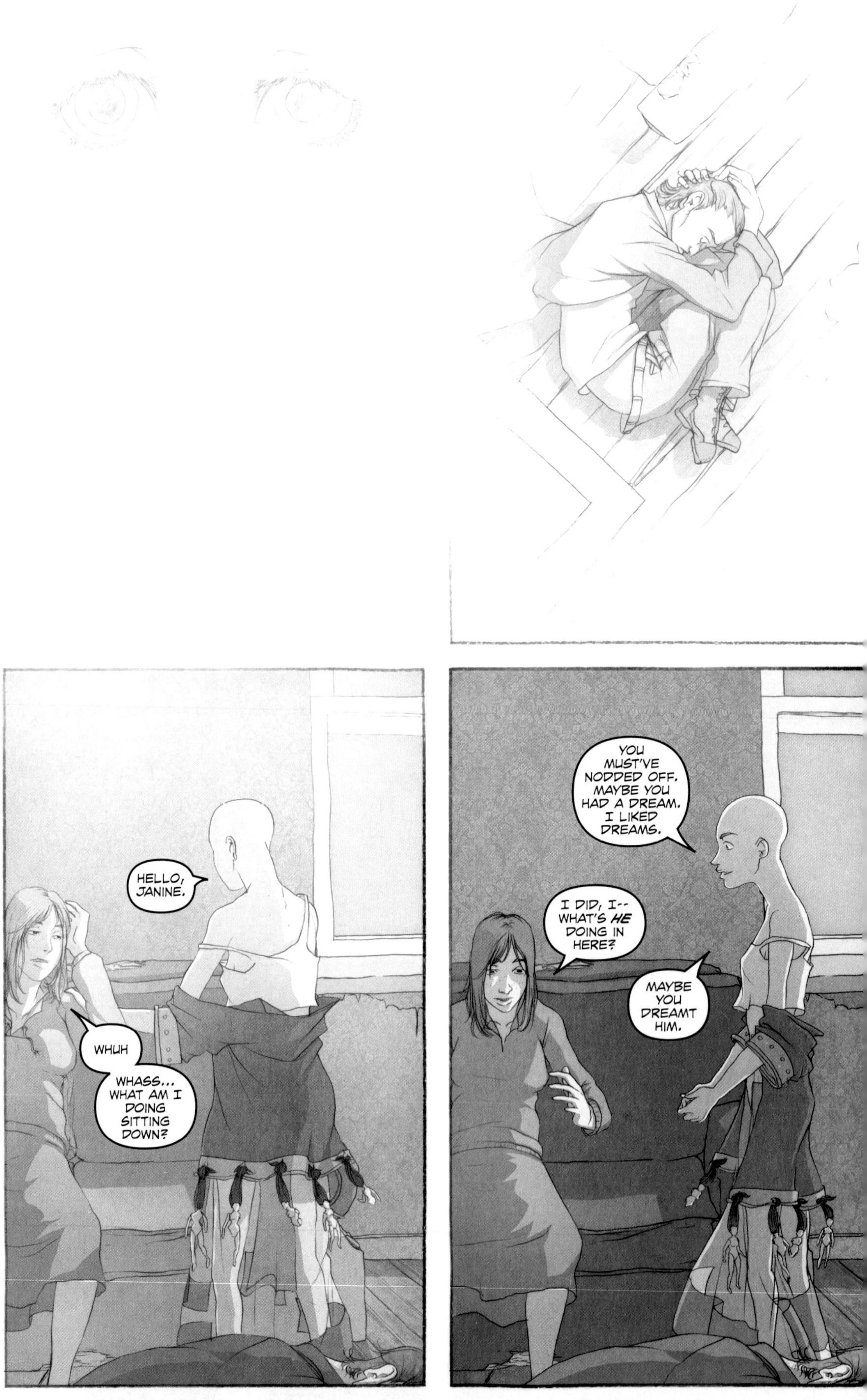
HELLO, JANINE.
WHUH
WHASS... WHAT AM I DOING SITTING DOWN?
YOU MUST'VE NODDED OFF. MAYBE YOU HAD A DREAM. I LIKED DREAMS.
I DID, I-- WHAT'S *HE* DOING IN HERE?
MAYBE YOU DREAMT HIM.

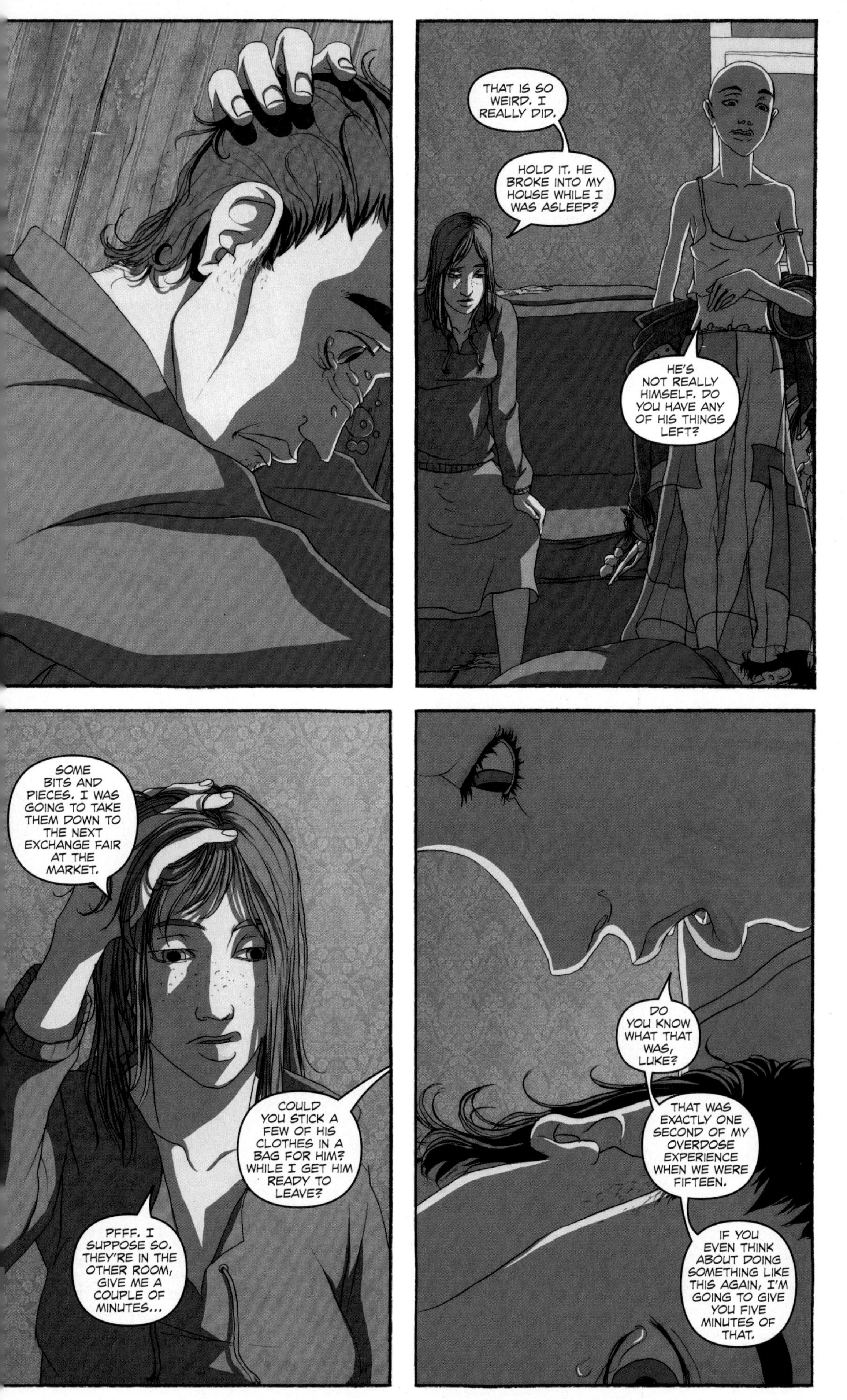
THAT IS SO WEIRD. I REALLY DID.
HOLD IT. HE BROKE INTO MY HOUSE WHILE I WAS ASLEEP?
HE'S NOT REALLY HIMSELF. DO YOU HAVE ANY OF HIS THINGS LEFT?
SOME BITS AND PIECES. I WAS GOING TO TAKE THEM DOWN TO THE NEXT EXCHANGE FAIR AT THE MARKET.
COULD YOU STICK A FEW OF HIS CLOTHES IN A BAG FOR HIM? WHILE I GET HIM READY TO LEAVE?
PFFF. I SUPPOSE SO. THEY'RE IN THE OTHER ROOM, GIVE ME A COUPLE OF MINUTES...
DO YOU KNOW WHAT THAT WAS, LUKE?
THAT WAS EXACTLY ONE SECOND OF MY OVERDOSE EXPERIENCE WHEN WE WERE FIFTEEN.
IF YOU EVEN THINK ABOUT DOING SOMETHING LIKE THIS AGAIN, I'M GOING TO GIVE YOU FIVE MINUTES OF THAT.

YESTERDAY, LUKE, I KNEW EXACTLY WHEN YOU'D DIE. RIGHT NOW, I DON'T.
DO YOU UNDERSTAND? YESTERDAY, YOU WERE GOING TO CONTROL AND ASSAULT JANINE, AND SIRKKA WAS GOING TO PICK UP ON IT.
THERE WAS GOING TO BE A BIG GROUP TRIAL, AND YOU WERE GOING TO LOSE YOUR TEMPER, AND EVERYONE WAS GOING TO GET TOGETHER AND KILL YOU.
NO.
YES. AS OF RIGHT NOW, I DON'T KNOW WHEN YOU DIE. YOU UNDERSTAND WHY, DON'T YOU?
NEVER DO ANYTHING LIKE THIS AGAIN. I'LL KNOW.
THERE. AND DON'T COME BACK, LUKE. WE'RE DONE.
I... I JUST... FUCK... I WANT TO...
GO.
BYE, LUKE. SEE YOU SOON.
GET THOSE TROUSERS WASHED. THEY'RE STINKY.

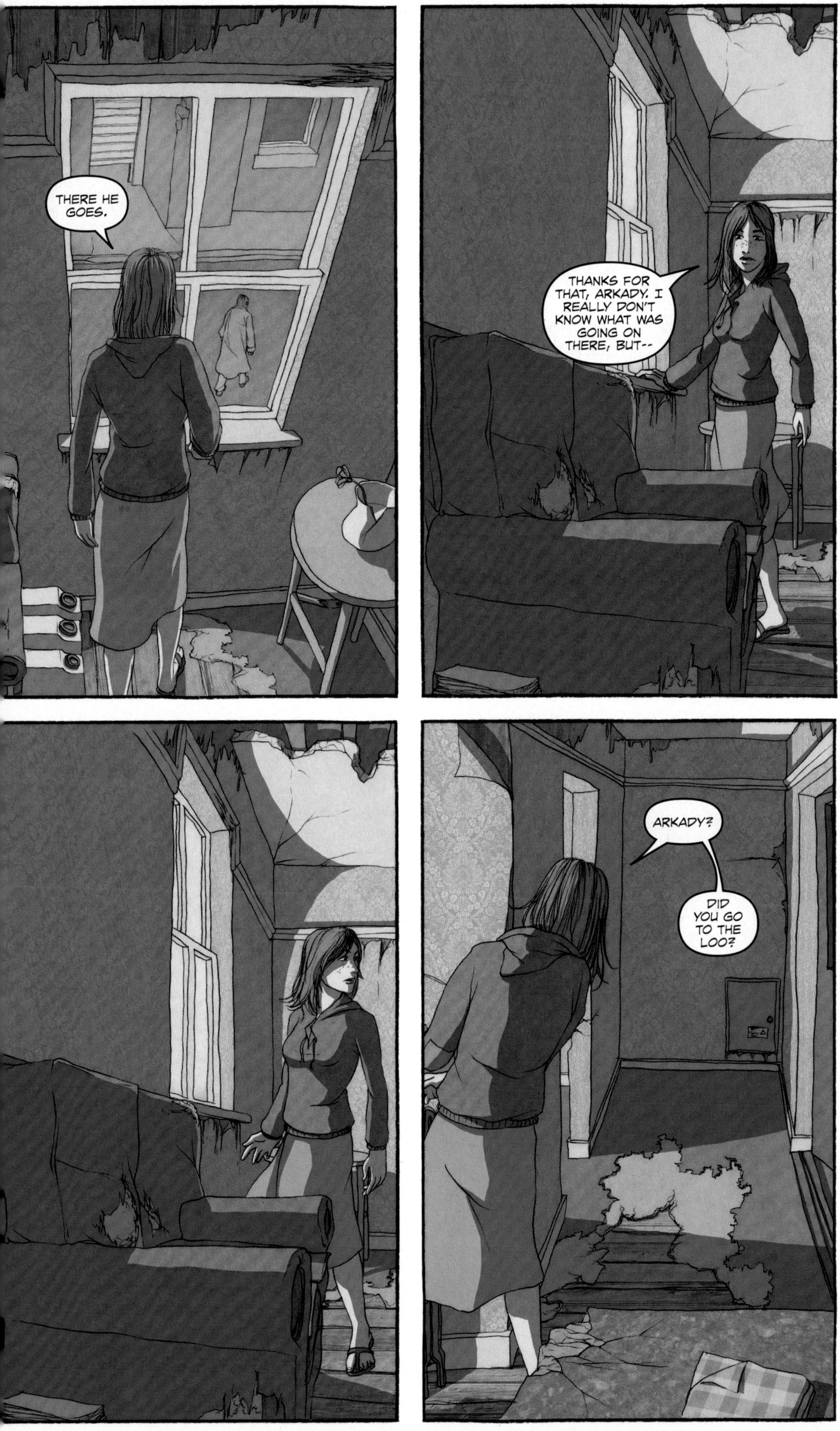
THERE HE GOES.
THANKS FOR THAT, ARKADY. I REALLY DON'T KNOW WHAT WAS GOING ON THERE, BUT--
ARKADY?
DID YOU GO TO THE LOO?

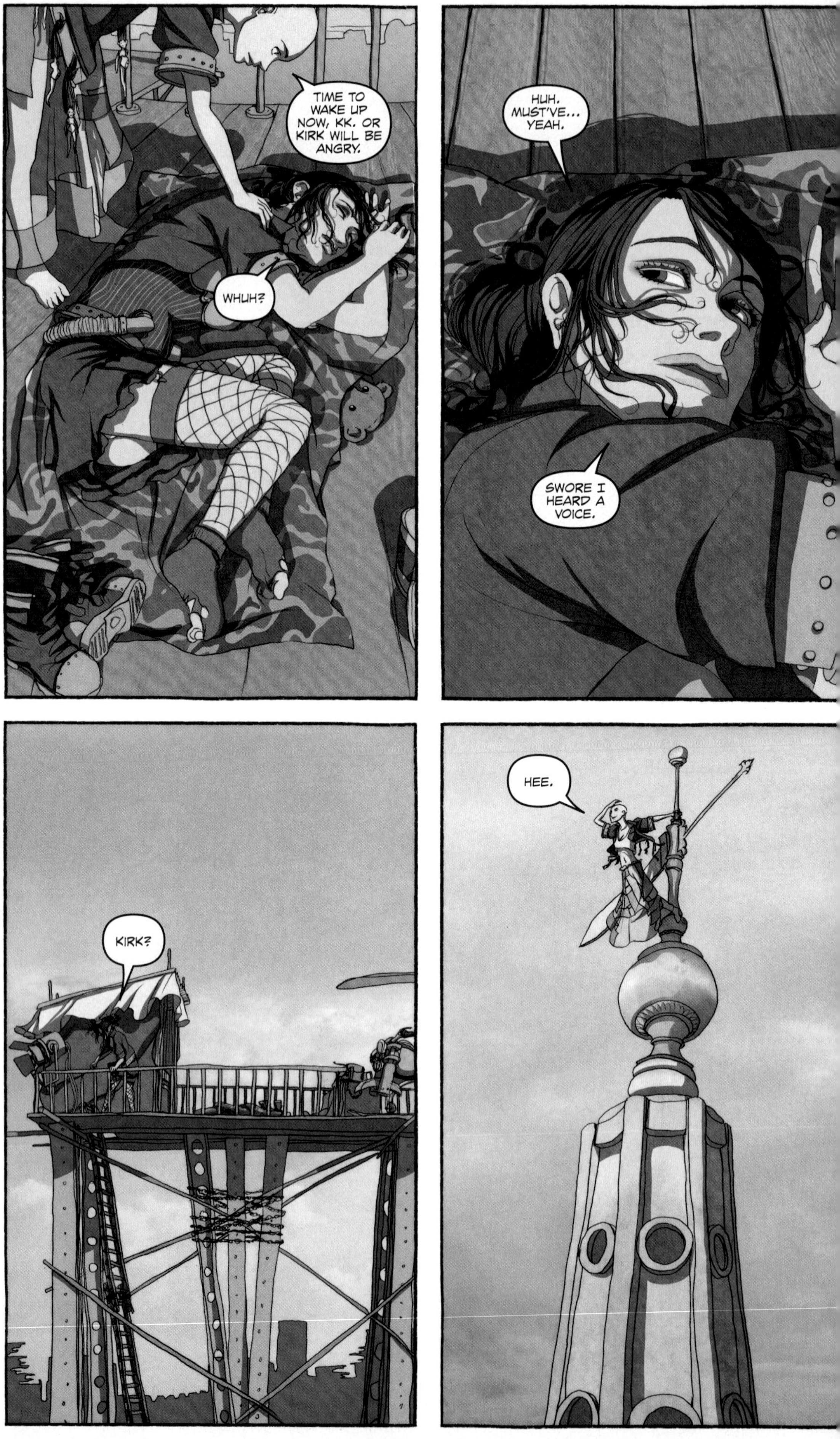
TIME TO WAKE UP NOW, KK. OR KIRK WILL BE ANGRY.
WHUH?
HUH. MUST'VE... YEAH.
SWORE I HEARD A VOICE.
KIRK?
HEE.

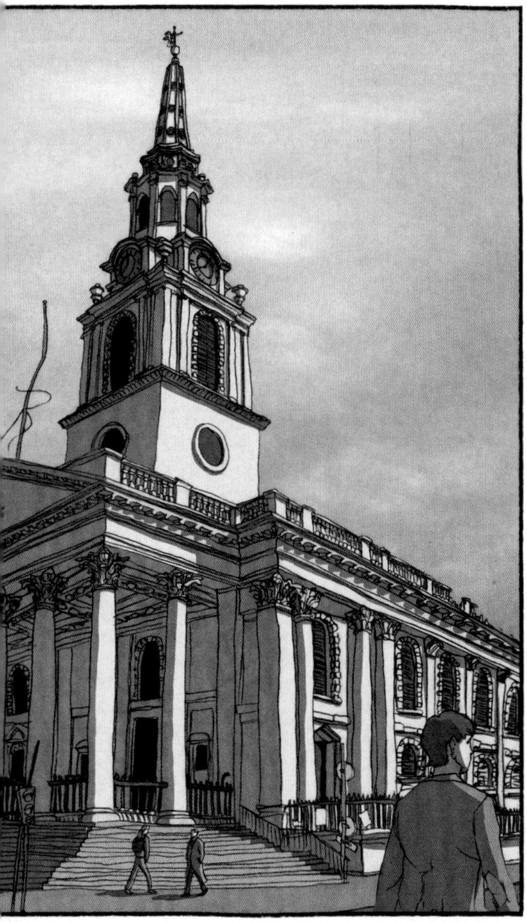

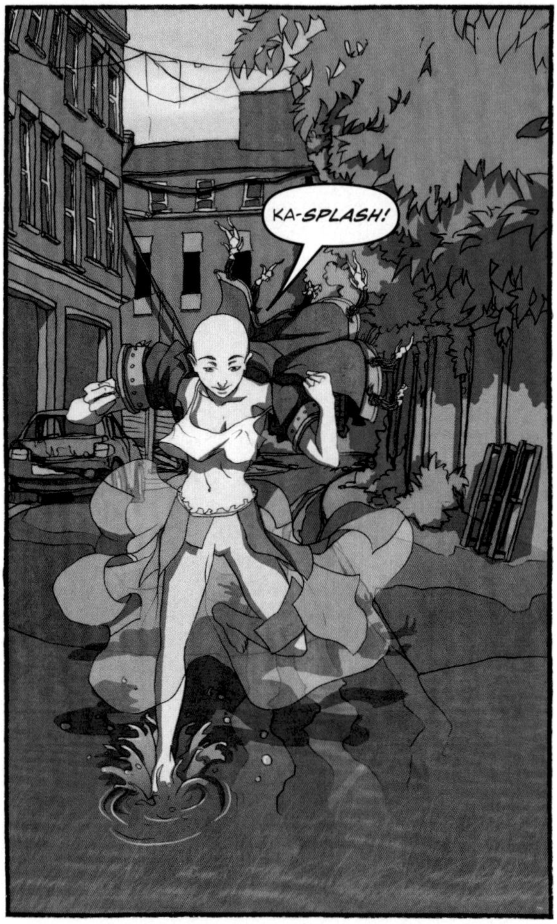
KA-SPLASH!

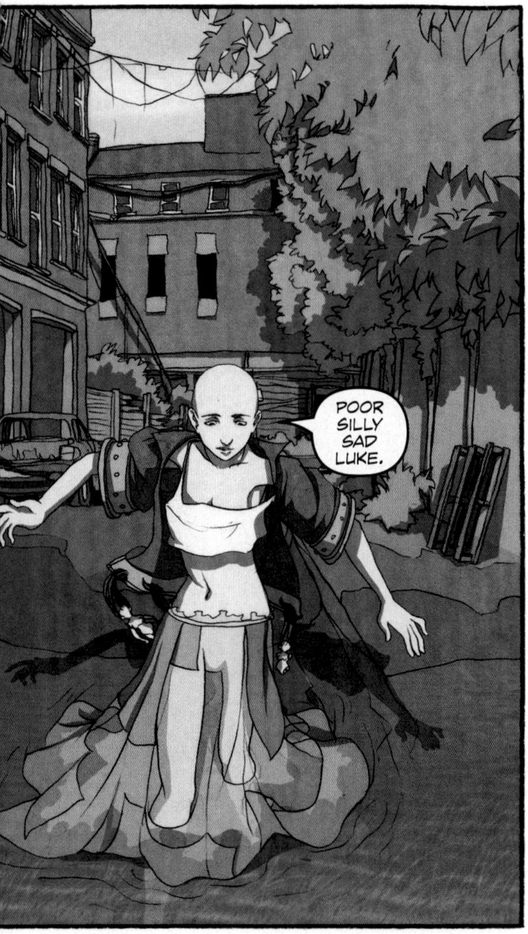
POOR SILLY SAD LUKE.

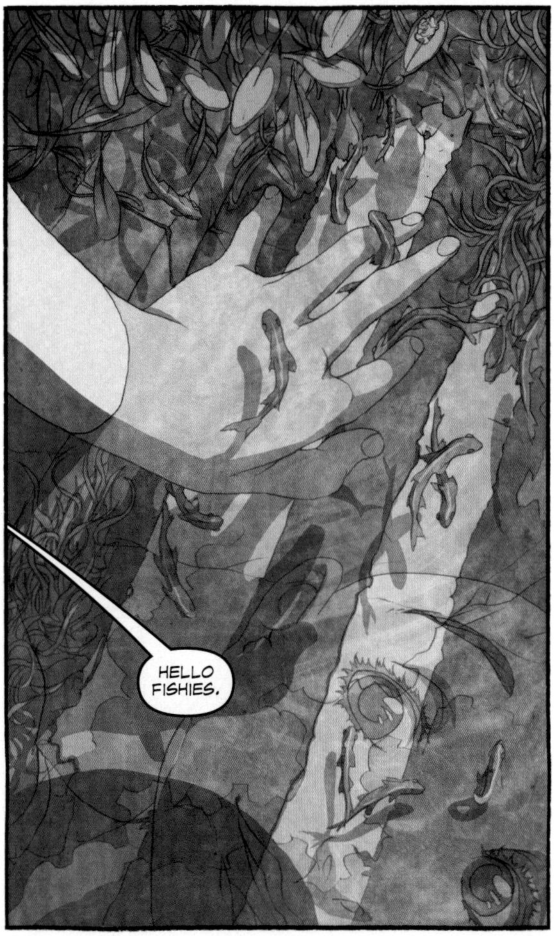
HELLO FISHIES.

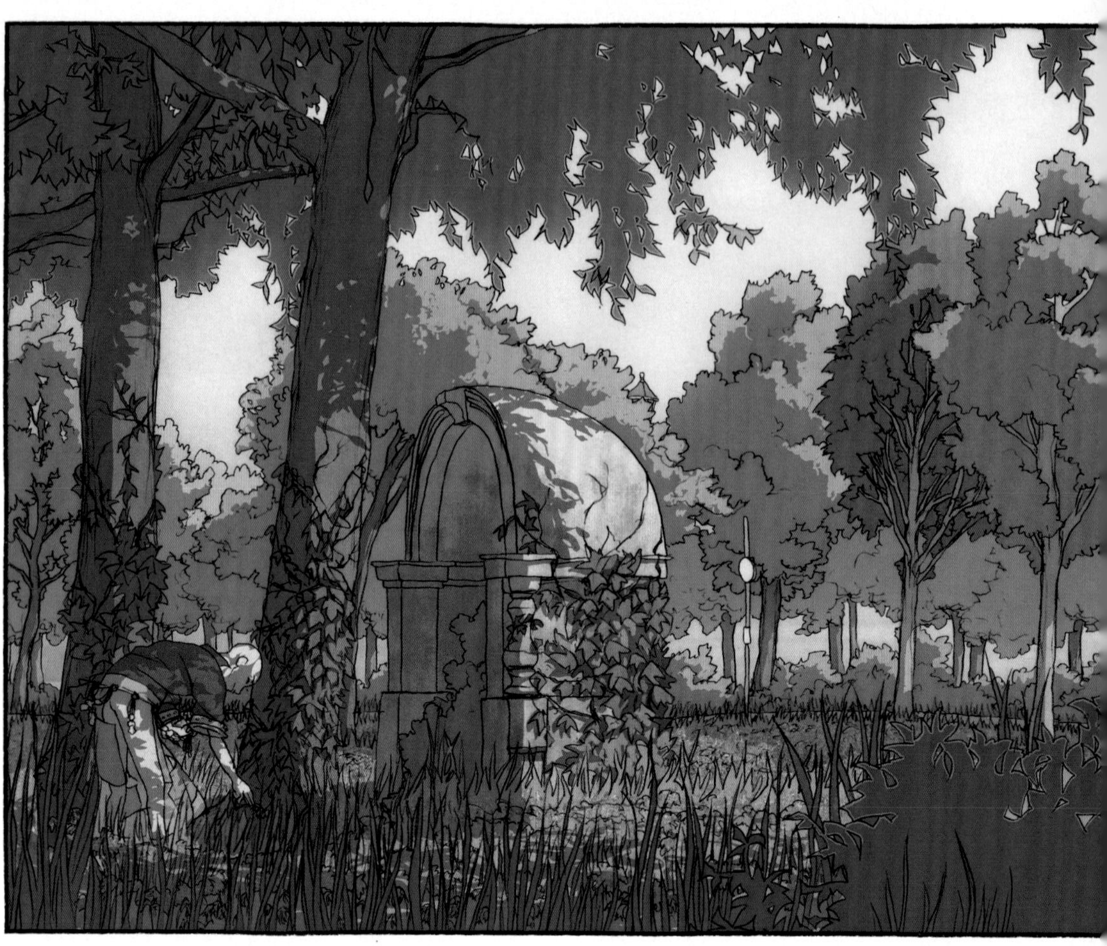

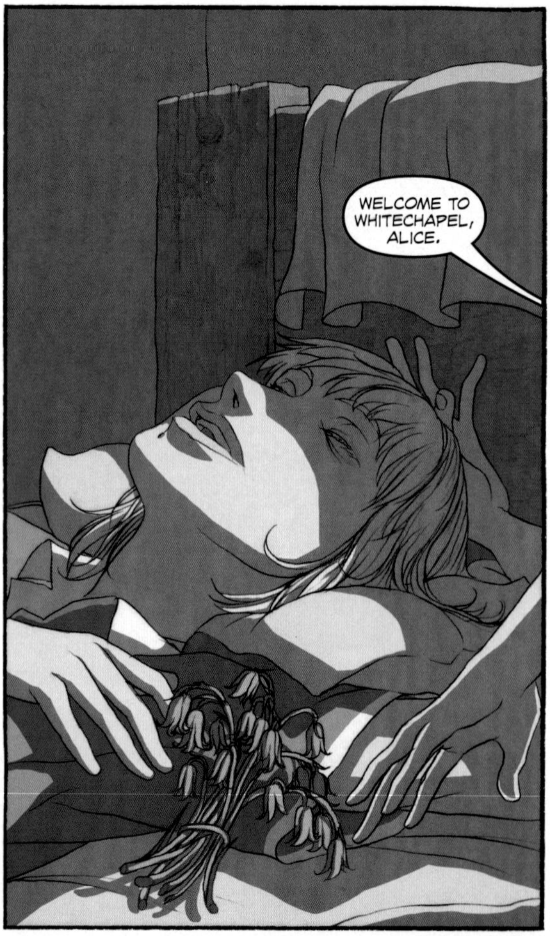
WELCOME TO WHITECHAPEL, ALICE.

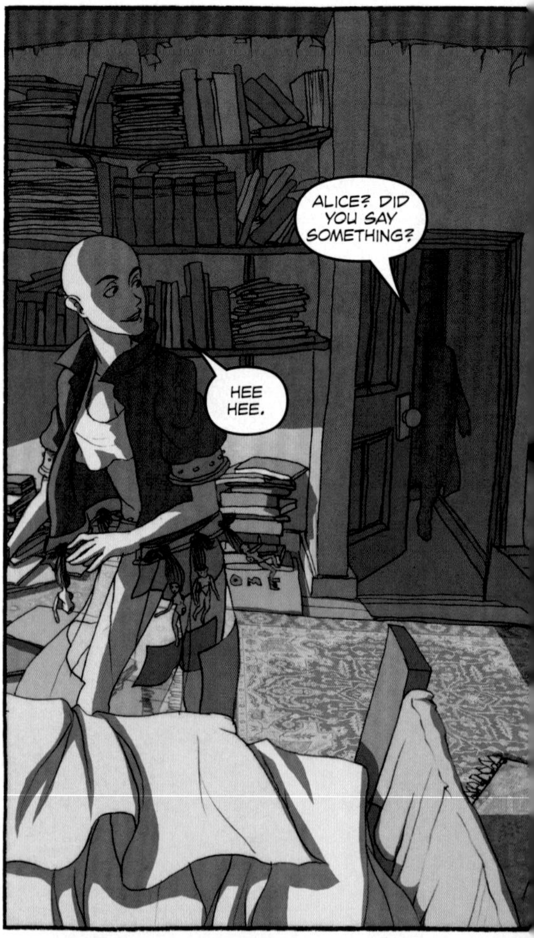
ALICE? DID YOU SAY SOMETHING?
HEE HEE.

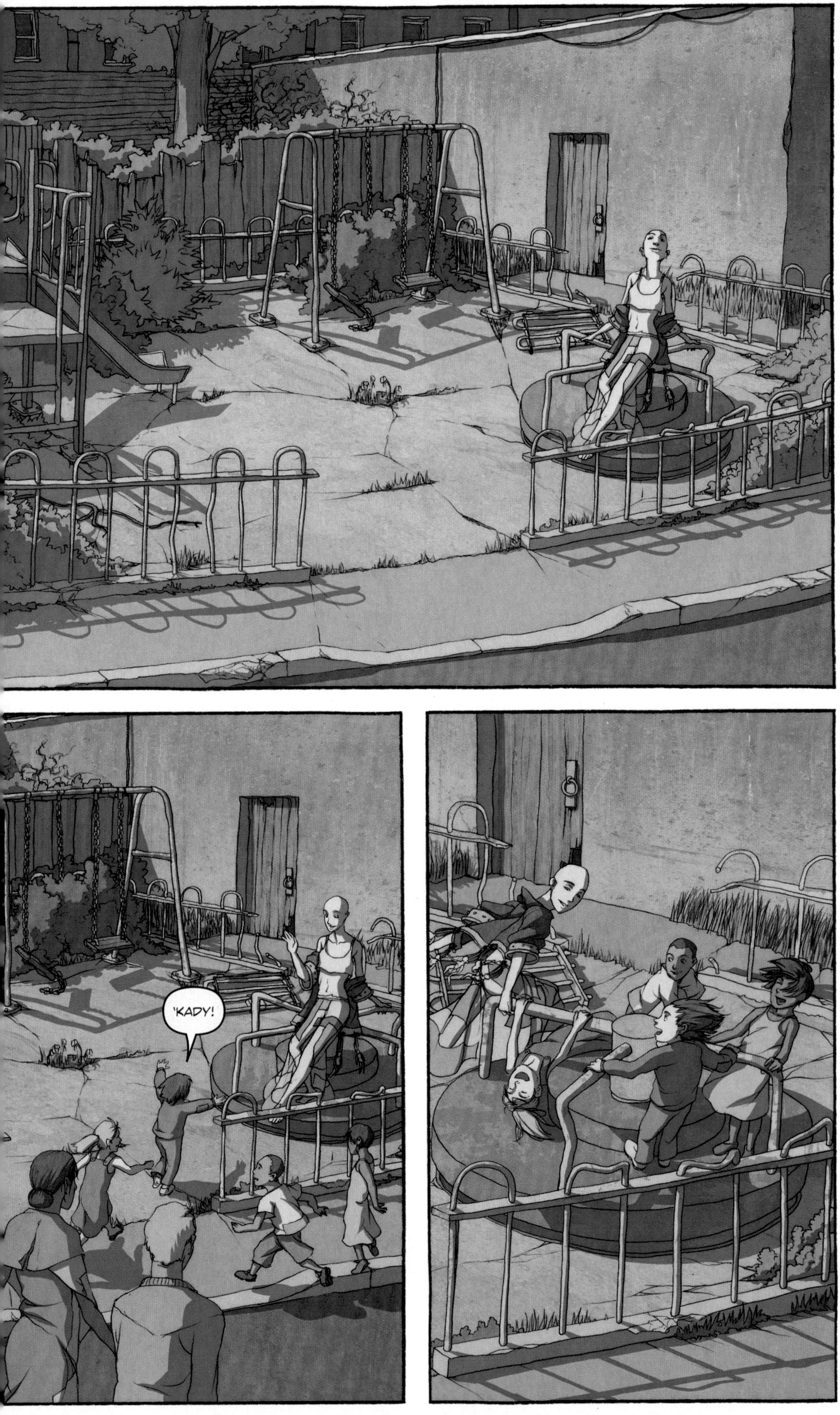
'KADY!

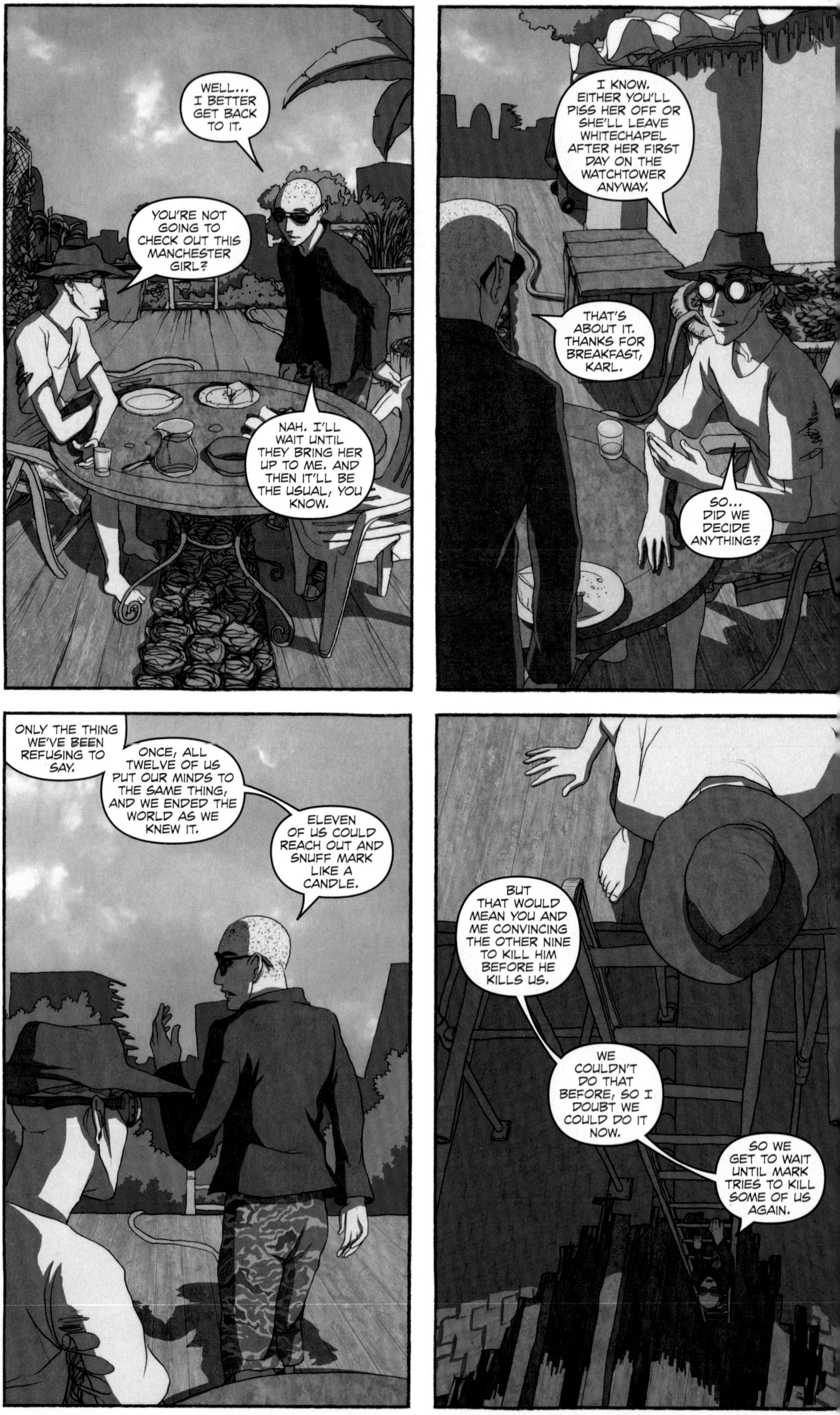
WELL... I BETTER GET BACK TO IT.
YOU'RE NOT GOING TO CHECK OUT THIS MANCHESTER GIRL?
NAH. I'LL WAIT UNTIL THEY BRING HER UP TO ME. AND THEN IT'LL BE THE USUAL, YOU KNOW.
I KNOW. EITHER YOU'LL PISS HER OFF OR SHE'LL LEAVE WHITECHAPEL AFTER HER FIRST DAY ON THE WATCHTOWER ANYWAY.
THAT'S ABOUT IT. THANKS FOR BREAKFAST, KARL.
SO... DID WE DECIDE ANYTHING?
ONLY THE THING WE'VE BEEN REFUSING TO SAY.
ONCE, ALL TWELVE OF US PUT OUR MINDS TO THE SAME THING, AND WE ENDED THE WORLD AS WE KNEW IT.
ELEVEN OF US COULD REACH OUT AND SNUFF MARK LIKE A CANDLE.
BUT THAT WOULD MEAN YOU AND ME CONVINCING THE OTHER NINE TO KILL HIM BEFORE HE KILLS US.
WE COULDN'T DO THAT BEFORE, SO I DOUBT WE COULD DO IT NOW.
SO WE GET TO WAIT UNTIL MARK TRIES TO KILL SOME OF US AGAIN.

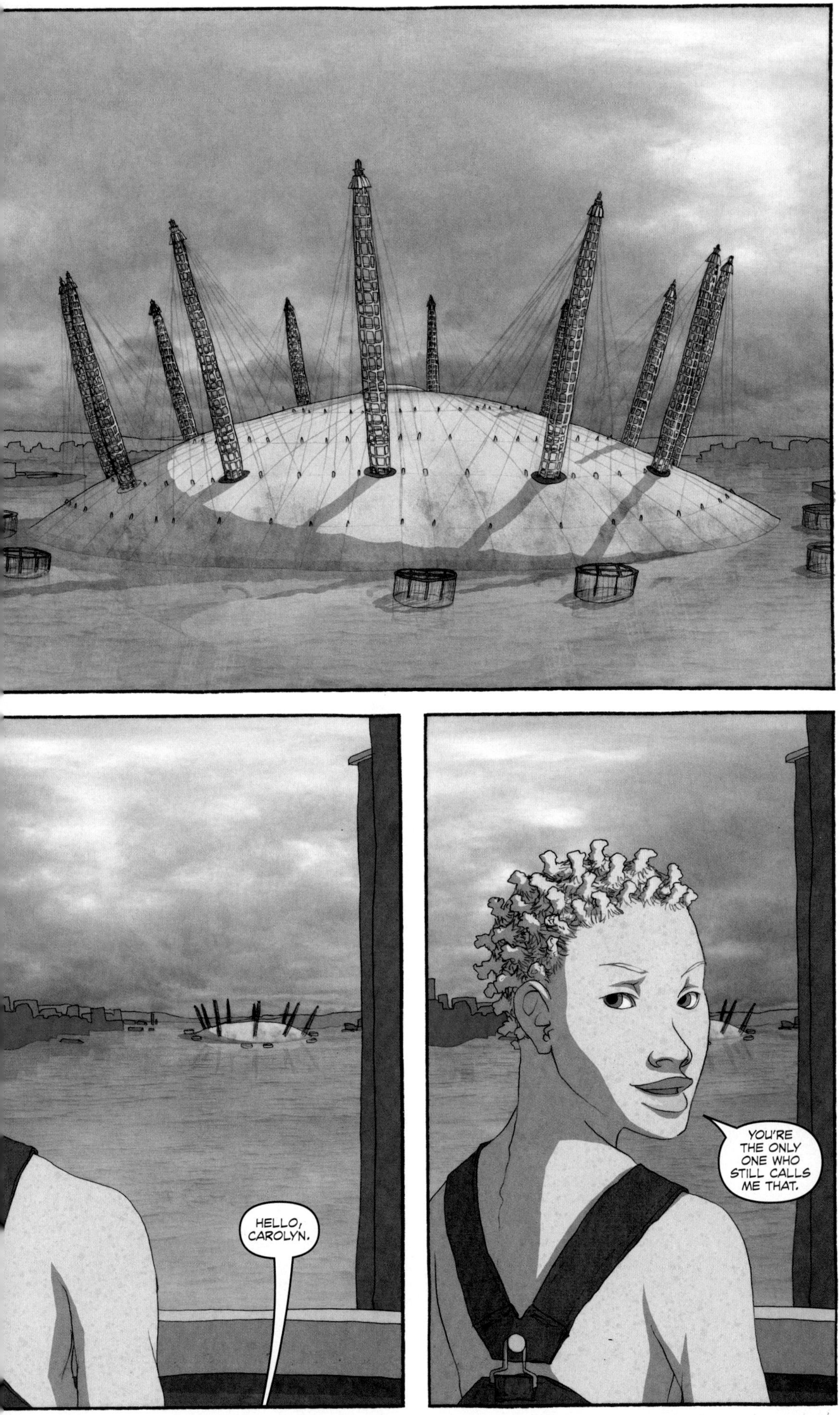
HELLO, CAROLYN.
YOU'RE THE ONLY ONE WHO STILL CALLS ME THAT.

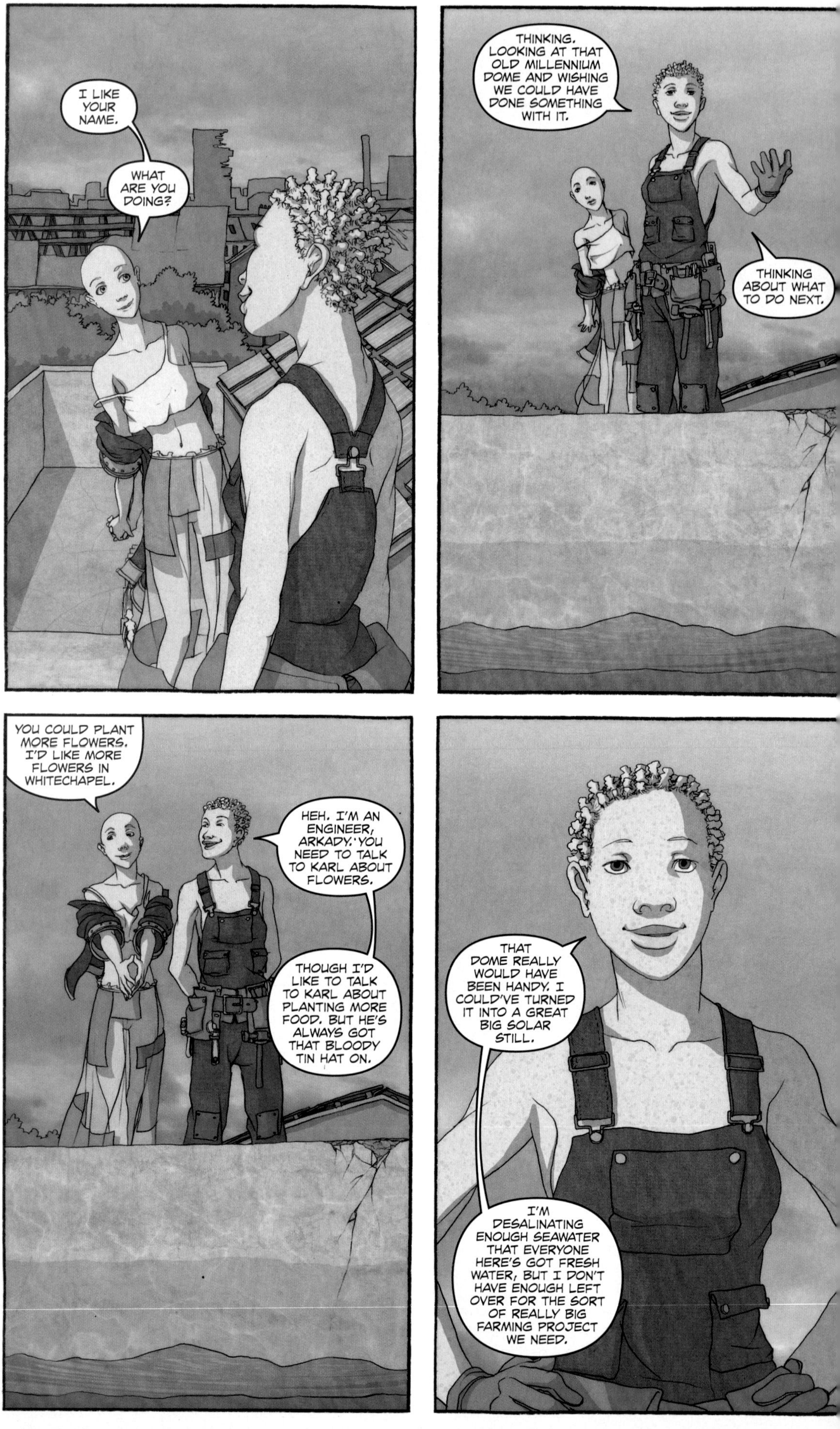
I LIKE YOUR NAME.
WHAT ARE YOU DOING?
THINKING. LOOKING AT THAT OLD MILLENNIUM DOME AND WISHING WE COULD HAVE DONE SOMETHING WITH IT.
THINKING ABOUT WHAT TO DO NEXT.
YOU COULD PLANT MORE FLOWERS. I'D LIKE MORE FLOWERS IN WHITECHAPEL.
HEH. I'M AN ENGINEER, ARKADY. YOU NEED TO TALK TO KARL ABOUT FLOWERS.
THOUGH I'D LIKE TO TALK TO KARL ABOUT PLANTING MORE FOOD. BUT HE'S ALWAYS GOT THAT BLOODY TIN HAT ON.
THAT DOME REALLY WOULD HAVE BEEN HANDY. I COULD'VE TURNED IT INTO A GREAT BIG SOLAR STILL.
I'M DESALINATING ENOUGH SEAWATER THAT EVERYONE HERE'S GOT FRESH WATER, BUT I DON'T HAVE ENOUGH LEFT OVER FOR THE SORT OF REALLY BIG FARMING PROJECT WE NEED.

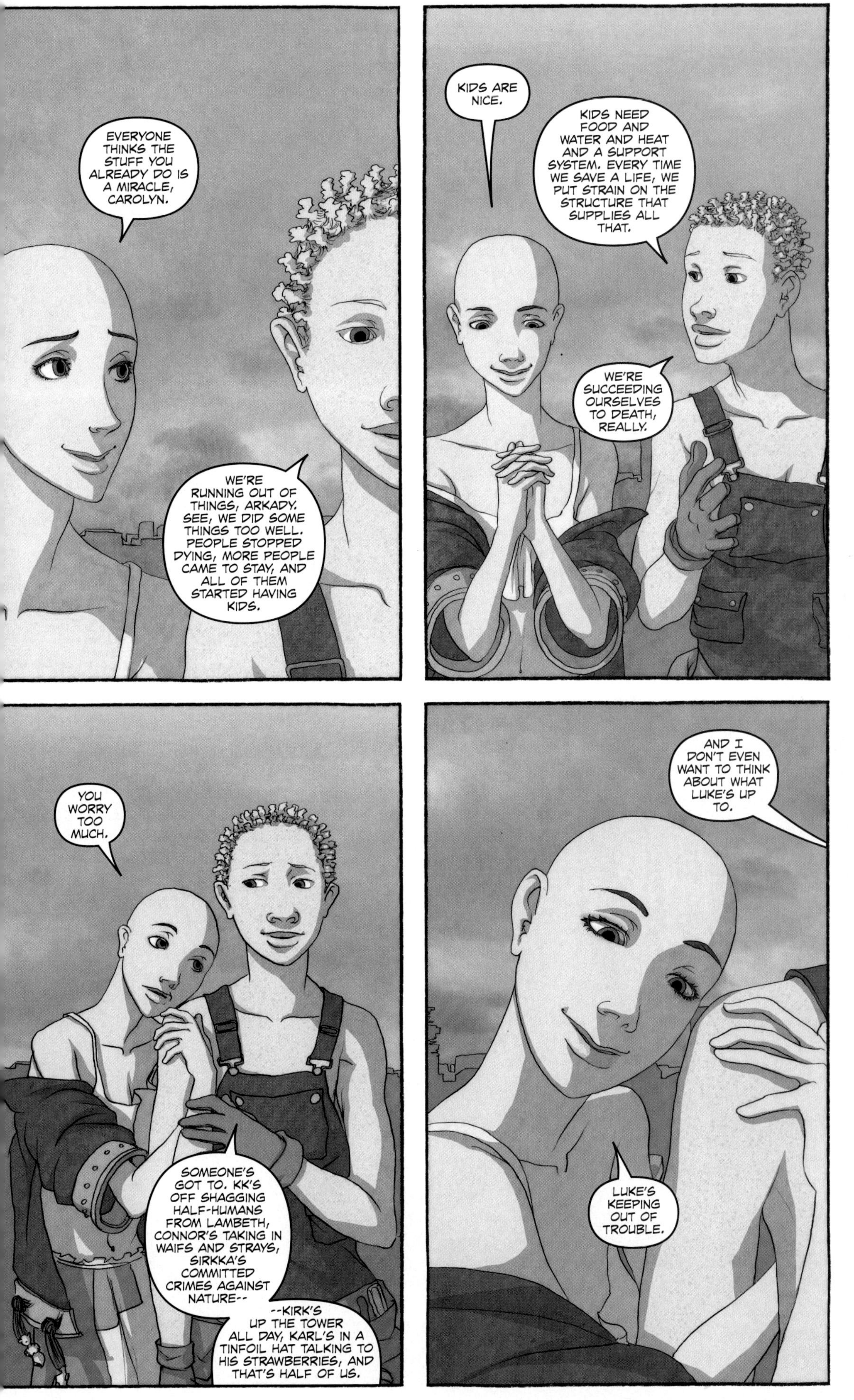
EVERYONE THINKS THE STUFF YOU ALREADY DO IS A MIRACLE, CAROLYN.
WE'RE RUNNING OUT OF THINGS, ARKADY. SEE, WE DID SOME THINGS TOO WELL. PEOPLE STOPPED DYING, MORE PEOPLE CAME TO STAY, AND ALL OF THEM STARTED HAVING KIDS.
KIDS ARE NICE.
KIDS NEED FOOD AND WATER AND HEAT AND A SUPPORT SYSTEM. EVERY TIME WE SAVE A LIFE, WE PUT STRAIN ON THE STRUCTURE THAT SUPPLIES ALL THAT.
WE'RE SUCCEEDING OURSELVES TO DEATH, REALLY.
YOU WORRY TOO MUCH.
SOMEONE'S GOT TO. KK'S OFF SHAGGING HALF-HUMANS FROM LAMBETH, CONNOR'S TAKING IN WAIFS AND STRAYS, SIRKKA'S COMMITTED CRIMES AGAINST NATURE--
--KIRK'S UP THE TOWER ALL DAY, KARL'S IN A TINFOIL HAT TALKING TO HIS STRAWBERRIES, AND THAT'S HALF OF US.
AND I DON'T EVEN WANT TO THINK ABOUT WHAT LUKE'S UP TO.
LUKE'S KEEPING OUT OF TROUBLE.

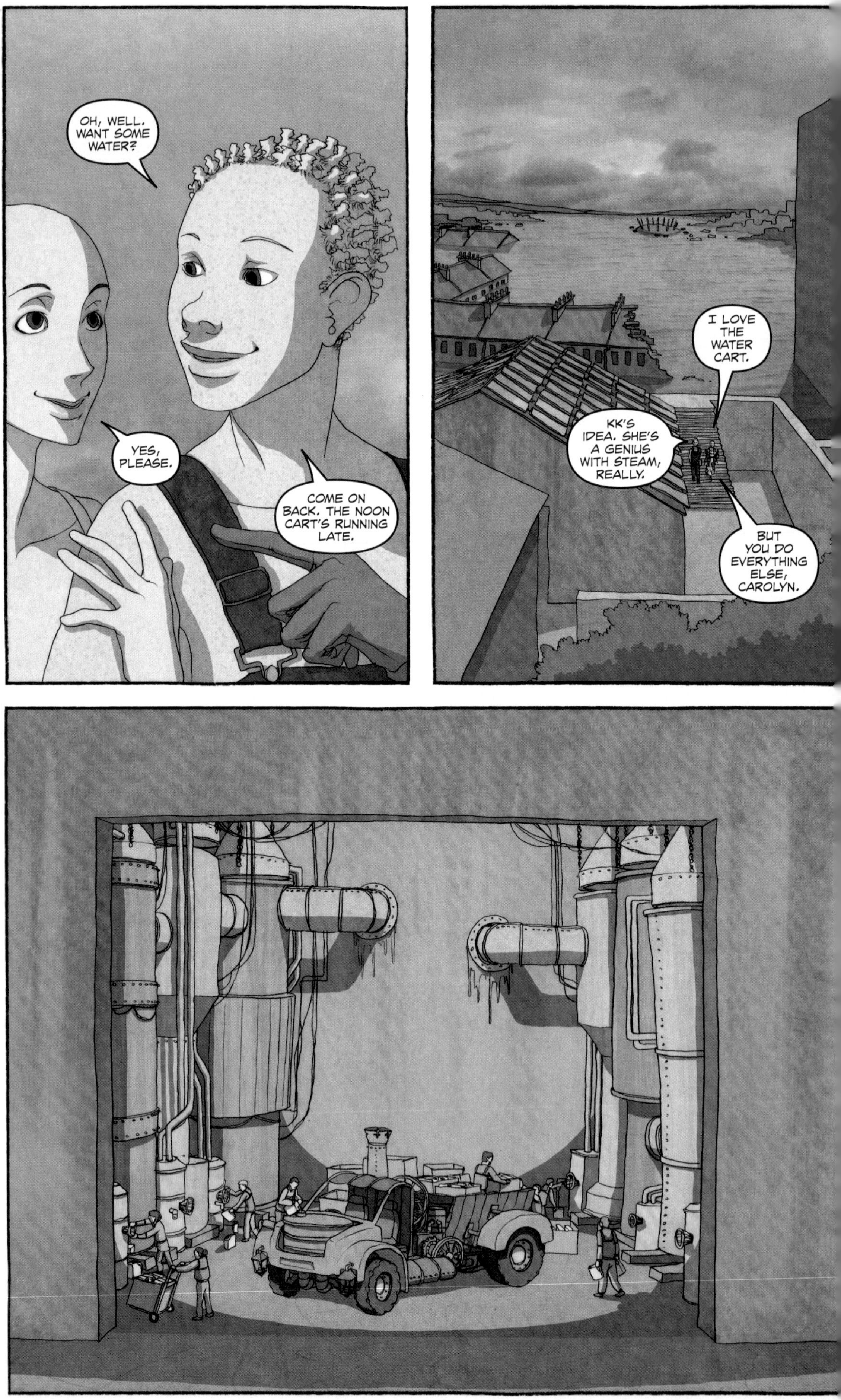
OH, WELL. WANT SOME WATER?
YES, PLEASE.
COME ON BACK. THE NOON CART'S RUNNING LATE.
I LOVE THE WATER CART.
KK'S IDEA. SHE'S A GENIUS WITH STEAM, REALLY.
BUT YOU DO EVERYTHING ELSE, CAROLYN.

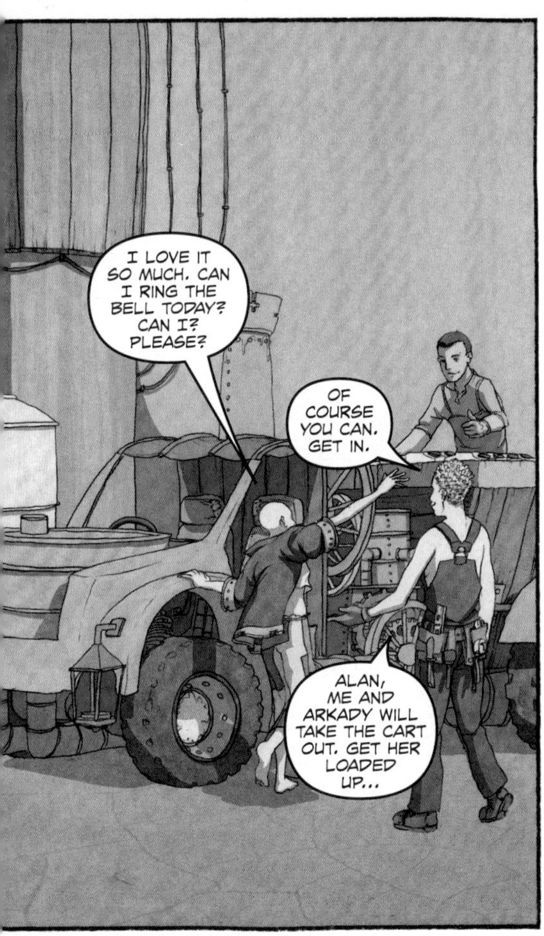
I LOVE IT SO MUCH. CAN I RING THE BELL TODAY? CAN I? PLEASE?
OF COURSE YOU CAN. GET IN.
ALAN, ME AND ARKADY WILL TAKE THE CART OUT. GET HER LOADED UP...

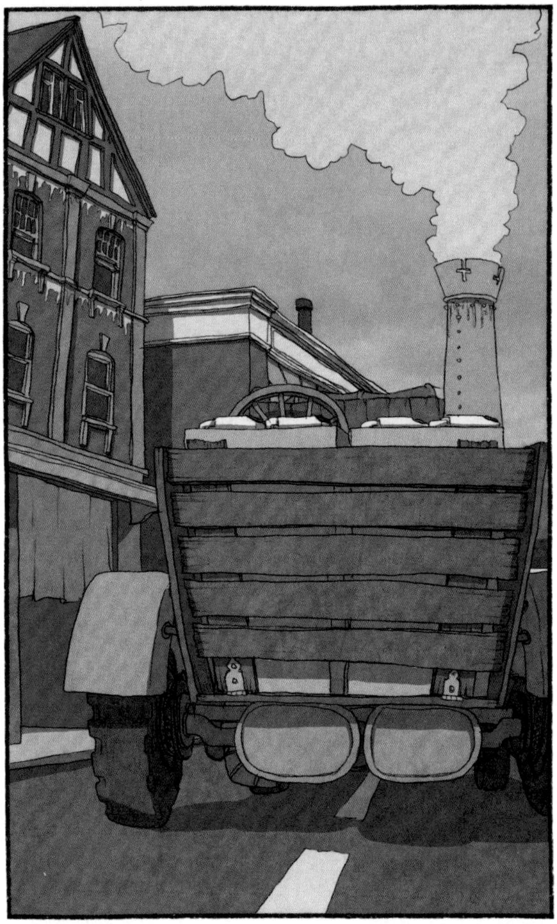

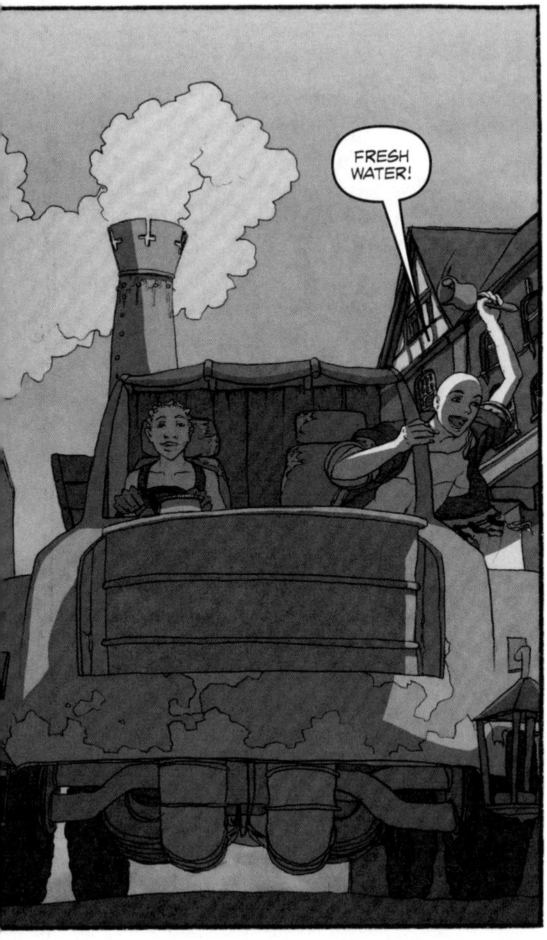
FRESH WATER!

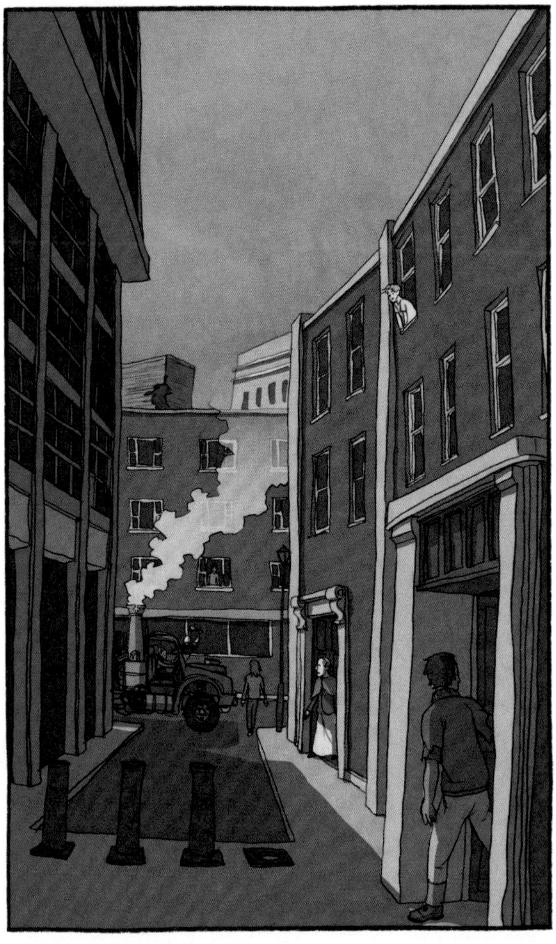

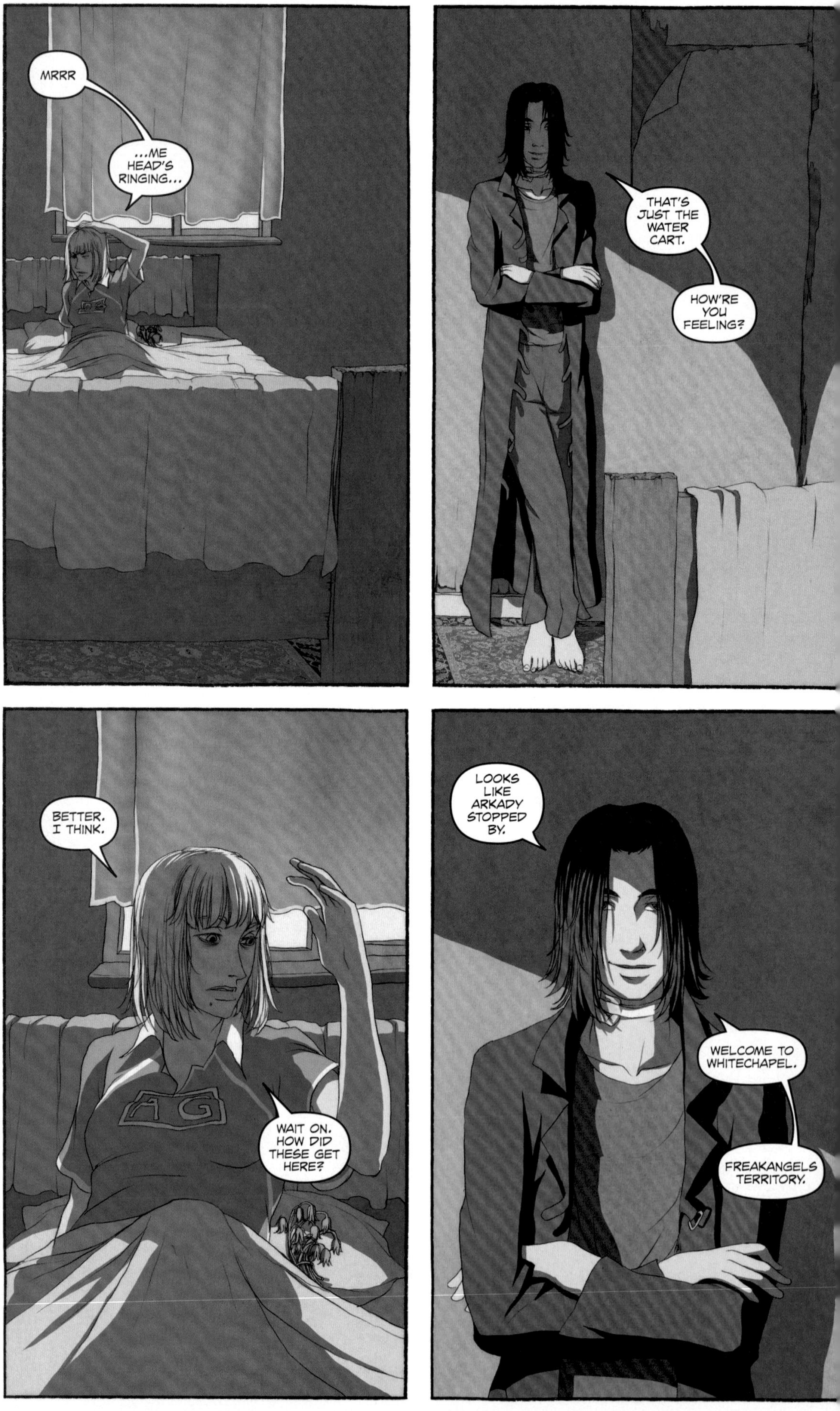
MRRR
...ME HEAD'S RINGING...
THAT'S JUST THE WATER CART.
HOW'RE YOU FEELING?
BETTER. I THINK.
WAIT ON. HOW DID THESE GET HERE?
LOOKS LIKE ARKADY STOPPED BY.
WELCOME TO WHITECHAPEL.
FREAKANGELS TERRITORY.

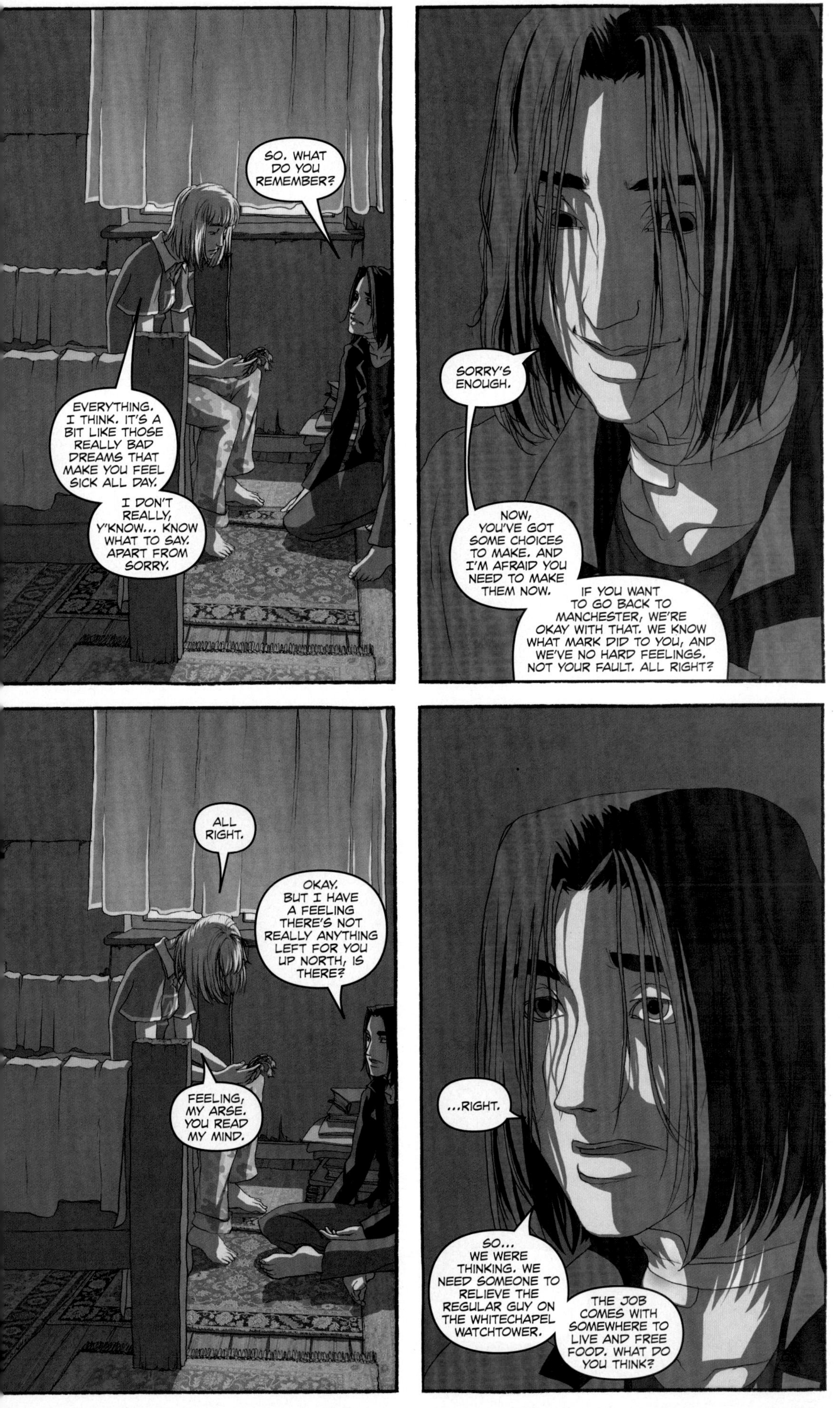
SO. WHAT DO YOU REMEMBER?
EVERYTHING. I THINK. IT'S A BIT LIKE THOSE REALLY BAD DREAMS THAT MAKE YOU FEEL SICK ALL DAY.
I DON'T REALLY, Y'KNOW... KNOW WHAT TO SAY. APART FROM SORRY.
SORRY'S ENOUGH.
NOW, YOU'VE GOT SOME CHOICES TO MAKE. AND I'M AFRAID YOU NEED TO MAKE THEM NOW.
IF YOU WANT TO GO BACK TO MANCHESTER, WE'RE OKAY WITH THAT. WE KNOW WHAT MARK DID TO YOU, AND WE'VE NO HARD FEELINGS. NOT YOUR FAULT. ALL RIGHT?
ALL RIGHT.
OKAY. BUT I HAVE A FEELING THERE'S NOT REALLY ANYTHING LEFT FOR YOU UP NORTH, IS THERE?
FEELING, MY ARSE. YOU READ MY MIND.
...RIGHT.
SO... WE WERE THINKING. WE NEED SOMEONE TO RELIEVE THE REGULAR GUY ON THE WHITECHAPEL WATCHTOWER.
THE JOB COMES WITH SOMEWHERE TO LIVE AND FREE FOOD. WHAT DO YOU THINK?

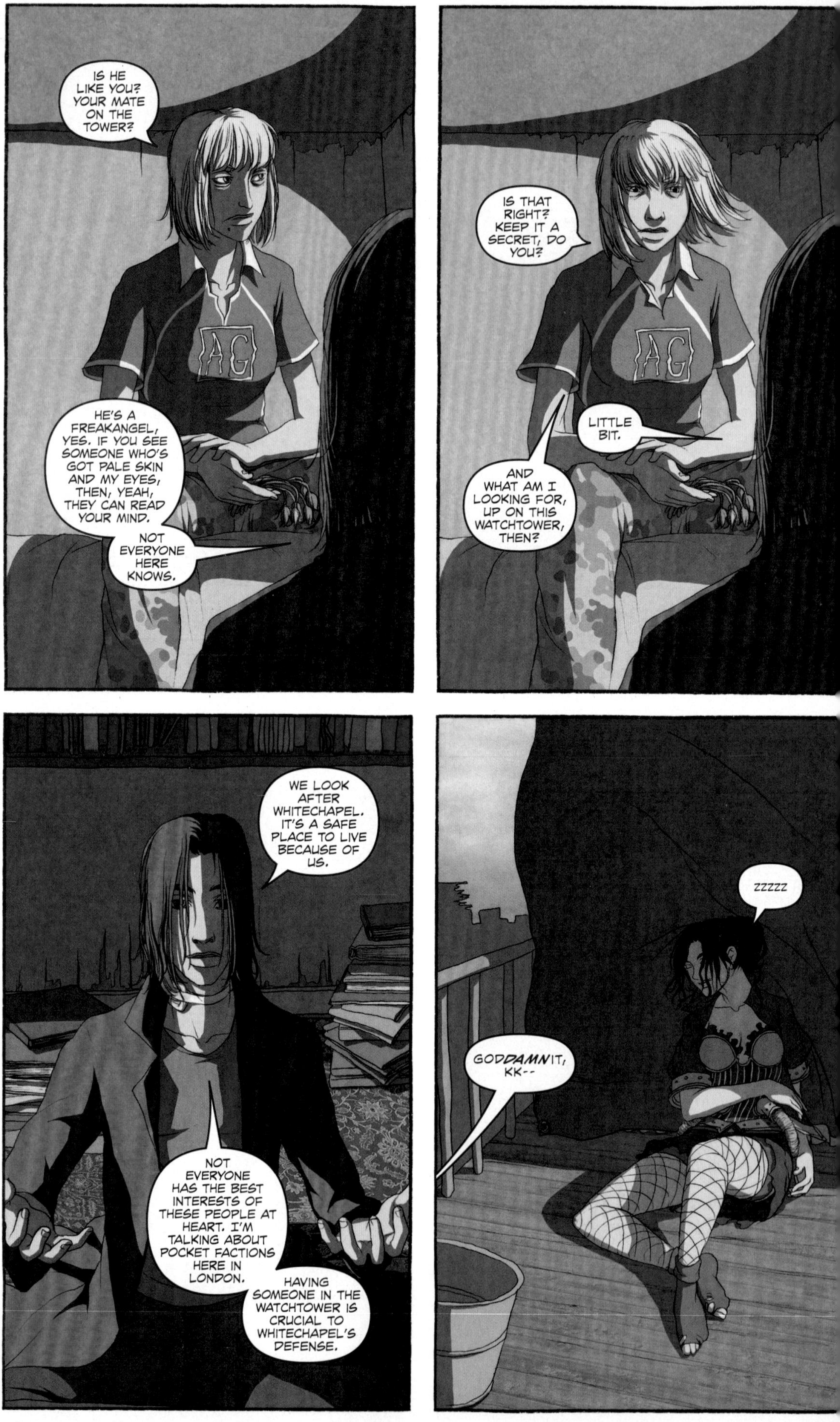
IS HE LIKE YOU? YOUR MATE ON THE TOWER?
HE'S A FREAKANGEL, YES. IF YOU SEE SOMEONE WHO'S GOT PALE SKIN AND MY EYES, THEN, YEAH, THEY CAN READ YOUR MIND.
NOT EVERYONE HERE KNOWS.
IS THAT RIGHT? KEEP IT A SECRET, DO YOU?
LITTLE BIT.
AND WHAT AM I LOOKING FOR, UP ON THIS WATCHTOWER, THEN?
WE LOOK AFTER WHITECHAPEL. IT'S A SAFE PLACE TO LIVE BECAUSE OF US.
NOT EVERYONE HAS THE BEST INTERESTS OF THESE PEOPLE AT HEART. I'M TALKING ABOUT POCKET FACTIONS HERE IN LONDON.
HAVING SOMEONE IN THE WATCHTOWER IS CRUCIAL TO WHITECHAPEL'S DEFENSE.
ZZZZZ
GOD*DAMN*IT, KK--

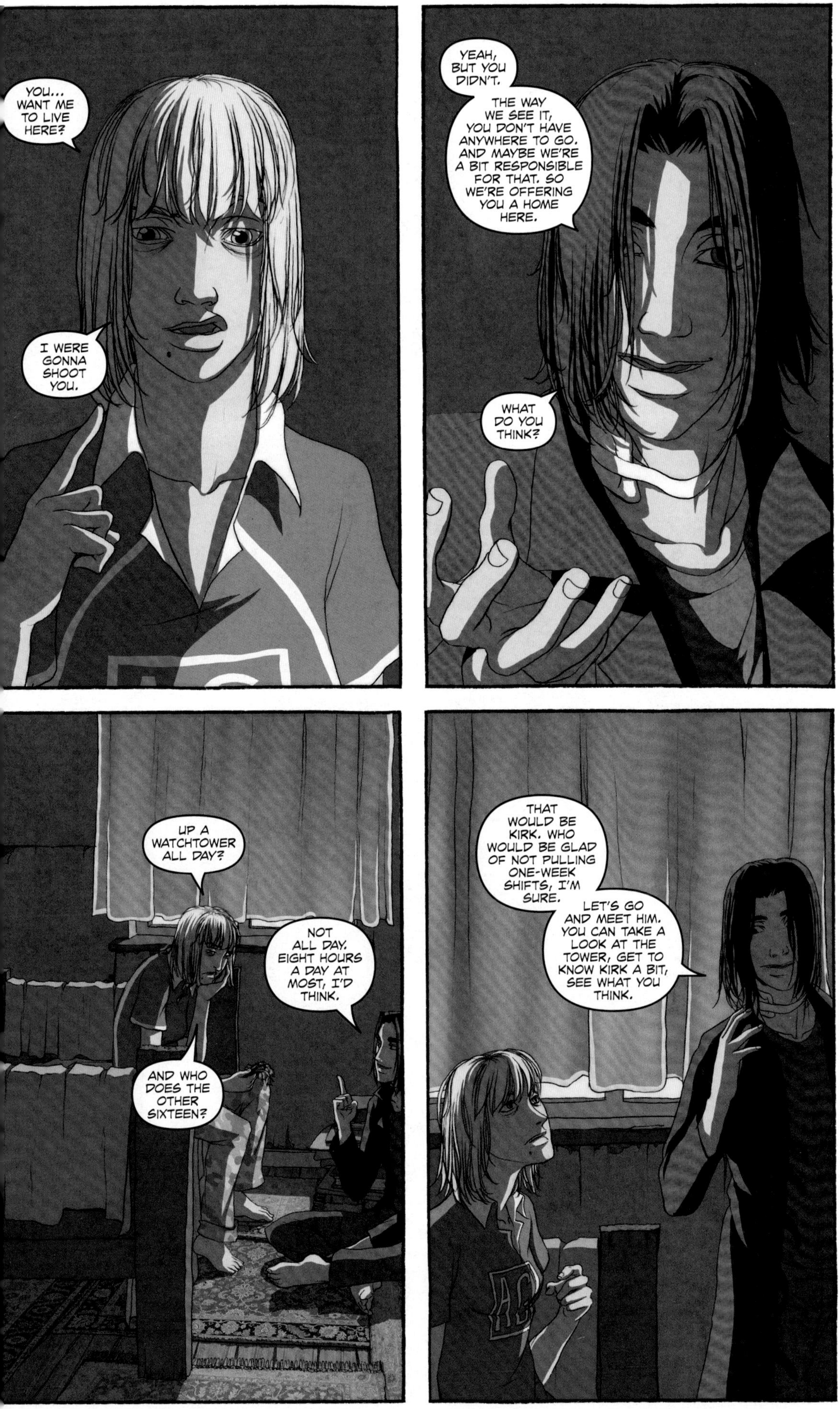
YOU... WANT ME TO LIVE HERE?
I WERE GONNA SHOOT YOU.
YEAH, BUT YOU DIDN'T.
THE WAY WE SEE IT, YOU DON'T HAVE ANYWHERE TO GO. AND MAYBE WE'RE A BIT RESPONSIBLE FOR THAT. SO WE'RE OFFERING YOU A HOME HERE.
WHAT DO YOU THINK?
UP A WATCHTOWER ALL DAY?
NOT ALL DAY. EIGHT HOURS A DAY AT MOST, I'D THINK.
AND WHO DOES THE OTHER SIXTEEN?
THAT WOULD BE KIRK. WHO WOULD BE GLAD OF NOT PULLING ONE-WEEK SHIFTS, I'M SURE.
LET'S GO AND MEET HIM. YOU CAN TAKE A LOOK AT THE TOWER, GET TO KNOW KIRK A BIT, SEE WHAT YOU THINK.

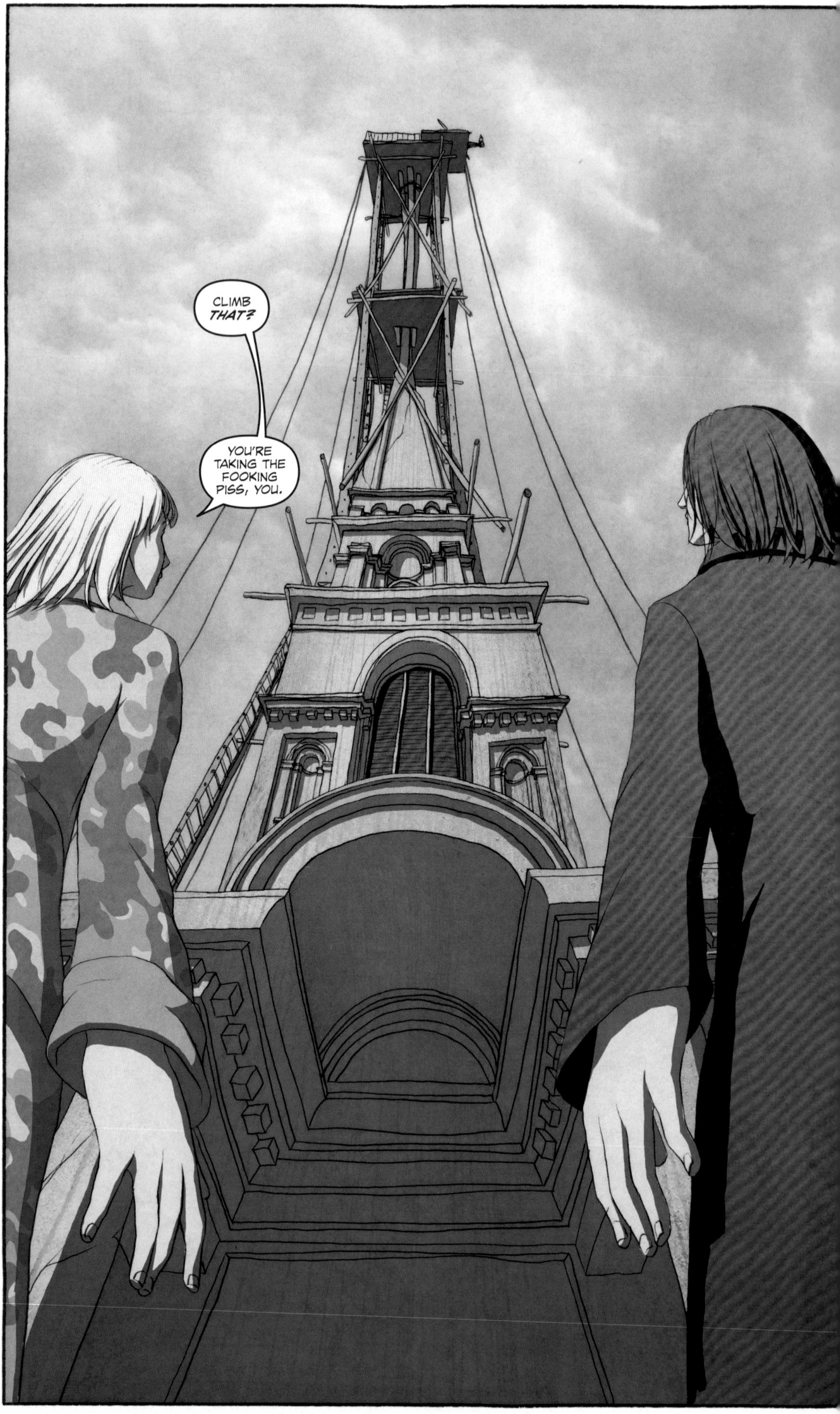
CLIMB *THAT?*
YOU'RE TAKING THE FOOKING PISS, YOU.

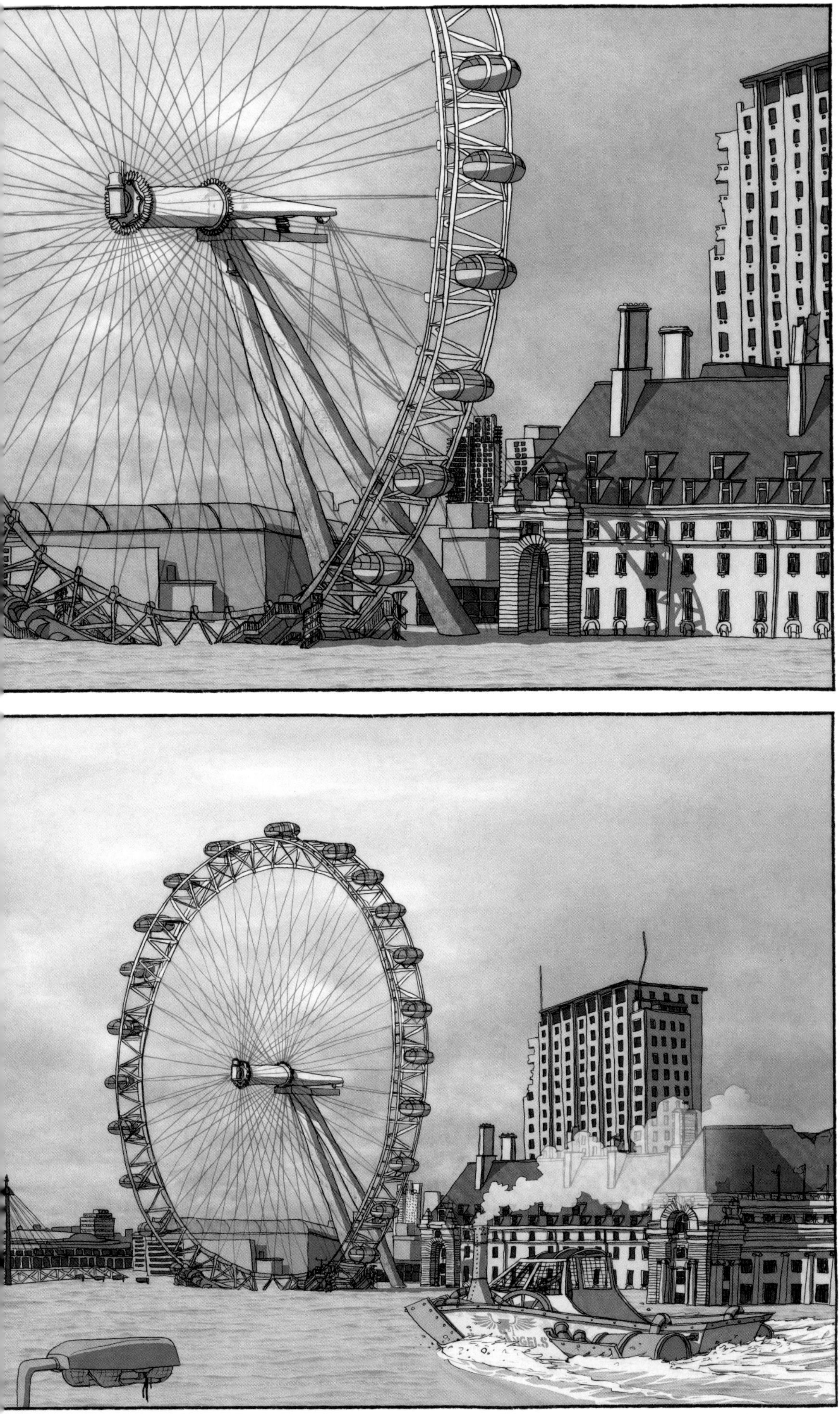

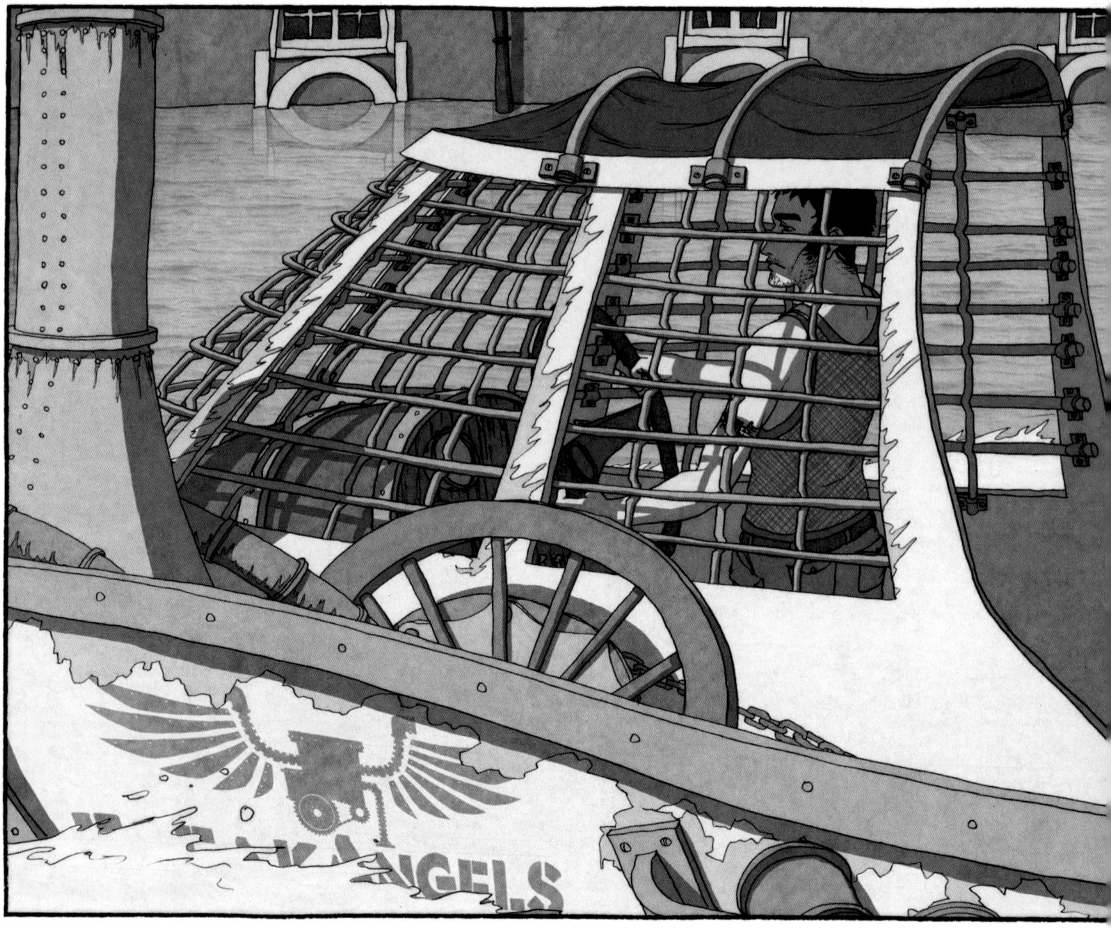

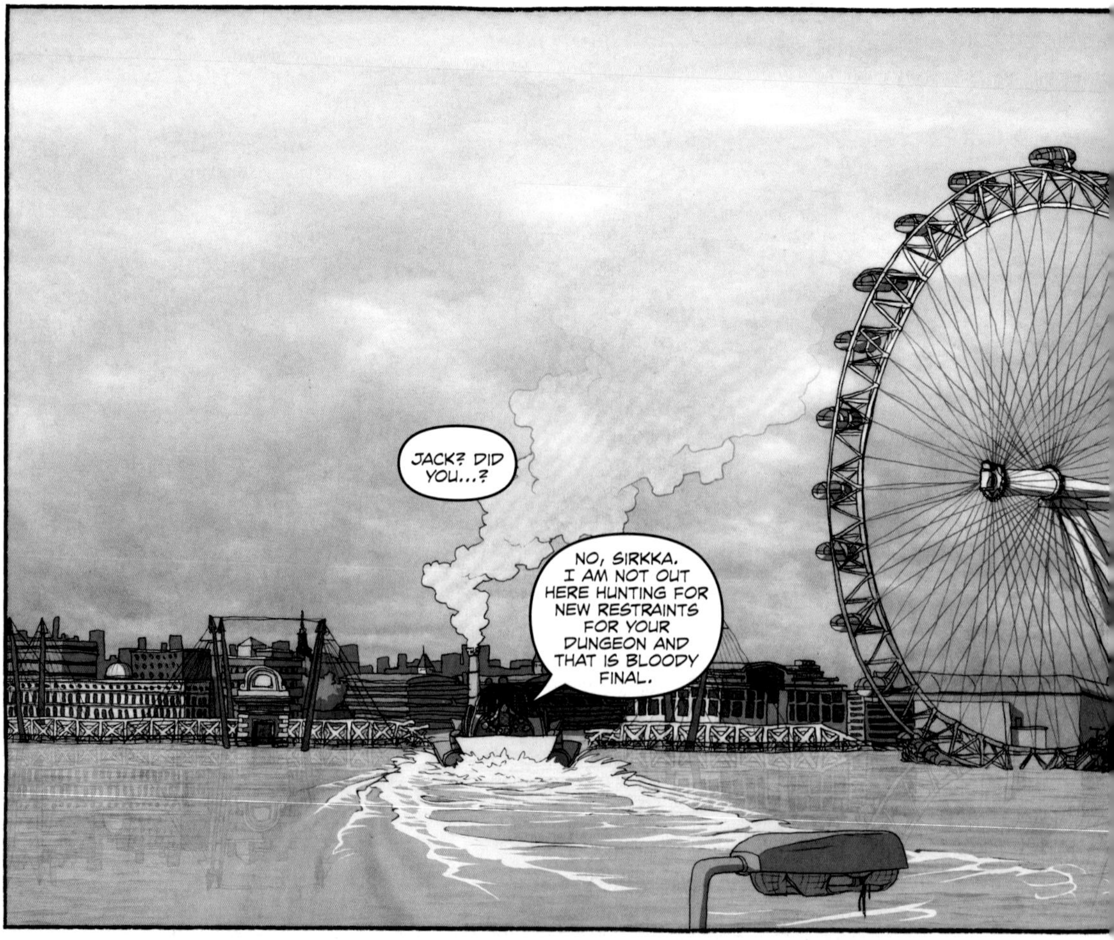
JACK? DID YOU...?
NO, SIRKKA. I AM NOT OUT HERE HUNTING FOR NEW RESTRAINTS FOR YOUR DUNGEON AND THAT IS BLOODY FINAL.

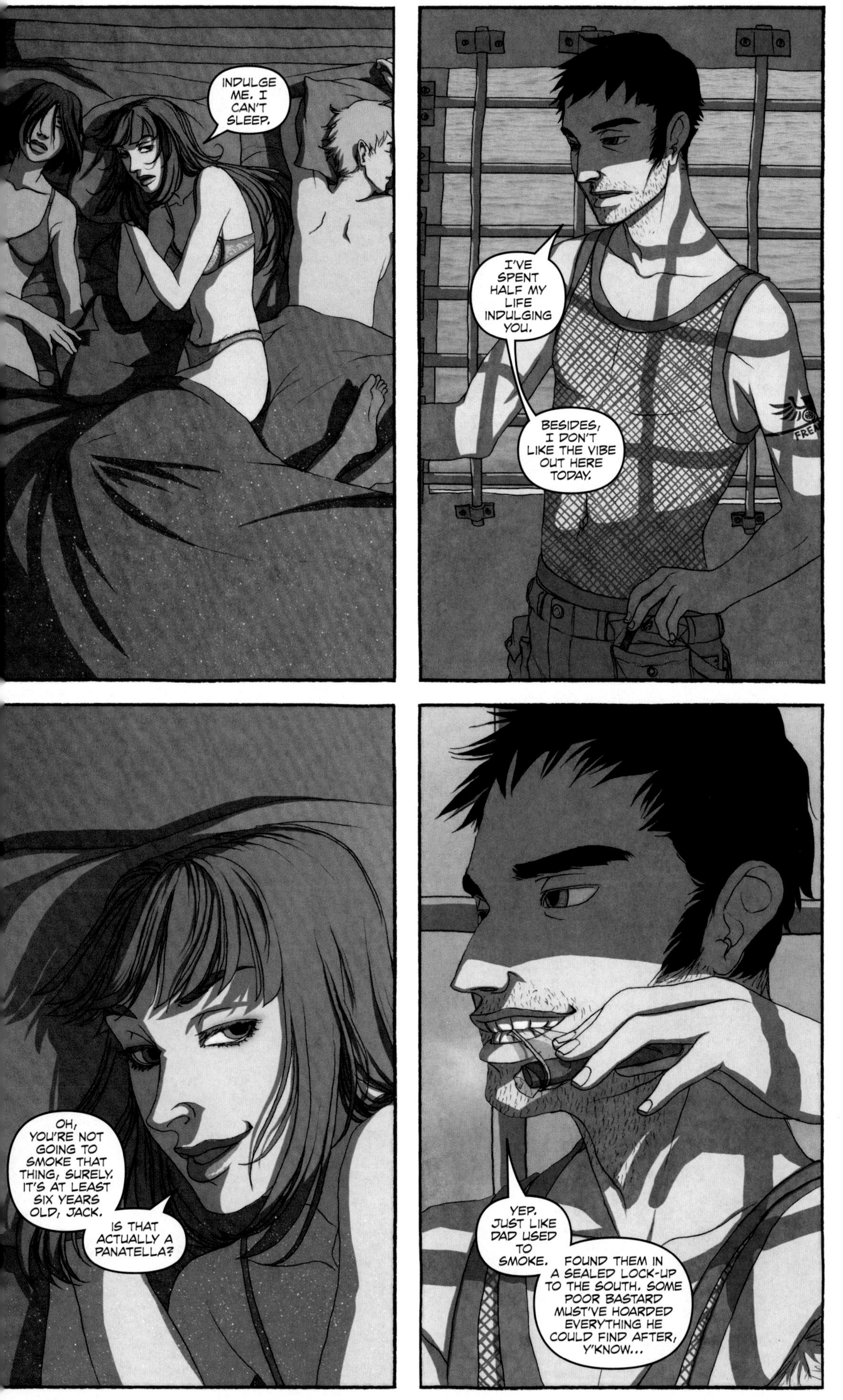
INDULGE ME. I CAN'T SLEEP.
I'VE SPENT HALF MY LIFE INDULGING YOU.
BESIDES, I DON'T LIKE THE VIBE OUT HERE TODAY.
OH, YOU'RE NOT GOING TO SMOKE THAT THING, SURELY. IT'S AT LEAST SIX YEARS OLD, JACK.
IS THAT ACTUALLY A PANATELLA?
YEP. JUST LIKE DAD USED TO SMOKE.
FOUND THEM IN A SEALED LOCK-UP TO THE SOUTH. SOME POOR BASTARD MUST'VE HOARDED EVERYTHING HE COULD FIND AFTER, Y'KNOW...

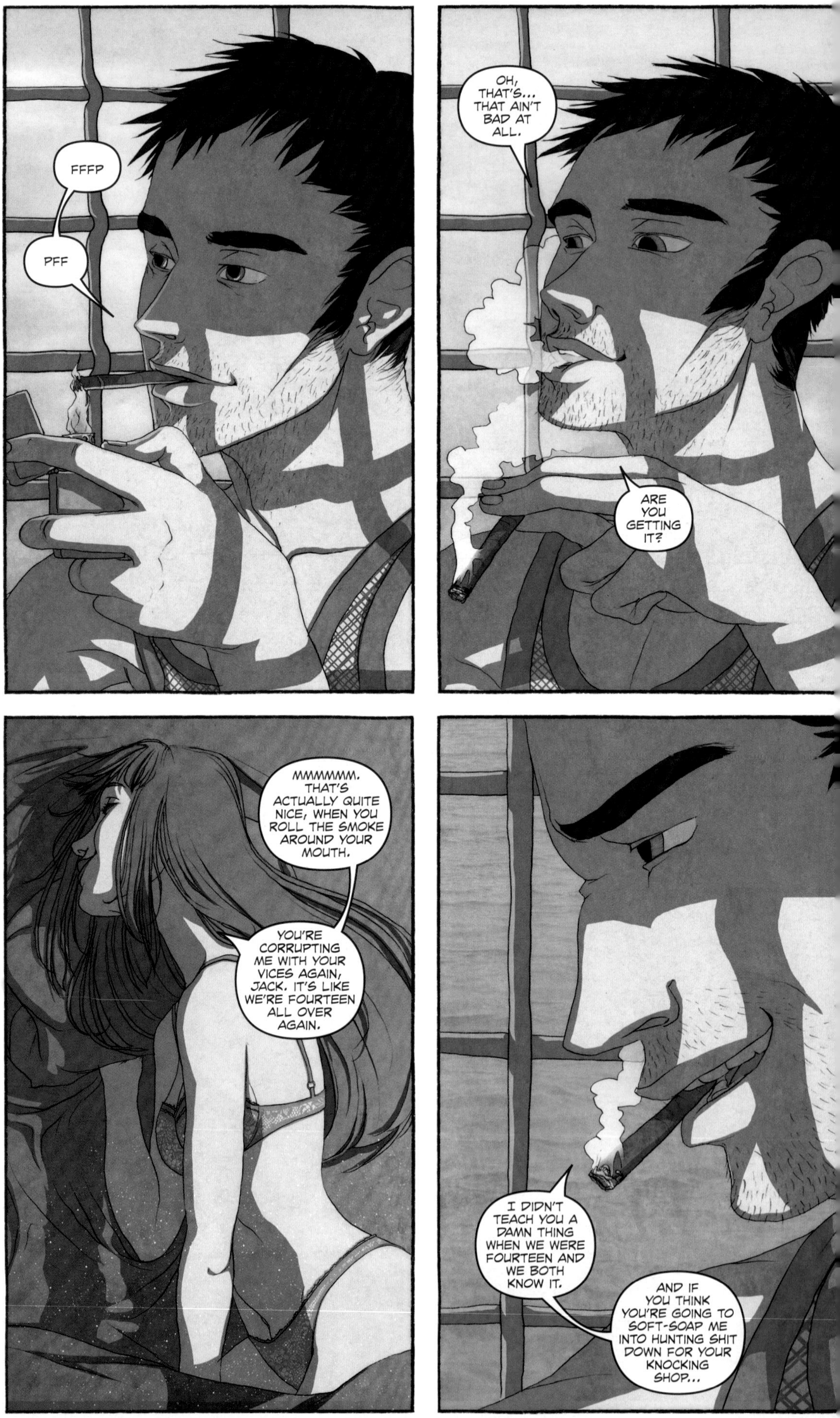
FFFP
PFF
OH, THAT'S... THAT AIN'T BAD AT ALL.
ARE YOU GETTING IT?
MMMMMM. THAT'S ACTUALLY QUITE NICE, WHEN YOU ROLL THE SMOKE AROUND YOUR MOUTH.
YOU'RE CORRUPTING ME WITH YOUR VICES AGAIN, JACK. IT'S LIKE WE'RE FOURTEEN ALL OVER AGAIN.
I DIDN'T TEACH YOU A DAMN THING WHEN WE WERE FOURTEEN AND WE BOTH KNOW IT.
AND IF YOU THINK YOU'RE GOING TO SOFT-SOAP ME INTO HUNTING SHIT DOWN FOR YOUR KNOCKING SHOP...

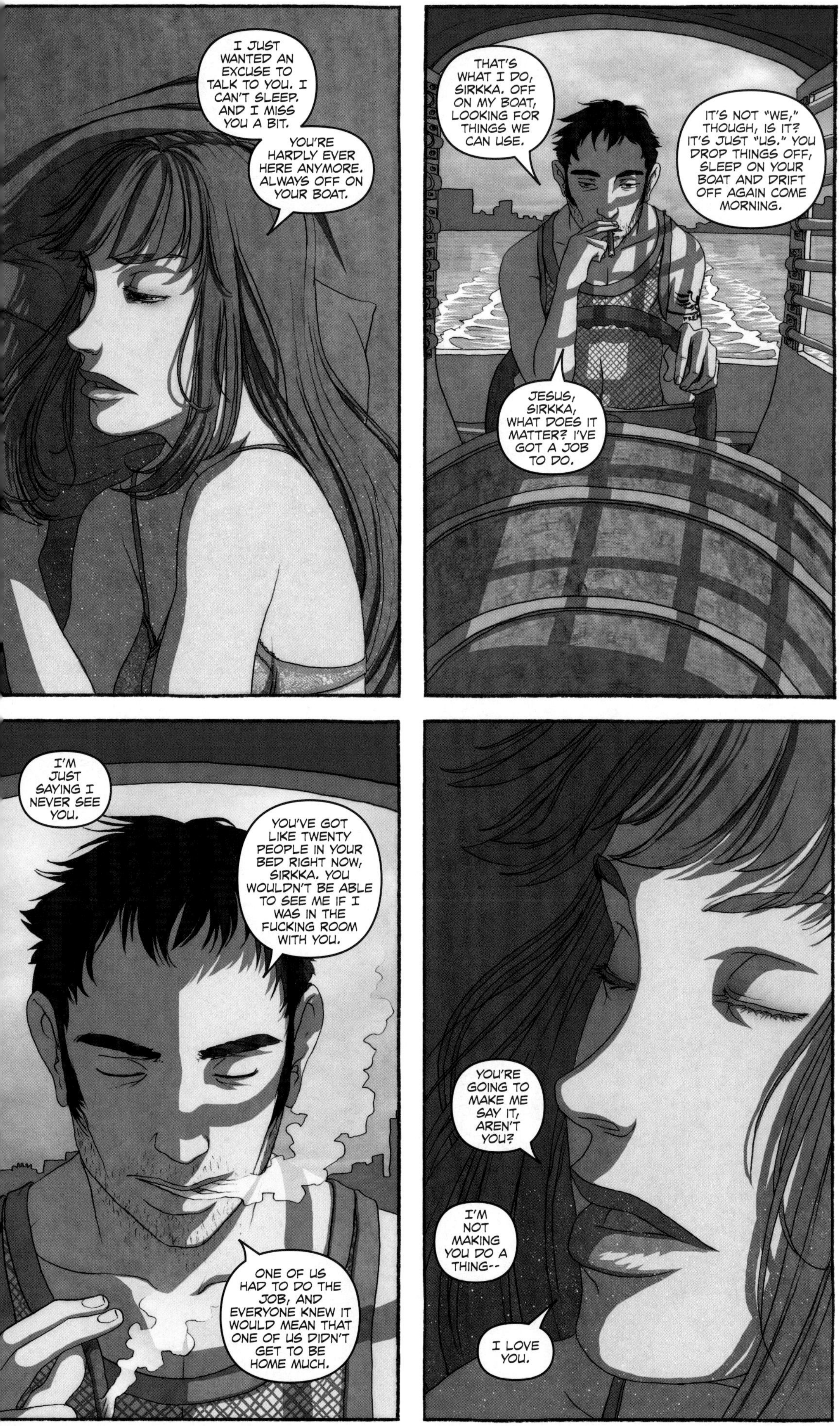
I JUST WANTED AN EXCUSE TO TALK TO YOU. I CAN'T SLEEP. AND I MISS YOU A BIT.
YOU'RE HARDLY EVER HERE ANYMORE. ALWAYS OFF ON YOUR BOAT.
THAT'S WHAT I DO, SIRKKA. OFF ON MY BOAT, LOOKING FOR THINGS WE CAN USE.
IT'S NOT "WE," THOUGH, IS IT? IT'S JUST "US." YOU DROP THINGS OFF, SLEEP ON YOUR BOAT AND DRIFT OFF AGAIN COME MORNING.
JESUS, SIRKKA, WHAT DOES IT MATTER? I'VE GOT A JOB TO DO.
I'M JUST SAYING I NEVER SEE YOU.
YOU'VE GOT LIKE TWENTY PEOPLE IN YOUR BED RIGHT NOW, SIRKKA. YOU WOULDN'T BE ABLE TO SEE ME IF I WAS IN THE FUCKING ROOM WITH YOU.
ONE OF US HAD TO DO THE JOB, AND EVERYONE KNEW IT WOULD MEAN THAT ONE OF US DIDN'T GET TO BE HOME MUCH.
YOU'RE GOING TO MAKE ME SAY IT, AREN'T YOU?
I'M NOT MAKING YOU DO A THING--
I LOVE YOU.

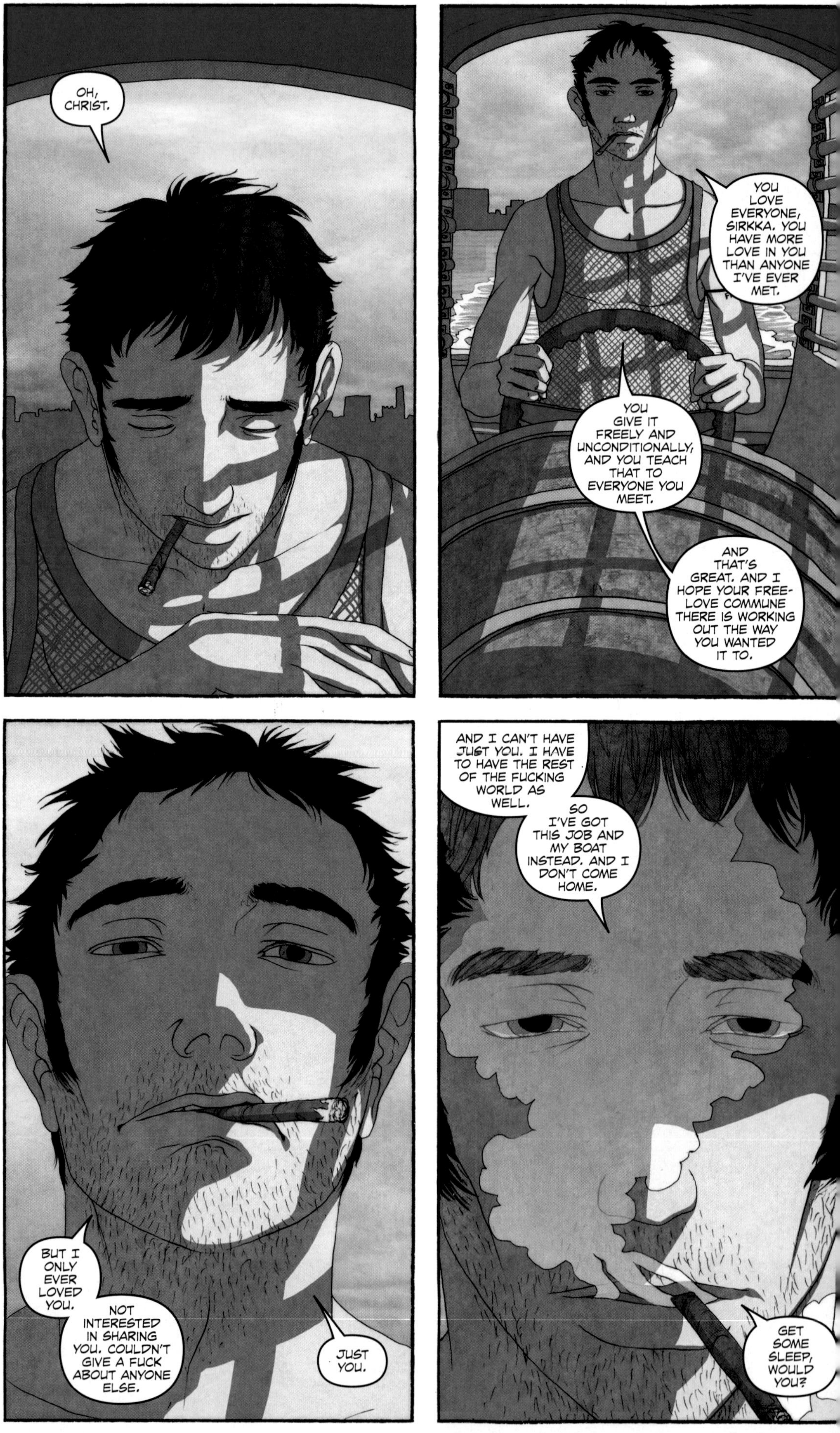
OH, CHRIST.
YOU LOVE EVERYONE, SIRKKA. YOU HAVE MORE LOVE IN YOU THAN ANYONE I'VE EVER MET.
YOU GIVE IT FREELY AND UNCONDITIONALLY, AND YOU TEACH THAT TO EVERYONE YOU MEET.
AND THAT'S GREAT. AND I HOPE YOUR FREE-LOVE COMMUNE THERE IS WORKING OUT THE WAY YOU WANTED IT TO.
BUT I ONLY EVER LOVED YOU.
NOT INTERESTED IN SHARING YOU. COULDN'T GIVE A FUCK ABOUT ANYONE ELSE.
JUST YOU.
AND I CAN'T HAVE JUST YOU. I HAVE TO HAVE THE REST OF THE FUCKING WORLD AS WELL.
SO I'VE GOT THIS JOB AND MY BOAT INSTEAD. AND I DON'T COME HOME.
GET SOME SLEEP, WOULD YOU?

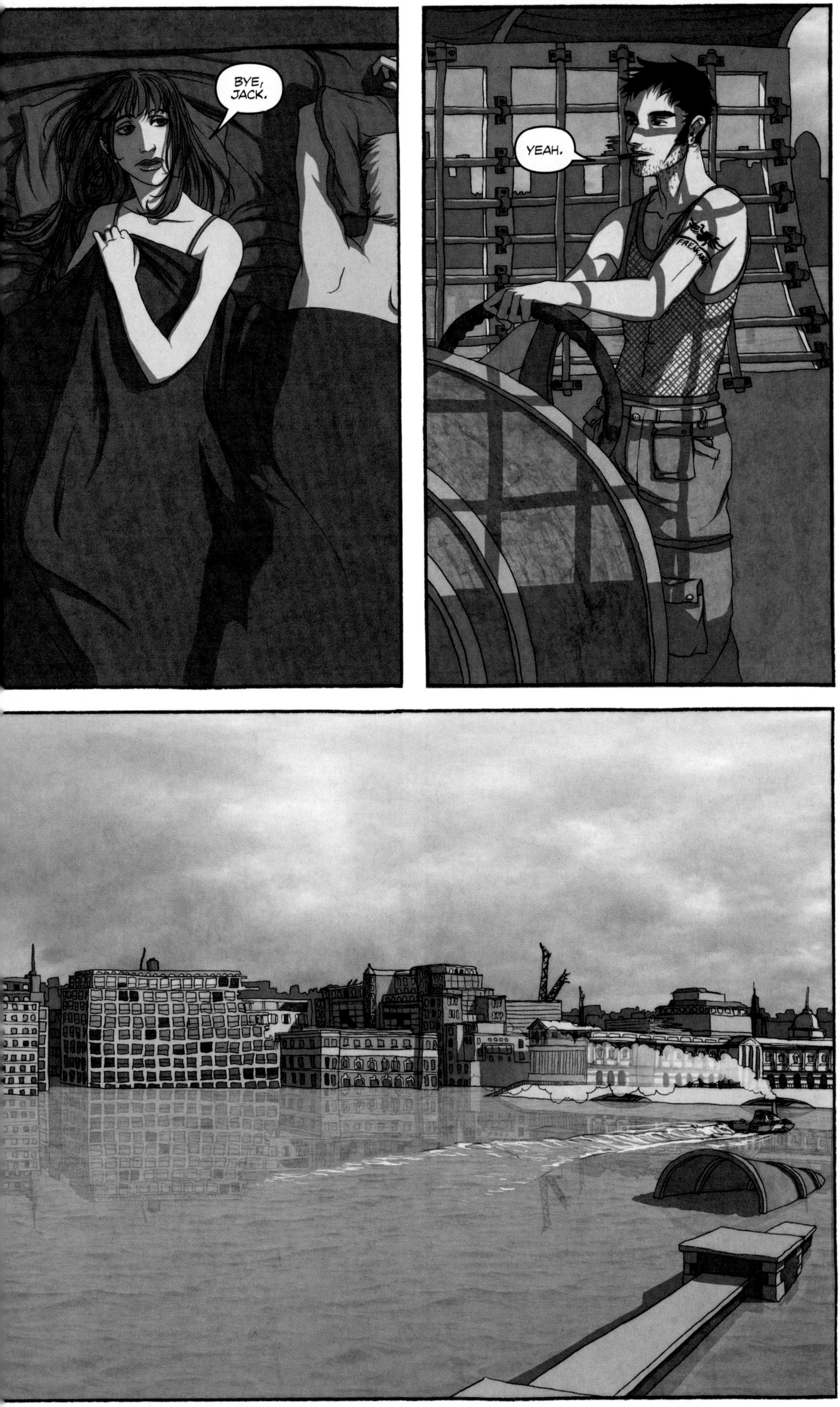
BYE, JACK.
YEAH.

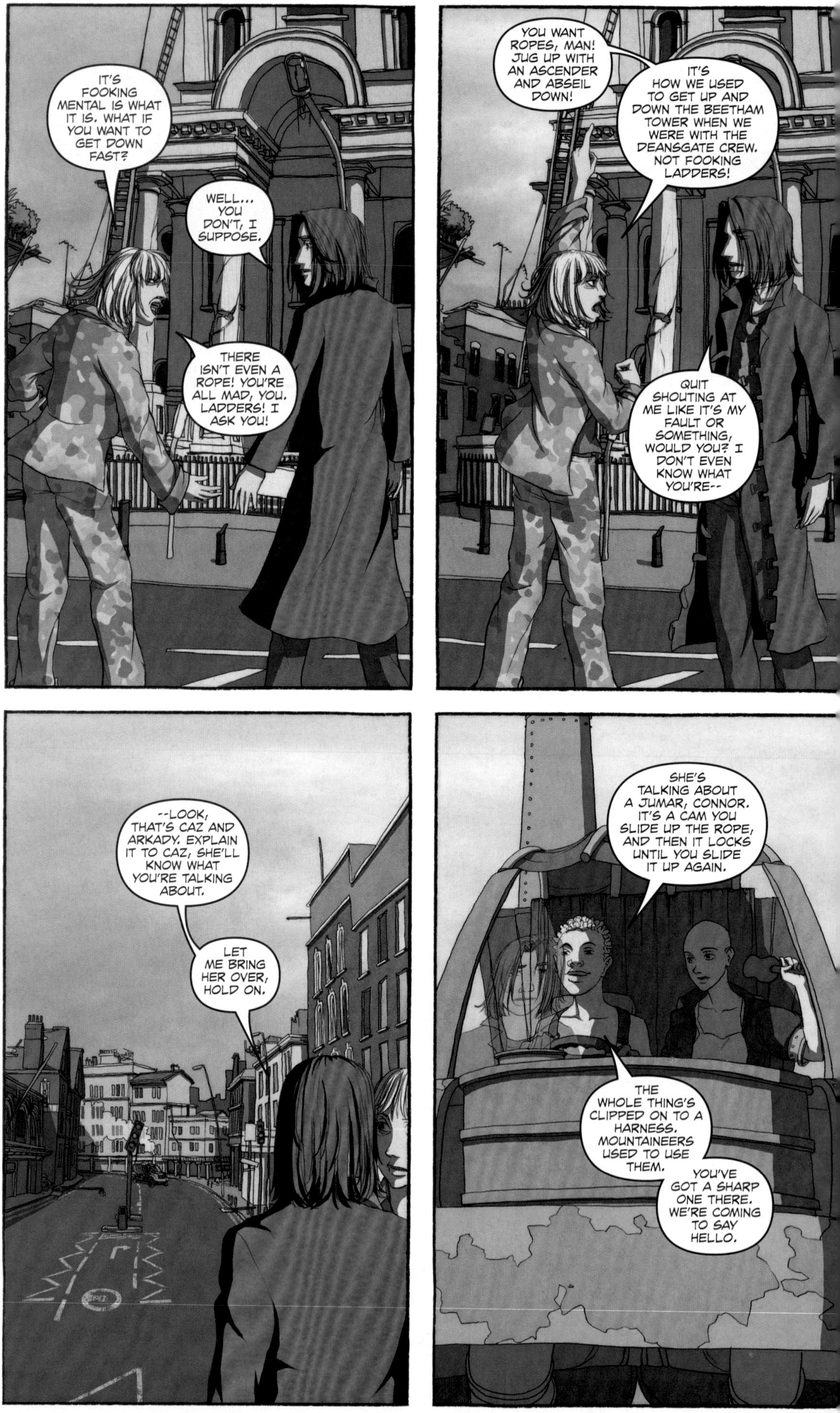
IT'S FOOKING MENTAL IS WHAT IT IS. WHAT IF YOU WANT TO GET DOWN FAST?
WELL... YOU DON'T, I SUPPOSE.
THERE ISN'T EVEN A ROPE! YOU'RE ALL MAD, YOU. LADDERS! I ASK YOU!
YOU WANT ROPES, MAN! JUG UP WITH AN ASCENDER AND ABSEIL DOWN!
IT'S HOW WE USED TO GET UP AND DOWN THE BEETHAM TOWER WHEN WE WERE WITH THE DEANSGATE CREW. NOT FOOKING LADDERS!
QUIT SHOUTING AT ME LIKE IT'S MY FAULT OR SOMETHING, WOULD YOU? I DON'T EVEN KNOW WHAT YOU'RE--
--LOOK, THAT'S CAZ AND ARKADY. EXPLAIN IT TO CAZ, SHE'LL KNOW WHAT YOU'RE TALKING ABOUT.
LET ME BRING HER OVER, HOLD ON.
SHE'S TALKING ABOUT A JUMAR, CONNOR. IT'S A CAM YOU SLIDE UP THE ROPE, AND THEN IT LOCKS UNTIL YOU SLIDE IT UP AGAIN.
THE WHOLE THING'S CLIPPED ON TO A HARNESS. MOUNTAINEERS USED TO USE THEM.
YOU'VE GOT A SHARP ONE THERE. WE'RE COMING TO SAY HELLO.

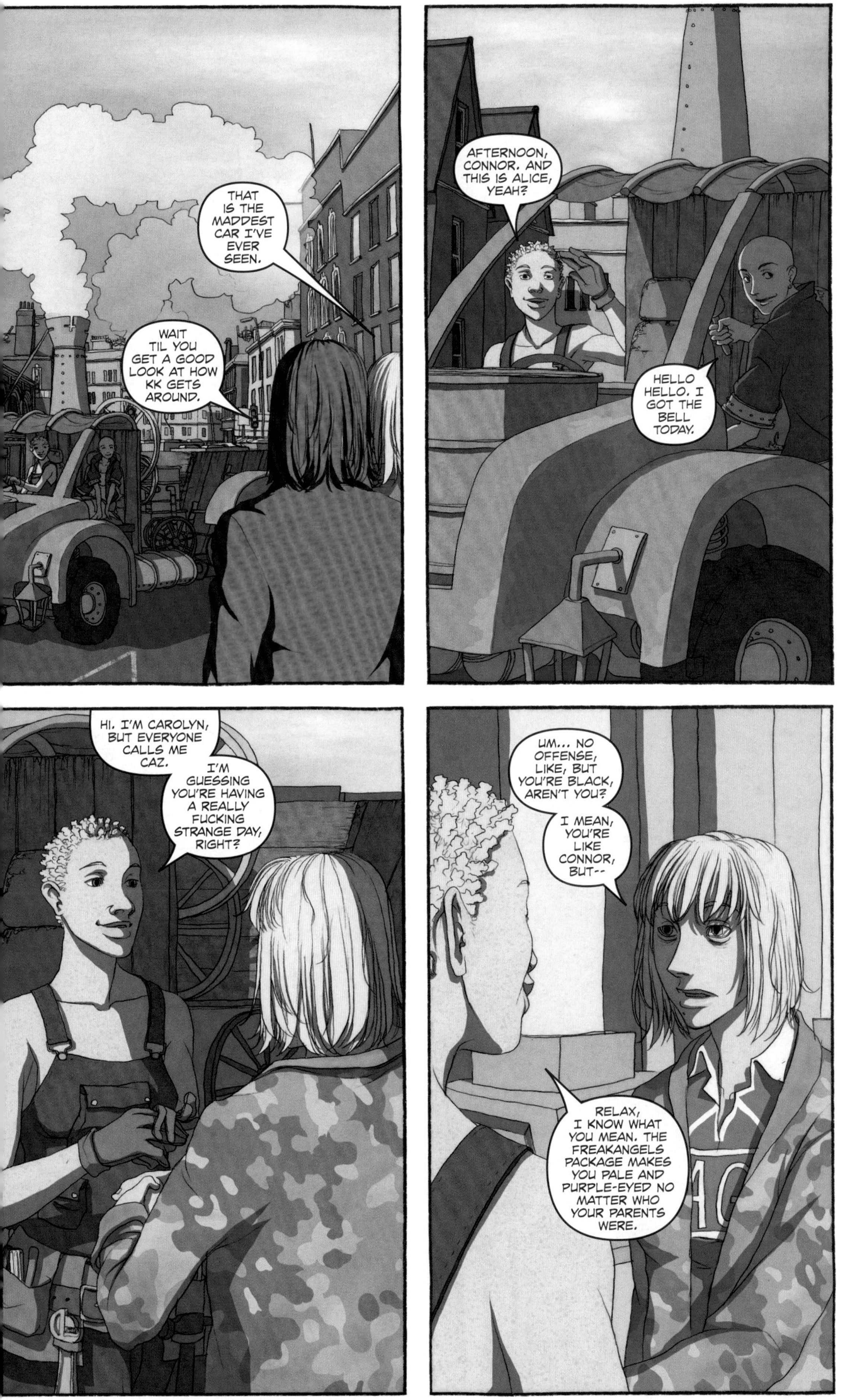
THAT IS THE MADDEST CAR I'VE EVER SEEN.
WAIT TIL YOU GET A GOOD LOOK AT HOW KK GETS AROUND.
AFTERNOON, CONNOR. AND THIS IS ALICE, YEAH?
HELLO HELLO. I GOT THE BELL TODAY.
HI. I'M CAROLYN, BUT EVERYONE CALLS ME CAZ.
I'M GUESSING YOU'RE HAVING A REALLY FUCKING STRANGE DAY, RIGHT?
UM... NO OFFENSE, LIKE, BUT YOU'RE BLACK, AREN'T YOU?
I MEAN, YOU'RE LIKE CONNOR, BUT--
RELAX, I KNOW WHAT YOU MEAN. THE FREAKANGELS PACKAGE MAKES YOU PALE AND PURPLE-EYED NO MATTER WHO YOUR PARENTS WERE.

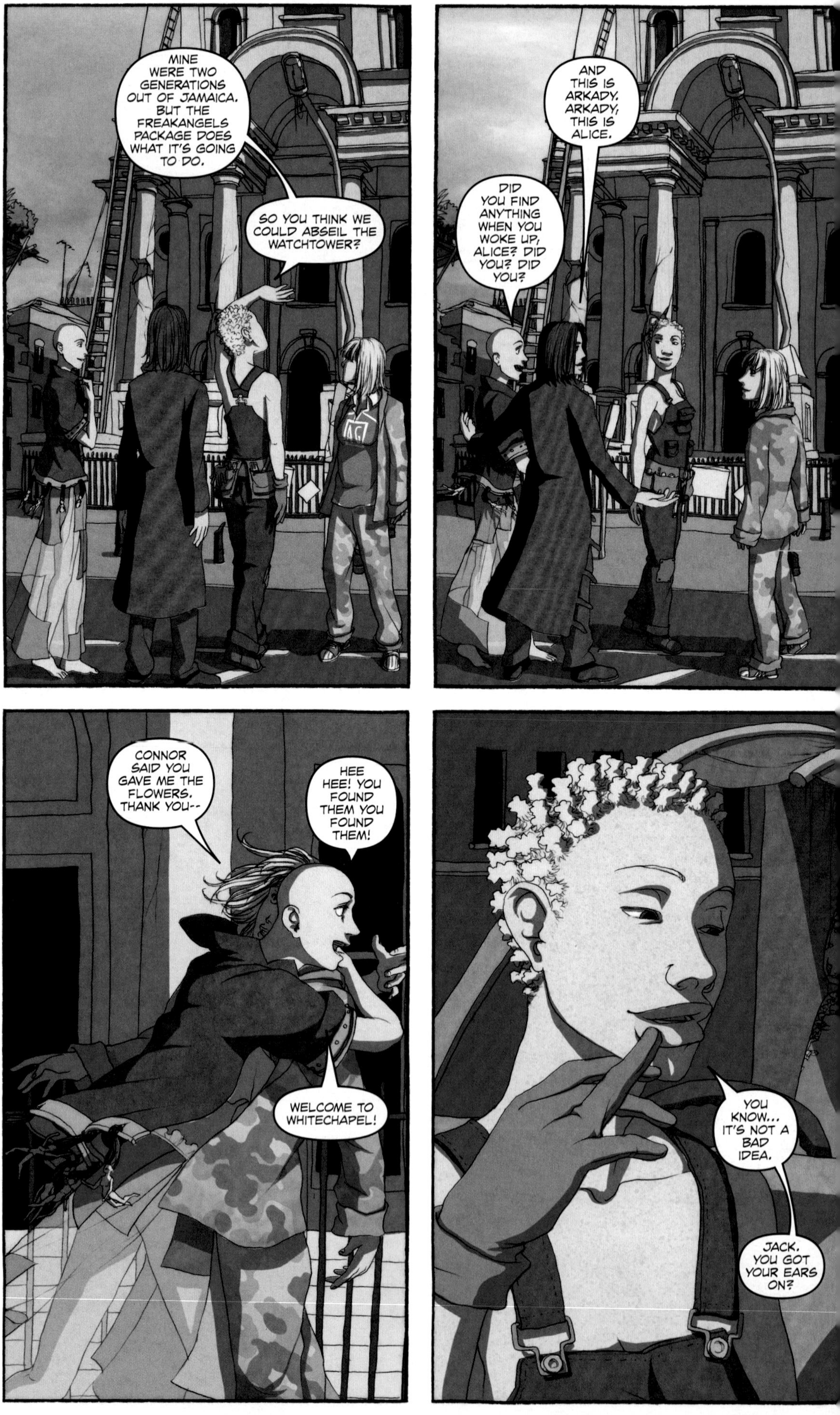
MINE WERE TWO GENERATIONS OUT OF JAMAICA. BUT THE FREAKANGELS PACKAGE DOES WHAT IT'S GOING TO DO.
SO YOU THINK WE COULD ABSEIL THE WATCHTOWER?
AND THIS IS ARKADY. ARKADY, THIS IS ALICE.
DID YOU FIND ANYTHING WHEN YOU WOKE UP, ALICE? DID YOU? DID YOU?
CONNOR SAID YOU GAVE ME THE FLOWERS. THANK YOU--
HEE HEE! YOU FOUND THEM YOU FOUND THEM!
WELCOME TO WHITECHAPEL!
YOU KNOW... IT'S NOT A BAD IDEA.
JACK. YOU GOT YOUR EARS ON?

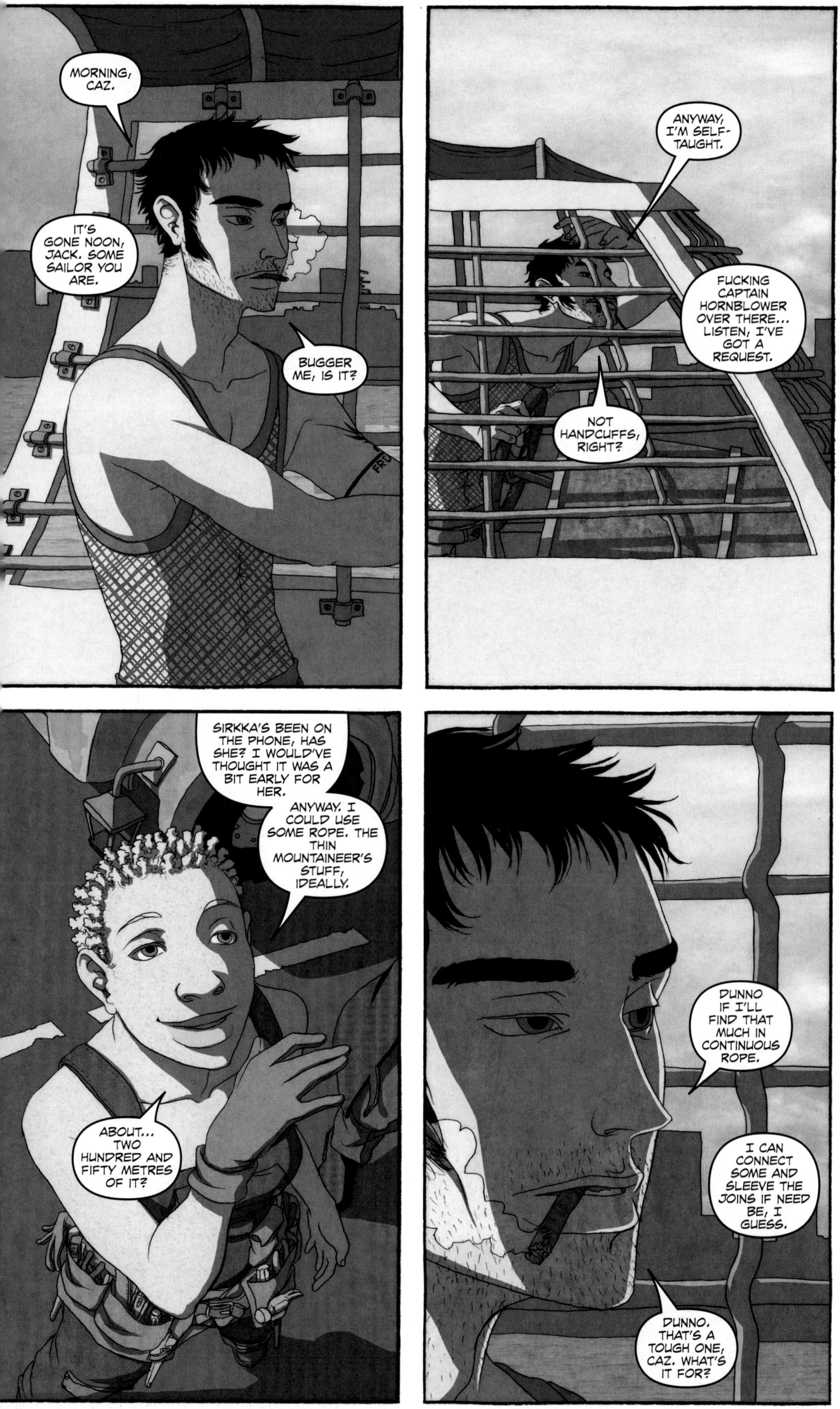
MORNING, CAZ.
IT'S GONE NOON, JACK. SOME SAILOR YOU ARE.
BUGGER ME, IS IT?
ANYWAY, I'M SELF-TAUGHT.
FUCKING CAPTAIN HORNBLOWER OVER THERE... LISTEN, I'VE GOT A REQUEST.
NOT HANDCUFFS, RIGHT?
SIRKKA'S BEEN ON THE PHONE, HAS SHE? I WOULD'VE THOUGHT IT WAS A BIT EARLY FOR HER.
ANYWAY. I COULD USE SOME ROPE. THE THIN MOUNTAINEER'S STUFF, IDEALLY.
ABOUT... TWO HUNDRED AND FIFTY METRES OF IT?
DUNNO IF I'LL FIND THAT MUCH IN CONTINUOUS ROPE.
I CAN CONNECT SOME AND SLEEVE THE JOINS IF NEED BE, I GUESS.
DUNNO. THAT'S A TOUGH ONE, CAZ. WHAT'S IT FOR?

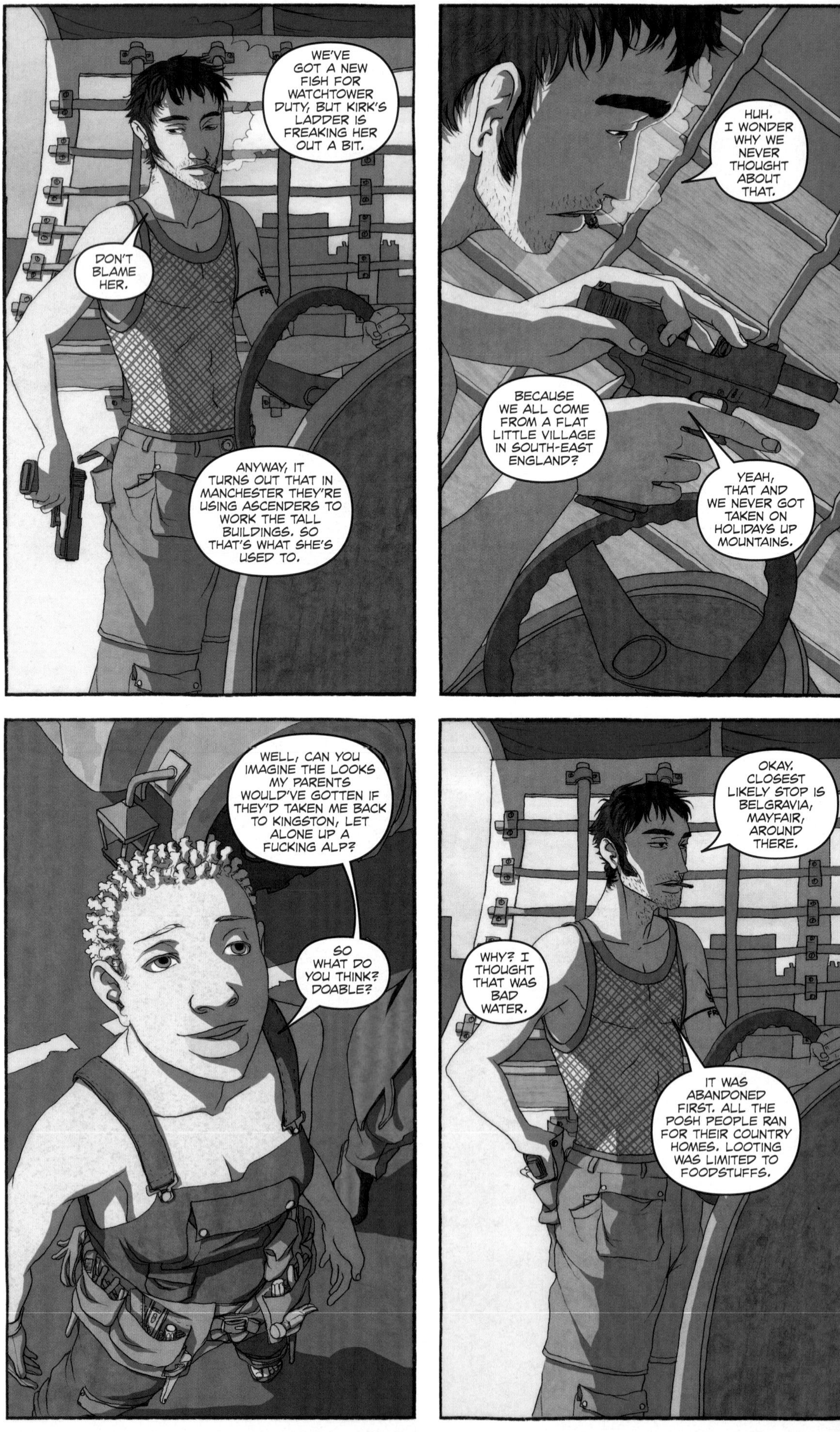
WE'VE GOT A NEW FISH FOR WATCHTOWER DUTY, BUT KIRK'S LADDER IS FREAKING HER OUT A BIT.
DON'T BLAME HER.
ANYWAY, IT TURNS OUT THAT IN MANCHESTER THEY'RE USING ASCENDERS TO WORK THE TALL BUILDINGS. SO THAT'S WHAT SHE'S USED TO.
HUH. I WONDER WHY WE NEVER THOUGHT ABOUT THAT.
BECAUSE WE ALL COME FROM A FLAT LITTLE VILLAGE IN SOUTH-EAST ENGLAND?
YEAH, THAT AND WE NEVER GOT TAKEN ON HOLIDAYS UP MOUNTAINS.
WELL, CAN YOU IMAGINE THE LOOKS MY PARENTS WOULD'VE GOTTEN IF THEY'D TAKEN ME BACK TO KINGSTON, LET ALONE UP A FUCKING ALP?
SO WHAT DO YOU THINK? DOABLE?
OKAY. CLOSEST LIKELY STOP IS BELGRAVIA, MAYFAIR, AROUND THERE.
WHY? I THOUGHT THAT WAS BAD WATER.
IT WAS ABANDONED FIRST. ALL THE POSH PEOPLE RAN FOR THEIR COUNTRY HOMES. LOOTING WAS LIMITED TO FOODSTUFFS.

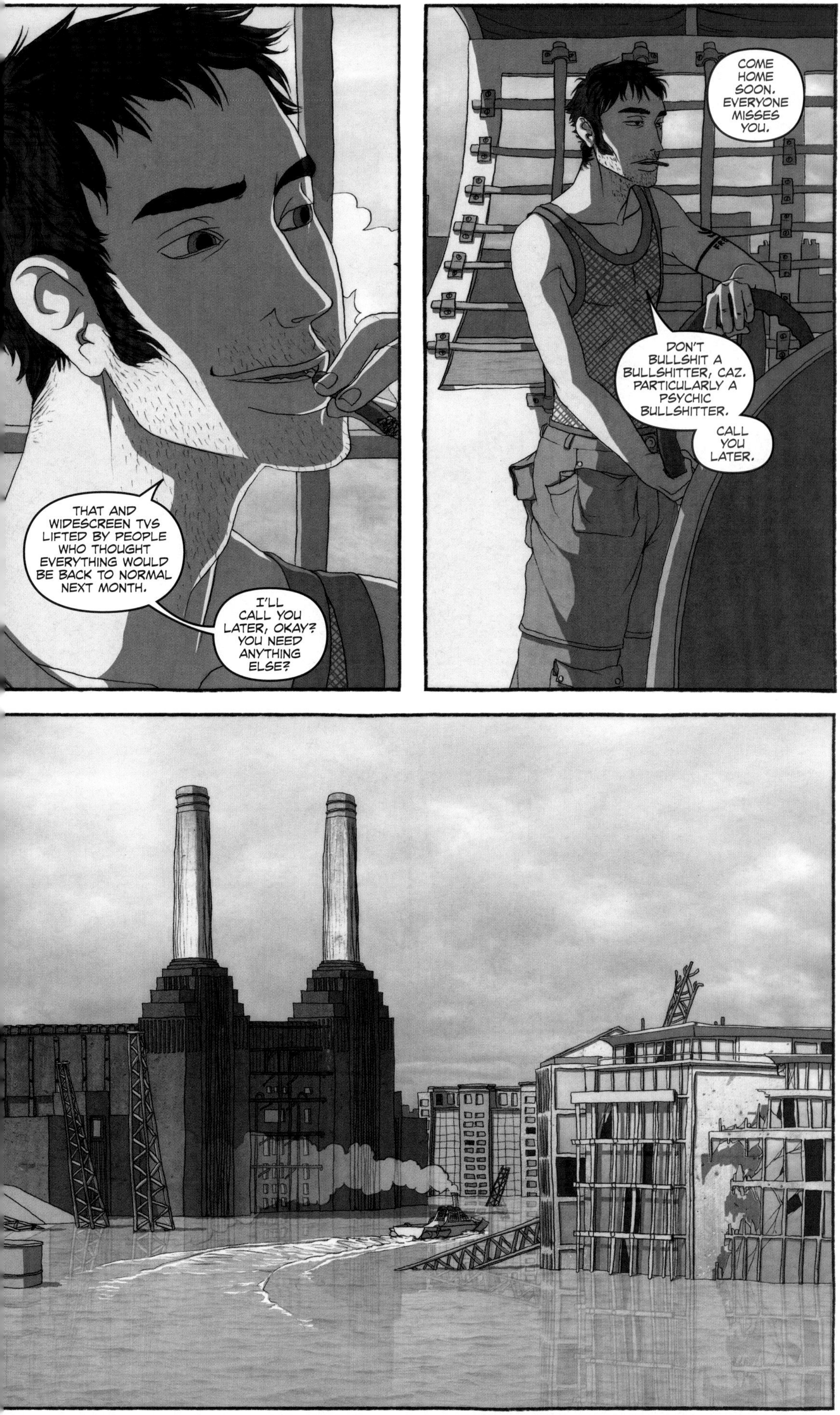
THAT AND WIDESCREEN TVS LIFTED BY PEOPLE WHO THOUGHT EVERYTHING WOULD BE BACK TO NORMAL NEXT MONTH.
I'LL CALL YOU LATER, OKAY? YOU NEED ANYTHING ELSE?
COME HOME SOON. EVERYONE MISSES YOU.
DON'T BULLSHIT A BULLSHITTER, CAZ. PARTICULARLY A PSYCHIC BULLSHITTER.
CALL YOU LATER.

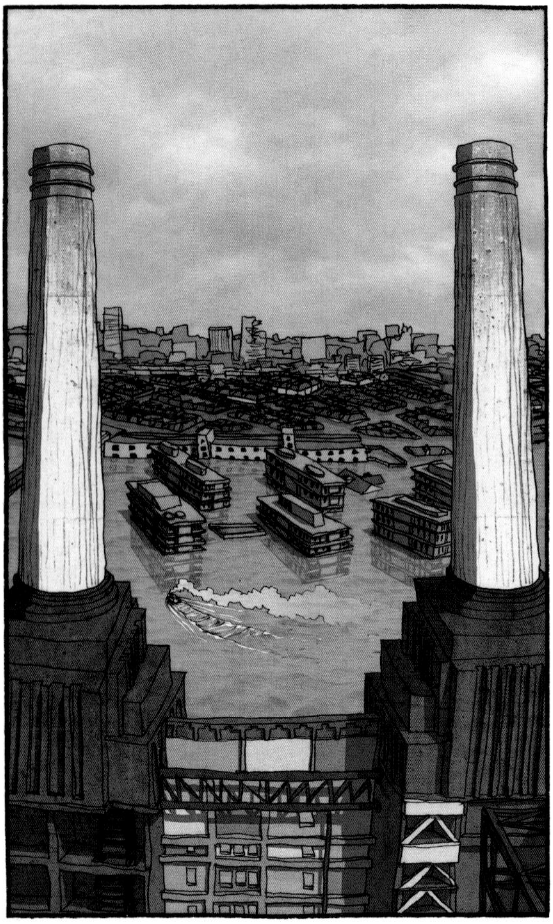
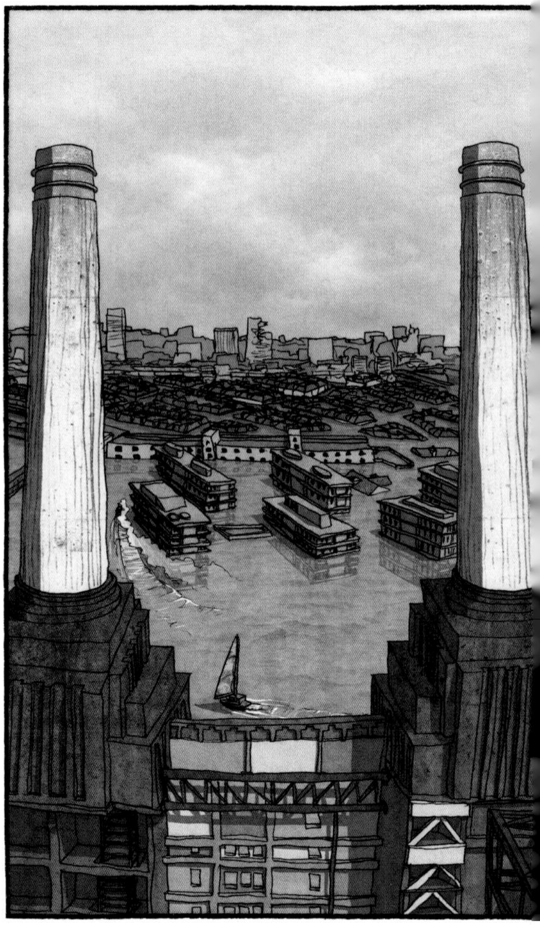
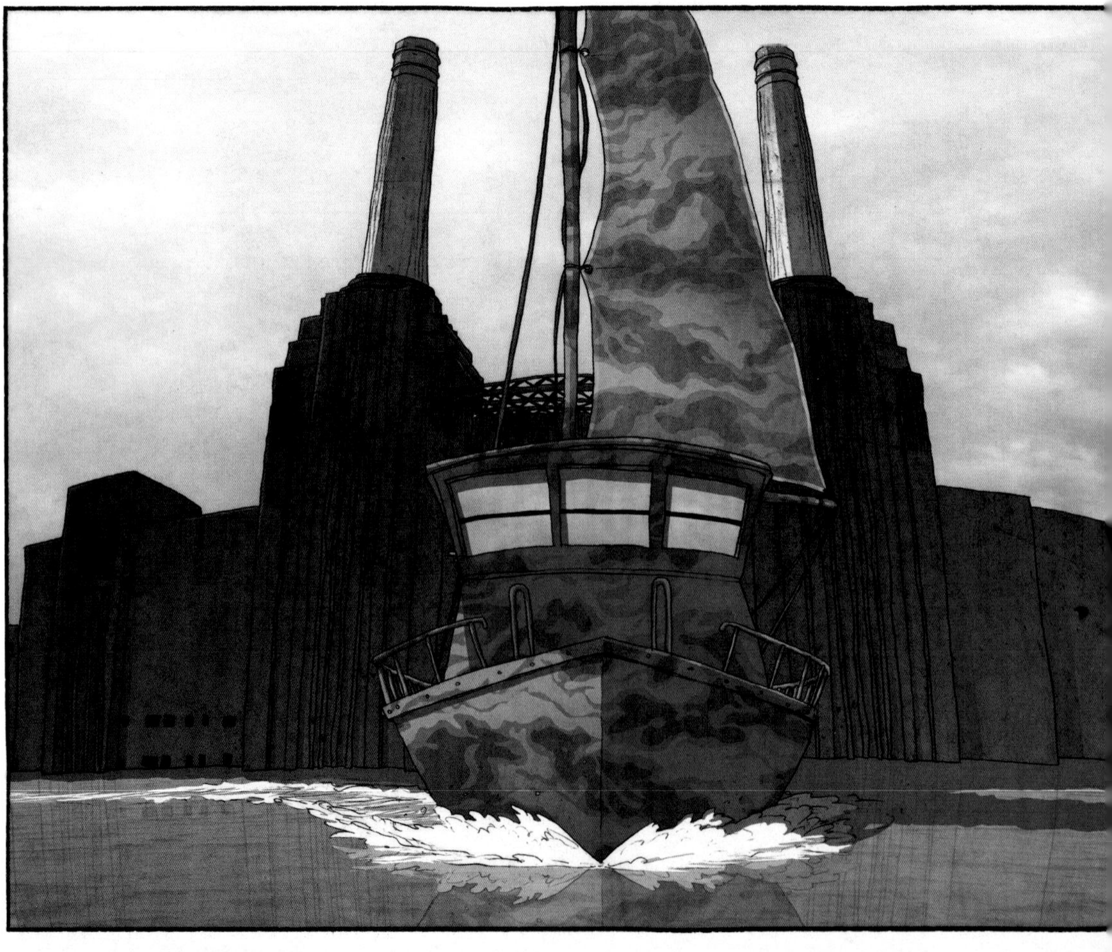

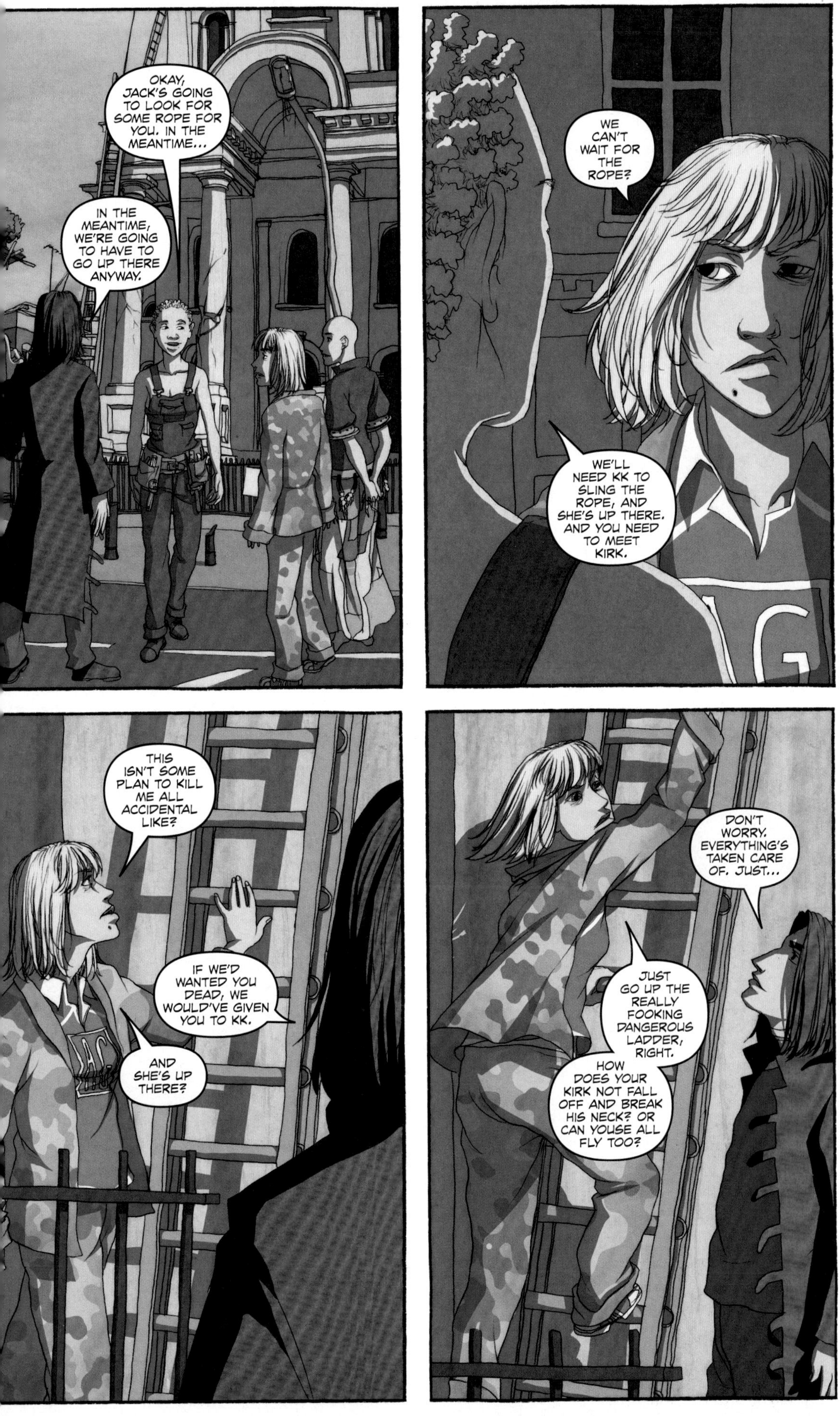
OKAY, JACK'S GOING TO LOOK FOR SOME ROPE FOR YOU. IN THE MEANTIME...
IN THE MEANTIME, WE'RE GOING TO HAVE TO GO UP THERE ANYWAY.
WE CAN'T WAIT FOR THE ROPE?
WE'LL NEED KK TO SLING THE ROPE, AND SHE'S UP THERE. AND YOU NEED TO MEET KIRK.
THIS ISN'T SOME PLAN TO KILL ME ALL ACCIDENTAL LIKE?
IF WE'D WANTED YOU DEAD, WE WOULD'VE GIVEN YOU TO KK.
AND SHE'S UP THERE?
DON'T WORRY. EVERYTHING'S TAKEN CARE OF. JUST...
JUST GO UP THE REALLY FOOKING DANGEROUS LADDER, RIGHT.
HOW DOES YOUR KIRK NOT FALL OFF AND BREAK HIS NECK? OR CAN YOUSE ALL FLY TOO?

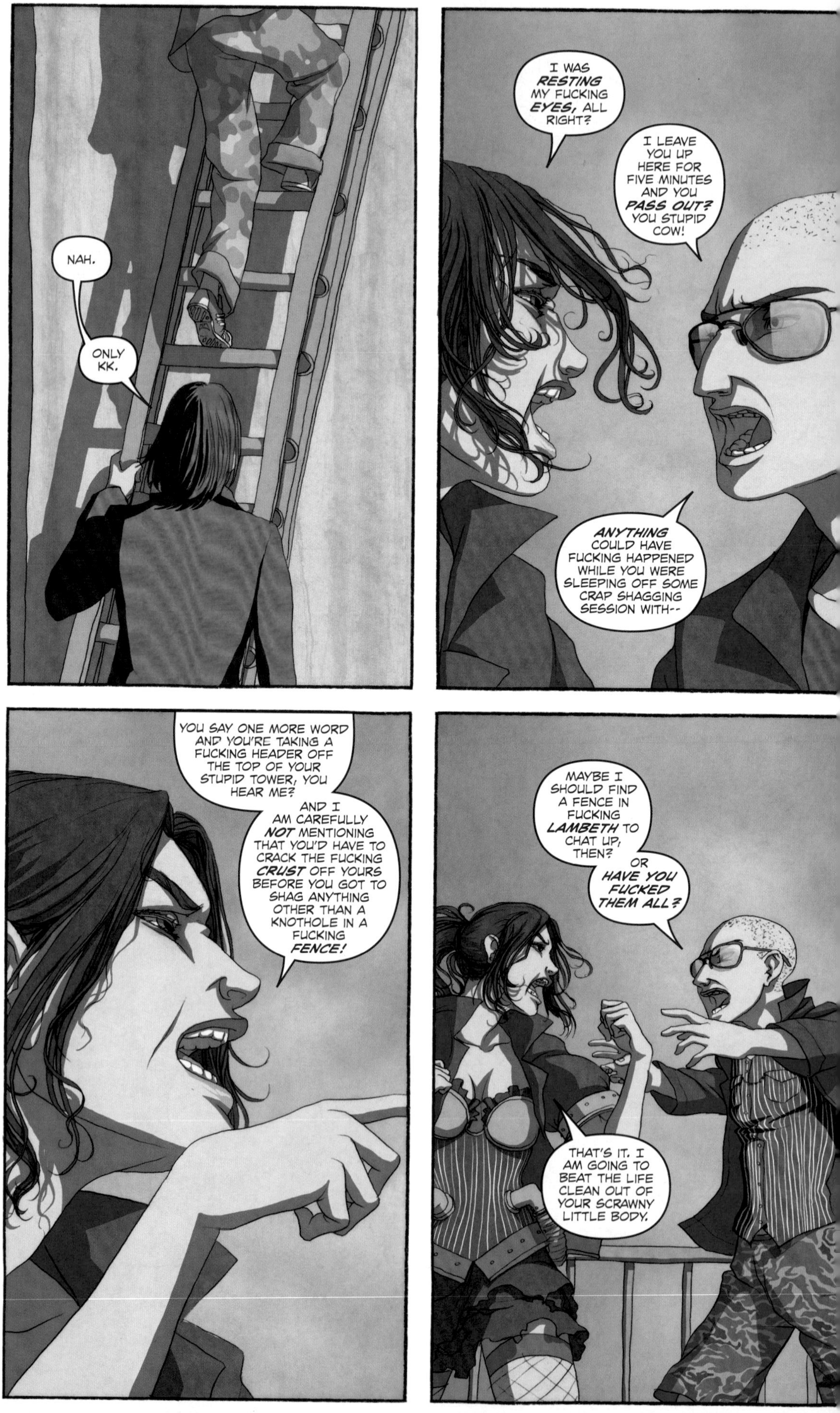
NAH.
ONLY KK.
I WAS RESTING MY FUCKING EYES, ALL RIGHT?
I LEAVE YOU UP HERE FOR FIVE MINUTES AND YOU PASS OUT? YOU STUPID COW!
ANYTHING COULD HAVE FUCKING HAPPENED WHILE YOU WERE SLEEPING OFF SOME CRAP SHAGGING SESSION WITH--
YOU SAY ONE MORE WORD AND YOU'RE TAKING A FUCKING HEADER OFF THE TOP OF YOUR STUPID TOWER, YOU HEAR ME?
AND I AM CAREFULLY NOT MENTIONING THAT YOU'D HAVE TO CRACK THE FUCKING CRUST OFF YOURS BEFORE YOU GOT TO SHAG ANYTHING OTHER THAN A KNOTHOLE IN A FUCKING FENCE!
MAYBE I SHOULD FIND A FENCE IN FUCKING LAMBETH TO CHAT UP, THEN?
OR HAVE YOU FUCKED THEM ALL?
THAT'S IT. I AM GOING TO BEAT THE LIFE CLEAN OUT OF YOUR SCRAWNY LITTLE BODY.

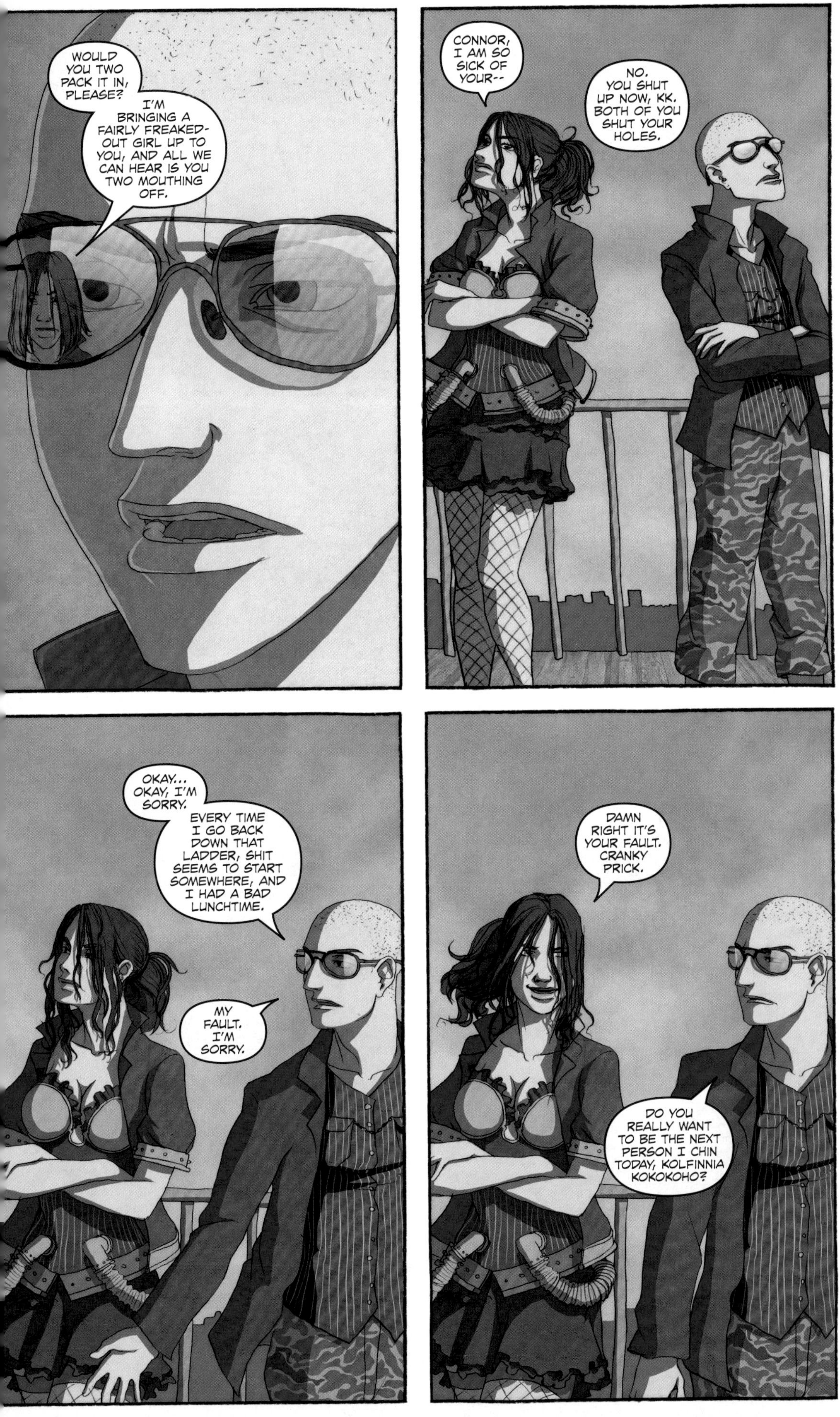
WOULD YOU TWO PACK IT IN, PLEASE?
I'M BRINGING A FAIRLY FREAKED-OUT GIRL UP TO YOU, AND ALL WE CAN HEAR IS YOU TWO MOUTHING OFF.
CONNOR, I AM SO SICK OF YOUR--
NO. YOU SHUT UP NOW, KK. BOTH OF YOU SHUT YOUR HOLES.
OKAY... OKAY, I'M SORRY.
EVERY TIME I GO BACK DOWN THAT LADDER, SHIT SEEMS TO START SOMEWHERE, AND I HAD A BAD LUNCHTIME.
MY FAULT. I'M SORRY.
DAMN RIGHT IT'S YOUR FAULT. CRANKY PRICK.
DO YOU REALLY WANT TO BE THE NEXT PERSON I CHIN TODAY, KOLFINNIA KOKOKOHO?

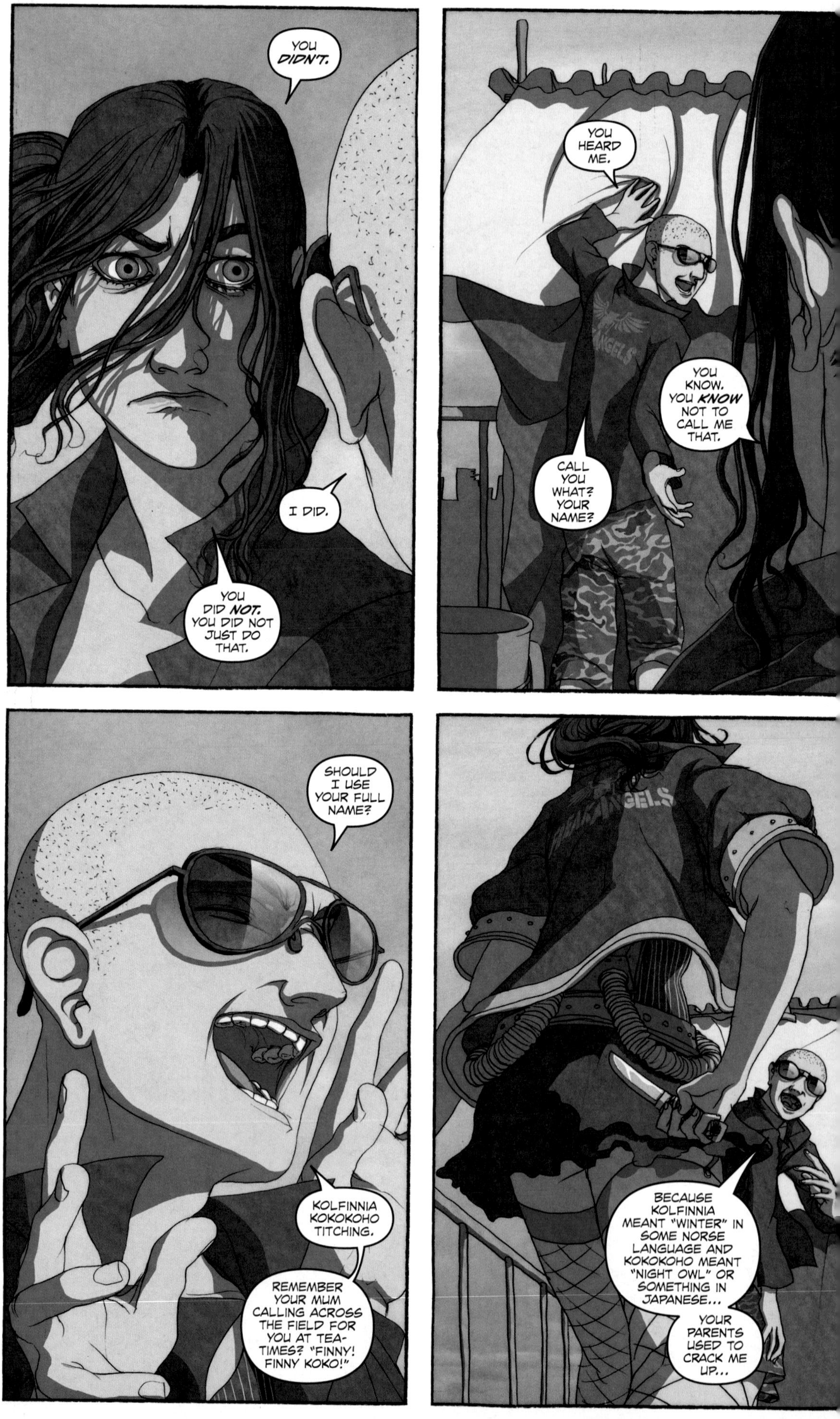
YOU *DIDN'T.*
I DID.
YOU DID *NOT.* YOU DID NOT JUST DO THAT.
YOU HEARD ME.
YOU KNOW. YOU *KNOW* NOT TO CALL ME THAT.
CALL YOU WHAT? YOUR NAME?
SHOULD I USE YOUR FULL NAME?
KOLFINNIA KOKOKOHO TITCHING.
REMEMBER YOUR MUM CALLING ACROSS THE FIELD FOR YOU AT TEA-TIMES? "FINNY! FINNY KOKO!"
BECAUSE KOLFINNIA MEANT "WINTER" IN SOME NORSE LANGUAGE AND KOKOKOHO MEANT "NIGHT OWL" OR SOMETHING IN JAPANESE...
YOUR PARENTS USED TO CRACK ME UP...

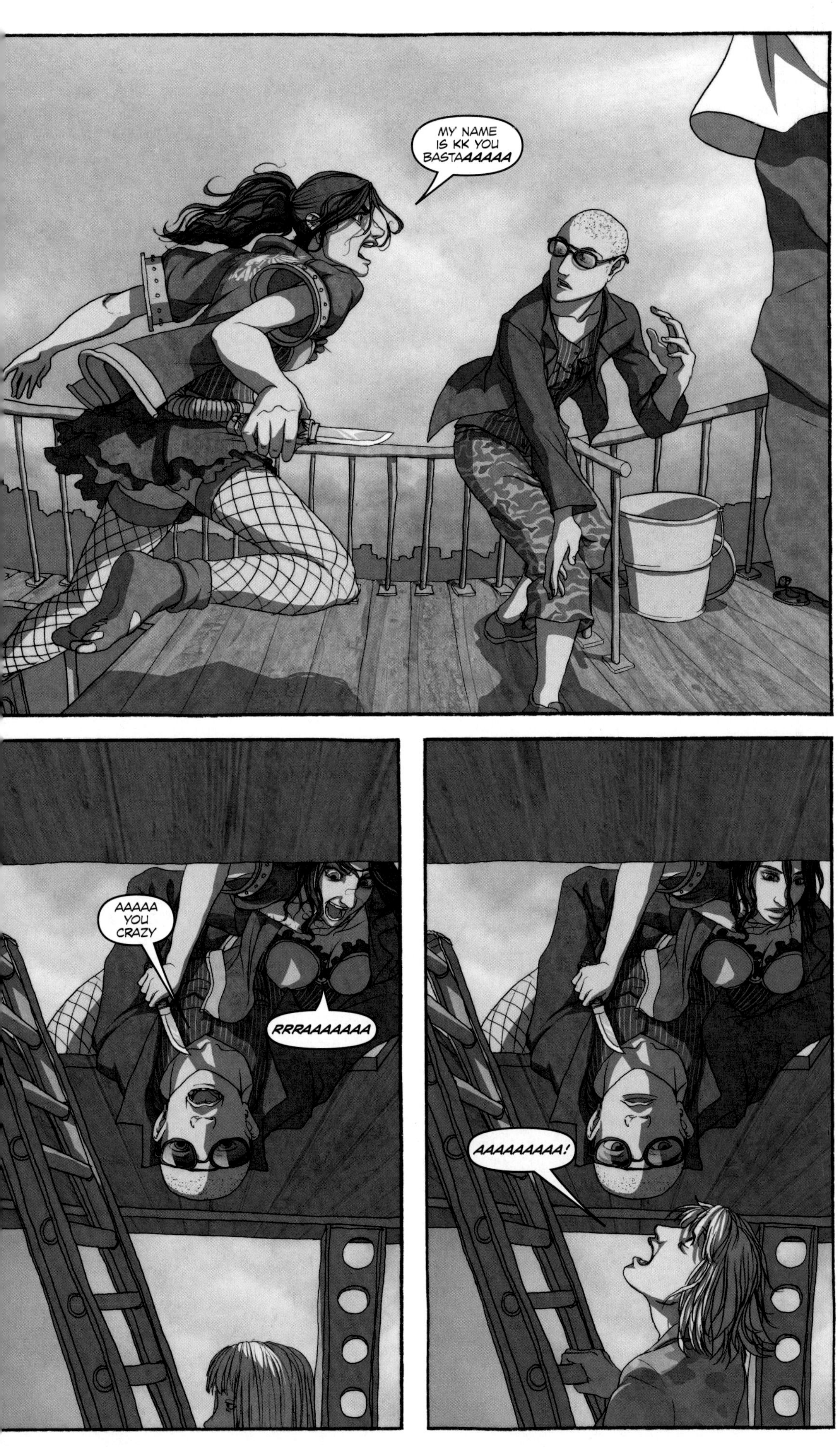
MY NAME IS KK YOU BASTAAAAAA
AAAAA YOU CRAZY
RRRAAAAAAAA
AAAAAAAAA!

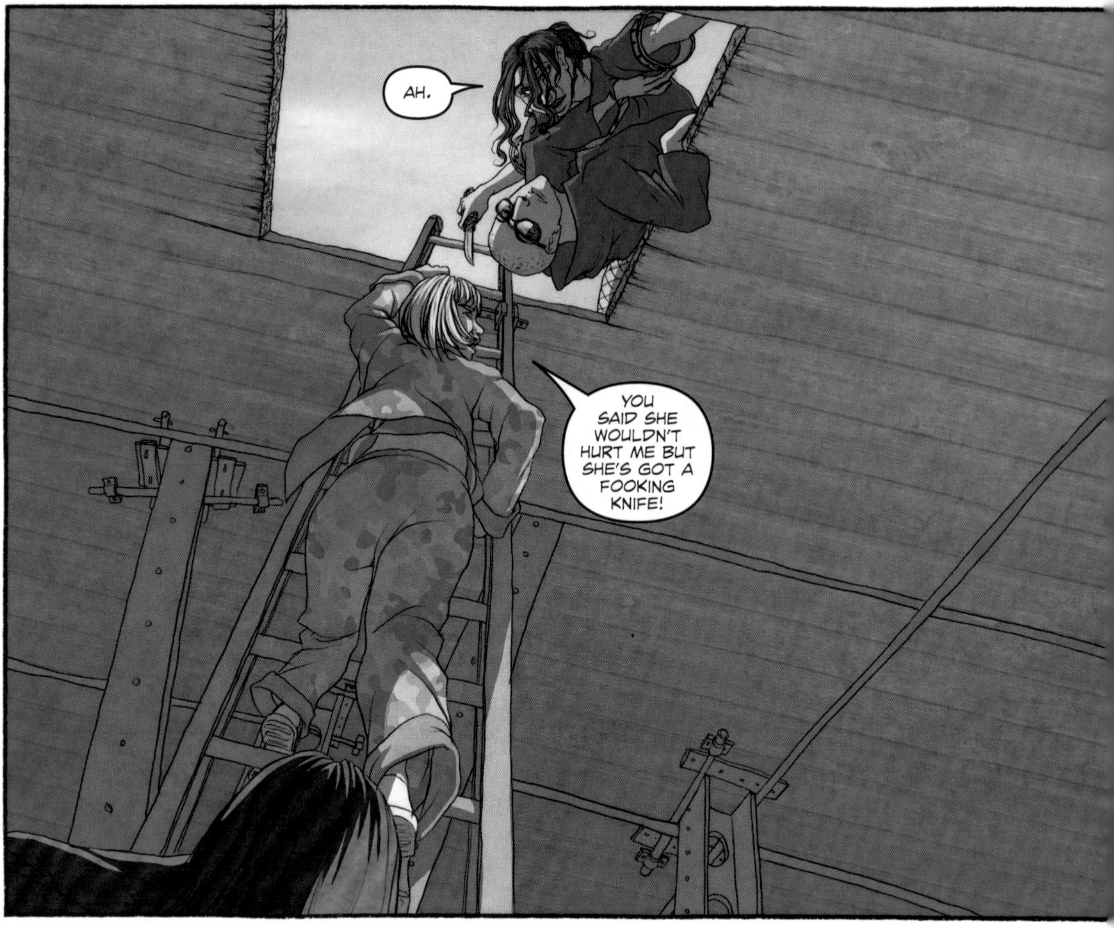
AH.
YOU SAID SHE WOULDN'T HURT ME BUT SHE'S GOT A FOOKING KNIFE!

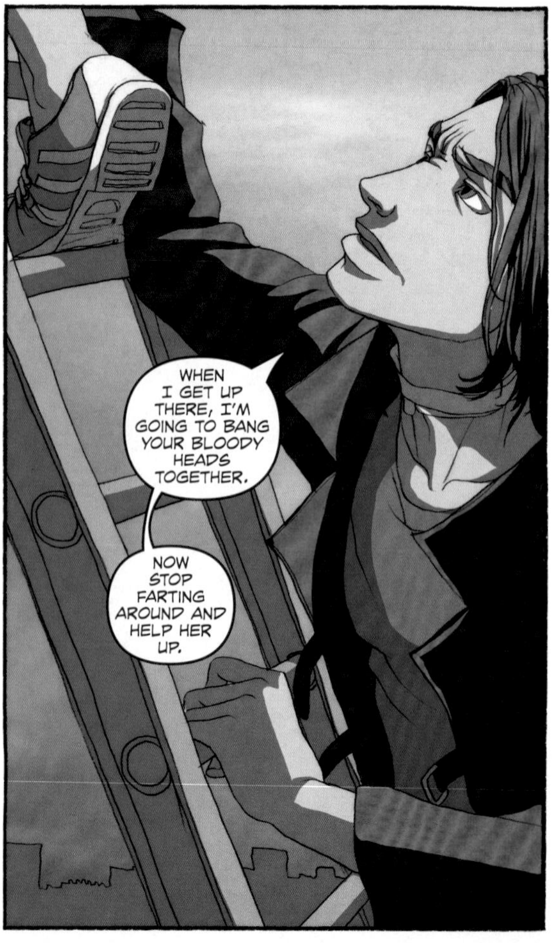
WHEN I GET UP THERE, I'M GOING TO BANG YOUR BLOODY HEADS TOGETHER.
NOW STOP FARTING AROUND AND HELP HER UP.

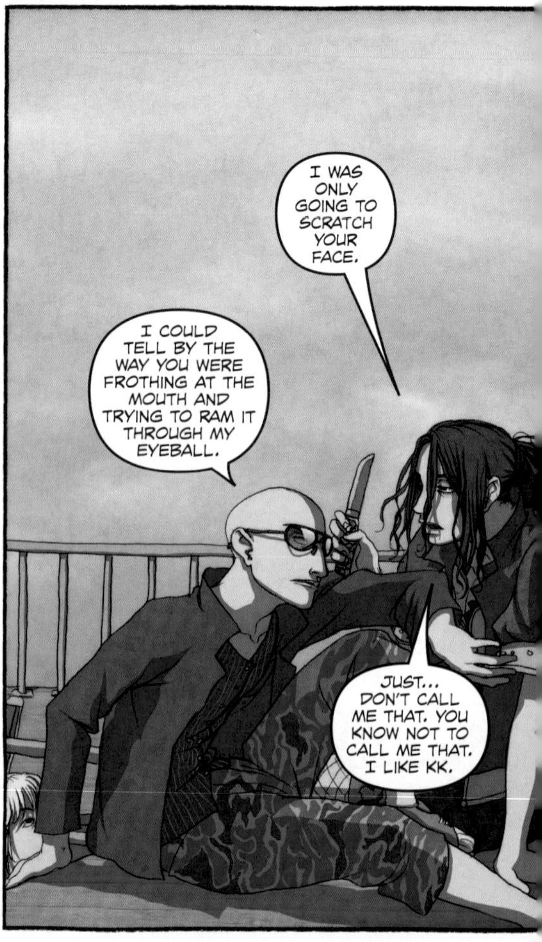
I WAS ONLY GOING TO SCRATCH YOUR FACE.
I COULD TELL BY THE WAY YOU WERE FROTHING AT THE MOUTH AND TRYING TO RAM IT THROUGH MY EYEBALL.
JUST... DON'T CALL ME THAT. YOU KNOW NOT TO CALL ME THAT. I LIKE KK.

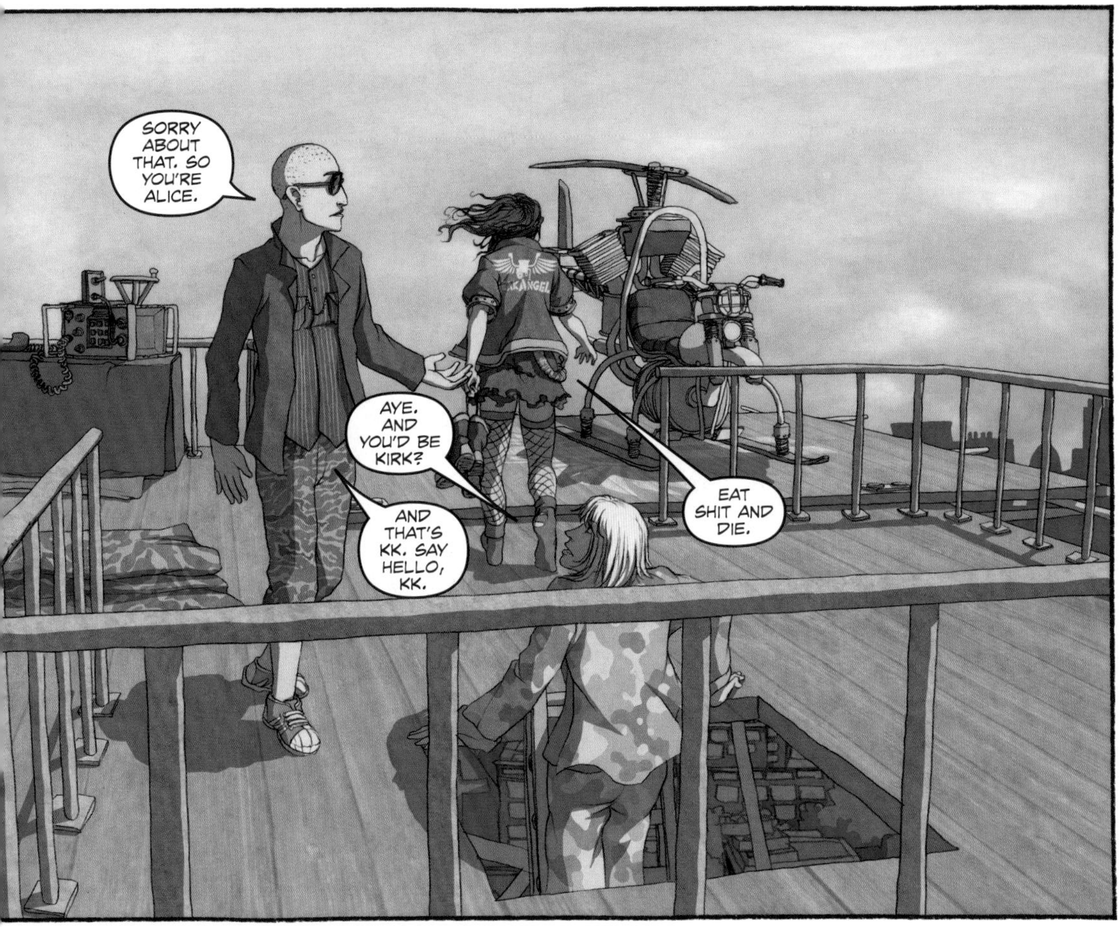
SORRY ABOUT THAT. SO YOU'RE ALICE.
AYE. AND YOU'D BE KIRK?
EAT SHIT AND DIE.
AND THAT'S KK. SAY HELLO, KK.

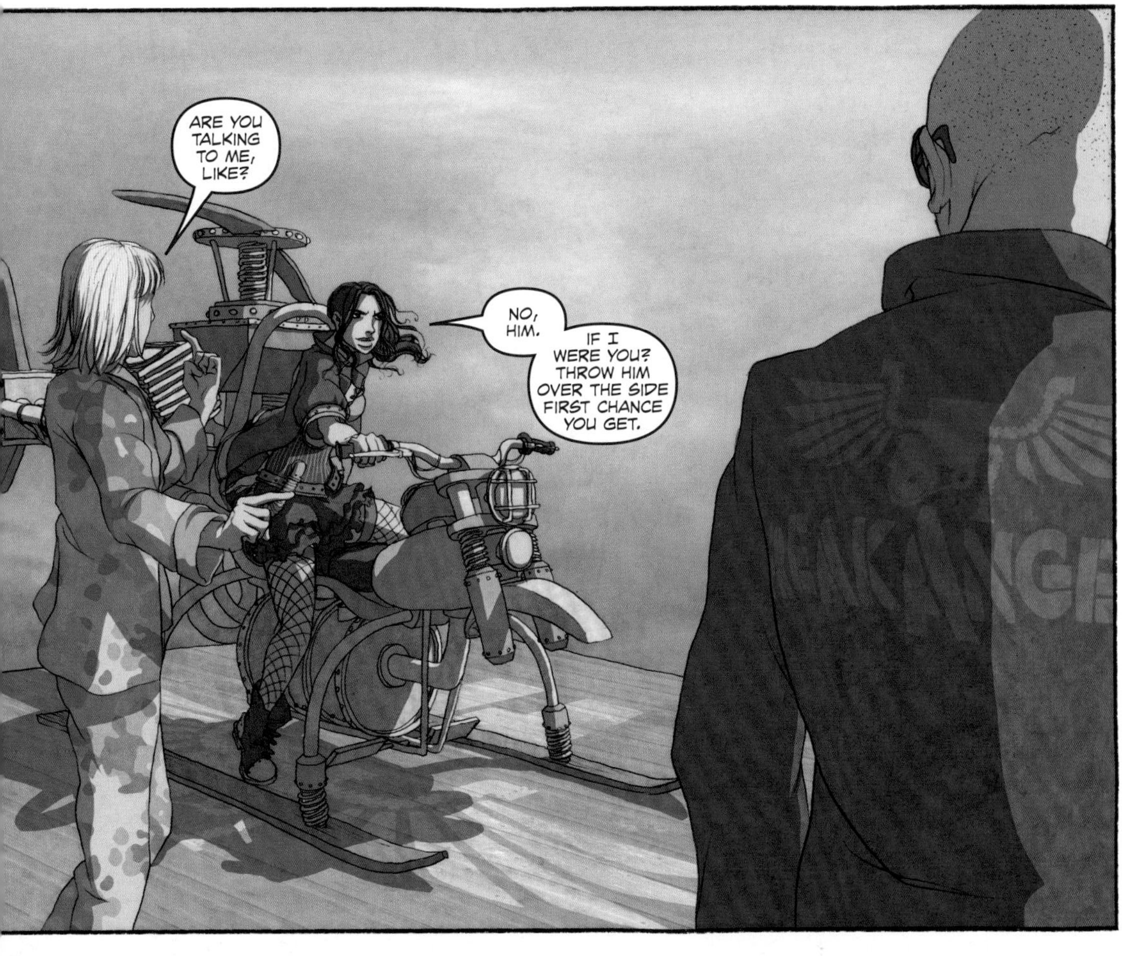
ARE YOU TALKING TO ME, LIKE?
NO, HIM.
IF I WERE YOU? THROW HIM OVER THE SIDE FIRST CHANCE YOU GET.

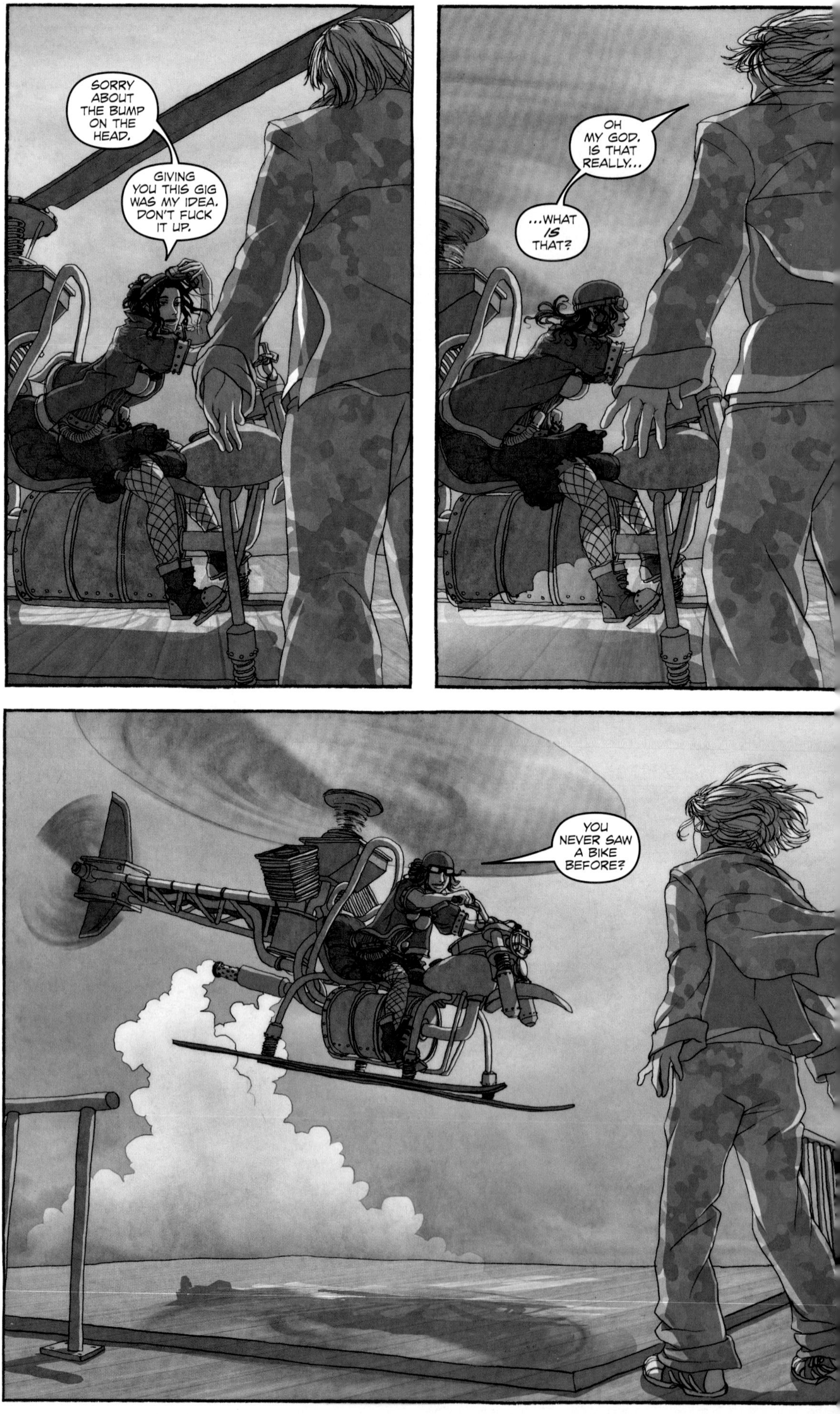
SORRY ABOUT THE BUMP ON THE HEAD.
GIVING YOU THIS GIG WAS MY IDEA. DON'T FUCK IT UP.
OH MY GOD. IS THAT REALLY...
...WHAT IS THAT?
YOU NEVER SAW A BIKE BEFORE?

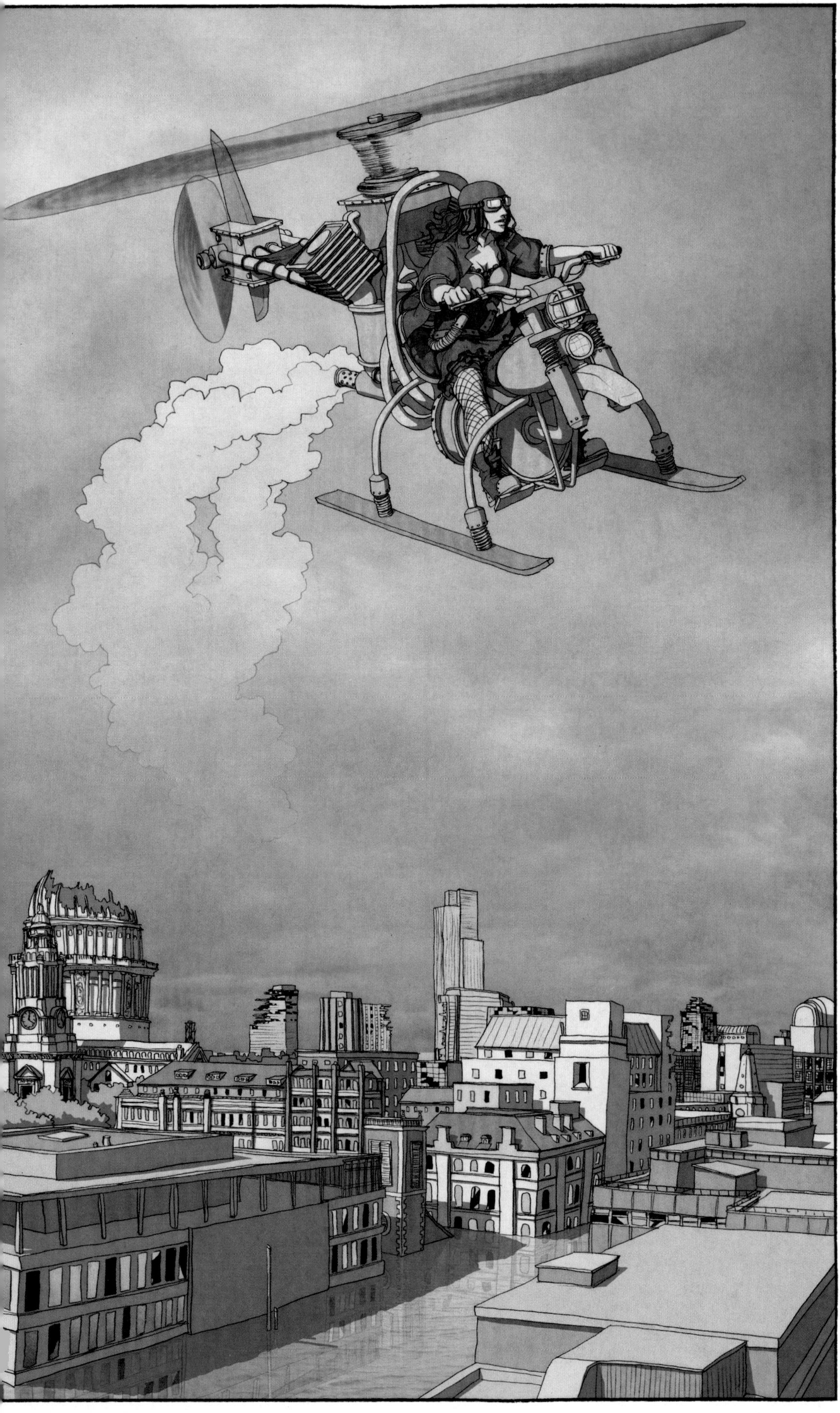

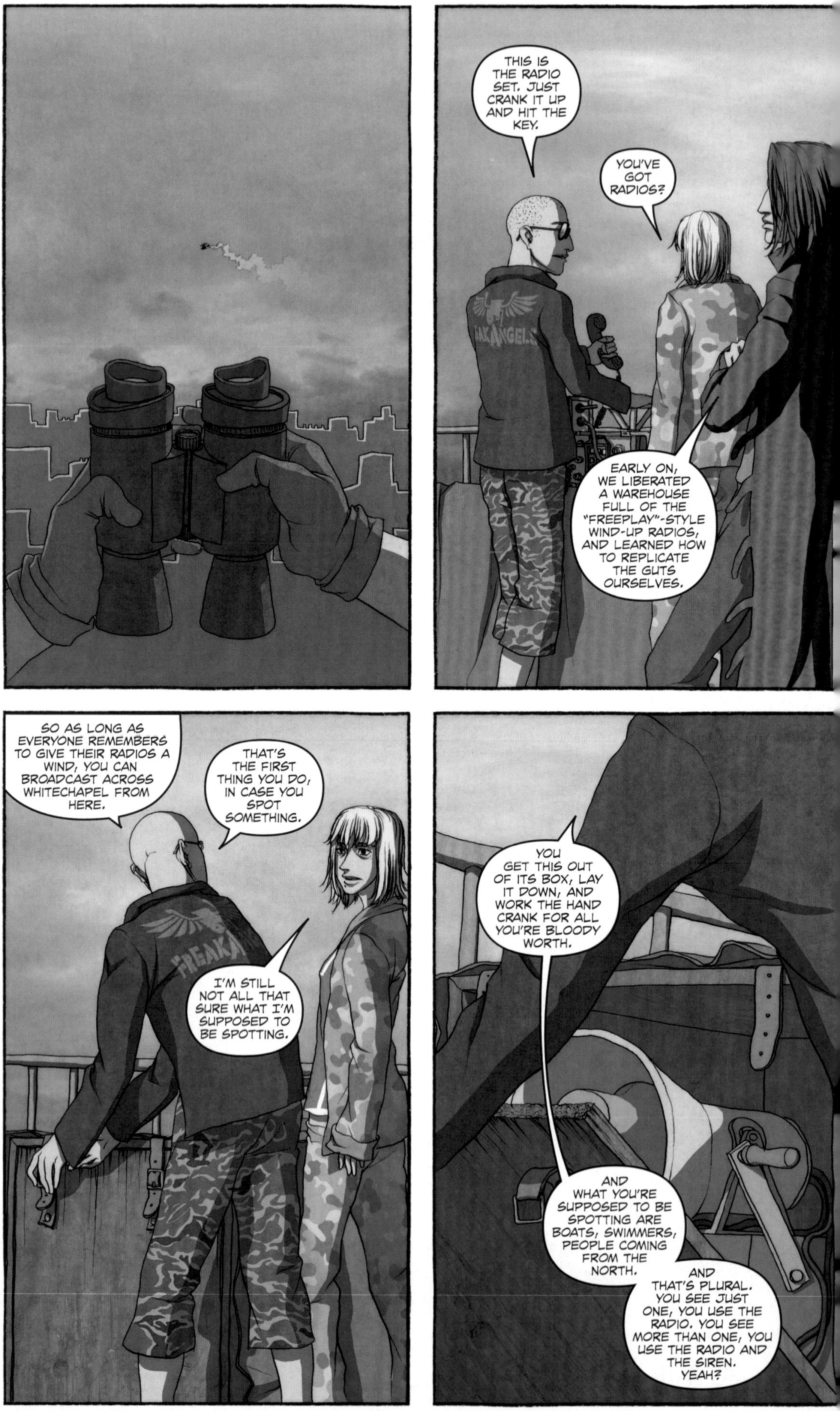
THIS IS THE RADIO SET. JUST CRANK IT UP AND HIT THE KEY.
YOU'VE GOT RADIOS?
EARLY ON, WE LIBERATED A WAREHOUSE FULL OF THE "FREEPLAY"-STYLE WIND-UP RADIOS, AND LEARNED HOW TO REPLICATE THE GUTS OURSELVES.
SO AS LONG AS EVERYONE REMEMBERS TO GIVE THEIR RADIOS A WIND, YOU CAN BROADCAST ACROSS WHITECHAPEL FROM HERE.
THAT'S THE FIRST THING YOU DO, IN CASE YOU SPOT SOMETHING.
I'M STILL NOT ALL THAT SURE WHAT I'M SUPPOSED TO BE SPOTTING.
YOU GET THIS OUT OF ITS BOX, LAY IT DOWN, AND WORK THE HAND CRANK FOR ALL YOU'RE BLOODY WORTH.
AND WHAT YOU'RE SUPPOSED TO BE SPOTTING ARE BOATS, SWIMMERS, PEOPLE COMING FROM THE NORTH.
AND THAT'S PLURAL. YOU SEE JUST ONE, YOU USE THE RADIO. YOU SEE MORE THAN ONE, YOU USE THE RADIO AND THE SIREN. YEAH?

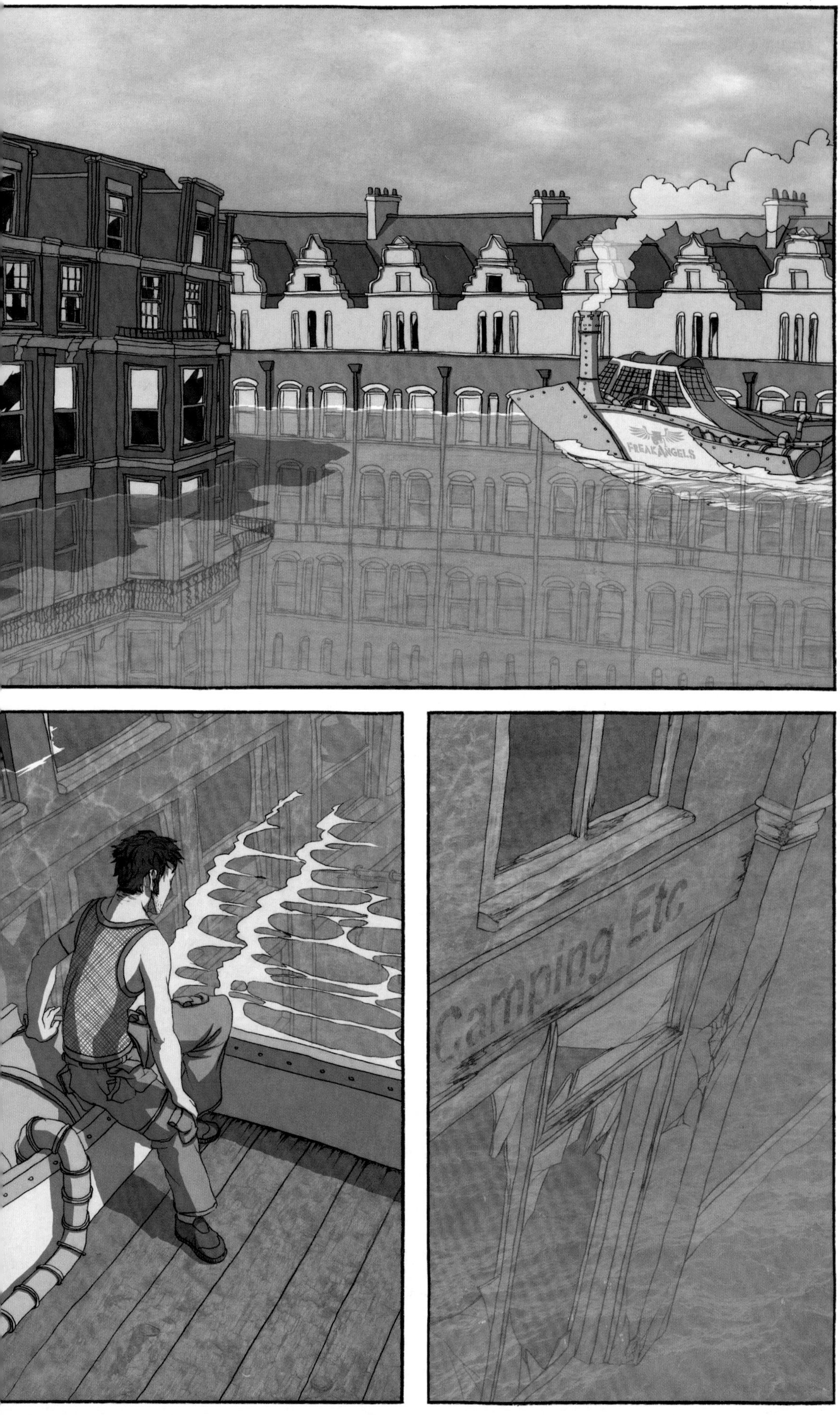
FREAKANGELS
Camping Etc

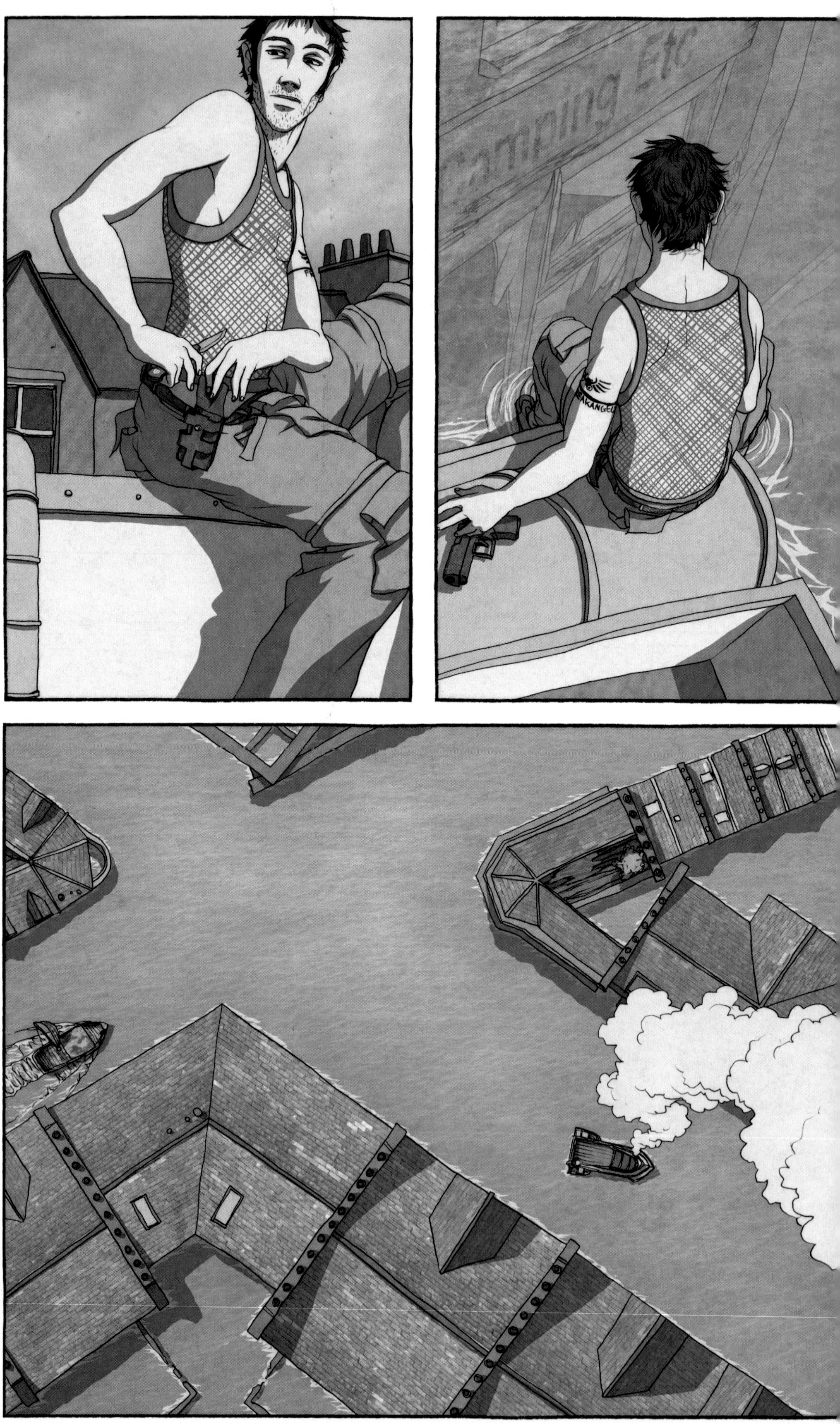
Etc

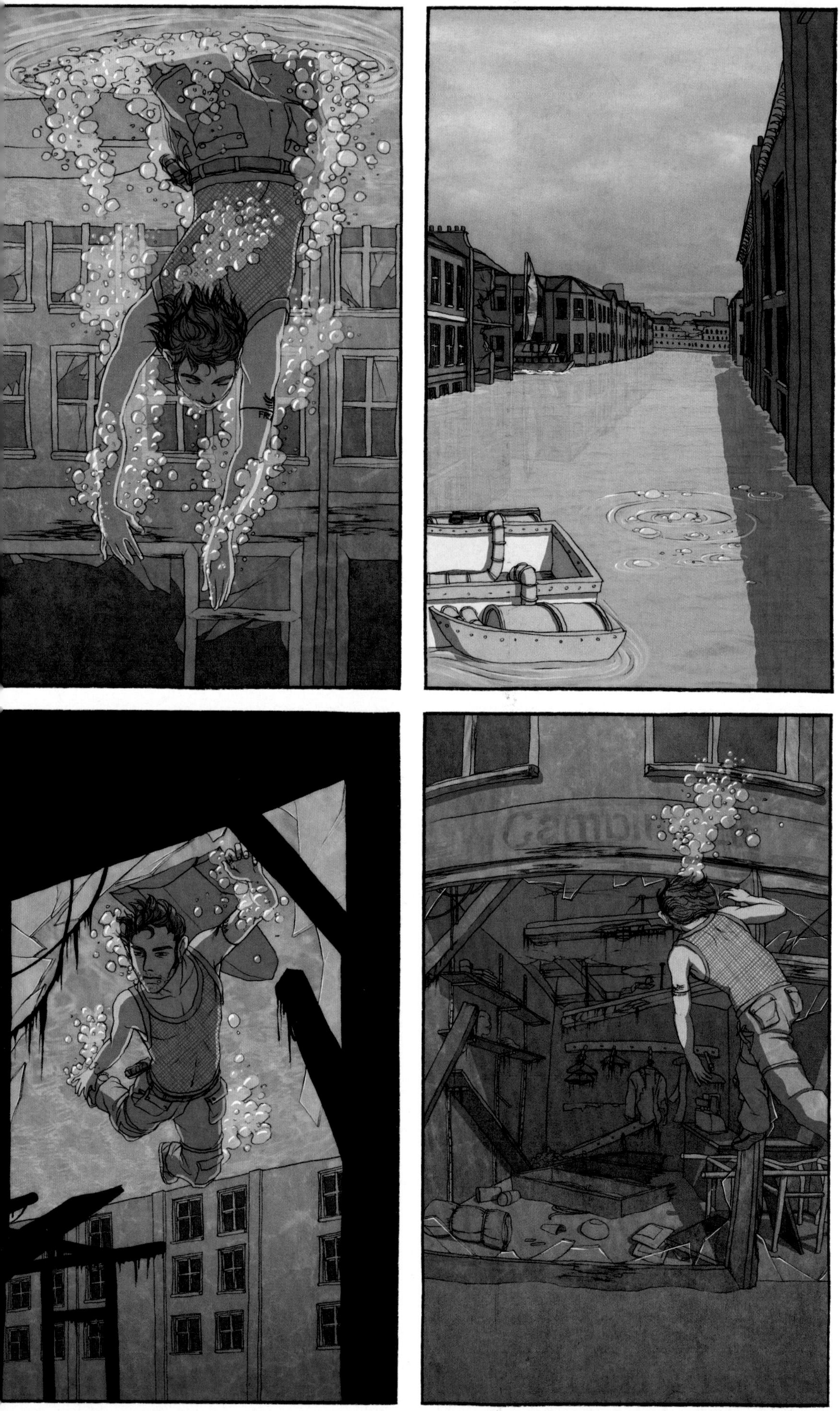

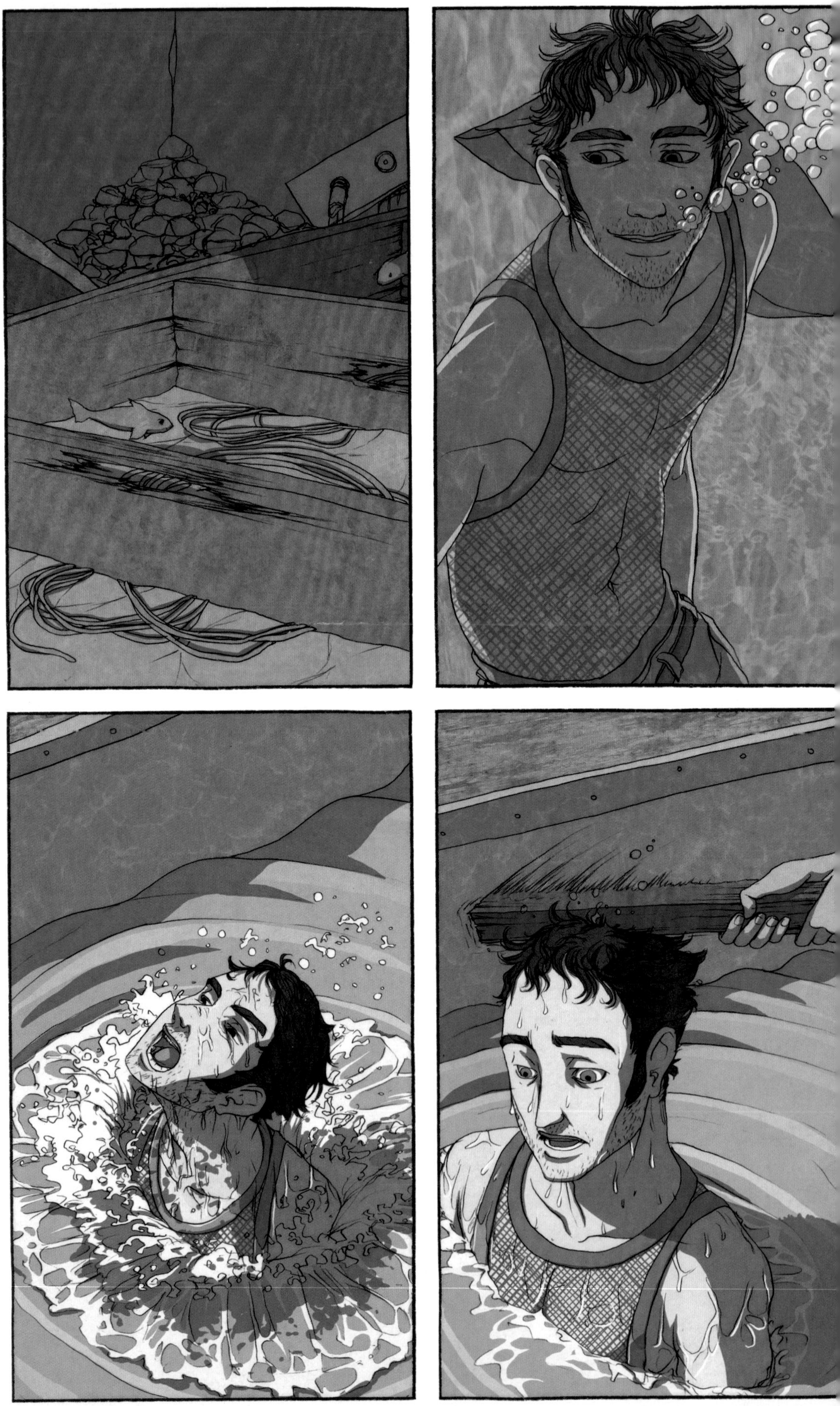

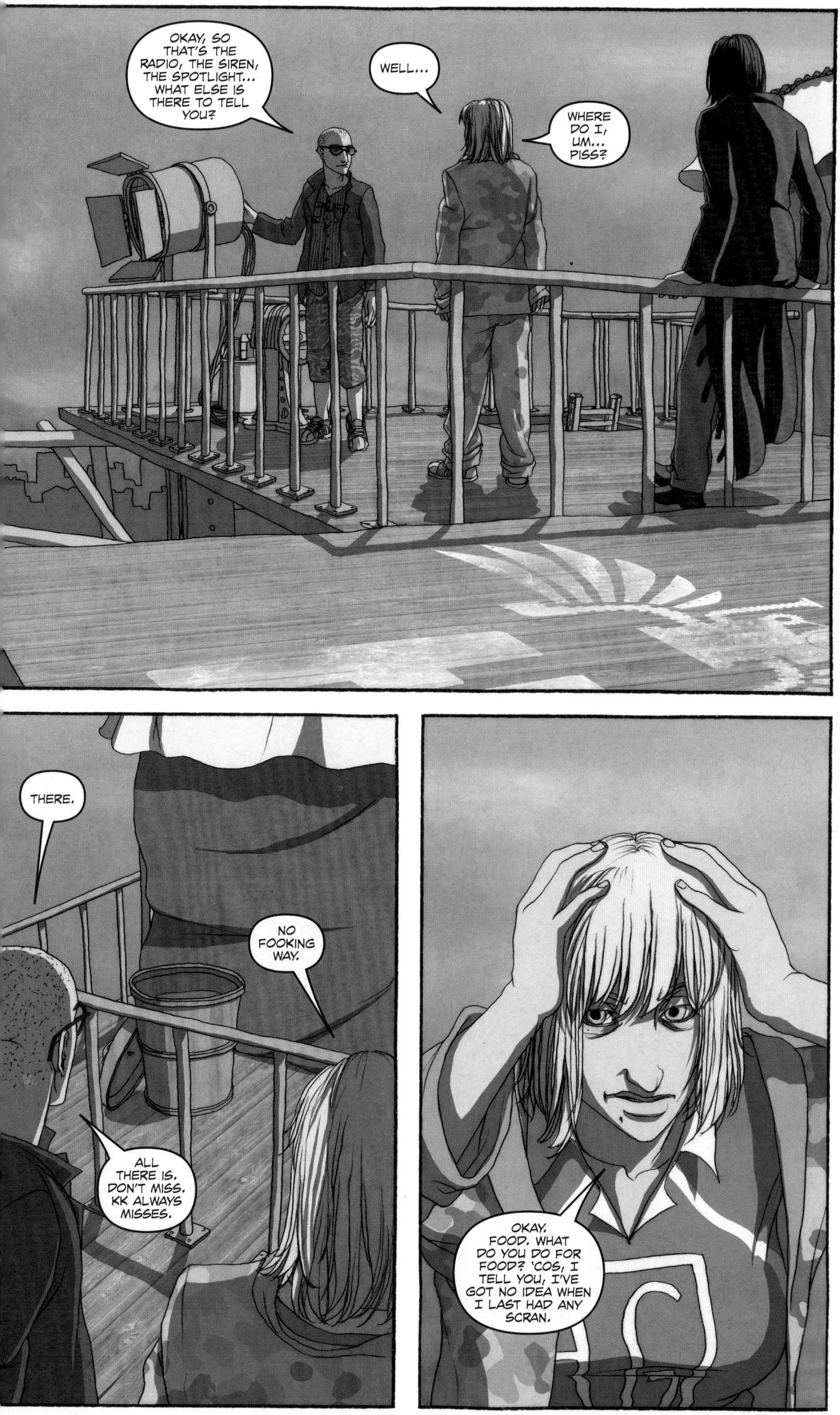
OKAY, SO THAT'S THE RADIO, THE SIREN, THE SPOTLIGHT... WHAT ELSE IS THERE TO TELL YOU?
WELL...
WHERE DO I, UM... PISS?
THERE.
NO FOOKING WAY.
ALL THERE IS. DON'T MISS. KK ALWAYS MISSES.
OKAY. FOOD. WHAT DO YOU DO FOR FOOD? 'COS, I TELL YOU, I'VE GOT NO IDEA WHEN I LAST HAD ANY SCRAN.

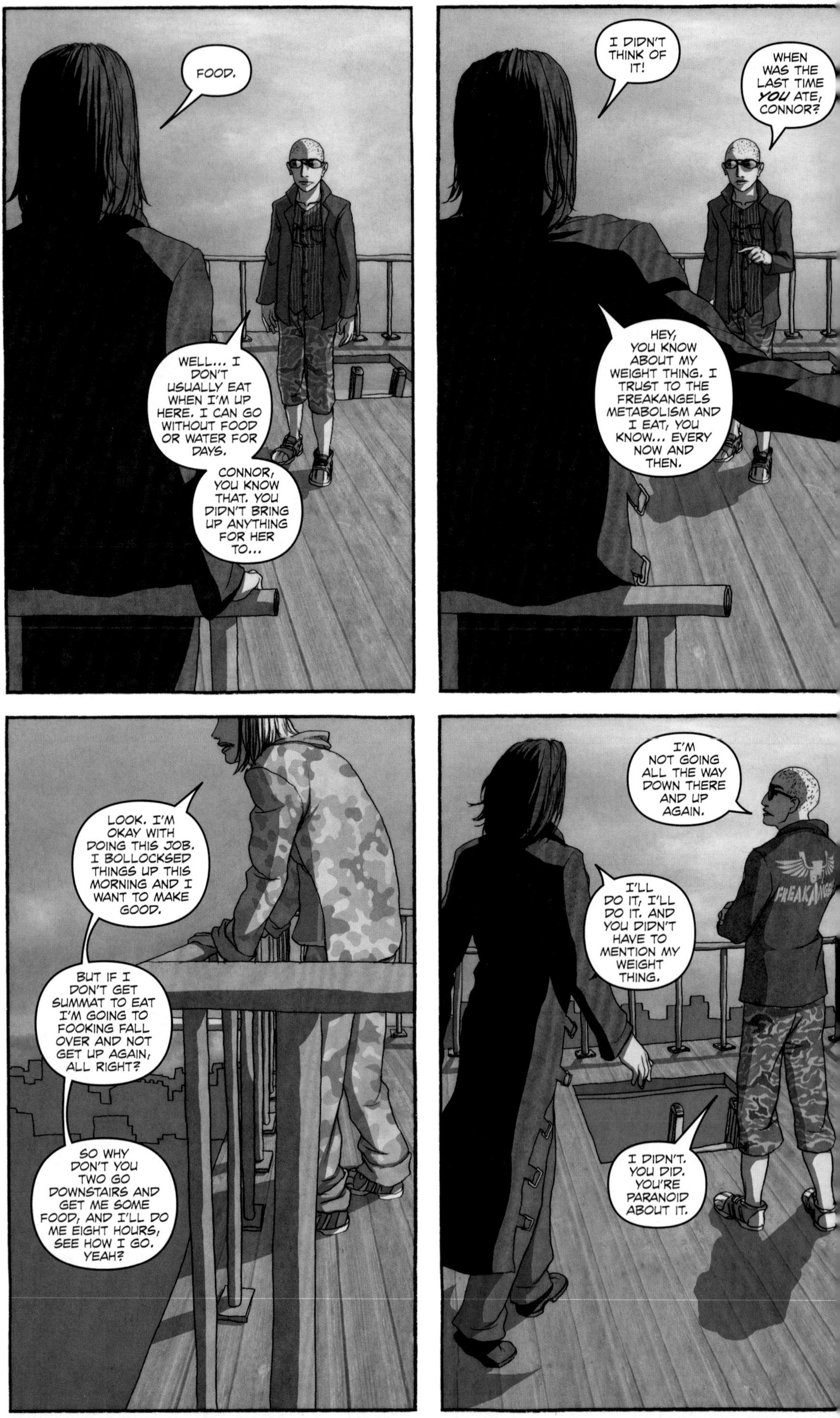
FOOD.
WELL... I DON'T USUALLY EAT WHEN I'M UP HERE. I CAN GO WITHOUT FOOD OR WATER FOR DAYS.
CONNOR, YOU KNOW THAT. YOU DIDN'T BRING UP ANYTHING FOR HER TO...
I DIDN'T THINK OF IT!
WHEN WAS THE LAST TIME YOU ATE, CONNOR?
HEY, YOU KNOW ABOUT MY WEIGHT THING. I TRUST TO THE FREAKANGELS METABOLISM AND I EAT, YOU KNOW... EVERY NOW AND THEN.
LOOK. I'M OKAY WITH DOING THIS JOB. I BOLLOCKSED THINGS UP THIS MORNING AND I WANT TO MAKE GOOD.
BUT IF I DON'T GET SUMMAT TO EAT I'M GOING TO FOOKING FALL OVER AND NOT GET UP AGAIN, ALL RIGHT?
SO WHY DON'T YOU TWO GO DOWNSTAIRS AND GET ME SOME FOOD, AND I'LL DO ME EIGHT HOURS, SEE HOW I GO. YEAH?
I'M NOT GOING ALL THE WAY DOWN THERE AND UP AGAIN.
I'LL DO IT, I'LL DO IT. AND YOU DIDN'T HAVE TO MENTION MY WEIGHT THING.
I DIDN'T. YOU DID. YOU'RE PARANOID ABOUT IT.

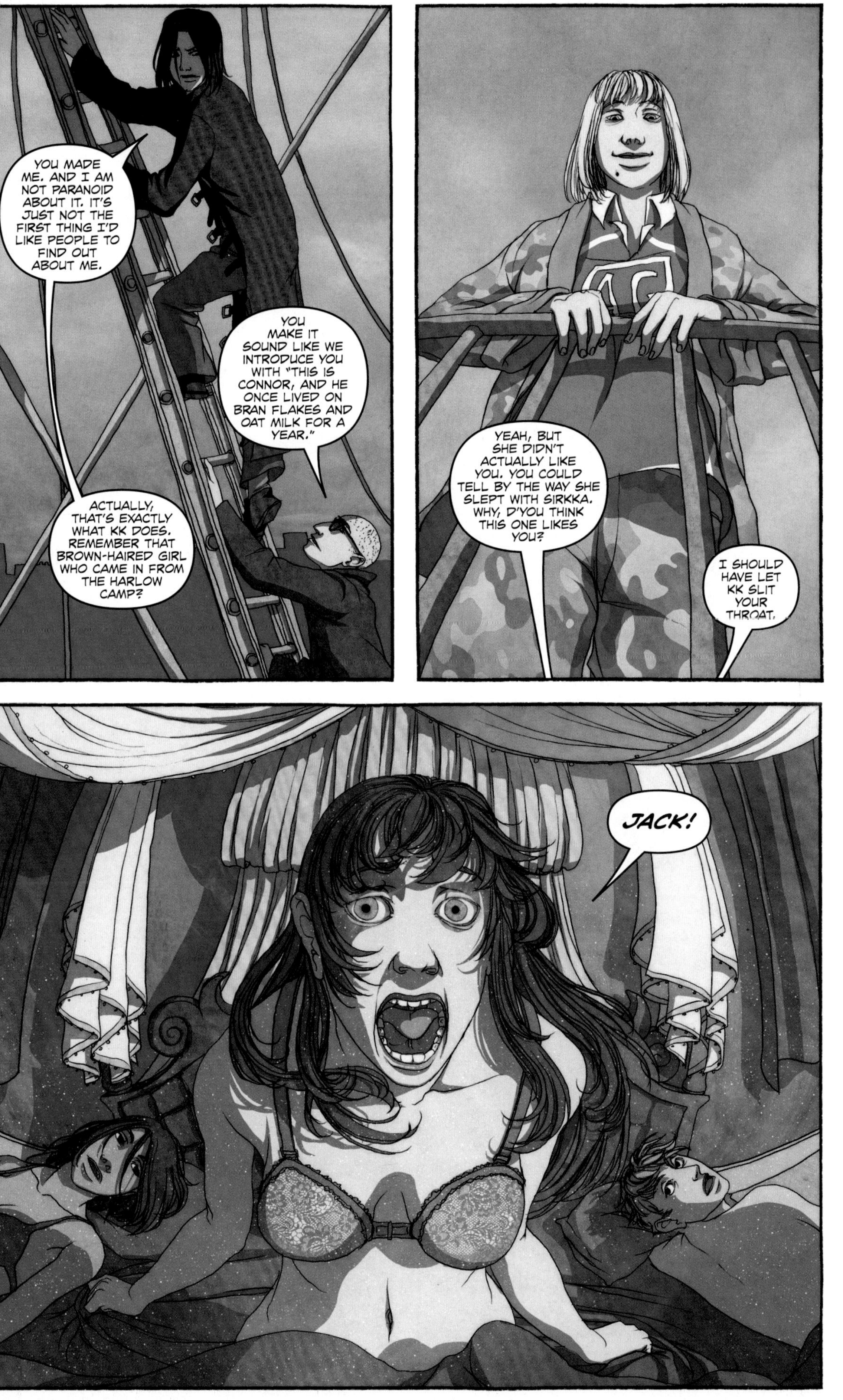
YOU MADE ME. AND I AM NOT PARANOID ABOUT IT. IT'S JUST NOT THE FIRST THING I'D LIKE PEOPLE TO FIND OUT ABOUT ME.
YOU MAKE IT SOUND LIKE WE INTRODUCE YOU WITH "THIS IS CONNOR, AND HE ONCE LIVED ON BRAN FLAKES AND OAT MILK FOR A YEAR."
ACTUALLY, THAT'S EXACTLY WHAT KK DOES. REMEMBER THAT BROWN-HAIRED GIRL WHO CAME IN FROM THE HARLOW CAMP?
YEAH, BUT SHE DIDN'T ACTUALLY LIKE YOU. YOU COULD TELL BY THE WAY SHE SLEPT WITH SIRKKA. WHY, D'YOU THINK THIS ONE LIKES YOU?
I SHOULD HAVE LET KK SLIT YOUR THROAT.
JACK!

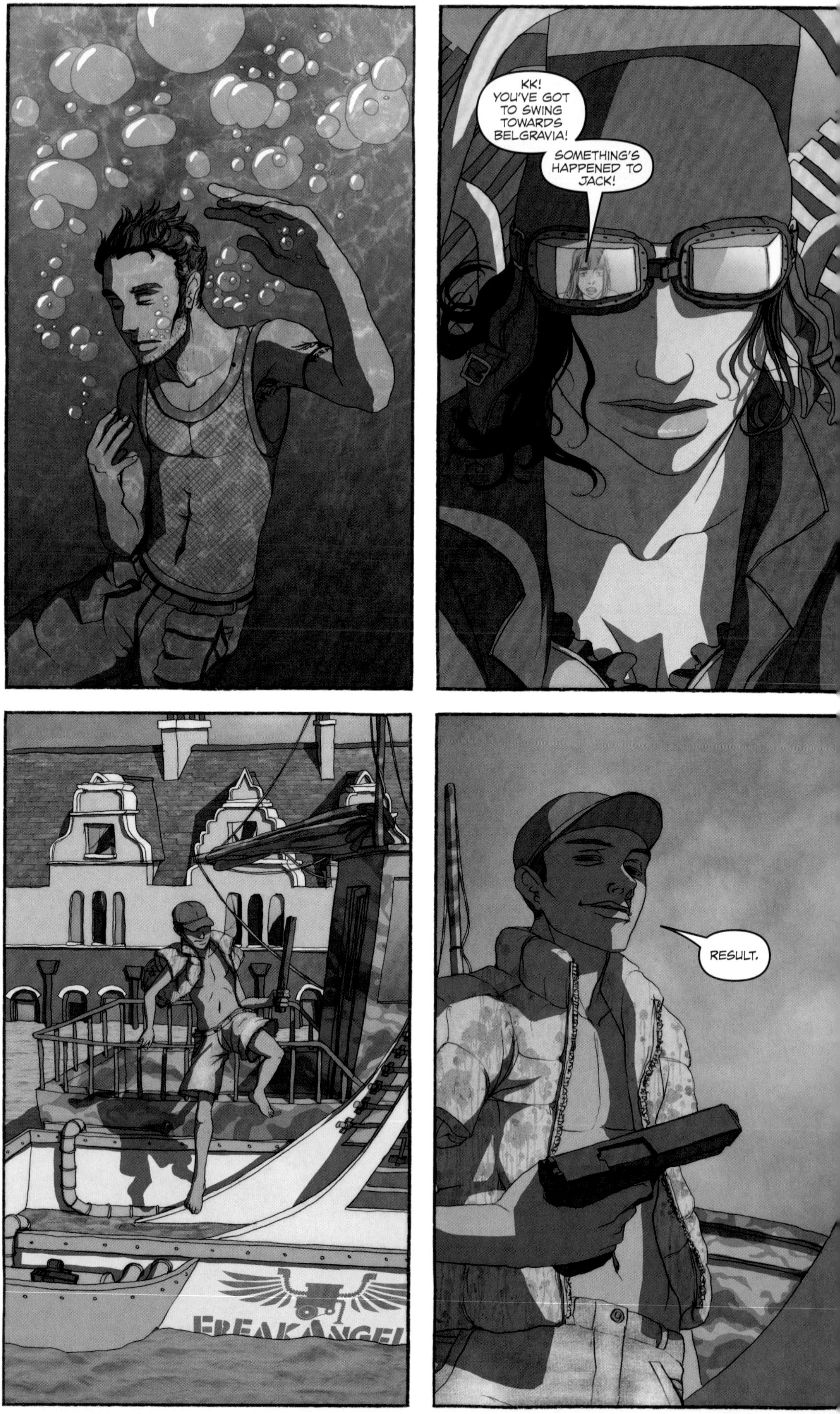
KK! YOU'VE GOT TO SWING TOWARDS BELGRAVIA!
SOMETHING'S HAPPENED TO JACK!
FREAKANGEL
RESULT.

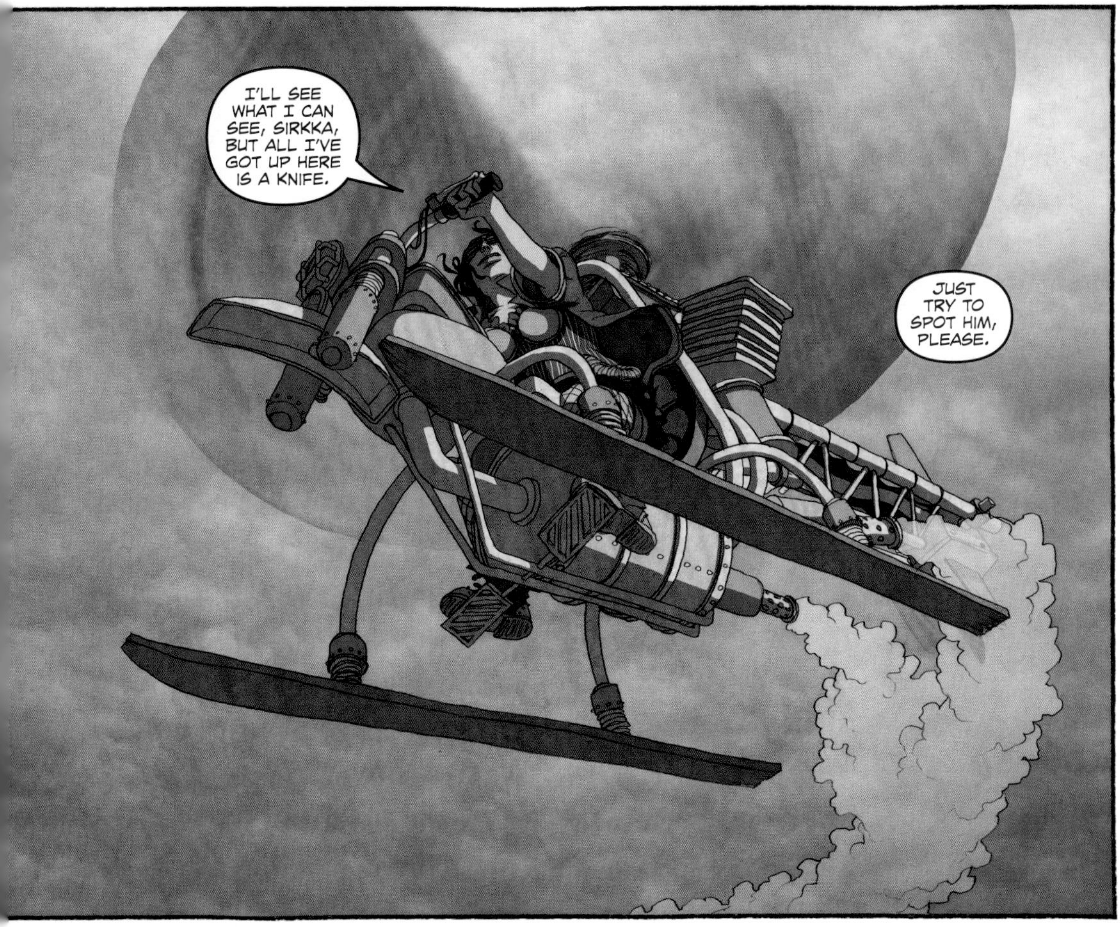
I'LL SEE WHAT I CAN SEE, SIRKKA, BUT ALL I'VE GOT UP HERE IS A KNIFE.
JUST TRY TO SPOT HIM, PLEASE.
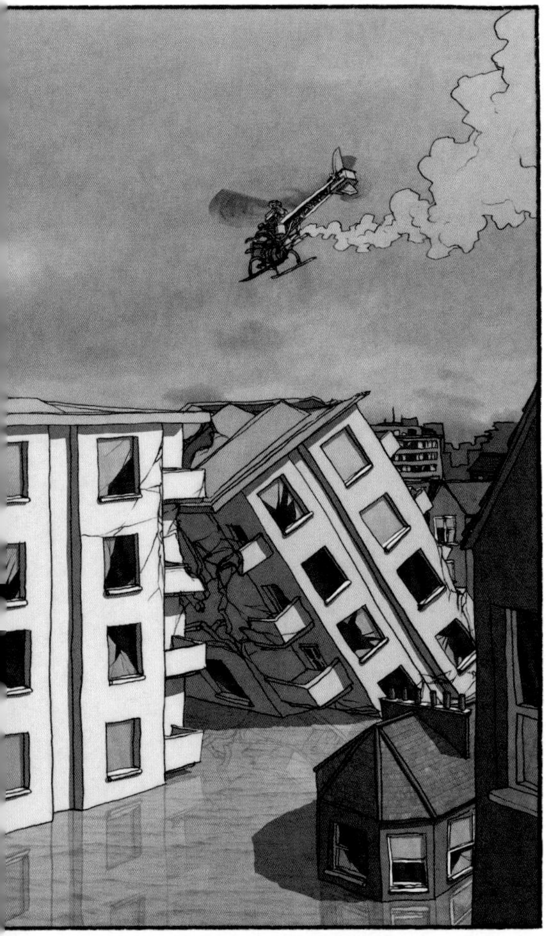
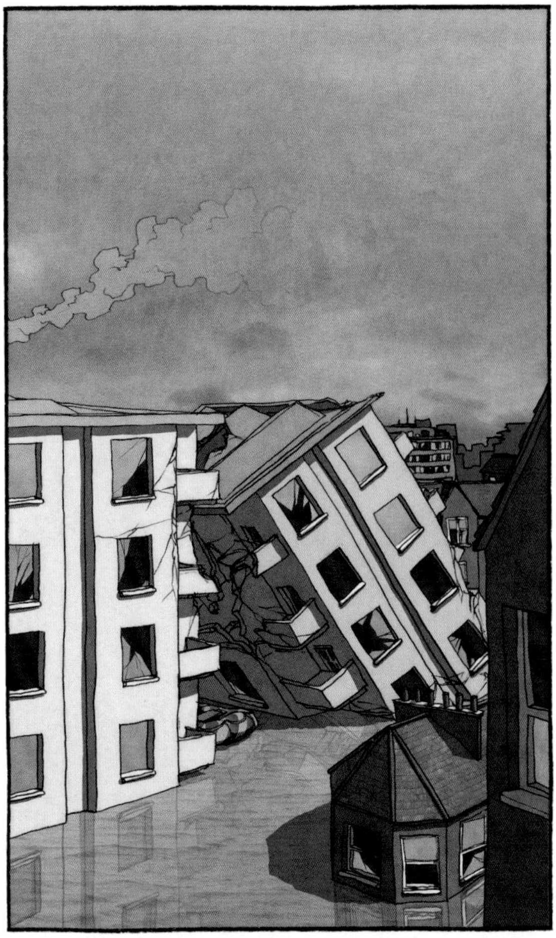

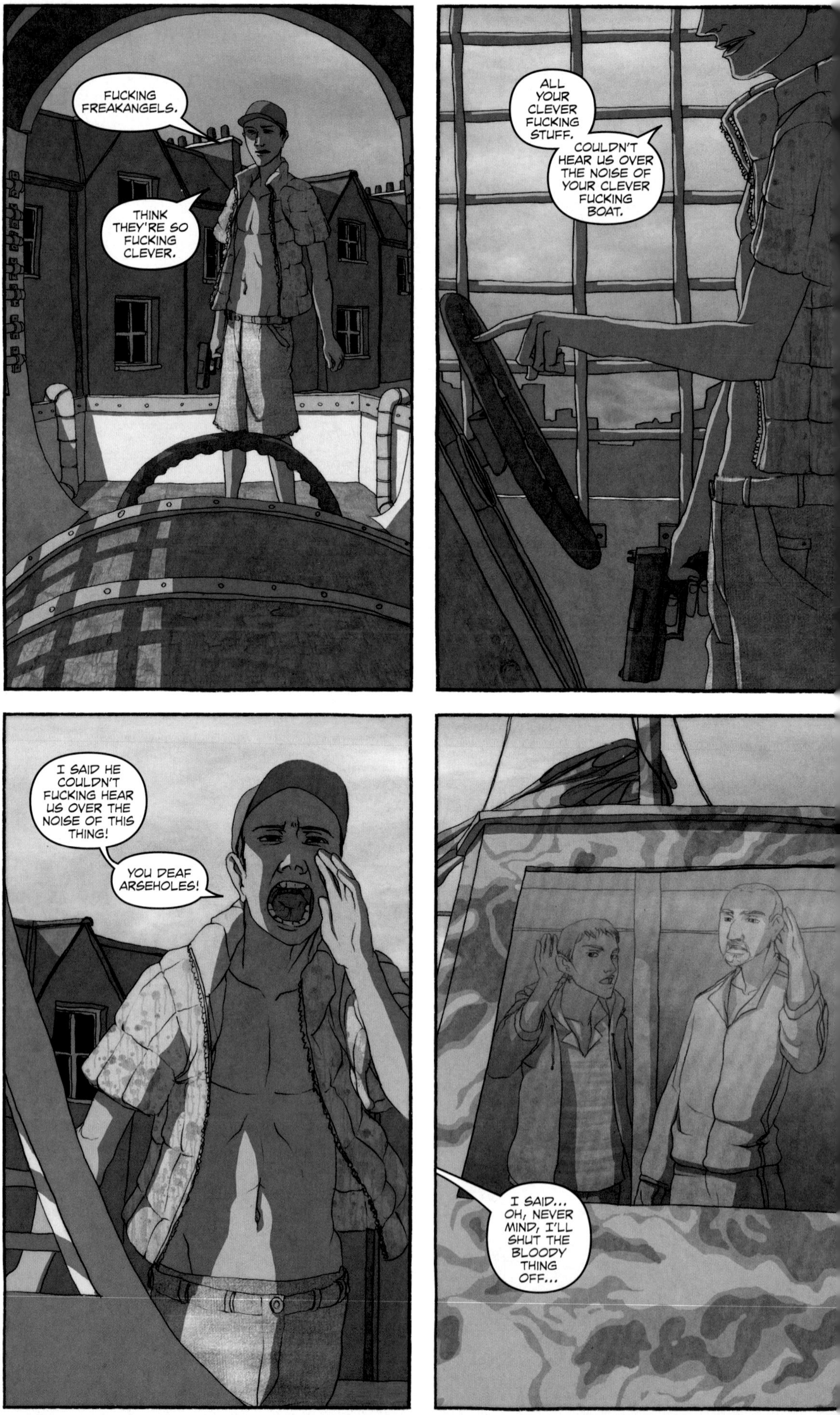
FUCKING FREAKANGELS.
THINK THEY'RE SO FUCKING CLEVER.
ALL YOUR CLEVER FUCKING STUFF.
COULDN'T HEAR US OVER THE NOISE OF YOUR CLEVER FUCKING BOAT.
I SAID HE COULDN'T FUCKING HEAR US OVER THE NOISE OF THIS THING!
YOU DEAF ARSEHOLES!
I SAID... OH, NEVER MIND, I'LL SHUT THE BLOODY THING OFF...

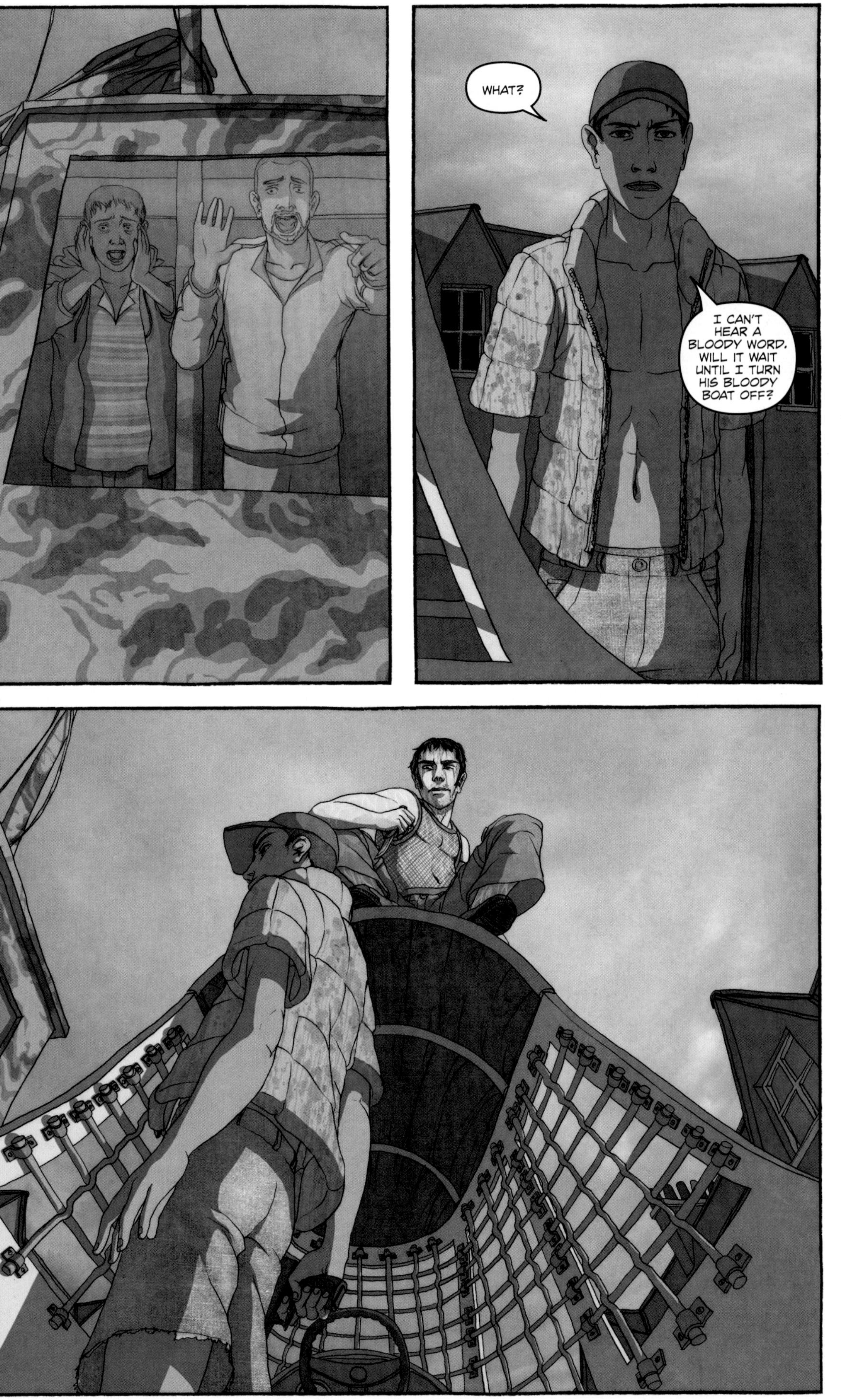
WHAT?
I CAN'T HEAR A BLOODY WORD. WILL IT WAIT UNTIL I TURN HIS BLOODY BOAT OFF?

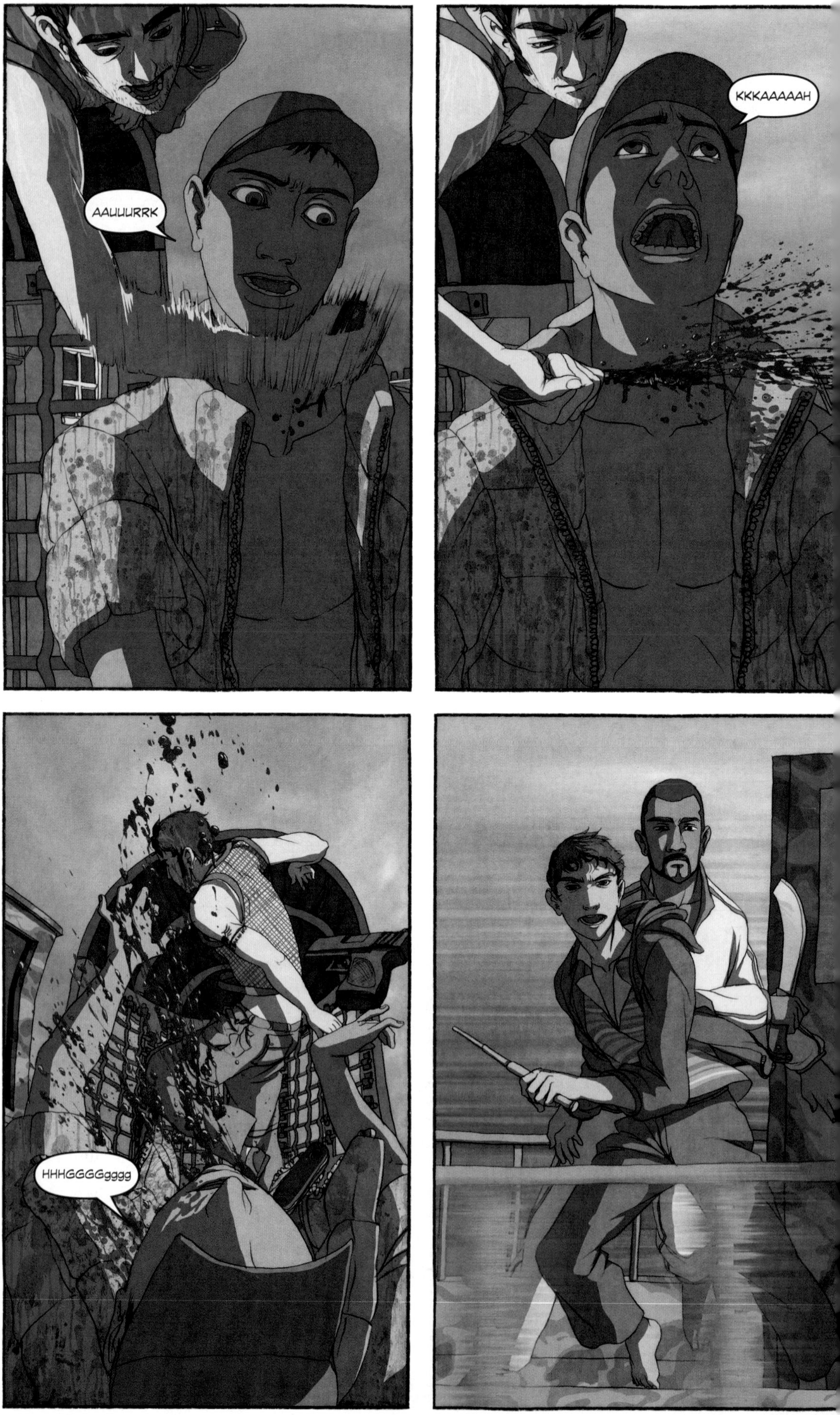
AAUUURRK
KKKAAAAAH
HHHGGGGgggg

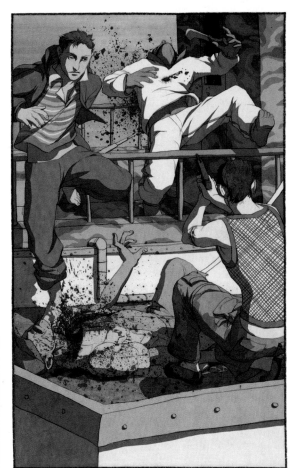

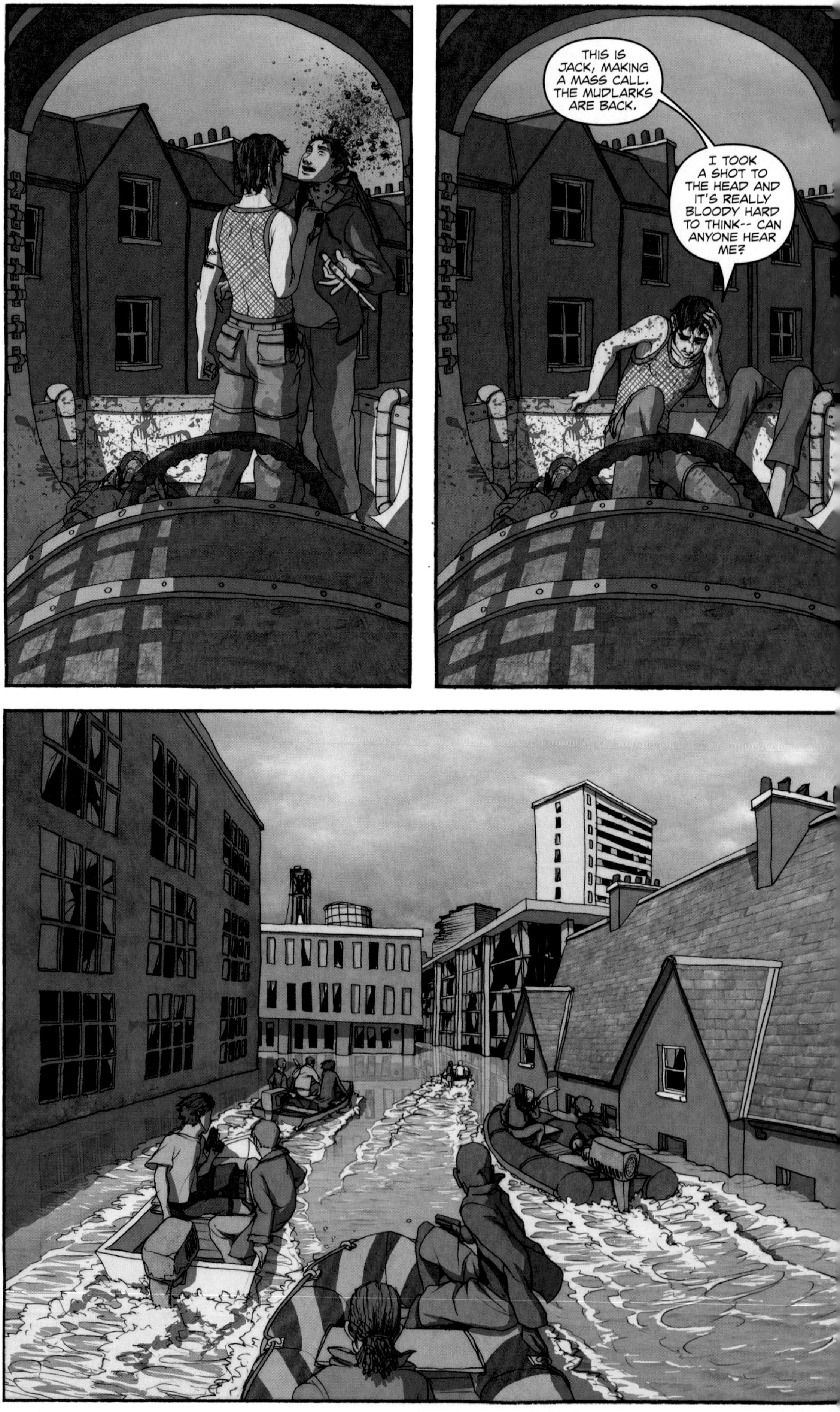
THIS IS JACK, MAKING A MASS CALL. THE MUDLARKS ARE BACK.
I TOOK A SHOT TO THE HEAD AND IT'S REALLY BLOODY HARD TO THINK-- CAN ANYONE HEAR ME?

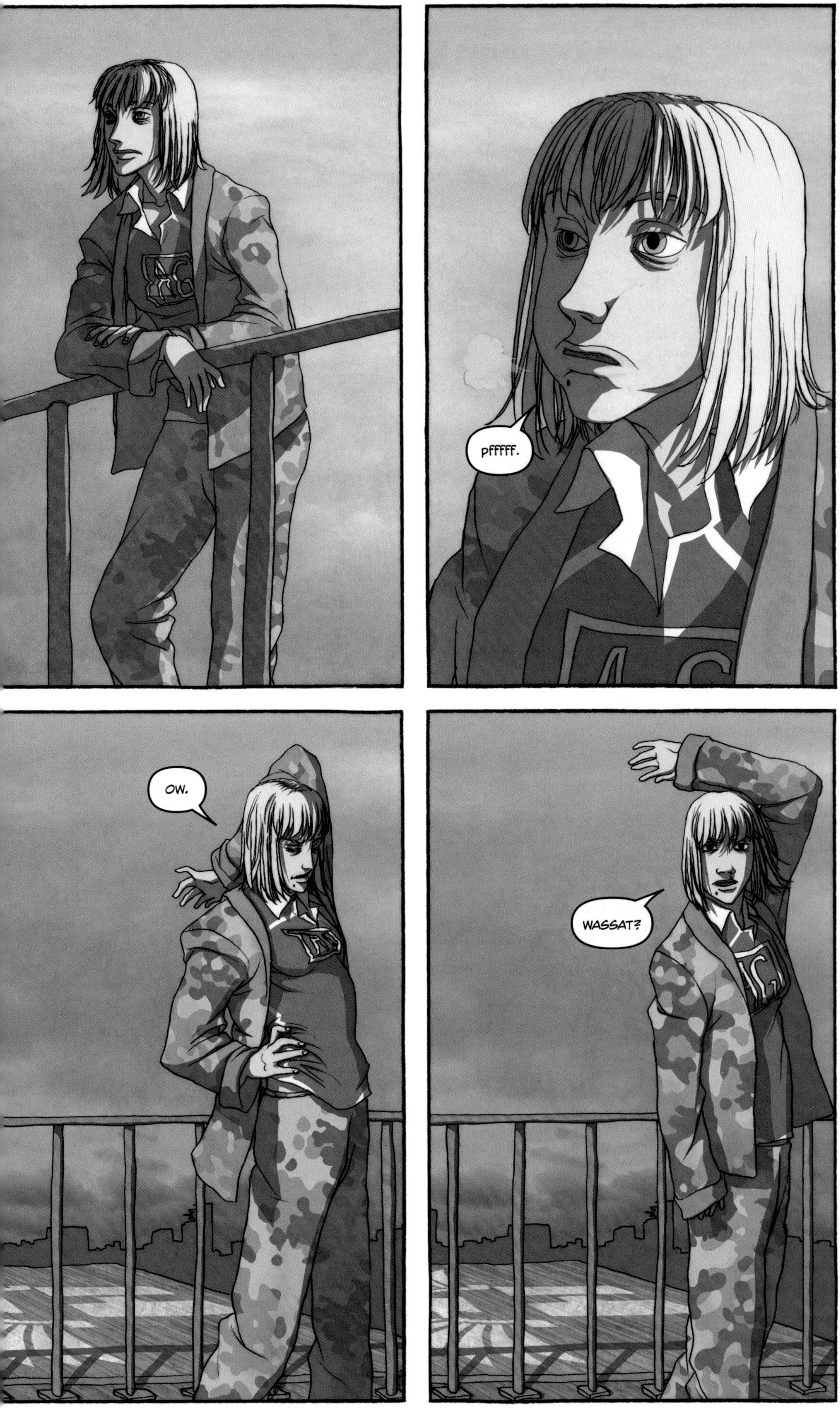
pfffff.
OW.
WASSAT?

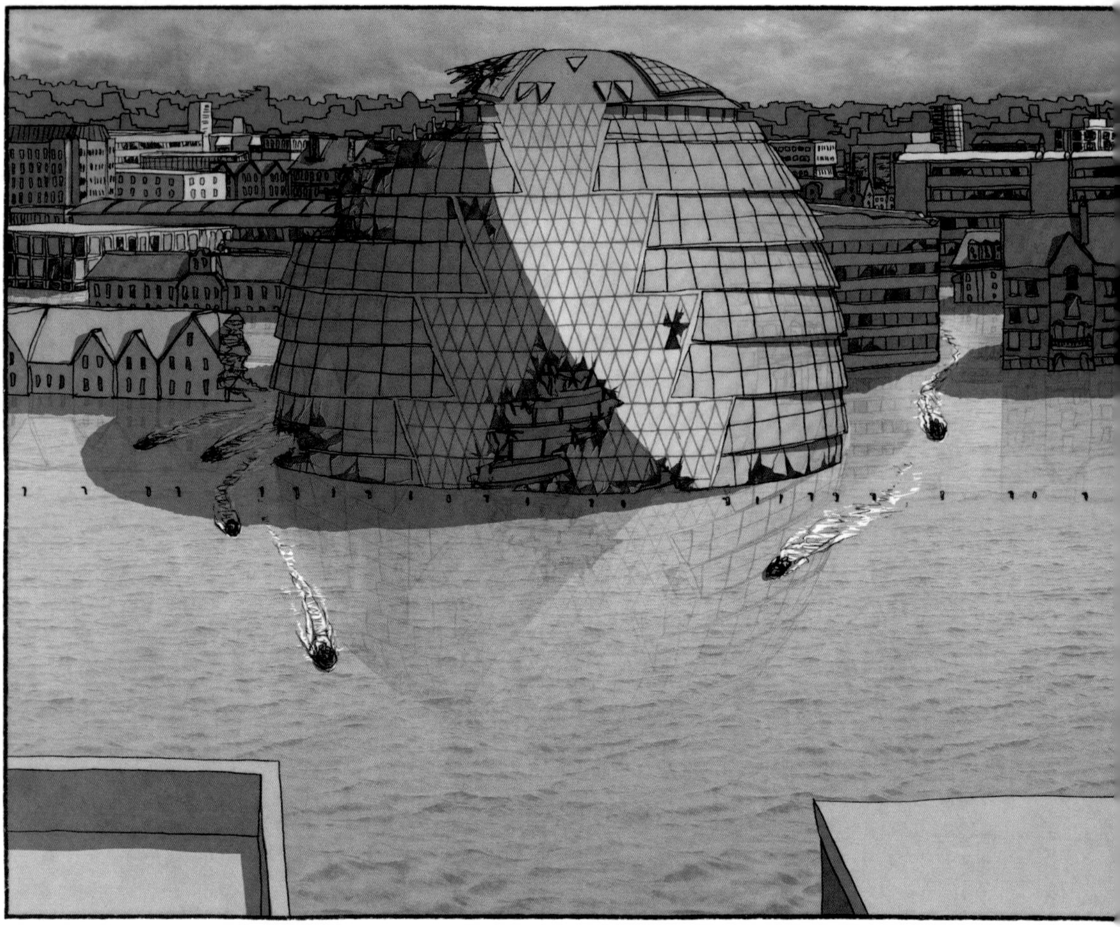
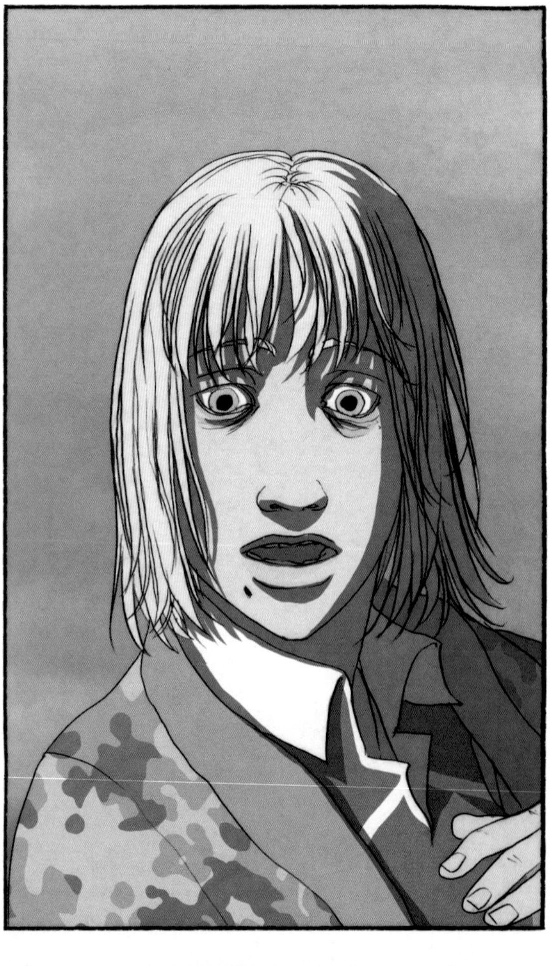
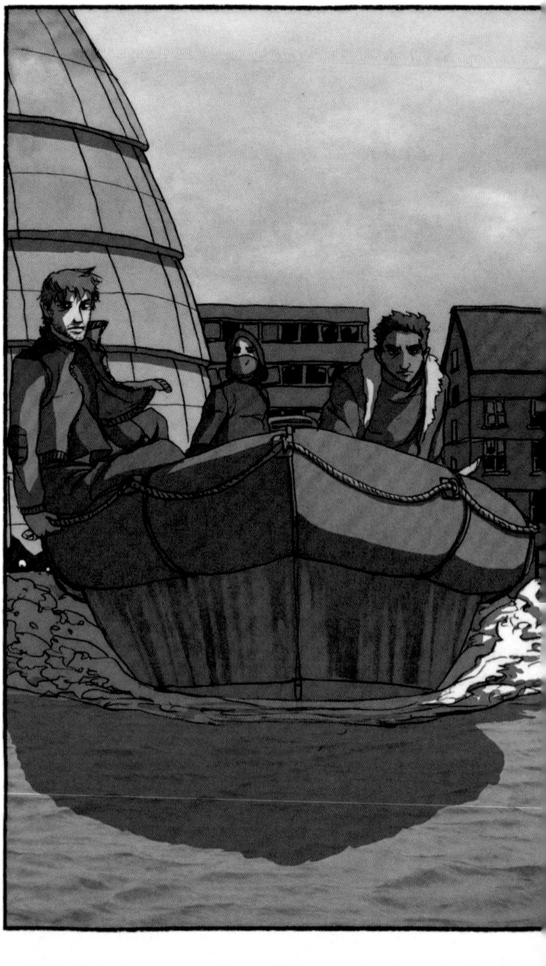

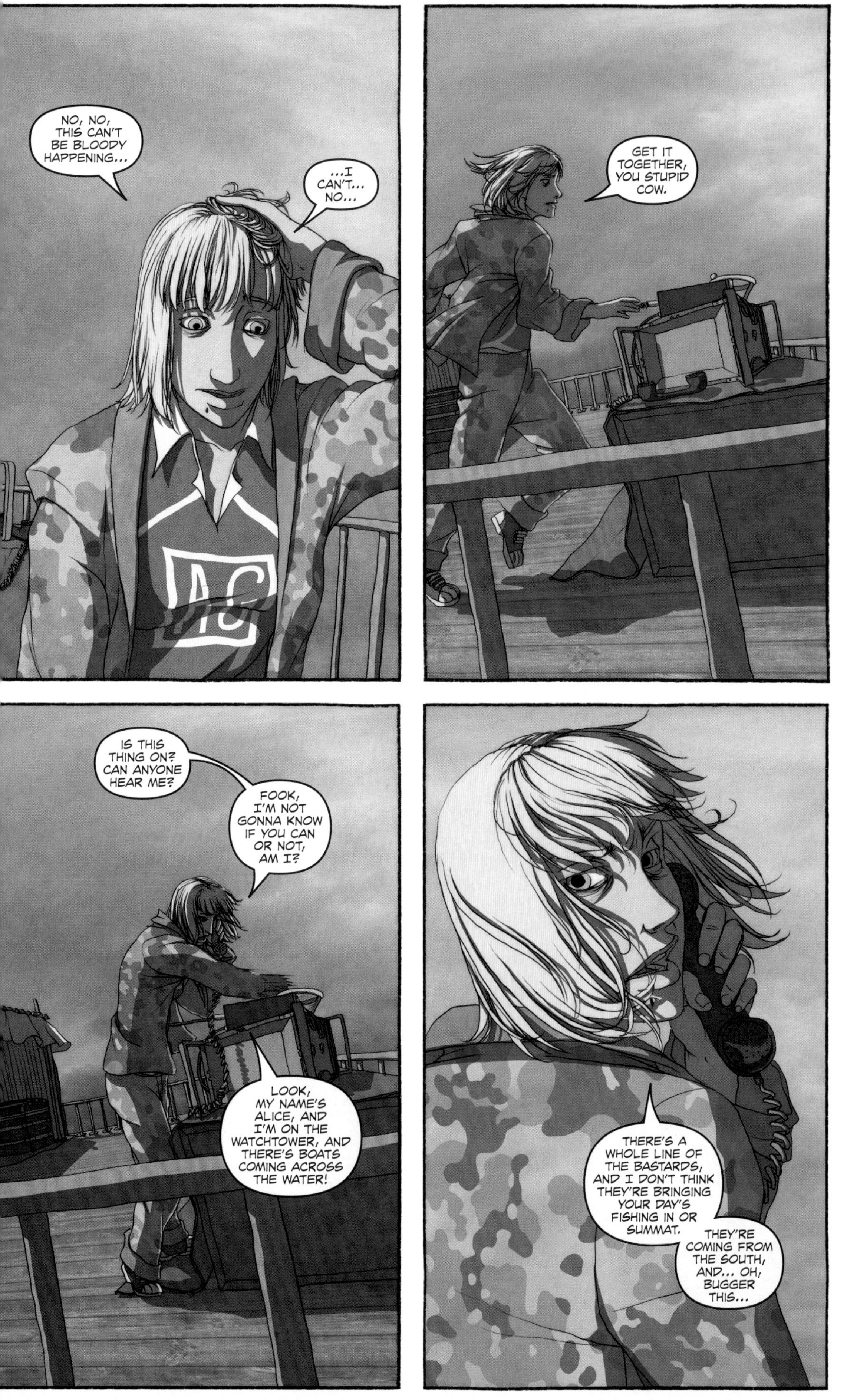
NO, NO, THIS CAN'T BE BLOODY HAPPENING...
...I CAN'T... NO...
GET IT TOGETHER, YOU STUPID COW.
IS THIS THING ON? CAN ANYONE HEAR ME?
FOOK, I'M NOT GONNA KNOW IF YOU CAN OR NOT, AM I?
LOOK, MY NAME'S ALICE, AND I'M ON THE WATCHTOWER, AND THERE'S BOATS COMING ACROSS THE WATER!
THERE'S A WHOLE LINE OF THE BASTARDS, AND I DON'T THINK THEY'RE BRINGING YOUR DAY'S FISHING IN OR SUMMAT.
THEY'RE COMING FROM THE SOUTH, AND... OH, BUGGER THIS...

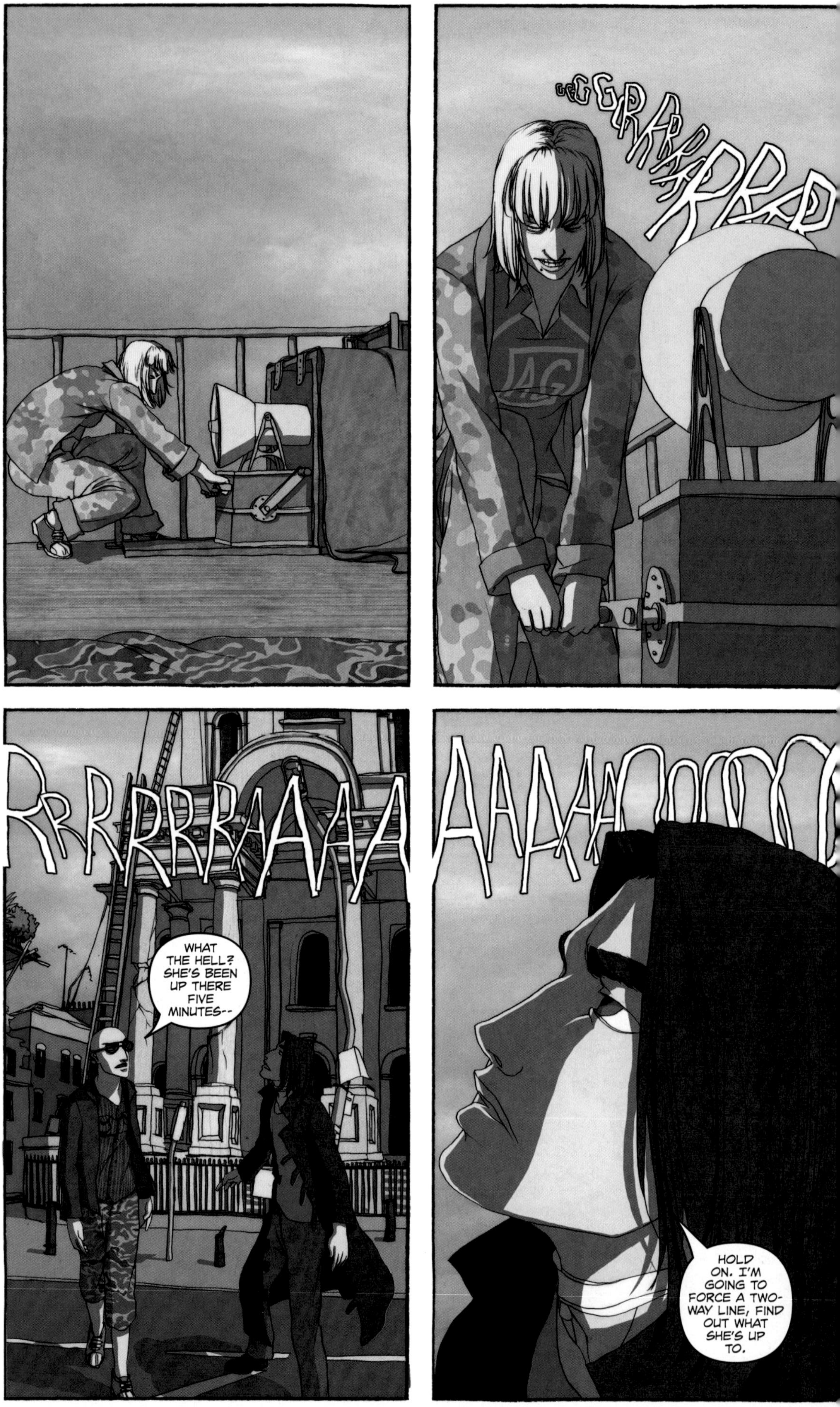
GGGGRRRRRRRRRRR
RRRRRRRAAAAAAAAAAAOOOOOO
WHAT THE HELL? SHE'S BEEN UP THERE FIVE MINUTES--
HOLD ON. I'M GOING TO FORCE A TWO-WAY LINE, FIND OUT WHAT SHE'S UP TO.

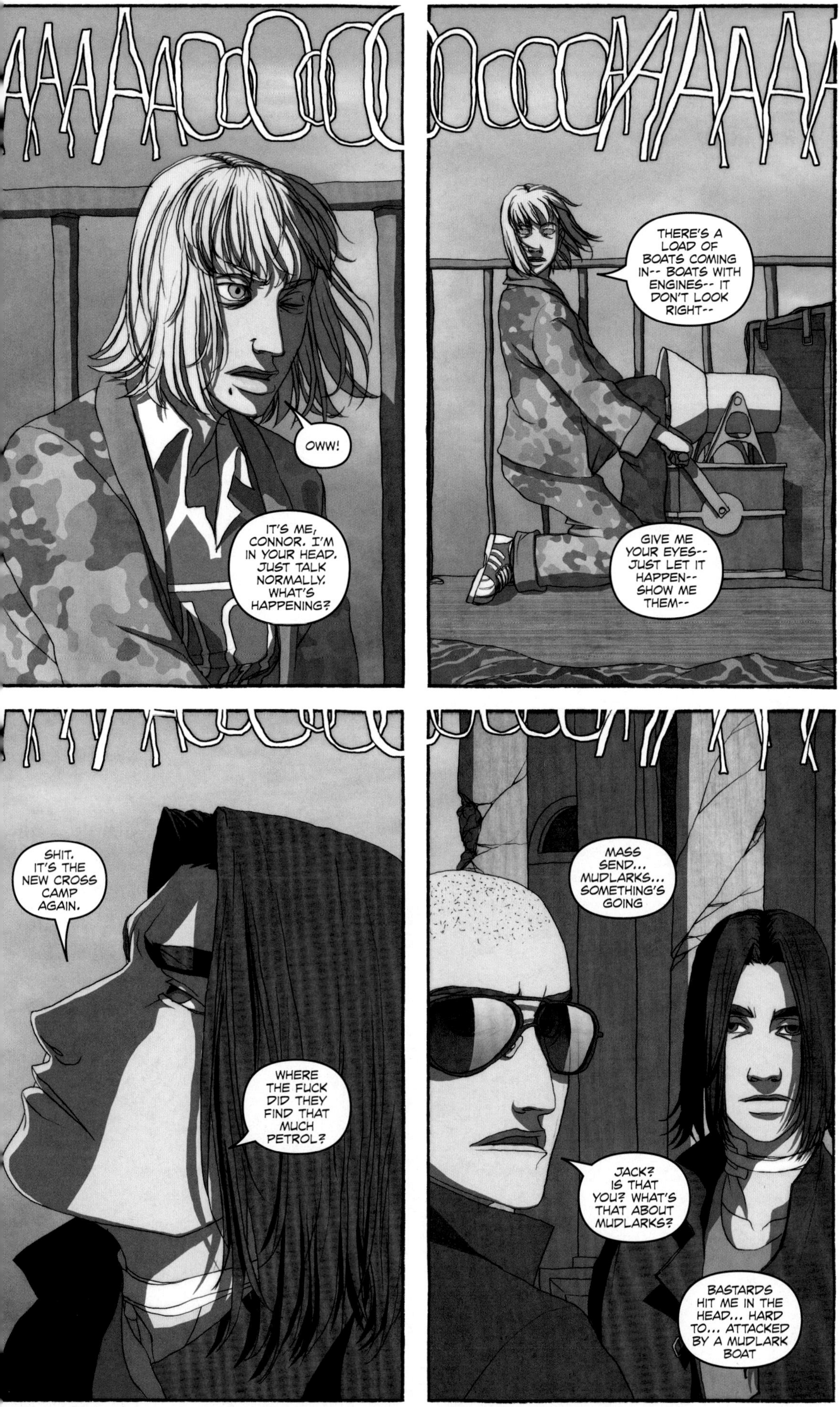
AAAAAOOOOOOOOOOOOOAAAAA
OWW!
IT'S ME, CONNOR. I'M IN YOUR HEAD. JUST TALK NORMALLY. WHAT'S HAPPENING?
THERE'S A LOAD OF BOATS COMING IN-- BOATS WITH ENGINES-- IT DON'T LOOK RIGHT--
GIVE ME YOUR EYES-- JUST LET IT HAPPEN-- SHOW ME THEM--
SHIT. IT'S THE NEW CROSS CAMP AGAIN.
WHERE THE FUCK DID THEY FIND THAT MUCH PETROL?
MASS SEND... MUDLARKS... SOMETHING'S GOING
JACK? IS THAT YOU? WHAT'S THAT ABOUT MUDLARKS?
BASTARDS HIT ME IN THE HEAD... HARD TO... ATTACKED BY A MUDLARK BOAT

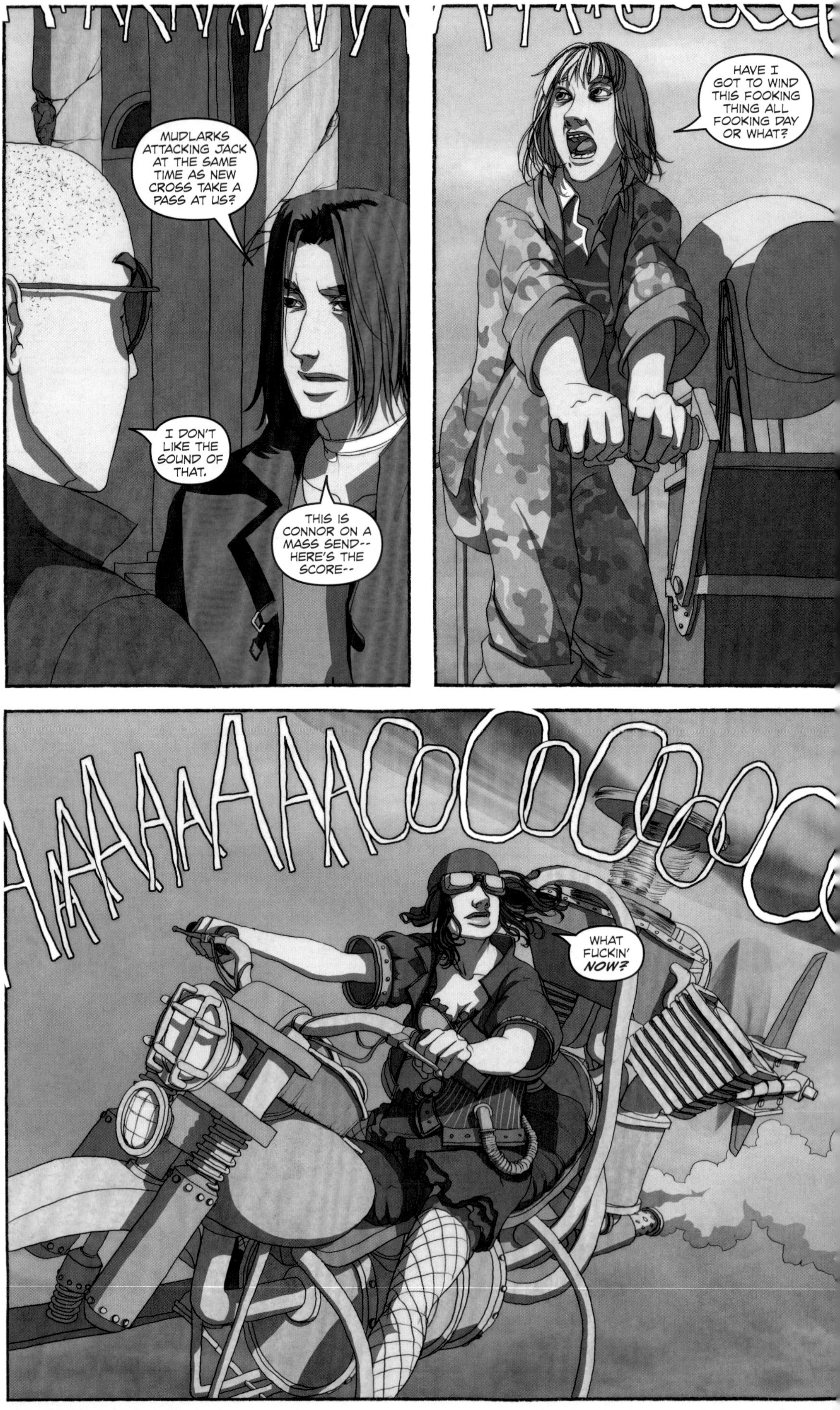
MUDLARKS ATTACKING JACK AT THE SAME TIME AS NEW CROSS TAKE A PASS AT US?
I DON'T LIKE THE SOUND OF THAT.
THIS IS CONNOR ON A MASS SEND-- HERE'S THE SCORE--
HAVE I GOT TO WIND THIS FOOKING THING ALL FOOKING DAY OR WHAT?
AAAAAAAAAAOOOOOOOOOOO
WHAT FUCKIN' *NOW?*

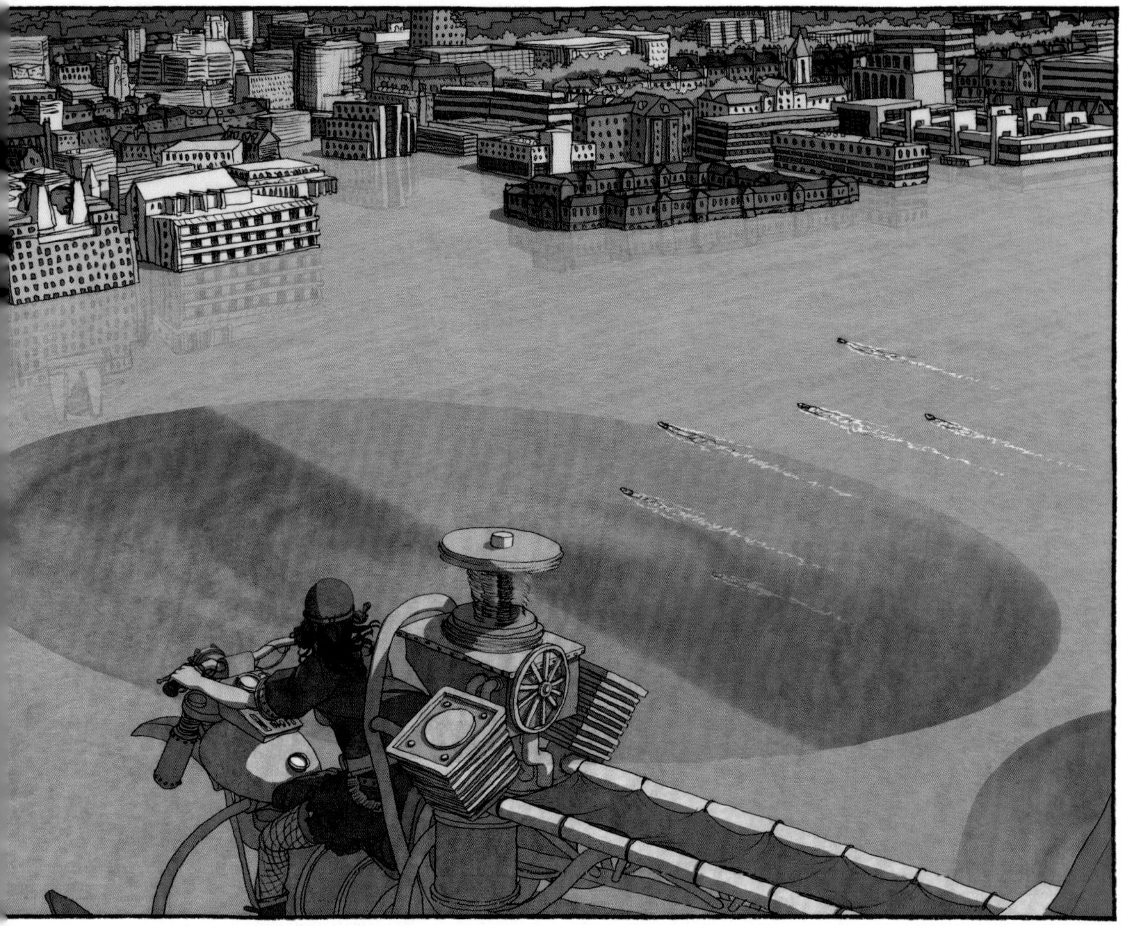

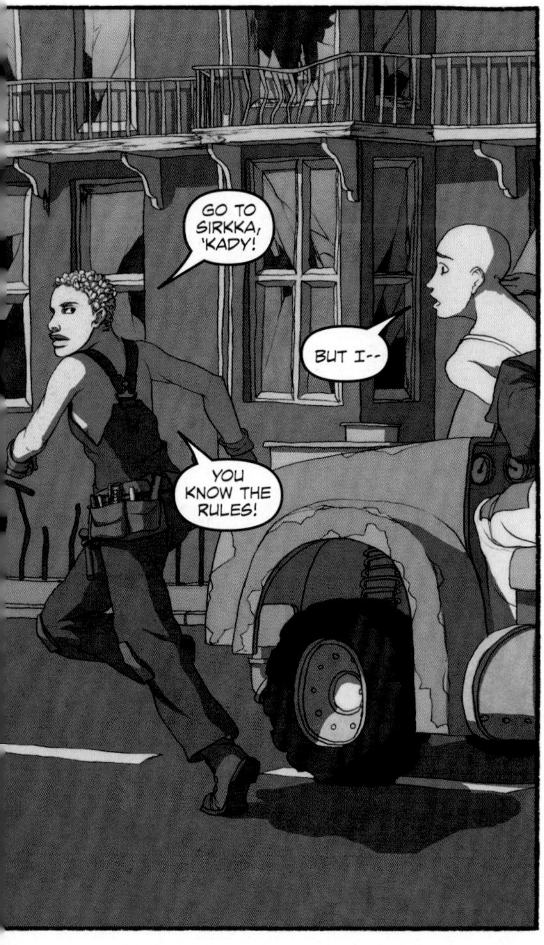
GO TO SIRKKA, 'KADY!
BUT I--
YOU KNOW THE RULES!

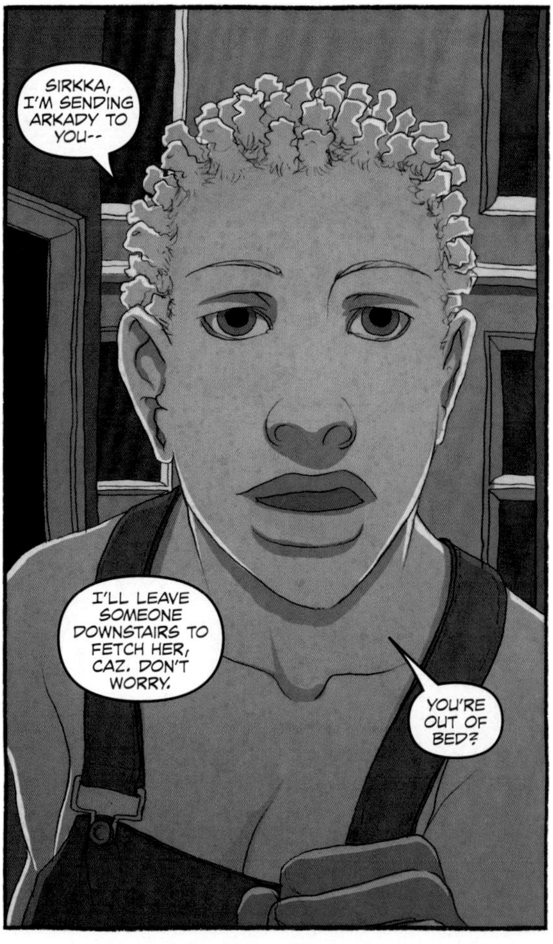
SIRKKA, I'M SENDING ARKADY TO YOU--
I'LL LEAVE SOMEONE DOWNSTAIRS TO FETCH HER, CAZ. DON'T WORRY.
YOU'RE OUT OF BED?

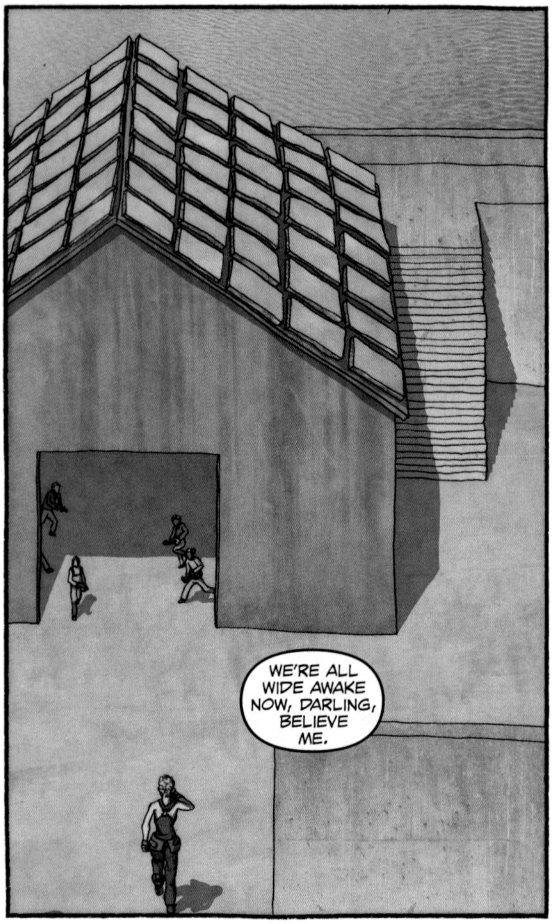
WE'RE ALL WIDE AWAKE NOW, DARLING, BELIEVE ME.

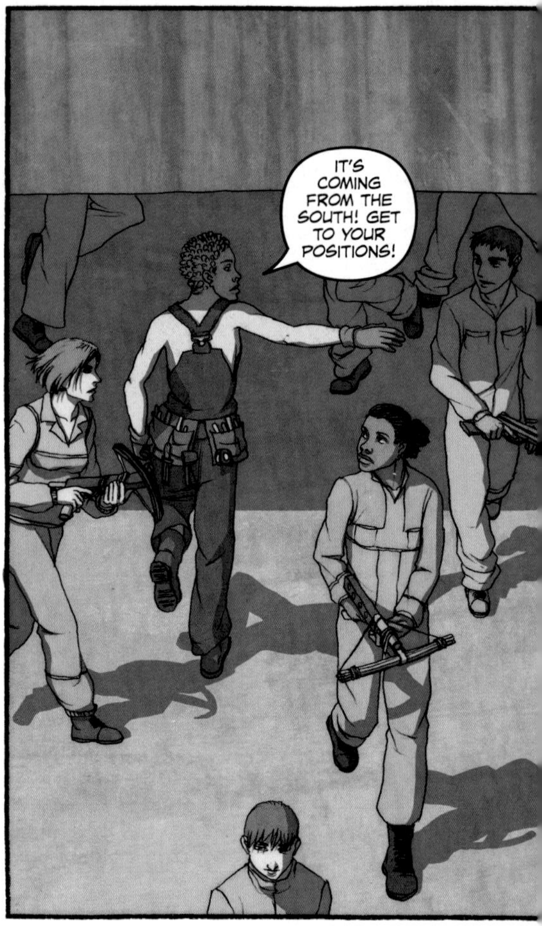
IT'S COMING FROM THE SOUTH! GET TO YOUR POSITIONS!

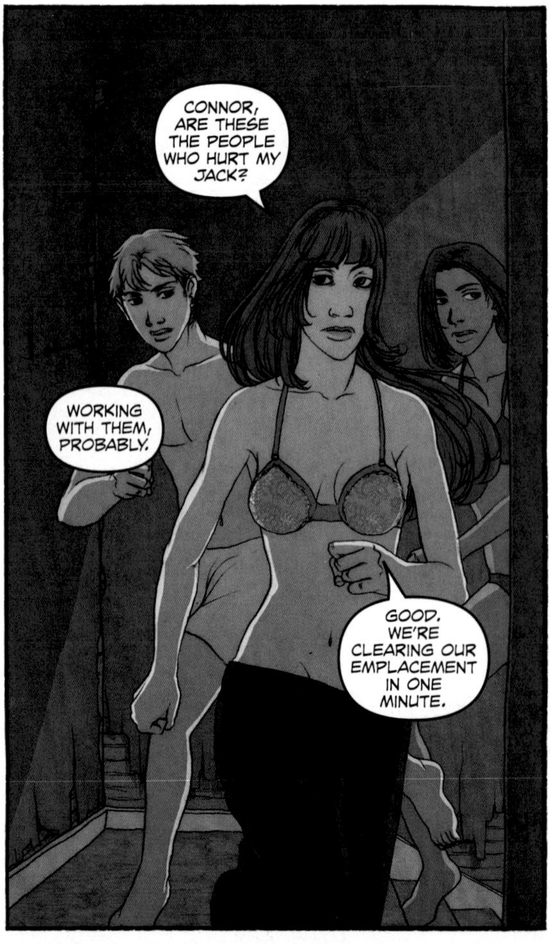
CONNOR, ARE THESE THE PEOPLE WHO HURT MY JACK?
WORKING WITH THEM, PROBABLY.
GOOD. WE'RE CLEARING OUR EMPLACEMENT IN ONE MINUTE.

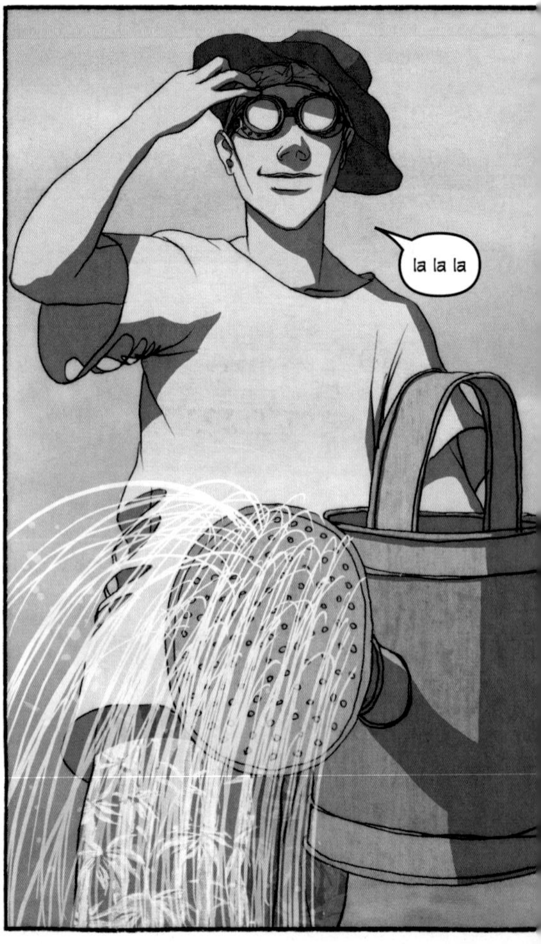
la la la

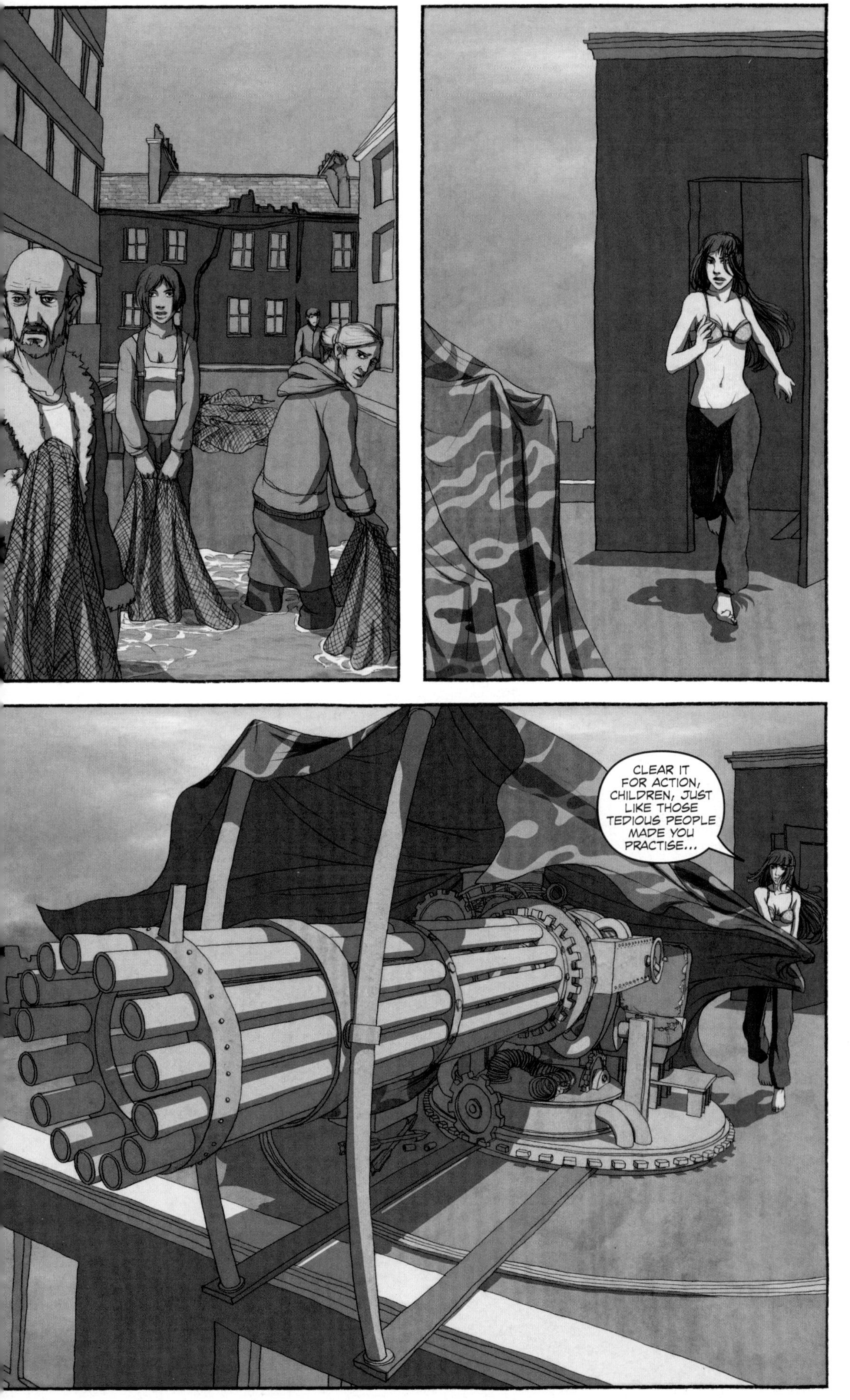
CLEAR IT FOR ACTION, CHILDREN, JUST LIKE THOSE TEDIOUS PEOPLE MADE YOU PRACTISE...

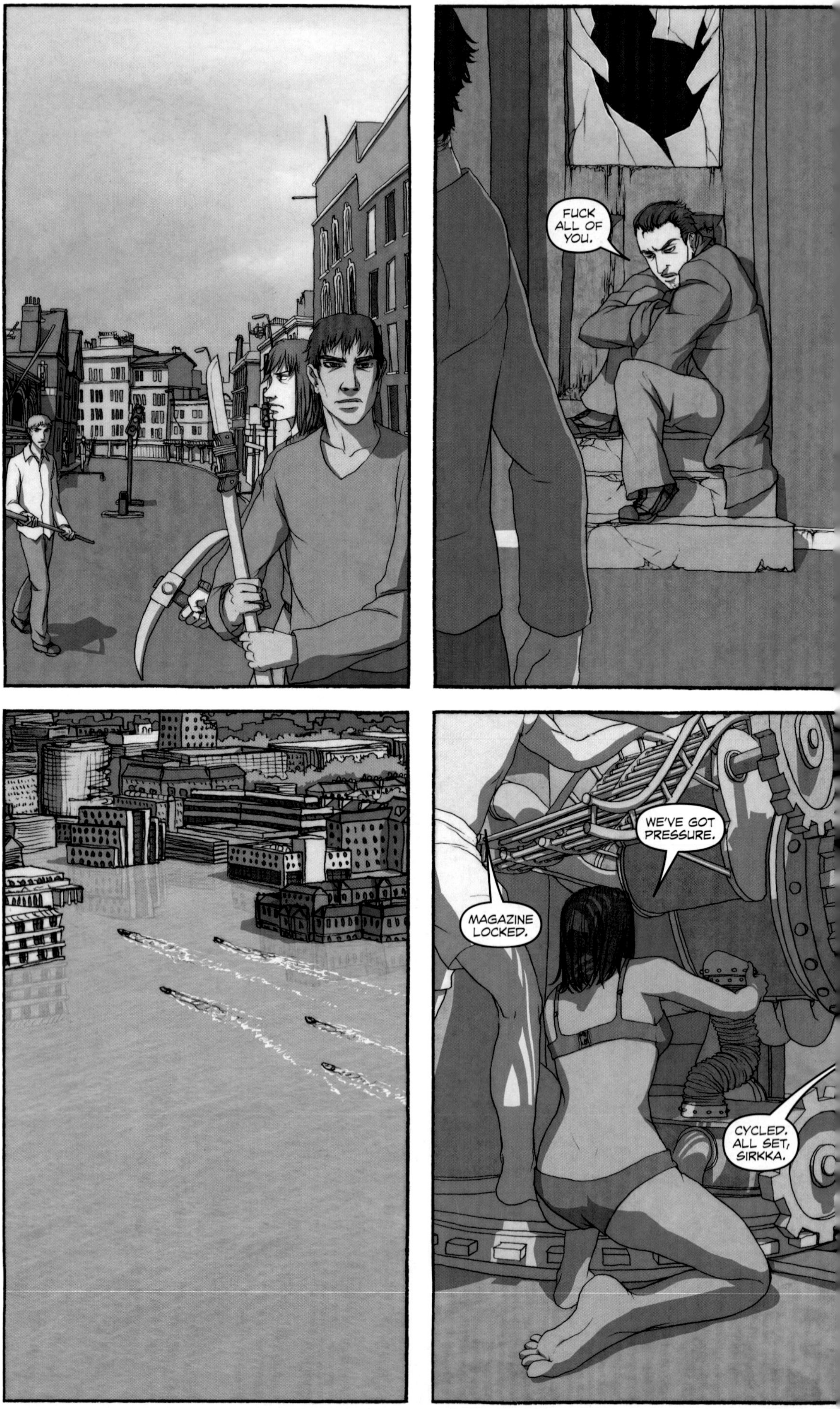
FUCK ALL OF YOU.
WE'VE GOT PRESSURE.
MAGAZINE LOCKED.
CYCLED. ALL SET, SIRKKA.

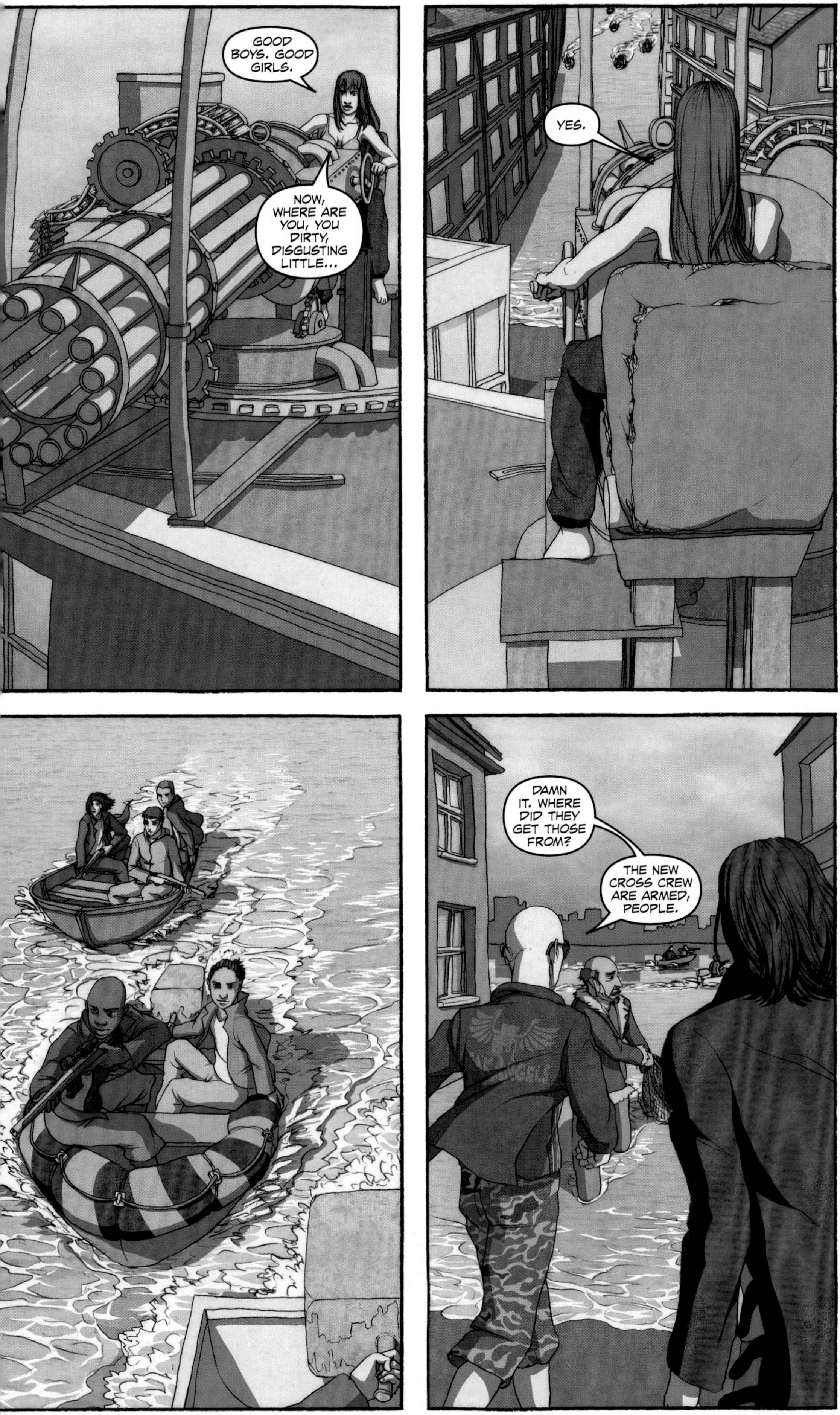
GOOD BOYS. GOOD GIRLS.
NOW, WHERE ARE YOU, YOU DIRTY, DISGUSTING LITTLE...
YES.
DAMN IT. WHERE DID THEY GET THOSE FROM?
THE NEW CROSS CREW ARE ARMED, PEOPLE.

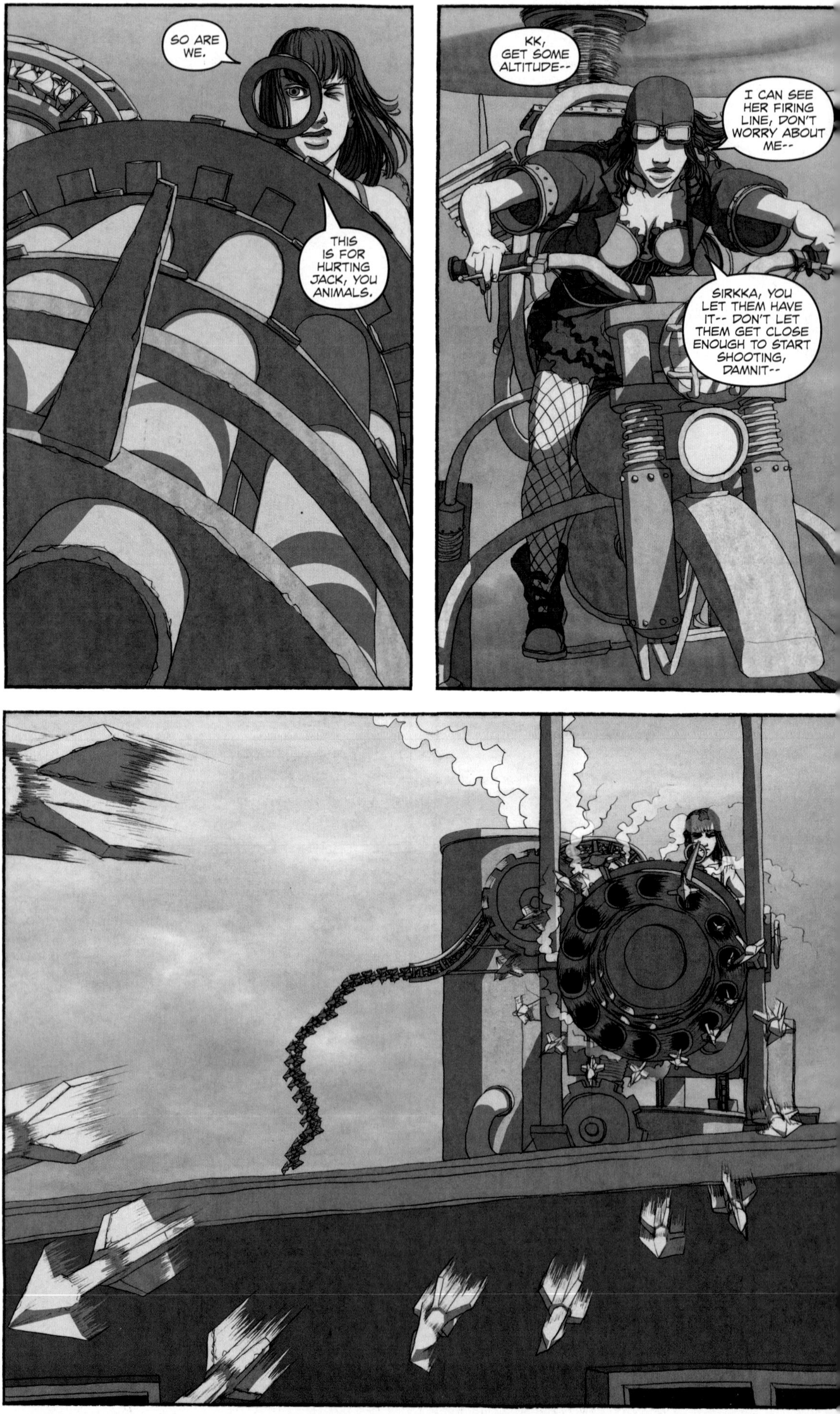
SO ARE WE.
THIS IS FOR HURTING JACK, YOU ANIMALS.
KK, GET SOME ALTITUDE--
I CAN SEE HER FIRING LINE, DON'T WORRY ABOUT ME--
SIRKKA, YOU LET THEM HAVE IT-- DON'T LET THEM GET CLOSE ENOUGH TO START SHOOTING, DAMNIT--

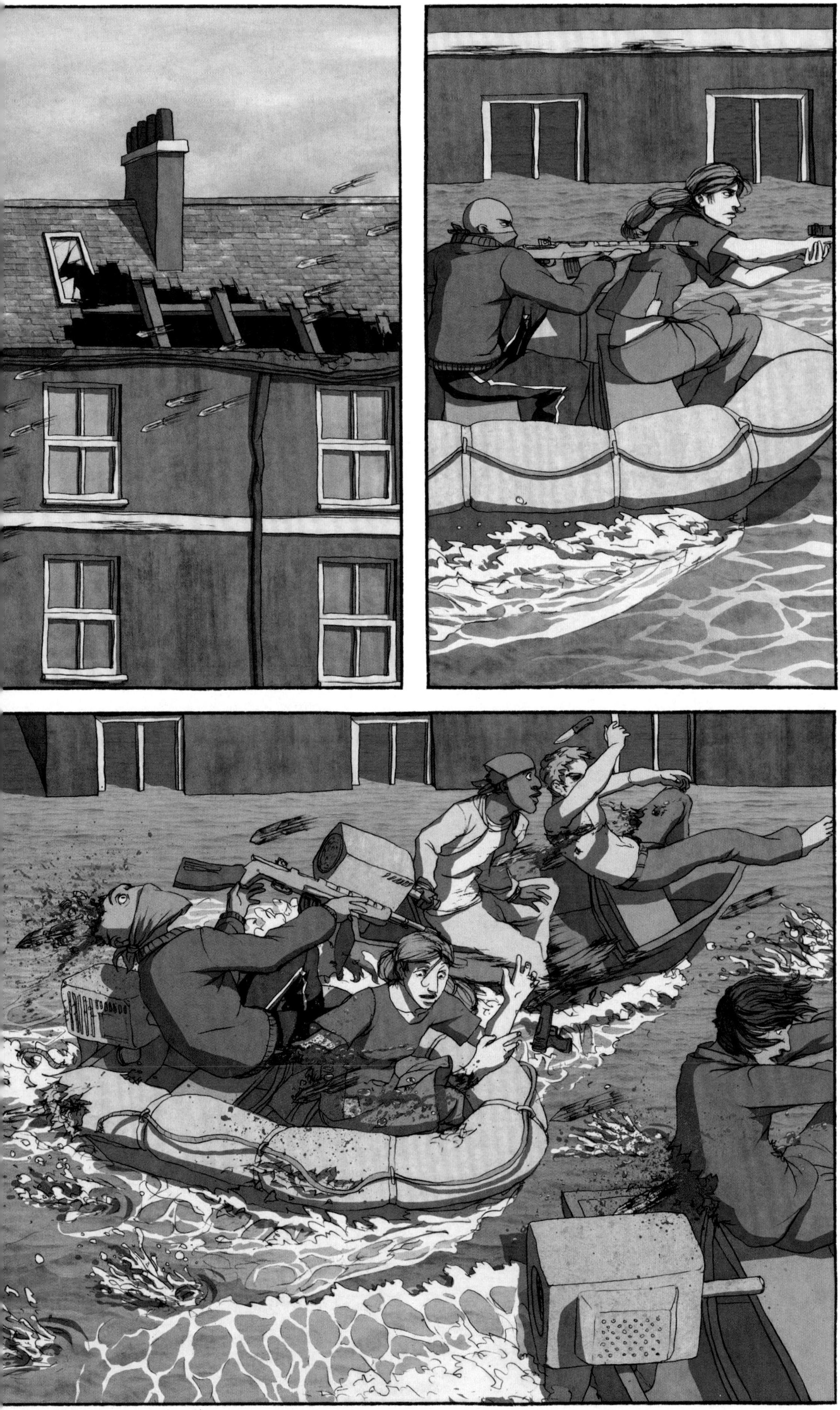

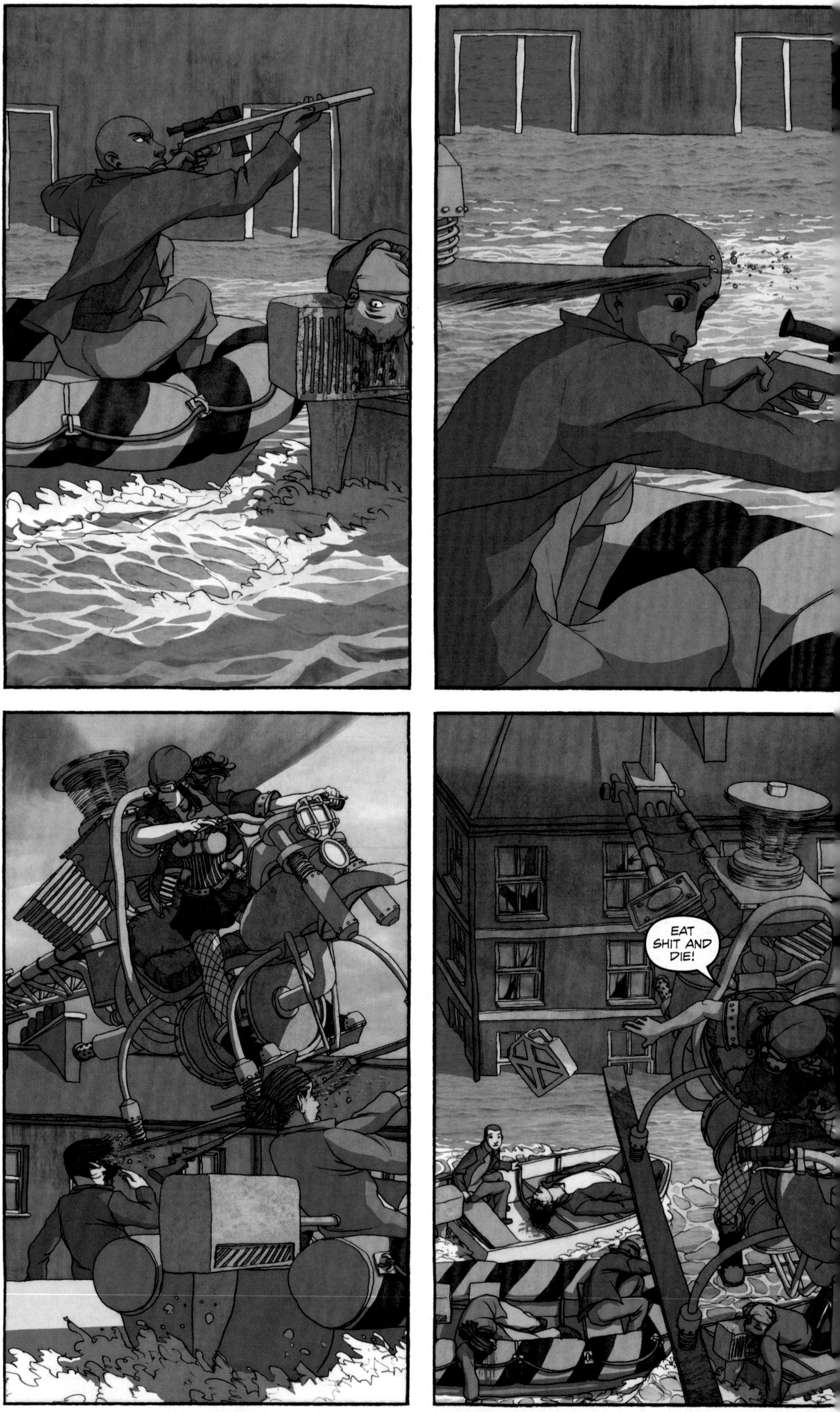
EAT SHIT AND DIE!

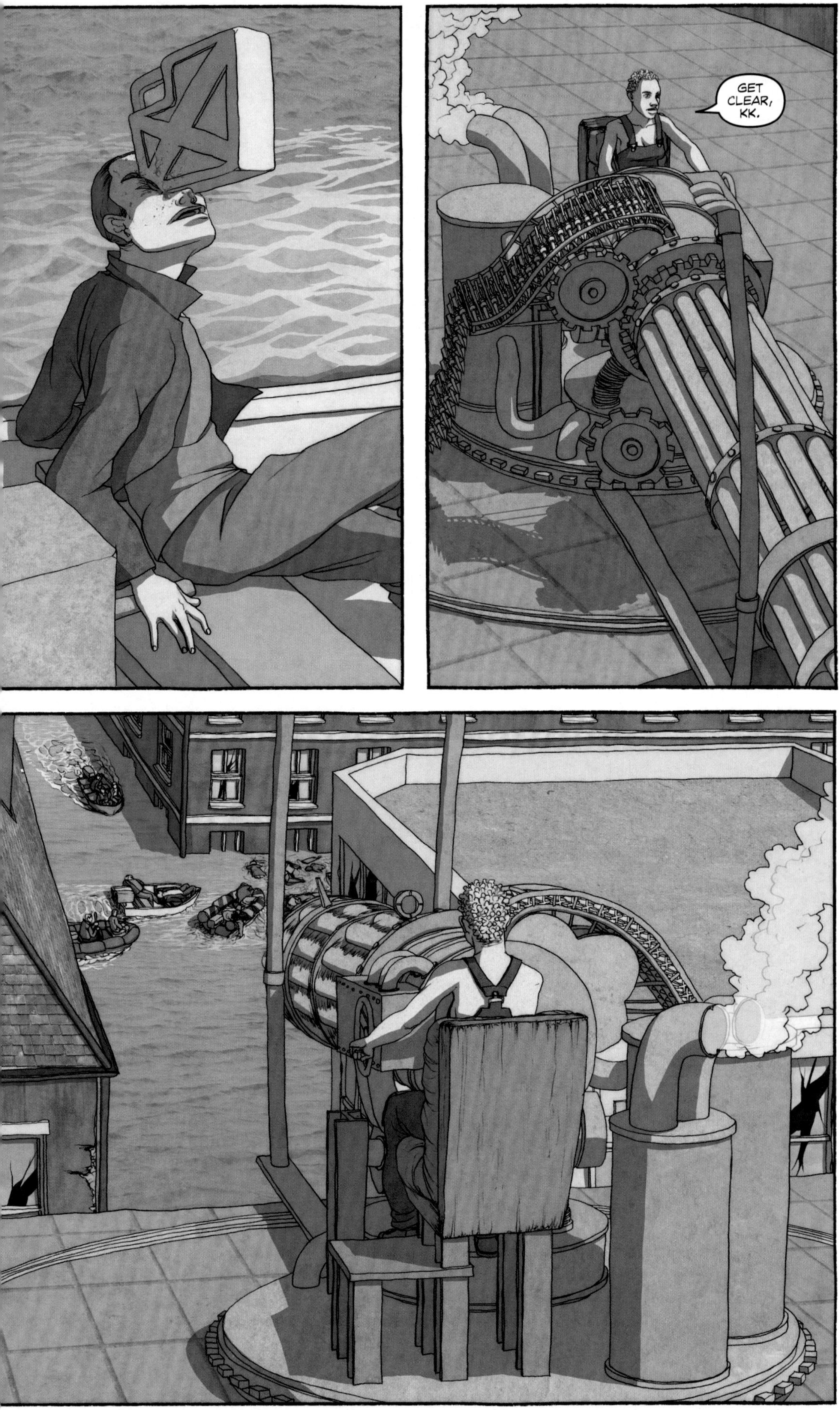
GET CLEAR, KK.

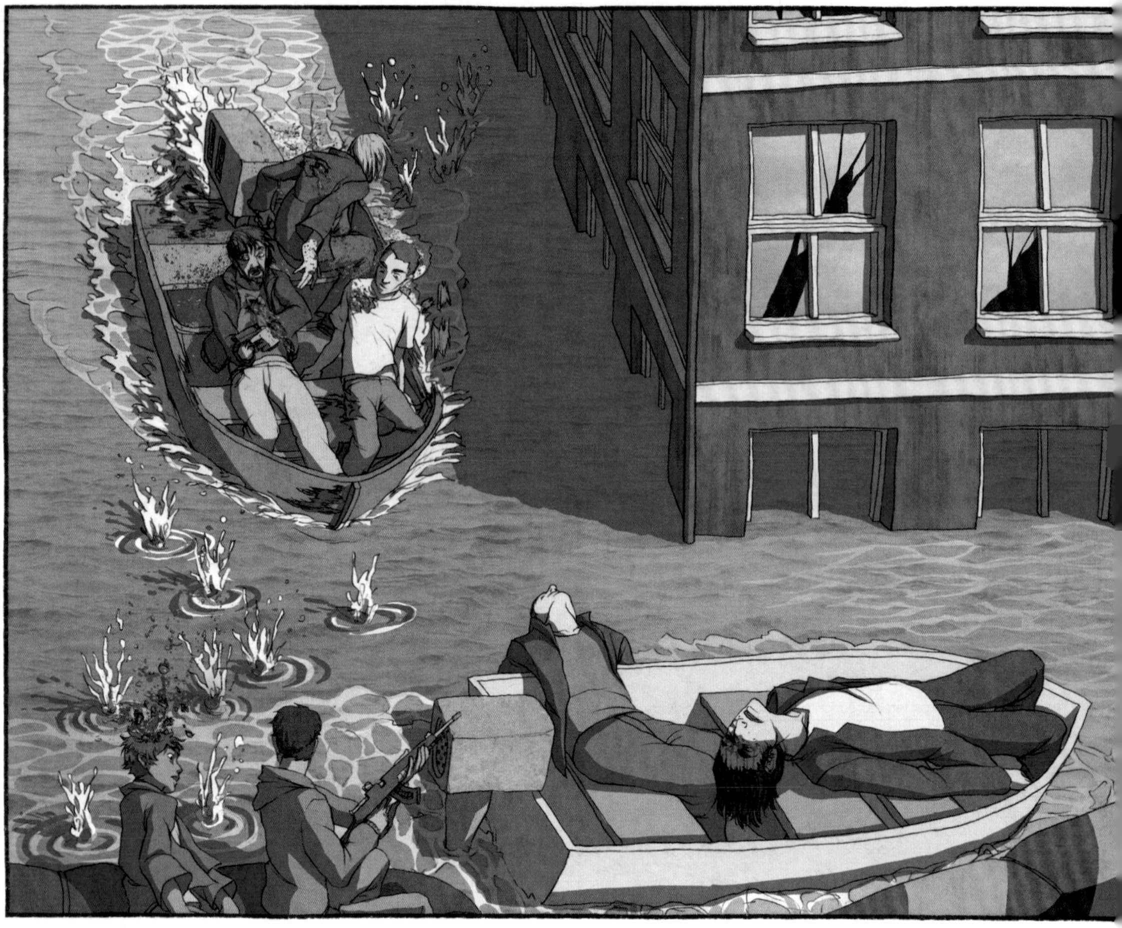

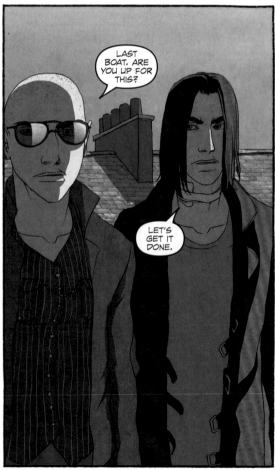

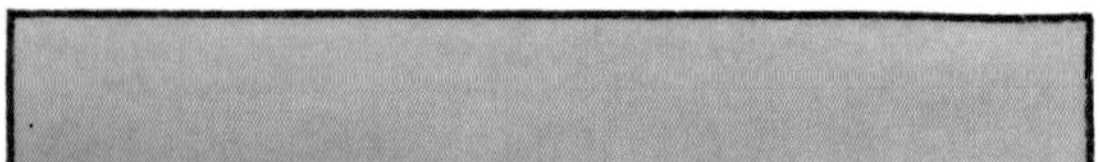
LAST BOAT. ARE YOU UP FOR THIS?
LET'S GET IT DONE.

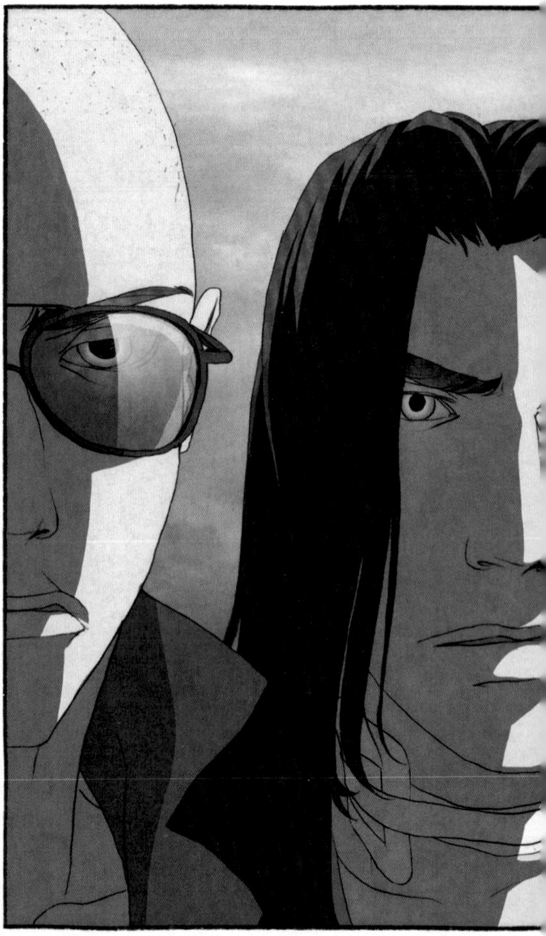

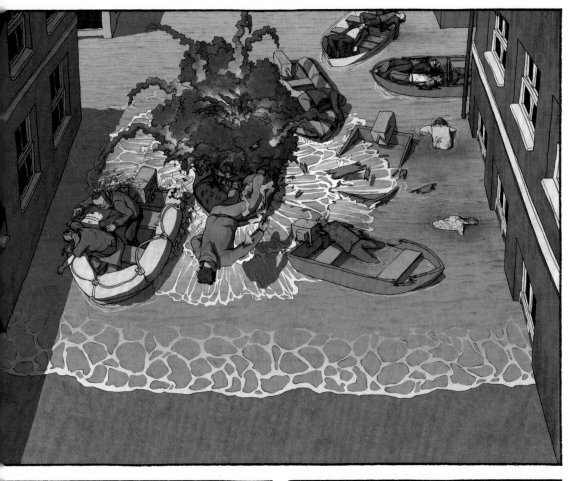

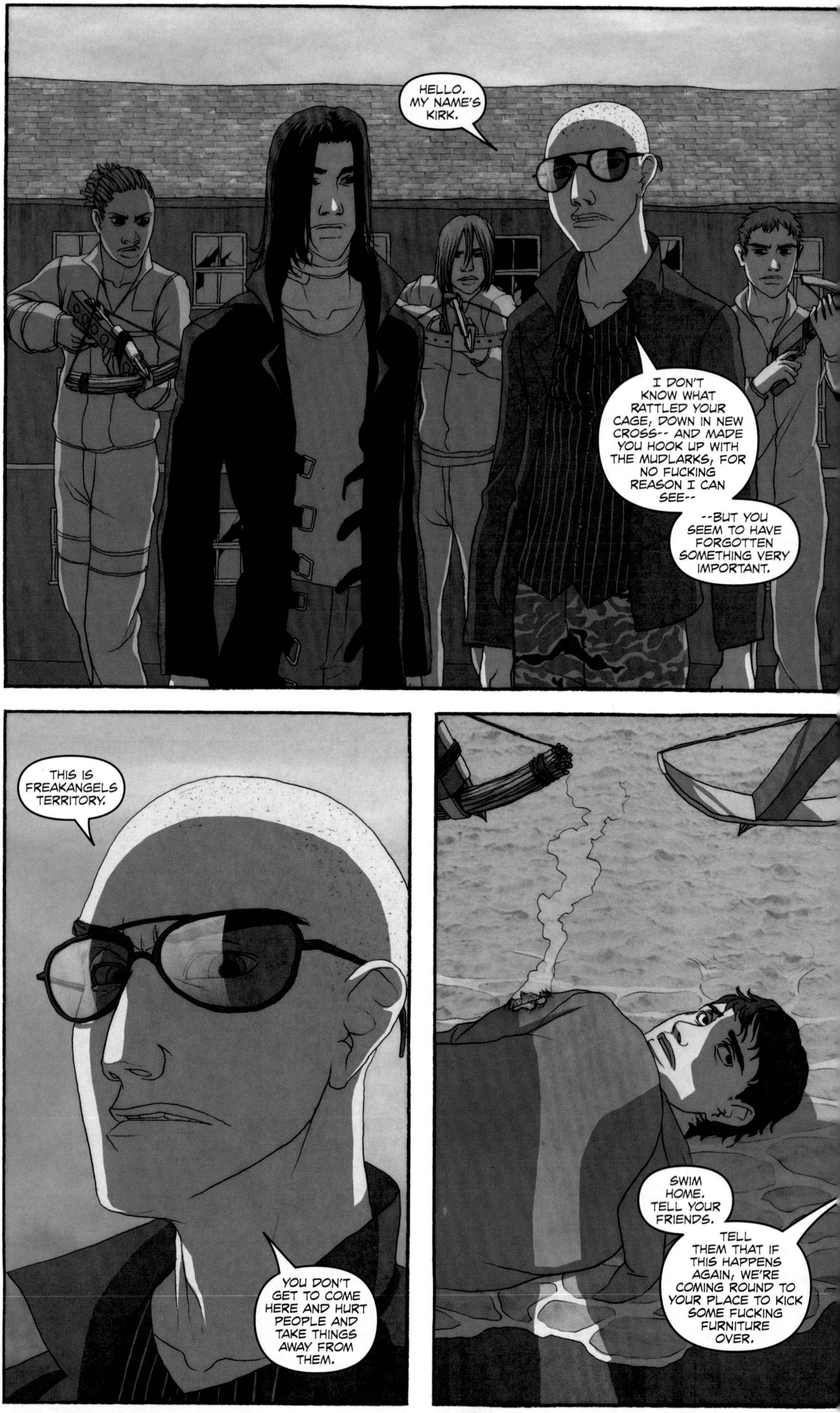
HELLO. MY NAME'S KIRK.
I DON'T KNOW WHAT RATTLED YOUR CAGE, DOWN IN NEW CROSS-- AND MADE YOU HOOK UP WITH THE MUDLARKS, FOR NO FUCKING REASON I CAN SEE--
--BUT YOU SEEM TO HAVE FORGOTTEN SOMETHING VERY IMPORTANT.
THIS IS FREAKANGELS TERRITORY.
YOU DON'T GET TO COME HERE AND HURT PEOPLE AND TAKE THINGS AWAY FROM THEM.
SWIM HOME. TELL YOUR FRIENDS.
TELL THEM THAT IF THIS HAPPENS AGAIN, WE'RE COMING ROUND TO YOUR PLACE TO KICK SOME FUCKING FURNITURE OVER.

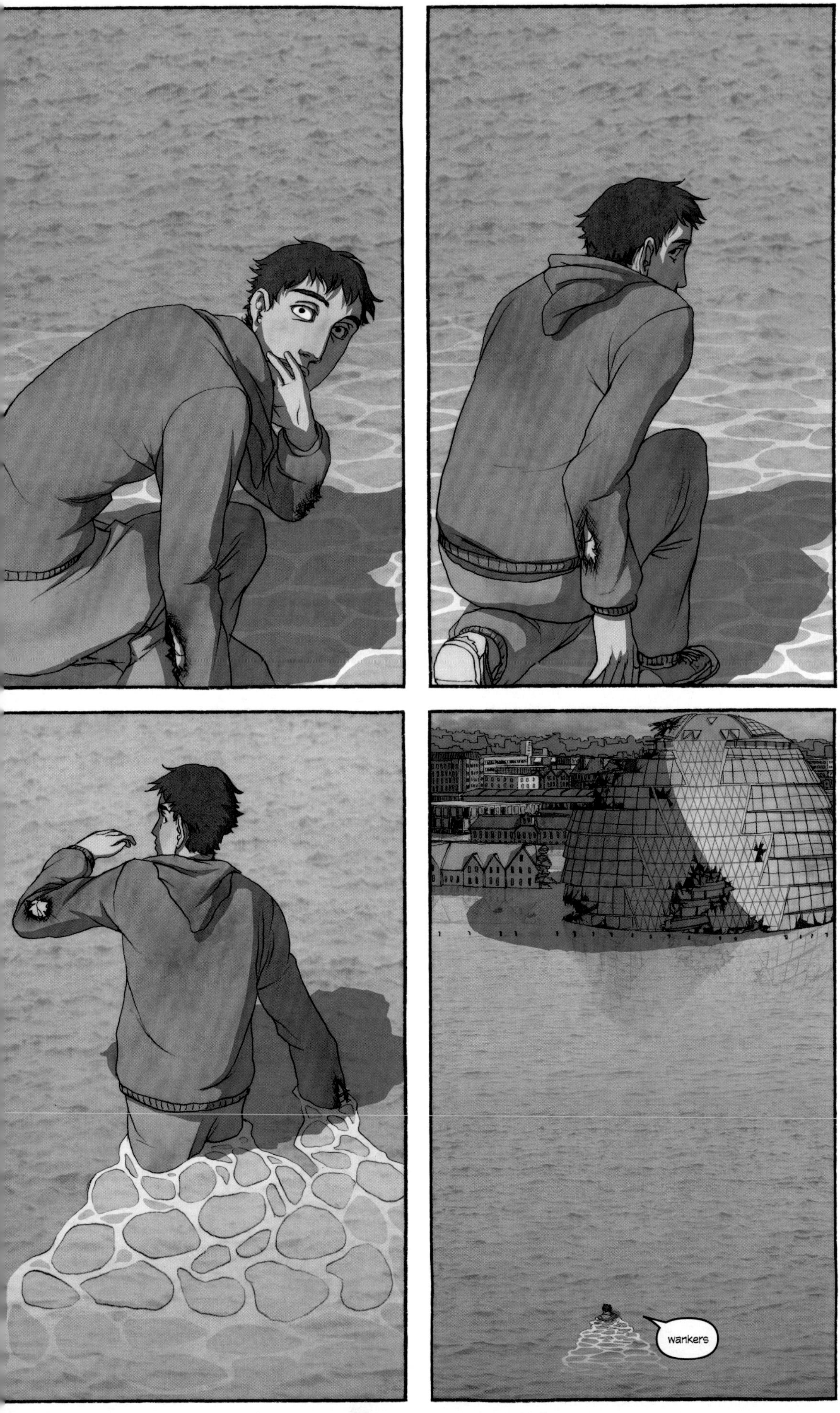
wankers

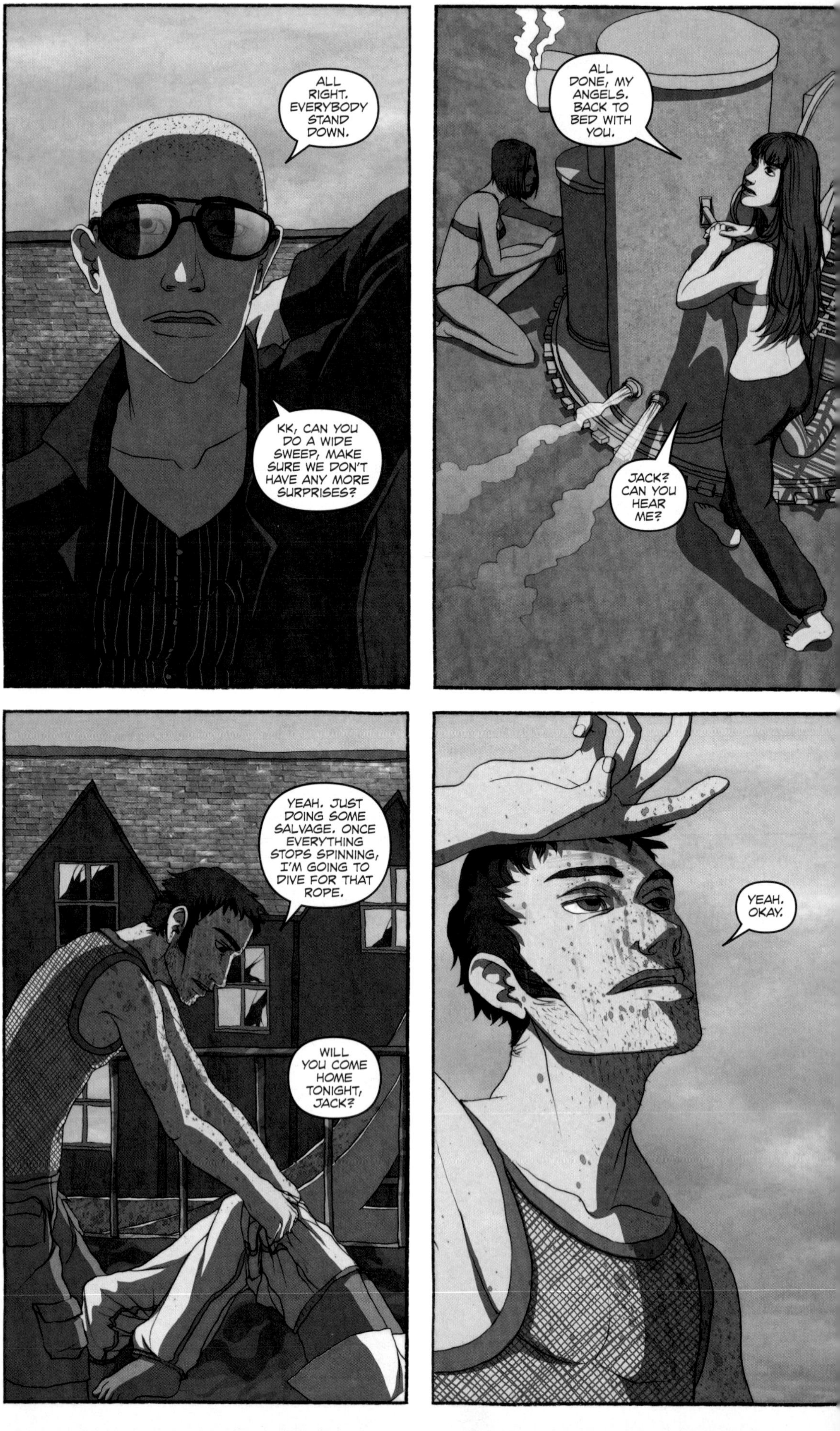
ALL RIGHT. EVERYBODY STAND DOWN.
KK, CAN YOU DO A WIDE SWEEP, MAKE SURE WE DON'T HAVE ANY MORE SURPRISES?
ALL DONE, MY ANGELS. BACK TO BED WITH YOU.
JACK? CAN YOU HEAR ME?
YEAH. JUST DOING SOME SALVAGE. ONCE EVERYTHING STOPS SPINNING, I'M GOING TO DIVE FOR THAT ROPE.
WILL YOU COME HOME TONIGHT, JACK?
YEAH. OKAY.

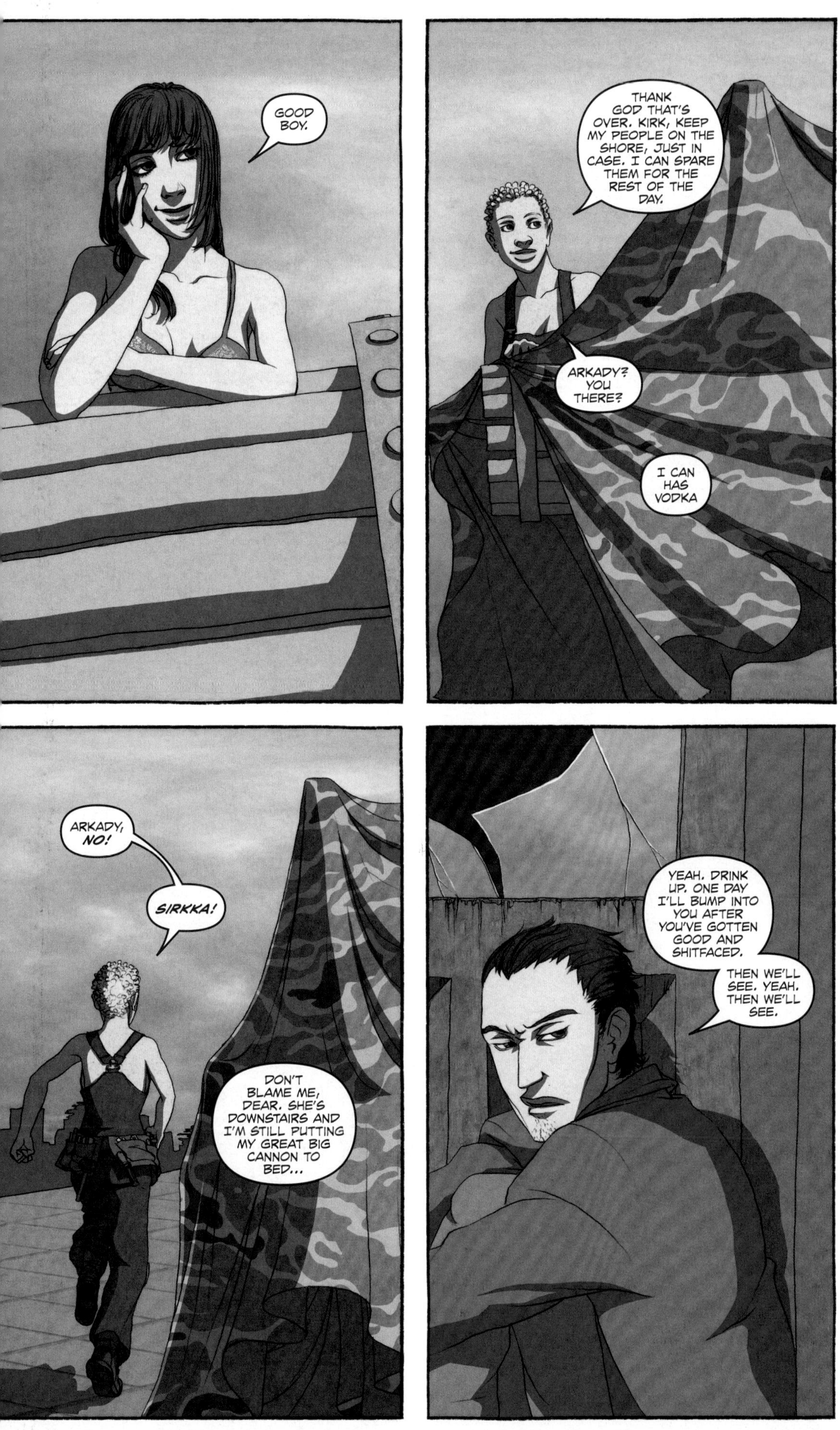
GOOD BOY.
THANK GOD THAT'S OVER. KIRK, KEEP MY PEOPLE ON THE SHORE, JUST IN CASE. I CAN SPARE THEM FOR THE REST OF THE DAY.
ARKADY? YOU THERE?
I CAN HAS VODKA
ARKADY, NO!
SIRKKA!
DON'T BLAME ME, DEAR. SHE'S DOWNSTAIRS AND I'M STILL PUTTING MY GREAT BIG CANNON TO BED...
YEAH. DRINK UP. ONE DAY I'LL BUMP INTO YOU AFTER YOU'VE GOTTEN GOOD AND SHITFACED.
THEN WE'LL SEE. YEAH. THEN WE'LL SEE.

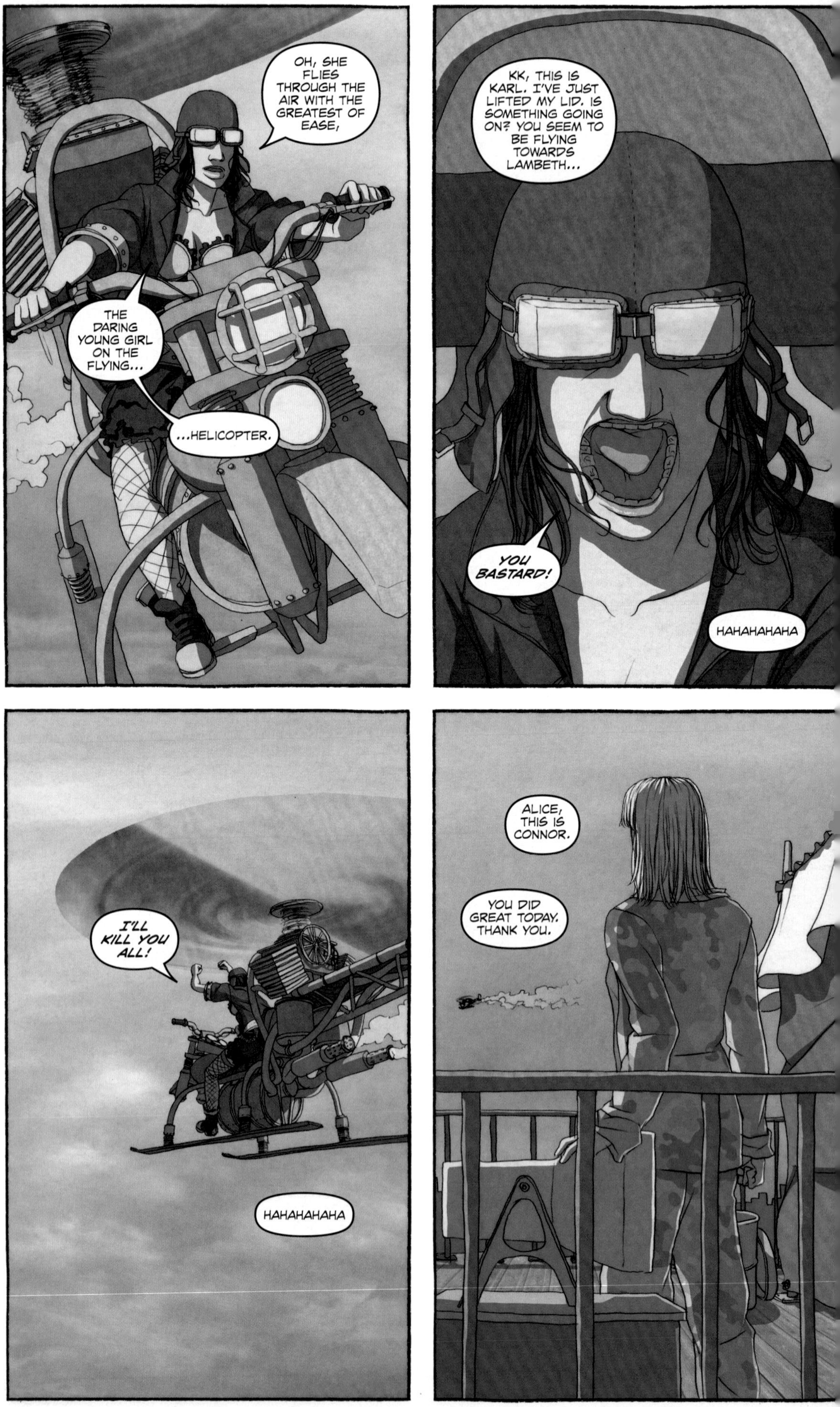
OH, SHE FLIES THROUGH THE AIR WITH THE GREATEST OF EASE,
THE DARING YOUNG GIRL ON THE FLYING...
...HELICOPTER.
KK, THIS IS KARL. I'VE JUST LIFTED MY LID. IS SOMETHING GOING ON? YOU SEEM TO BE FLYING TOWARDS LAMBETH...
YOU BASTARD!
HAHAHAHAHA
I'LL KILL YOU ALL!
HAHAHAHAHA
ALICE, THIS IS CONNOR.
YOU DID GREAT TODAY. THANK YOU.

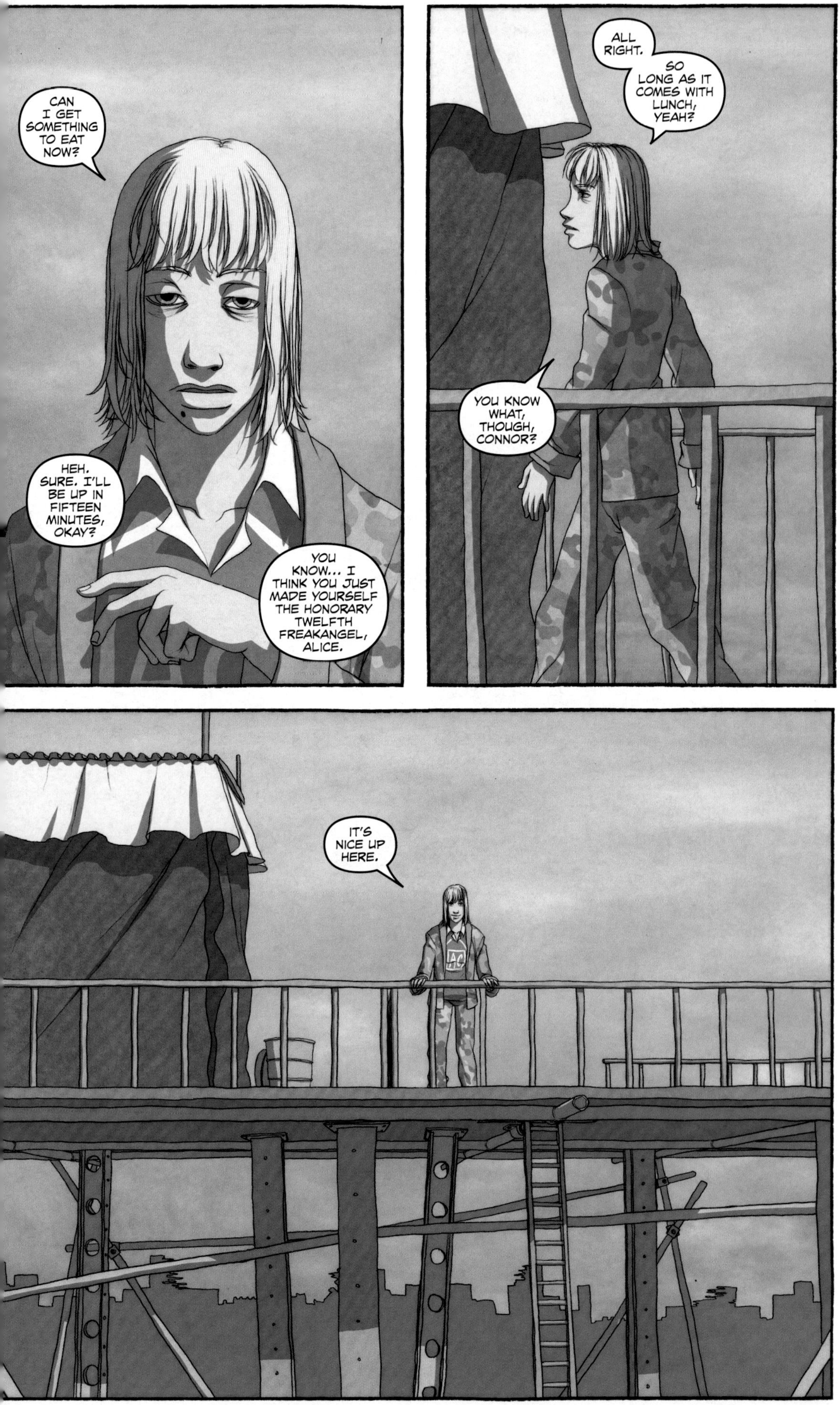
CAN I GET SOMETHING TO EAT NOW?
HEH. SURE. I'LL BE UP IN FIFTEEN MINUTES, OKAY?
YOU KNOW... I THINK YOU JUST MADE YOURSELF THE HONORARY TWELFTH FREAKANGEL, ALICE.
ALL RIGHT.
SO LONG AS IT COMES WITH LUNCH, YEAH?
YOU KNOW WHAT, THOUGH, CONNOR?
IT'S NICE UP HERE.

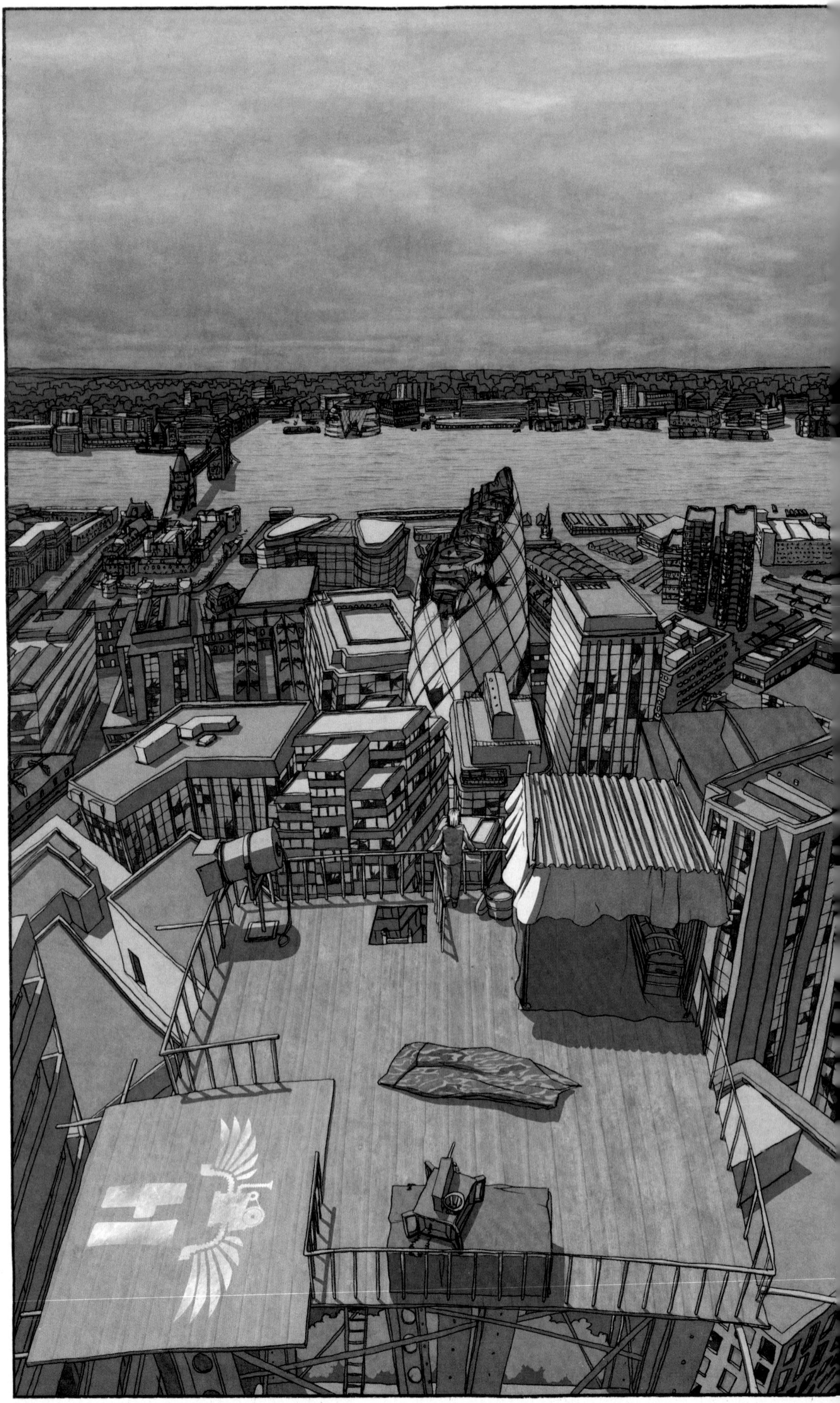